Business, Ethics and Institutions

This book is the first systematic scholarly study on the business history of Turkey and its predecessor the Ottoman Empire from the nineteenth century until the present. It aims to place the distinctive characteristics of capitalism in Turkey within a global and comparative perspective, dealing with three related issues. First, it examines the institutional context that shaped capitalist development in Turkey. Second, it focuses on the corporate actors, entrepreneurs, and business enterprises that have led national economic growth. Third, it explores the ethical foundations and social responsibility of business enterprises in the country. The comparative and historical approach sets the volume apart from previous books on the subject.

Business, Ethics and Institutions aims to strengthen scholarly and policy-related understandings of Turkish capitalism and the diversified business groups dominating the economy by providing a deep analysis of the evolution of political and social institutions that shaped corporate activity. It demonstrates the key role played by large family-owned business groups in Turkey's development. It also seeks to identify both the similarities and the differences in the Turkish pattern of economic development, making comparisons with Japan, an early example of catch-up, and a more successful model than Turkey. The comparative perspective makes the book highly relevant to business practitioners and policy makers, and to a wide range of scholars and students interested in the institutional foundations of modern capitalism, business and economic history, ethics, organizational studies, and entrepreneurship.

Asli M. Colpan is a Professor of Corporate Strategy at the Graduate School of Management and Graduate School of Economics, Kyoto University, Japan, and Visiting Professor at Koç University, Turkey.

Geoffrey Jones is Isidor Straus Professor of Business History at the Harvard Business School, Boston, United States.

Routledge International Studies in Business History

Series editors:
Jeffrey Fear and Christina Lubinski

Multinational Business and Transnational Regions
A transnational business history of energy transition in the Rhine region, 1945–1973
Marten Boon

Making Managers in Canada, 1945–1995
Companies, Community Colleges, and Universities
Jason Russell

The Evolution of Business
Interpretative Theory, History and Firm Growth
Ellen Mølgaard Korsager

Multinational Enterprise, Political Risk and Organisational Change
From Total War to Cold War
Edited by Neil Forbes, Takafumi Kurosawa and Ben Wubs

Co-operation and Globalisation
The British Co-operative Wholesales, the Co-operative Group and the World since 1863
Anthony Webster

The Age of Entrepreneurship
Business Proprietors, Self-employment and Corporations Since 1851
Robert J. Bennett, Harry Smith, Cary van Lieshout, Piero Montebruno and Gill Newton

Business, Ethics and Institutions
The Evolution of Turkish Capitalism in Global Perspectives
Edited by Asli M. Colpan and Geoffrey Jones

For more information about this series, please visit: www.routledge.com/Routledge-International-Studies-in-Business-History/book-series/SE0471

Business, Ethics and Institutions

The Evolution of Turkish Capitalism in Global Perspectives

Edited by
Asli M. Colpan and Geoffrey Jones

Routledge
Taylor & Francis Group
NEW YORK AND LONDON

First published 2020
by Routledge
605 Third Avenue, New York, NY 10017

and by Routledge
2 Park Square, Milton Park, Abingdon, Oxon, OX14 4RN

First issued in paperback 2021

Routledge is an imprint of the Taylor & Francis Group, an informa business

Library of Congress Cataloging-in-Publication Data
A catalog record for this book has been requested

ISBN 13: 978-0-367-77708-1 (pbk)
ISBN 13: 978-0-367-14290-2 (hbk)

Typeset in Sabon
by Apex CoVantage, LLC

Contents

Figures

Tables

Abbreviations

AKP	Justice and Development Party; in Turkish, *Adalet ve Kalkınma Partisi*
AP	Justice Party; in Turkish, *Adalet Partisi*
CHP	Republican People's Party; in Turkish, *Cumhuriyet Halk Partisi*
CSR	Corporate Social Responsibility
DP	Democratic Party; in Turkish, *Demokrat Parti*
EU	European Union
MÜSİAD	Association of Independent Industrialists and Businessmen; in Turkish, *Müstakil Sanayici ve İşadamları Derneği*
OECD	Organization for Economic Co-operation and Development
RP	Welfare Party; in Turkish, *Refah Partisi*
TÜRKONFED	Turkish Enterprise and Business Confederation; in Turkish, *Türk Girişim ve İş Dünyası Konfederasyonu*
TUSKON	Turkish Confederation of Businessmen and Industrialists; in Turkish, *Türkiye İşadamları ve Sanayiciler Konfederasyonu*
TÜSİAD	Turkish Industry and Business Association; in Turkish, *Türk Sanayicileri ve İş İnsanları Derneği*

Foreword

This book originated in the ambition of the Shibusawa Eiichi Memorial Foundation in Japan to celebrate and diffuse knowledge of the life and work of Shibusawa Eiichi. Shibusawa was a nineteenth-century Japanese venture capitalist and pioneer of the Confucian-inspired *gappon capitalism*, a form of ethical and stakeholder capitalism. The first volume of the project, dealing with Shibusawa's influence in Japan in comparative perspective, was published as *Ethical Capitalism: Shibusawa Eiichi and Business Leadership in Global Perspective* (Patrick Fridenson and Takeo Kikkawa, eds.; University of Toronto Press) in 2017. Subsequently the Foundation launched projects to explore the history of the varieties of ethical capitalism outside Japan, especially in emerging economies. The origins of the project explain why authors in this volume have sought to develop comparisons with Japan in their chapters. This has the additional advantage of preventing an unnecessary Eurocentric bias when seeking to put Turkey's experience in a global perspective.

There are many people to thank who have supported this project. The Shibusawa Eiichi Memorial Foundation supported three conferences in Japan to promote the research, and it has provided logistic and financial support for copyediting among other things. The President of the Foundation, Masahide Shibusawa, and the former managing director, Jun'etsu Komatsu, were key figures in making the project happen. We would also like to thank many Japanese colleagues who supported the project and enabled the authors to deepen comparisons with Japan. We would especially like to thank Takashi Hikino, Takeo Kikkawa, Masato Kimura, Masakazu Shimada and Kazuhiro Tanaka. We also would like to take this opportunity to thank Jeffrey Fear and Christina Lubinski, the editors of the Routledge book series International Studies in Business History. Finally, we thank our copyeditor Jim Runsdorf for his careful work on the whole volume.

This book cannot claim to be the last word in Turkish business history, as there remains much to be researched and explained, but the editors do hope that it will provide momentum for further research. We also hope to show why Turkey presents a fascinating case for anyone interested in the evolution of global capitalism.

Asli M. Colpan, Kyoto
Geoffrey Jones, Boston
June 11 2019

Part I

Institutions and Capitalist Development

1 Business, Ethics and Institutions

The Evolution of Turkish Capitalism in a Comparative Perspective[1]

Asli M. Colpan and Geoffrey Jones

This book seeks to provide a broad overview of the business history of Turkey and its predecessor, the Ottoman Empire. There are major scholarly studies on the economic history and political economy of Turkey, some written by authors in this volume.[2] The distinctive contribution of this book is the greater focus on business enterprises, and the attempt to explore the coevolution of business enterprises with the institutional, economic and social context in shaping Turkey's politics and institutions. The authors address the role of political and social institutions in corporate development, how business formation and change contributed to economic growth, and how ethics and corruption shaped both political and business developments. The book seeks to place the Turkish experience in a comparative context, and so show how the Turkish example can shed light on broader issues of economic development, corporate strategy, and organizational change.

At the broadest level, the Turkish experience forms an important case study in the debate that has raged among economic historians for a decade about the "Great Divergence." At some stage, which is still debated, incomes in Western Europe rose above those in Asia and elsewhere in the world. The Ottoman Empire appears to have broadly similar incomes to Western Europe around the sixteenth century, but then a gap opened. When modern economic growth started with the Industrial Revolution in eighteenth-century Britain, the gap in incomes between the developed West and the Rest grew wider still. A number of non-Western countries, beginning with Japan, caught up, but it was not the norm. The telling of this story has involved lengthy research in developing historical statistics, especially developing indices of GDP per capita and real wage levels.[3] Yet despite considerable scholarly work, a dearth of historical data remains, along with many continuing uncertainties.

The available data certainly confirms that the Ottoman Empire and Turkey were on the "wrong" side of the Great Divergence. Table 1.1 compares per capita GDP growth in the Ottoman Empire/Turkey with that of other nations.

Table 1.1 Real GDP Per Capita 1870–2016 in the Ottoman Empire/Turkey and Other Countries (in 2011 US$)

	1870	*1913*	*1950*	*1970*	*1980*	*1990*	*2016*
Ottoman/ Turkey	1,449	1,831	2,583	5,466	7,543	10,696	17,906
Argentina	2,578	6,670	8,579	12,826	14,414	11,300	18,875
China	754	786	637	1,115	1,539	2,379	12,569
India	710	855	824	1,155	1,300	1,742	6,125
South Korea	465	669	1,178	2,989	5,674	12,004	36,103
Japan	1,160	2,182	3,023	15,286	21,130	29,567	37,465
Britain	5,716	8,052	10,846	16,829	20,211	25,679	37,334
Germany	3,715	7,369	7,840	21,826	28,513	32,178	44,689
USA	3,736	8,101	15,241	23,958	29,613	36,982	53,015

Source: Madison Project Database 2018, www.rug.nl/ggdc/historicaldevelopment/maddison/releases/maddison-project-database-2018

According to this data, the Ottoman Empire was well behind the per capita GDP levels of developed Western countries such as Germany and the United States in 1870. It was also behind Argentina, which was beginning to grow rich through commodity exports. However, the Ottoman Empire was far more affluent than China, India, Japan and Korea. By 1913, Japan, which was undergoing modern economic growth following the opening of the country in the Meiji Restoration in 1868, had surpassed the Ottoman Empire, but Japan's per capita income levels were otherwise still far higher than those of the other Asian economies. This remained true in 1950: Indian real income levels had fallen during the last decades of British colonial rule, while China had been devastated by two decades of Japanese invasion and civil war. Turkey had not, however, caught up at all with the developed West. The gaps between Turkey and both the West and Japan grew much larger during the decades before 1980. By 1990, South Korea, which had been much poorer than Turkey before 1950, had surpassed Turkey in per capita income, and by 2016 the gap had become huge as South Korea grew wealthy rapidly. By 2016 Turkey's per capita income was still higher than China and India's, but both Asian countries began experiencing extremely rapid growth in 1990 and very sharply narrowed the gap between them and Turkey. Turkey never "caught up" with the West, and never achieved the growth spurts of China, Japan and South Korea.

Most of the research on why modern economic growth began in the West, and why countries in the Rest, such as the Ottoman Empire/Turkey, failed to catch up, has focused on macro-level explanations, of which three stand out. The earliest is the role of culture. Crudely put, the West had the "right" culture, and the Rest had "wrong" cultures for capitalist enterprise. Weber, Landes and Mokyr have made this argument in one form or another, as has Ferguson more recently when he identified the Protestant work ethic as one of the West's "killer apps."[4] As Chapter 2, by Ağır, argues, Muslims' attitudes on business were seen as a problem by late Ottoman intellectuals themselves. "Lack of striving for profit through trade, asceticism, and laziness" are cited as the cultural attributes of the "Ottoman man" that caused Muslims to fail in business activities. Thus, according to some authors, governmental attempts to fill the institutional void in order to develop the economy were doomed because of such cultural factors.[5]

The second proposed explanation is that, following the work of Douglass North, the West had the "right" institutions to promote capitalist economic growth, and the Rest did not.[6] This has led to debates about whether the long-term impact of particular colonial regimes, such as the British colonies in North America, had the "right" sort of colonialism, while the Rest did not, and whether countries with a common law system had the "right" legal regime for encouraging capitalist development, and the Rest not. A serious flaw in this theory is its use of property rights laws as a proxy for institutions.[7] It is not evident that the West's property rights regimes were superior to those of parts of the Rest. British India, for example, operated under the common law system. The widespread existence of market activities and the importance of private property in nineteenth-century (and earlier) China would not suggest an overwhelmingly poor property rights regime.[8] While the lack of company law in that country might have made capital raising difficult, when China finally introduced a Company Law Act enabling limited liability in 1904, few Chinese companies registered under the act.[9]

Whatever the weakness of some institutional theories, this line of thought has been influential in explaining Turkey and the Middle East's developmental challenges. In a study published in 2011, Kuran described Islamic law as a major developmental obstacle. He argued that the inheritance system fragmented the estates and property of successful business, the practice of polygamy dispersed wealth, and the ban on usury made it difficult for merchants to obtain credit. The bar on interest also meant that banks could not fully develop.[10] The Ottoman Empire did import French commercial law in 1850. This provided an organizational form that could be used to raise capital, but, as Ağır notes in Chapter 2, take-up was very low.

Finally, education (or lack of it) has been used to account for global wealth and poverty.[11] While plausible, the link with the development of modern business has never been clearly established. Eighteenth- and nineteenth-century China had widespread literacy, for example, which did not translate into the creation of modern firms.[12] Probably the greatest negative consequence of low education levels was raising the cost of skilled labor. In the case of colonial India, the high cost of skilled labor has been identified as one possible explanation for why the country remained inclined to small-scale traditional manufacture.[13] Whatever the exact consequences, and accepting that there are acute difficulties with the methodology of measuring and comparing education levels between countries, we may safely conclude that literacy levels were low in the Ottoman Empire and the Republic of Turkey. Using an adult literacy metric, we observe that Turkey had 8.2 percent literacy in 1925 and 30 percent in 1950. In comparison Argentina, which had the best education system in Latin America, had adult literacy rates of 60 and 87 percent in those years. In 1950 China had 47 percent adult literacy and Thailand 52 percent, although India had only 19 percent.[14]

This book does not seek to engage directly with these macro explanations of the Great Divergence, although it contains particularly rich insights on the development of institutions. It does seek to develop a more firm-specific lens through which to view the issues, something that has been notably absent from most of the Great Divergence literature.[15]

1.1 Is Turkish Business History Distinctive?

A recent survey of the business history of emerging markets observed considerable commonalities across Africa, Asia and Latin America arising from the fact that businesses based in these regions faced five common challenges.[16] Because Turkey encountered the same obstacles, its development experience was quite typical of many countries beyond Western Europe and North America. First, and most obviously, these countries had to catch up with the developed West. This left them with multiple impediments to building successful businesses, from finding skilled labor forces to breaking into markets already dominated by powerful Western incumbents. Naturally, in the broad picture there was much variation within individual countries. India may have been poor and rural before World War I, but the port cities of Bombay and Calcutta were important hubs of modern business enterprise.[17] In the Ottoman Empire, Istanbul was a large commercial and cultural center, quite different from the rural areas where most people lived.[18]

A second challenge faced by these countries was Western imperialism. In nineteenth- and early twentieth-century Africa and South Asia, and earlier in Latin America, the social, institutional and cultural impact of colonization was huge, enduring and more often negative than positive. The Ottoman Empire was one of the countries that escaped formal colonialization, but experienced long periods of constrained autonomy.

In the case of the Ottoman Empire, the West's political power was evident. The so-called "capitulation" treaties, especially those from the early nineteenth century, gave special privileges to Europeans and the non-Muslim minorities who lived in the Empire, primarily Greeks, Armenians and Jews. These communities were free to choose European legal jurisdictions besides the Ottoman Islamic judicial system in disputes involving non-Muslims, such as in contracting and dispute resolution. They were also exempted from several taxes and paid lower customs duties.[19] As the Ottoman Empire aimed to modernize itself during the *Tanzimat* (Reform) period (1839–1876), Muslim Turks could obtain jobs in the bureaucracy and viewed business as an inferior occupation. The overall result was that the Turkish Muslim majority was relatively absent from private business.[20]

The financial collapse and default of the Ottoman government in 1875 was a pivotal event in Ottoman history that rendered the government subject to restrictive Western controls. The Empire basically lost financial autonomy after the formation of the Public Debt Administration, dominated by European bondholder organizations, in 1881. The consequences, however, are debatable. Although this crisis is classically seen as an example of malign Western imperialism, Burdal paints a more nuanced picture, arguing that it enabled the Ottoman government to borrow at lower rates because of reduced risk, and especially resulted in a surge of foreign direct investment, which among other things facilitated the development of railroads.[21]

Third, almost all these countries went through long periods of state intervention. As noted by Fridenson in Chapter 6, government policies are often not exogenous to business, and must instead need to be regarded as a result of interaction. Yet in broad terms the importance of state policies is clear. Practically all private businesses in late Imperial China required state patronage.[22] As the countries sought modernization, there was more state intervention. In China after the Communist Revolution in 1949 capitalist enterprise was effectively abolished until the 1980s. Long periods of import substitution, planning, controls and other forms of state intervention were prevalent in South Asia, sub-Saharan Africa and Latin America between the 1950s and 1980s. These policies promoted industrialization, but often in a distorted fashion, and with a great deal of rent-seeking and corruption, as discussed in Chapter 10 by Hunter and Jones.

Governments also interacted directly with business by establishing their own firms. State-owned enterprises were very important in many developing countries between the 1930s and the 1980s, especially in public utilities, energy, resource extraction, and finance and banking. In Brazil, for example, the state-owned development bank BNDES became hugely important to the industrial sector.[23] However, the relative importance of state-owned businesses varied. Within Latin America, for instance, state-owned firms became very important in Argentina, Brazil and Mexico, but rather less so elsewhere.[24]

The Ottoman Empire and the Republic of Turkey broadly fit this overall pattern. As Chapter 2 explores, the Ottoman state closely watched market activities, although, as Ağır makes clear, it should not be described as "anti-capitalistic" as such. The state supervised the guilds that dominated economic activity before the late nineteenth century. The impact of these guilds, however, is less easy to generalize about. They created entry barriers and stifled competition, but they also generated social benefits.

As the following chapters, and especially Chapter 3, by Buğra, discuss, during the 1930s the Turkish government intervened extensively by establishing public enterprises, partly because indigenous private investment was stagnant. After World War II, which Turkey had stayed out of until almost the end, governments experimented with less interventionist policies, especially after Adnan Menderes of the Democrat Party, came to power in 1950 as the first democratically elected prime minister in the history of Turkey. However, policies soon shifted back towards increased state intervention.[25] The Foreign Capital Incentive Law was enacted in 1950 to encourage foreign direct investment (FDI), but in practice bureaucratic and legal complexities and hurdles resulted in few foreign firms entering Turkey.[26] The state's role continued to be critical for the accumulation of capital as import substitution and a protected domestic market from 1960 to the end of the 1970s further helped the enlargement of business groups. Those entrepreneurs who had established "contact" capabilities with the series of governments that ruled Turkey during these years were thus in a favorable position to grow.

Fourth, these non-Western countries have faced what are often described as "institutional voids" in their capital, labor and other markets.[27] The historical literature has fully documented many situations where land could be sold but only with difficulty and encumbrances, and where institutional credit was unavailable to the overwhelming majority of small businesses, which could obtain loans but only informally, often expensively, and from a very small range of potential suppliers.

Finally, most countries outside the West have witnessed much turbulence in their business environments. Political instability, expropriation, violence and extreme macroeconomic fluctuations—often a function of dependence on exports of primary commodities and abrupt policy reversals—have been the norm rather than the exception. Economic and political institutional instability became embedded in business life in Latin America over the long term, for example, with coups, military dictatorships and political shifts becoming the norm, except in a handful of countries such as Colombia and Mexico.[28] The impact on business of high turbulence was profound: for Argentinean entrepreneurs, for example, extended volatility and abrupt shifts in economic policy frequently led to a tactical rather than a strategic mind-set. The short-run became a matter of weeks.[29] Argentina's poor economic performance during the second half of the twentieth century, evident in Table 1.1, was one consequence.

Certainly, Turkey's modern history fits this turbulent pattern. The disintegration of the Ottoman Empire and its replacement by the Republic of Turkey in 1923 was one such enormous shock. Between the 1960s and the 1980s repeated military coups provided other shocks. After 1960, when an army coup overthrew the government, policies were characterized by planned economic development with protectionist trade policies. Local firms were given incentives to enter into the manufacturing sector, foreign exchange was allocated to favored industries, and state contracts were granted to enable construction and international trade. But the policies were poorly implemented. There was political turmoil with eight short-lived coalition governments and two military coups, in 1971 and 1980.[30] There was hyper-inflation between the 1970s and 1990s. In 2001 a major economic crisis saw the stock market crash and interest rates at one point reach 3,000 percent. After a number of years of accelerated economic growth during the 2000s, there was a new bout of financial instability, culminating in a major currency and debt crisis in 2018.

If the challenges faced by business in the Ottoman Empire/Turkey have many parallels elsewhere, so do the responses. In Turkey, as in many emerging markets, family business was the dominant organizational form.[31] Larger businesses also took the form of diversified business groups. These appeared quite early, before World War I in Asian countries such as India, and Latin American countries such as Argentina. Examples included the Tata group in India and the Tornquist group in Argentina.[32] These organizations have continued to dominate modern business in most of the non-Western world. For decades such diversified business groups were practically nonexistent and/or stereotyped in the mainstream economic development, strategy and management literatures. More recently they have no longer automatically been seen as rent-seeking and inefficient legacies of the past, or second-best alternatives to Western-style corporations, and instead have been re-interpreted as rational responses to institutional voids, which could be highly productive and were certainly durable.[33]

Turkey was somewhat late in creating modern business groups. Before the establishment of the Turkish Republic, there were larger firms in the Ottoman Empire, especially in agriculture, food-processing, banking, trading, mining and railroads, but as noted earlier they mostly belonged to minorities such as Armenians, Greeks and Jews. Creating a national business class became an objective of the new government, which actively supported private business development by Muslim Turks. The government thus gave tax allowances and exemptions; awarded customs exemptions for importing industrial machinery and apparatus; granted land parcels to those who would build factories; provided various types of financial incentives; and assigned profitable sectors to private enterprises. These policies facilitated the emergence of the first cohort of business groups.[34]

In spite of the dramatic turn of economic policies towards liberalization and opening of the domestic markets beginning in the 1980s, as Chapters 3 and 4 show, diversified business groups remained resilient forms of business organizations in the economy, even if individual groups failed and new ones appeared. Turkish business groups continued to display many similarities to groups elsewhere, including their formation of internal capital and labor markets, pursuit of their private interests, and dependence on government for business. As Chapter 7 by Yurtoğlu and Chapter 8 by Üsdiken show, Turkish business groups shared a reluctance to incorporate salaried professional managers in top decision making, which can be found in many other emerging markets, although there was a noteworthy contrast with the Japanese business groups, known as *zaibatsu*, which were formed in the Meiji period and incorporated professional managers into strategic decision making from early on.[35]

A number of aspects of Turkish business history were more distinctive. A noteworthy feature of many countries seeking to "catch up" from their relatively low nineteenth-century per capita GDP was the role of minorities, diaspora and immigrants. The reasons have been the subject of much discussion. While some have emphasized the distinctive values of such groups, others have pointed to advantages in capital raising and access to knowledge. The pattern is clear, however. In India, particular ethnicities such as Parsis, which included the Tata family, and certain Hindu castes, dominated modern entrepreneurship. By the interwar years Marwari families, such as Birla, had become prominent.[36] Elsewhere in Asia, economic growth was driven by the entrepreneurial activities of Hokkien Chinese in Java and the Philippines, the Chinese mestizos in the Philippines and Chettiars in Burma.[37]

The business elites of Latin America were heavily populated by immigrant minorities. The families behind the big business groups in Argentina were typically immigrants, especially Italian.[38] In the case of Mexico, French, Spanish and German immigrants were highly significant as entrepreneurs.[39] Even in Colombia, which attracted few immigrants, the few hundred Europeans who settled in the country's Caribbean ports from the late nineteenth century became prominent within the local business elites.[40]

The Ottoman Empire initially fitted the pattern of minorities being important in business well, given the preeminence of Armenians, Greeks and Jews. However the events during World War I surrounding the end of the Empire and the creation of the Republic of Turkey transformed this situation. Non-Muslim minorities were distrusted, as they were seen to engage in their own territorial claims, collaborating with the imperialist forces.[41] The Armenian tragedy of 1915 and later the population exchange with Greece sharply reduced the most entrepreneurial elements in Ottoman society.[42] The residual non-Muslim population thereafter was subject to overt discrimination, which reached another peak during World War II with the Wealth Tax in 1942.[43]

There are few other cases of such decimation of a country's entrepreneurial elite. Perhaps the closest parallels are after the Russian Revolution in 1917 and the Chinese Revolution in 1949, when the capitalist classes were expropriated and/or forced to flee. In the Chinese case, the primary winners were the British colony of Hong Kong, Taiwan and Southeast Asian countries with large ethnic Chinese populations, which received an infusion of entrepreneurial talent. Another example was the expulsion of the Asian community in Uganda in 1972. The 50,000 Asians expelled owned 90 percent of the country's businesses. However, their return after two decades enabled them in time to resume a prominent role in Uganda's business sector.[44] In the case of Turkey, there were few returnees, although some expelled from the Ottoman Empire became highly successful entrepreneurs elsewhere, including Aristotle Onassis, who acquired Argentinean and later Greek citizenship after he and his family fled from their homes in Smyrna (İzmir) in 1922 and between the 1950s and 1970s became a prominent shipping magnate.[45]

The attempt to build a new Muslim national business class through tax allowances and exemptions, customs exemptions for importing industrial machinery and equipment granting land parcels to those who would build factories, and other financial incentives proved challenging. As Chapter 2 observes, a new series of changes to legal institutions, especially the introduction of a new commercial code in 1926 based on a French code of commerce revised the same year, was executed in a fashion that prioritized the creation of a Muslim business class, even if it involved legitimizing rent-seeking and illicit gains. As striking was how Anatolia-based conservative Muslim business grew large enough to challenge the secular Istanbul business class, a development examined by Fabbe, Özlale, and Balıkçıoğlu in Chapter 5.

Again, parallels are hard to find. The most direct might be Malaysia, where ethnic Chinese dominated the modern business sector after independence from Britain in 1957. Beginning in the 1980s, government support for ethnic Muslim Malays helped build large business groups. The outcomes were not good. The largest Malay group was Renong, a group of companies closely linked to the ruling political party. The venture grew rapidly through government contracts to build motorways, telecoms networks, and other infrastructure projects, primarily with money borrowed from banks. However, the Asian financial crisis of 1997 exposed the weakness of the entire structure, which included systemic attempts to cheat minority shareholders. In 2001 Renong was taken over by the country's sovereign wealth fund Khazanah Nasional Bhd on the grounds that the group had too much debt and posed a systemic risk to the banking system. The Renong episode, and similar episodes in the country, was illustrative of the corrupt business system co-created by the Malaysian government and Malay business leaders during the 1980s. The system displayed almost no evidence of innovation whilst delivering scandals at the highest levels of business and government.[46]

A final distinctive feature of the business history of the Republic of Turkey was the remarkably small role of foreign-owned business. This was not true of the Ottoman period. The Imperial Ottoman Bank, the state bank founded in 1856 was managed from Paris and London. And there was extensive FDI in the country apart from finance, including in insurance, ports, docks and tobacco. Geyikdagi among others has explored how these investments were often entangled with Western political interests, and has argued that they had a broadly negative impact on Ottoman development.[47]

Nationalistic policies and economic instability subsequently made the Republic of Turkey very inhospitable for foreign firms. Ford's disastrous experience trying to manufacture automobiles in interwar Turkey is discussed in Chapter 4. During the postwar decades few foreign companies sought to invest in Turkey. Exchange controls which made profit remittances difficult and government policies to block wholly-owned foreign businesses made Turkey, like India and Japan, deeply unattractive as a host country for global firms. In 1980 the ratio of the stock of inward FDI to GDP was 0.2 percent. This was almost the lowest in the non-Communist developing world. In the same year the ratio for India, another country whose government sought to restrict foreign ownership, was 0.7 percent. The ratios were 1.8 percent for South Korea, 7.4 percent for Brazil, 14 percent for Indonesia, 21 percent for Malaysia and 53 percent for Singapore.[48]

Koç's lengthy endeavors to entice US automobile manufactures to invest in Turkey, discussed in Chapter 4, was indicative of the unwillingness of foreign firms to consider Turkey as a location in this era. The Anglo-Dutch consumer goods company Unilever did enter Turkey in 1950 when it established Unilever-İş, which included a 20-percent equity holding by the government-owned İş Bank. The company launched a highly successful vegetable ghee called Vita, and developed a large market for margarine in the country, and by the mid-1960s accounted for one-third of all fats consumed in Turkey, including butter and olive oil. However by the 1970s the business was being badly constrained by government controls and restrictions, including a prohibition on remitting any dividends. The company resolved to stay in Turkey until government policies changed, as they did in the 1980s, but few other multinationals had the size or the patience to do business in the country, opting instead to work with agents or license technologies.[49]

The low participation by foreign companies was matched by low exposure to international economy in trade. Figure 1.1 shows the low ratio of exports and imports to GDP during most of the period, with the ratios only moving upwards after 1980 as liberalization and internationalization was put in place.

During the 2000s Turkey became a much more attractive host economy. Inward FDI grew from $18 billion in 2000 to $180 billion in 2017. Many of the biggest investments came from Asia and the Middle East, particularly Qatar.[50] However, by that time India held twice as

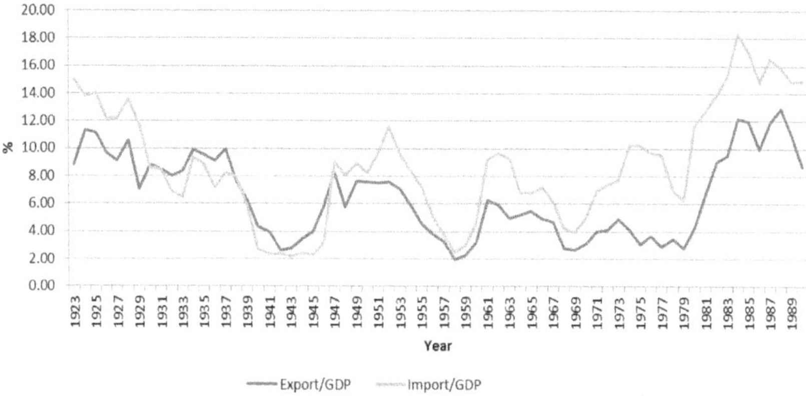

Figure 1.1 Turkish Exports and Imports as a Percentage of GDP, 1923–1990

Source: Compiled from statistical data (*Yıllara Göre Dış Ticaret, Gayri Safi Yurtiçi Hasıla*) at Türkiye İstatistik Kurumu at www.tuik.gov

much inward FDI, while countries like Brazil, Indonesia and Thailand far exceeded the stock of Turkey. While a preference for local ownership rather than reliance on foreign multinationals was not necessarily a developmental handicap—both Japan and South Korea experienced economic miracles led by local firms—in the case of Turkey it probably contributed to weaker economic performance as the country's local firms were not particularly innovative. Nor were the local affiliates of foreign firms.

The business history of Turkey, then, has many commonalities with other emerging markets, including extensive government intervention, large institutional voids and considerable turbulence. The business group organizational form became preeminent, and family ownership was the norm rather than the exception. The really big exceptions were related to matters of ethnicity and religion, seen in the expropriation of the primary entrepreneurial groups in the 1910s and 1920s, and subsequently the bifurcation of modern business into secular and religious components during the late twentieth century. The very limited role of foreign-owned business in the Republic of Turkey was noteworthy too. It probably reduced opportunities for significant technological transfer, which had to use licensing modes instead, and it also limited the competitive structure of the economy.

1.2 Ethical Capitalism and Responsibility

In recent years there has been renewed interest in the history of corporate responsibility and ethical capitalism, although much of this research is still focused on the developed West. As industrialization took hold, some business leaders in Europe and the United States engaged in various forms of paternalism towards their workers, from providing welfare benefits to building company towns. In the United States there was also the advent of business philanthropy. From steel magnate Andrew Carnegie's establishment of the Carnegie Foundation in 1911 onwards, a succession of business leaders has devoted enormous sums of money to charitable foundations. Bill Gates, Warren Buffet, George Kaiser, and the Walton family are among the American business leaders who have continued this distinctive tradition until the present day.[51]

The huge wealth created by the affluent but economically stratified society of the United States provided the resources to fund these foundations, while the limited role of the state provided gaps to fill. These factors fueled the ambitions of successful business leaders to shape the future. Large individual wealth was combined with a distinctive value system that was highly individualistic yet had a strong sense of community. Religion also played its part in shaping the mental attitudes of the early business philanthropists in the United States. Later in life Carnegie became an active Presbyterian. The Rockefeller family, who created the Rockefeller Foundation in 1913, were Baptists. The hotelier Conrad Hilton, who established a foundation in 1944 to "relieve the suffering, the distressed, and the destitute," was a fervent Roman Catholic. Meanwhile, industrial paternalism was often associated with particular religious sects, such as the Quakers.[52]

Despite receiving much less attention, a concern for social, and sometimes ecological, responsibility has also been found to be a common feature in the business history of emerging markets.[53] In Latin America, an important driver of the business response to social responsibility was the influence of the Roman Catholic Church, and especially Social Catholic Doctrine, usually dated from Pope Leo XIII's 1891 encyclical letter *Rerum novarum*, which condemned both capitalism and socialism.[54]

A belief in the broad responsibility of business to society emerged early in the modern industrialization of India in the nineteenth century. Parsis followed Zorastrian beliefs about the importance of doing good works in the material world. The Tata family, for example, was an early advocate of the responsibilities of business.[55] During the interwar years, the independence campaigner Mohandas Gandhi proposed that businesses should act as trustees or stewards, sharing profits among multiple stakeholders and maintaining the highest ethical standards. These views, derived variously from Western writers such as John Ruskin and aspects of Hindu and Jain traditional philosophies and practices, influenced a number of business practitioners, including the prominent business leaders G.D. Birla and Jamnalal Bajaj.[56]

Whether in Latin America or India, businesses committed to wider social purposes were never the norm, though in some cases—like the

Parsi firms in India—they were significant components of the business sector. There are other cases too where the same historical and institutional context provided radically different models about the responsibility of business to society. The different business models that appeared in Japan after the Meiji Restoration in 1868 provide a striking example. Iwasaki Yataro's shipping company, Mitsubishi, was very profit focused. It was one of the pioneers of the *zaibatsu*-style diversified business group. This contrasted considerably with the venture capitalist Shibusawa Eiichi's evolving concept of *gappon shugi*, a form of stakeholder capitalism that has been examined extensively in recent research.[57]

A very early trip to Europe in 1867 and 1868, where he was impressed with the status of business leaders in national policy-making, seems to have stimulated Shibusawa to radically reconsider traditional Confucian teachings.[58] Gappon capitalism can be understood as a system to achieve sustainable catch-up growth.[59] It was heavily shaped by the institutional voids faced by the country. In order to overcome capital shortages that deterred the industrialization of Japan, Shibusawa introduced the joint stock company concept in 1869 through which he accumulated capital from numerous shareholders, mainly wealthy members of the nobility, merchants and landlords.[60] He founded or invested in new ventures or in other start-ups, and raised additional capital from other potential investors. He then often opened up these firms to the public by listing them on the stock exchange in order to raise additional capital. Once the companies he invested in achieved a healthy growth pattern, Shibusawa would sell off his shares and use the earnings to reinvest in the next promising businesses.[61] To support this business model, Shibusawa founded the Tokyo Stock Exchange and the "First National Bank" of Japan as the first *private* commercial bank in the country.[62]

Shibusawa also aimed to correct failures in the labor market, especially in the managerial class, by supporting the foundation of the Tokyo Commercial School (later Hitotsubashi University) for business education in 1920 and other institutions for the study of commerce and law.[63] Furthermore, professional managers were nurtured in the enterprises founded by Shibusawa and, when necessary, transferred to other enterprises he had founded. He himself acted as "an official and unpaid management development center (in these enterprises) . . . setting up all kinds of courses, seminars and discussion groups" designed to nurture young executives.[64] In these enterprises, Shibusawa gave the salaried professional managers autonomy and responsibility, and even promoted them to the directorship positions. These salaried professional managers who became directors were granted share ownership in the companies and would hold a strong grip on the strategic control of their businesses.

The other leg of Shibusawa's *gappon* capitalism was related to the *goal* towards which the gappon entrepreneur conducted the institutional void-filling activities. He sought not only to achieve short-term private profits from his business activity, but also enhancement of public welfare. He was not prepared to take on a business activity that generated profits by immoral or illegal means. Shibusawa developed a set of ideas he called the "inseparability of economy and morality," bringing together Confucian ethics with market capitalism. This was different from and beyond simple compliance to regulatory requirements and social expectations; it meant a voluntary and active commitment to the social good.[65]

In Shibusawa's *gappon* businesses, ownership was dispersed among numerous shareholders.[66] The board of the companies consisted of investor-directors—usually both the original shareholders and salaried professional managers who had received some shareholding in the company. Execution would be left mostly to the salaried professional managers. Thanks to this arrangement the *gappon* enterprise theoretically had fewer agency problems as large investors who were represented on the boards were supposed to effectively monitor managers' decisions. The principal-principal problems—that is, problems between different shareholders, majority and minority—were actively mediated by Shibusawa himself and other investor-directors. Shibusawa promoted the concept of "long-term goal orientation," which is necessary to integrate private profits with the public interest, and actively emphasized that approach in order to secure common interest among different shareholders. Shibusawa believed that only by taking such a long-term perspective could companies produce results for the public good, and not simply for their shareholders. Concentration of shareholding among a number of limited shareholders each with large equity stakes, who were also interested in the sustainability of their enterprises, facilitated patient capital.

As Chapter 2 by Ağır and Chapter 7 by Yurtoğlu discuss in detail, Turkey has a rich history of philanthropy rooted in the institution of "*waqf*," an inalienable charitable endowment under Islamic law, which played a central role as an instrument of public policy in the social and economic life of Ottoman pre-modern cities. As the Ottoman Empire undertook the project of modernization, which was pursued more aggressively during the young Republic, the activities of the *waqf* were transferred to the government. In 1954 the *waqf* activities were abolished and their capital put in the Bank of Awqaf. Neither the Turkish Civil Code nor the Code of Commerce made use of the Turkish word for *waqf*, (i.e., *vakıf*) and instead used the word *tesis*, or establishment. In 1967, however, new legislation provided for the establishment of secular *waqf* with Islamic principles. The Turkish Civil Code replaced the word *tesis* with *vakıf*, which were given a judicial role. Soon afterwards the large business groups began establishing philanthropic foundations.[67]

The closest corporate counterpart to Japan's Shibusawa in terms of impact on the Turkish economy and society was Vehbi Koç and his business group. As Colpan and Jones show in Chapter 4, as Koç grew his business, he did not have easy access to capital as the capital markets were underdeveloped; nor did he have easy access to educated human talent. Koç aimed to overcome these barriers often by establishing complex shareholding across his companies, which would then fund other newly establishing companies that individually also had separate partners; and, beginning in the 1970s, partially opening their shares to the public. He also employed inter-company transfers of employees for managerial training, and in 1982 even founded the Koç Holding Training and Development Center to provide business education for his group employees. Yet, unlike Shibusawa and much like the Japanese *zaibatsu* business groups, the Koç organization remained a family business group, and Koç and his family maintained effective control of the Koç companies.

During all these endeavors Koç, like Shibusawa, became increasingly attentive to business ethics. The Koç group's case was somewhat unusual as its founder early on began shifting his emphasis to generating public good alongside private profits, claiming: "I live and prosper with my country. As long as democracy exists and thrives, so do we. We shall do our utmost to strengthen our economy. As our economy prospers, so will democracy and our standing in the world."[68] He was committed to the moral conduct of business and even, as noted in Chapter 4, apologized publicly when his companies failed to adhere to his high standards during World War II.

Koç's social responsibility extended to his philanthropic activities, especially in education, health and culture. Early philanthropic endeavors included the donation of dormitories to Ankara University in 1951 and to Middle East Technical University in 1968, a donation for the building of the Vehbi Koç Eye Bank within the Ankara University Medical School in 1962, and the building of the Admiral Bristol Vehbi Koç Cancer Pavilion in 1967.[69] In 1969 he formally established the Vehbi Koç Foundation, donating eight percent of Koç Holding's shares, which were equivalent to 12 million liras ($1.3 million) at the time. Unlike Shibusawa, Koç continued such efforts not only individually but especially through the projects undertaken together with the Koç Foundation as well as Koç Holding and its several affiliated companies. Koç's actions set a benchmark which others sought to emulate. In 1992 the Koç Group established its own university. Other families controlling large business groups followed suit: the Sabancı, Yaşar and Özyeğin families, for example, founding, respectively, Sabancı University (1996), Yaşar University (2001) and Özyeğin University (2007).[70]

Business leaders also invested in other educational projects, including targeting girls' education. In 1993 Hüsnü Özyeğin, the founder of Fiba Group, a multi-billion investment holding company with diversified interests, together with his wife created the Mother and Child Education Foundation, which trained unprivileged mothers to raise their children better and prepare them for school. By 2013, it had trained about 850,000 women and young preschool children in every province of Turkey.

Murat Vargı, after working for several decades for Koç, founded his own diversified group, MV Holding, which provides scholarships to deserving girls as part of its corporate philanthropy. He noted in a recent interview that "It's the mother who raises the children. . . . If they remain ignorant mothers, so their children also remain ignorant."[71]

A final reflection on ethical capitalism must move beyond individual firms and institutions to consider the overall situation that shapes business responsibility and ethical capitalism. First, as Chapter 10 observes, Turkey is characterized by very low trust levels within society beyond the confined domains of family and community, one of the consequences of which is that although individual philanthropy levels are quite high, little is given to civil society organizations. Most acts of philanthropy are directed towards family members and neighbors. Second, as Chapters 9 and 10 observe, Turkey has a long history of corruption, which has seeped into the political economy, and has been exacerbated in certain periods by government policies. While business leaders see corruption as a critical issue, interestingly, Çarkoğlu suggests that Turkish public perceptions of corruption have much to do with media coverage patterns. Corruption appears to drop from public attention if the media does not see it as a problem.

1.3 Concluding Remarks

Turkish business over the last century and a half was shaped in an institutional context similar to those in many developing countries. The country missed out on the first wave of modern industrialization during the Ottoman era and developed in a somewhat skewed way, with minority religious and ethnic groups dominating business, in part because of policies imposed by the Western powers. As in many developing countries, business in the Ottoman Empire faced the daunting task of catching up with the developed West. Unlike most other countries, however, the elimination of entrepreneurial minority groups greatly complicated the task, and gave it some distinct characteristics. At the center of this distinctiveness was the role of the government in the early Turkish Republic, which pursued a nationalistic and secular agenda in a Muslim country. Turkish business (in contrast to, say, that of India) grew in an insular fashion, largely unable to develop strong international competitive advantages compared to some of its South Asian and Latin American counterparts. Turkey's business groups were, as elsewhere, a response to institutional voids and the importance of contact capabilities but even the best of them remained primarily focused on the domestic market, and mostly functioned as licensors of foreign technologies rather than as drivers of innovation.[72]

The last three decades have seen a remarkable development as long-established business groups have faced a new set of challenges from the provincial towns of Anatolia, which are characterized by their religious beliefs and links to political Islam. They created their own associations and utilized institutions that have roots in traditional Islamic and Ottoman history, such as the *vakıf*, to raise capital. Strikingly, this sector of the business community emerges in Chapter 5 as more resilient and responsive to the global economy than do their secular counterparts. Anatolian capitalism has thus become a source of renewal and growth for the Turkish economy, albeit one in which persistent problems of corruption and rent-seeking have appeared in new forms.

Notes

1. The authors would like to thank Behlül Üsdiken for helpful comments on an earlier draft of this chapter.
2. A. Buğra, *State and Business in Modern Turkey: A Comparative Study*, New York: State University of New York Press, 1994; A. Buğra and O. Savaşkan, *New Capitalism in Turkey: The Relationship Between Politics, Religion and Business*, Northampton, MA: Edward Elgar Publishing, 2014.
3. G. Jones, "The Great Divergence and the Great Convergence," in T. Lopes, C. Lubinski, and H.J.S. Tworek (eds.) *The Routledge Companion to the Makers of Global Business*, New York: Routledge, 2019.
4. M. Weber, *The Protestant Ethic and the Spirit of Capitalism*, reprint, Oxford: Oxford University Press, 2011; D.S. Landes, *The Wealth and Poverty of Nations*, New York: W.W. Norton, 1998; J. Mokyr, *The Lever of Riches*, Oxford: Oxford University Press, 1990; N. Ferguson, *Civilization: The West and the Rest*, London: The Penguin Press 2011.
5. See Chapter 2, section 2.3.
6. D.C. North, *Institutions, Institutional Change and Economic Performance*, Cambridge: Cambridge University Press, 1990; D.C. North, *Understanding the Process of Economic Change*, Princeton, NJ: Princeton University Press, 2005.
7. G. Jones, *Entrepreneurship and Multinationals: Global Business and the Making of the Modern World*, Northampton, MA: Edward Elgar Publishing, 2013, pp. 14–18.
8. K. Deng, "A Critical Survey of Recent Research in Chinese Economic History," *Economic History Review*, v.53, n. 1 2000, pp. 1–28; D.A. Faure, *China and Capitalism*, Hong Kong: Hong Kong University Press, 2006.
9. W.C. Kirby, "China Unincorporated: Company Law and Business Enterprise in Twentieth-Century China," *Journal of Asian Studies*, v.54, 1995, pp. 43–63.
10. T. Kuran, *The Long Divergence: How Islamic Law Held Back the Middle East*, Princeton, NJ: Princeton University Press, 2011.
11. R.A. Easterlin, "Why Isn't the Whole World Developed?" *Journal of Economic History*, v.41, n. 1, 1981, pp. 1–19.
12. Deng, "A Critical Survey."
13. T. Roy, *The Economic History of India 1857–1947*, New Delhi: Oxford University Press, 2000, Chapter 7.
14. Adult Literacy Rates, www.hbs.edu/businesshistory/courses/resources/historical-data-visualization/Pages/details.aspx?data_id=31, accessed April 21, 2019.
15. Jones, "The Great Divergence."

16. G. Austin, C. Davila, and G. Jones, "The Alternative Business History: Business in Emerging Markets," *Business History Review*, v.91, n. 3, 2017, pp. 537–569.
17. T. Roy, "Beyond Divergence: Rethinking the Economic History of India," *Economic History of Developing Regions*, v.27, n. 1, 2012, pp. 57–65.
18. Y. Bahadıroğlu "Osmanlı Devletinin nüfüsu ne kadardı?" *Yeni Akit*, September 6, 2017, https://m.yeniakit.com.tr/yazarlar/yavuz-bahadiroglu/osmanli-devletinin-nufusu-ne-kadardi-20921.html
19. Kuran, *Long Divergence*; Artunç, "The Protégé System."
20. Buğra, *State*; Y. Kepenek and N. Yentürk, *Türkiye Ekonomisi*, Istanbul: Remzi Kitabevi, 2000; H. Şahin, *Türkiye Ekonomisi*, Bursa: Ezgi Kitabevi Yayınları, 2002.
21. M. Burdal, *The Political Economy of Ottoman Public Debt: Insolvency and European Financial Control in the Late Nineteenth Century*, London: Tauris Academic Studies, 2010.
22. Faure, *China and Capitalism.*
23. Carlos Marichal, "Archival Note: Banking History and Archives in Latin America," *Business History Review*, v.82, n. 3, 2008, pp. 595–596.
24. A. Musacchio and S. Lazzarini, *Reinventing State Capitalism: Leviathan in Business, Brazil and Beyond*, Cambridge, MA: Harvard University Press, 2014.
25. Buğra, *State.*
26. L. Yılmaz, "4875 Sayılı Doğrudan Yabancı Yatırımlar Kanunu'nun Getirdiği Yenilikler," *İstanbul Ticaret Üniversitesi Sosyal Bilimler Dergisi*, v.5, n. 10, 2006, pp. 173–190; A. Zarakolu, "Yabancı Sermayeyi Teşvik Kanunu," 1954, http://auhf.ankara.edu.tr/dergiler/auhfd-arsiv/AUHF-1954-11-01-02/AUHF-1954-11-01-02-Zarakolu.pdf, accessed April 14, 2013.
27. C. Gao, T. Zuzul, G. Jones, and T. Khanna, "Overcoming Institutional Voids: A Reputation-Based View of Long-Run Survival," *Strategic Management Journal*, v.38, n. 11, 2017, pp. 2147–2167.
28. Austin, Davila and Jones, "Alternative."
29. G. Jones and A. Lluch, "Argentine and Chilean Business in the Second Global Economy," in G. Jones and A. Lluch (eds.) *The Impact of Globalization on Argentina and Chile: Business Enterprises and Entrepreneurship*, Northampton, MA: Edward Elgar Publishing, 2015, pp. 261–262.
30. Buğra, *State.*
31. For recent historical research on family business in emerging markets, see especially P. Fernández and A. Lluch (eds.), *Evolution of Family Business: Continuity and Change in Latin America and Spain*, Northampton, MA: Edward Elgar Publishing, 2016.
32. M.I. Barbero, "Business Groups, in Nineteenth and Twentieth Century Argentina," in Jones and Lluch (eds.) *Impact*, pp. 6–44; M. Raianu, "The Incorporation of India: The Tata Business Firm Between Empire and Nation, ca. 1860–1970," unpublished Harvard PhD dissertation, 2017.
33. A.M. Colpan, T. Hikino, and J.R. Lincoln (eds.), *The Oxford Handbook of Business Groups,* Oxford: Oxford University Press, 2010.
34. A.M. Colpan, "Business Groups in Turkey," in Colpan, Hikino, and Lincoln (eds.) *Oxford Handbook*, pp. 486–525.
35. W. M. Fruin, *The Japanese Enterprise System: Competitive Strategies and Cooperative Structures*, Oxford: Clarendon Press, 1992; H. Miyajima and S. Kawamoto, "Business Groups in Prewar Japan: Historical Formation and Legacy," in Colpan, Hikino, and Lincoln (eds.) *Oxford Handbook*, pp. 97–126.

36. A.V. Desai, "The Parsis: Entrepreneurial Success," in M.M. Kudaisya (ed.) *The Oxford India Anthology of Business History*, New Delhi: Oxford University Press, 2011, pp. 122–130; T.A. Timberg, *The Marwaris, from Traders to Industrialists*, New Delhi: Allen Lane, 1978; A. Hardgrove, *Community and Public Culture: The Marwaris in Calcutta, c. 1897–1997*, New York: Columbia University Press, 2002.
37. C. Dobbin, *Asian Entrepreneurial Minorities: Conjoint Communities in the Making of the World Economy 1570–1940*, Richmond: Curzon Press, 1996.
38. M. Barbero and A. Lluch, "Family Capitalism in Argentina: Changes and Continuities Over the Course of a Century," in Fernández and Lluch (eds.) *Evolution*, pp. 123–156.
39. A. Gómez-Galvarriato, "Networks and Entrepreneurship: The Modernization of the Textile Business in Porfirian Mexico," *Business History Review*, v.82, n. 3, 2008, pp. 475–502.
40. C. Dávila, *Empresas y empresarios en la Historia de Colombia: Siglos XIX y XX*, Bogota: Editorial Norma, 2003.
41. See Chapter 2.
42. See Chapter 3.
43. S. Ağır and C. Artunç, "The Wealth Tax of 1942 and the Disappearance of Non-Muslim Enterprises in Turkey," *Journal of Economic History*, v.79, n. 1, 2019, pp. 201–243; A. Aktar, "Tax Me to the End of My Life!": Anatomy of an Anti-Minority Tax Legislation (1942–3)," in B.C. Fortna, S. Katsikas, D. Kamouzis, and P. Konortas (eds.) *State-Nationalisms in the Ottoman Empire, Greece and Turkey : Orthodox and Muslims, 1830–1945*, New York: Routledge, 2013, pp. 188–221.
44. F. Dawood, "Ugandan Asians Dominate Economy After Exile," *BBC World News*, May 15, 2016, www.bbc.com/news/world-africa-36132151, accessed May 10, 2019; R.R. Ramchandani, *Uganda Asians: The End of an Enterprise: A Study of the Role of the People of Indian Origin in the Economic Development of Uganda and Their Expulsion, 1894–1972*, Bombay: United Asia Publications, 1976.
45. G. Harlaftis, *Creating Global Shipping: Aristotle Onassis, the Vagliano Brothers, and the Business of Shipping, c1820–1970*, Cambridge: Cambridge University Press, 2019.
46. Austin, Davila, and Jones, "Alternative."
47. V.N. Geyikdağı, *Foreign Investment in the Ottoman Empire: International Trade and Relations, 1854–1914*, London: I B Taurus, 2011; V.N. Geyikdağı, "French Direct Investments in the Ottoman Empire Before World War I," *Enterprise & Society*, v.12, n. 3, 2011, pp. 525–561. See also S. Pamuk, *The Ottoman Empire and European Capitalism, 1820–1913: Trade, Investment and Production*, Cambridge: Cambridge University Press, 1987.
48. J. Dunning and S.M. Lundan, *Multinational Enterprises and the Global Economy*, Northampton, MA: Edward Elgar Publishing, 2008, pp. 31–32.
49. Jones, *Entrepreneurship*, pp. 180–185.
50. World Investment Report, 2018, https://unctad.org/en/PublicationsLibrary/wir2018_en.pdf, accessed March 30, 2019.
51. G. Jones, "Gapponshugi in Global Perspective: Debating the Responsibility of Capitalism," in P. Fridenson and T. Kikkawa (eds.) *Ethical Capitalism: Shibusawa Eiichi and Business Leadership in Global Perspective*, Toronto: University of Toronto Press, 2017; O. Zunz, *Philanthropy in America: A History*, Princeton, NJ: Princeton University Press, 2011; C. Harvey, M. Maclean, and E. Shaw, "Andrew Carnegie and the Foundations of Contemporary Entrepreneurial Philanthropy," *Business History*, v.53, n. 3, 2011.

52. Jones, "Gapponshugi."
53. Austin, Davila, and Jones, "Alternative."
54. C. Sanborn and F. Portocarrero (eds.), *Philanthropy and Social Change in Latin America* Cambridge, MA: Harvard University Press, 2005; J.C. Dávila, C. Dávila, L. Grisales, and D. Schnarch, *Business Goals and Social Commitment: Shaping Organizational Capabilities—Colombia's Fundación Social, 1984–2011,* Bogotá: Ediciones Uniandes, 2014.
55. Jones, "Gapponshugi."
56. B.R. Nanda, *In Gandhi's Footsteps: The Life and Times of Jamnalal Bajaj*, New Delhi: Oxford University Press, 1990.
57. Fridenson and Kikkawa (eds.) *Ethical Capitalism.*
58. T. Kikkawa, "Introduction," in Fridenson and Kikkawa (eds.) *Ethical Capitalism.*
59. T. Kikkawa, "The Crisis of Capitalism and the Gappon-shugi of Shibusawa Eiichi, Gappon Capitalism," in Fridenson and Kikkawa, (eds.). *Ethical Capitalism.*
60. M. Shimada, "The Tensions Between the Open Market Model and Closed Zaibatsu Model," in Fridenson and Kikkawa, (eds.) *Ethical Capitalism.*
61. M. Shimada, "Gappon Capitalism and Emerging Markets," Draft Paper for the Workshop on Gappon Capitalism and Emerging Markets, May 20–21, 2016, Tokyo.
62. M. Shimada, *The Entrepreneur Who Built Modern Japan: Shibusawa Eichi,* Tokyo, Japan: Japan Publishing Industry Foundation for Culture, 2017.
63. M. Kimura, "The Gapponshugi Project from the First Phase to the Second Phase," Draft note for the Workshop on Gappon Capitalism and Emerging Markets, 2015, May 20–21, 2016.
64. P. Drucker, *The Age of Discontinuity: Guidelines to Our Changing Society*, New York: Harper & Row, 1969.
65. K. Tanaka, "Harmonization Between Morality and Economy," Draft Paper for the Workshop on Gappon Capitalism and Emerging Markets, May 20–21, 2016.
66. Shimada, "Gappon Capitalism and Emerging Markets."
67. See Chapter 6; "Survival & Restoration of Waqfs in Turkey," https://islamicmarkets.com/education/survival-restoration-of-waqfs-in-turkey, accessed May 11, 2019.
68. Koc Group Corporate Social Responsibility Report, 2006–07.
69. See Chapter 4.
70. V. Giacomin, G. Jones, and E.H. Salvaj, "Business Investment in Education in Emerging Markets since the 1960s," *Business History*, forthcoming.
71. Interview with Murat Vargı, interviewed by Felix Oberholzer-Gee, September 17, 2014, Creating Emerging Markets Project, Baker Library Historical Collections, *Harvard Business School*, www.hbs.edu/creating-emerging-markets; Giacomin, Jones, and Salvaj, "Business Investment."
72. See Chapters 4 and 9; Colpan, "Business Groups in Turkey."

2 Institutions and Business Organizations in the Late Ottoman Empire and Early Turkish Republic

Seven Ağır

This chapter examines historical factors shaping the adoption and spread of business organizational forms in Turkey and their implications for economic development and social welfare. In particular, it focuses on the institutions—legal and moral codes—defining the responsibilities and opportunities associated with business activity in the late Ottoman Empire and the way they shaped the later evolution of business law and culture in Turkey. Through this analysis, the chapter will highlight peculiarities of the Turkish case by referring to other cases without offering a fully fledged comparison. Thus, it aims to present the peculiarities of the Turkish case in a way that would support or challenge generalizations about institutional conditions of a welfare-enhancing business environment.

Recent literature on economic history and finance shows that the availability of new forms of business organization has contributed to business performance and economic growth. The emergence of the joint-stock company and the private limited liability company, in particular, is shown to have provided business owners with a larger menu of tools to meet their various—sometimes conflicting—needs, such as facilitating access to finance, limiting liability, and preventing untimely dissolution. As the same time, however, these innovations gave rise to different sets of concerns such as moral hazard for external creditors and potential oppression of minority shareholders. The ability to develop the legal and cultural institutions that can balance such tradeoffs between different economic and moral concerns is regarded as an essential condition for economic growth. Moreover, in the case of late developing countries, business models aiming not only to make profit but also to foster modernization and enhance welfare have been shown to have contributed to economic development.[1] Accordingly, the question as to how societies could create legal and cultural institutions that align business activities with social welfare and economic development has become subject of extensive research. The cases that may not qualify as success stories, on the other hand, have generally remained unexamined. Studying such cases, however, might reveal the context-specific nature of institutional change and help us understand to what extent and how institutional borrowing might work.

Turkey is the country with arguably the most dynamic economy in the Middle East, offering lucrative opportunities for global businesses. Yet, the problems with business environment, such as weak property rights and corruption, are more evident than ever before. In hindsight, despite its dynamism, Turkey seems to have failed to create an environment aligning business activities with long-term development and welfare.[2] In what follows, we aim to explore the historical factors, in particular the legacy of the late Ottoman institutions, that shaped the legal and cultural environment in which businesses have operated in modern Turkey.

The first part of the chapter provides a *longue durée* perspective on the Ottoman political economy by focusing on the two main institutions through which economic activity was organized—guilds and *waqfs*—with a focus on their implications not only for the capital accumulation and entrepreneurship, but also for the social and moral responsibilities associated with business. We show that these two institutions defined both the legal and moral constraints and collective-action opportunities of the urban economic activity in the Ottoman Empire. By doing so, they provided welfare-enhancing functions such as enabling businesses' access to finance, reducing risks associated with trade, and providing tools supporting contract enforcement. At the same time, however, they stifled competition and efficiency for the sake of stability and equity. More importantly, they constituted one of the key nexuses of state-business networks that persisted up to the Republican period. Although these institutions evolved over time due to the changes in the global context, they failed to generate growth-promoting enterprises.

The second part focuses on the adoption of modern institutions such as corporations and limited liability companies in the late Ottoman Empire, arguing that the preexisting institutional context examined in the first part shaped the nature of legal and institutional borrowing: The nature of state-business collaboration, embodied in *waqfs* and guilds, continued to play significant—albeit restricted—roles in both pooling capital and meeting certain social needs during the late Ottoman era, and also shaped the way modern instruments were adopted. Nationalist economic policies, along with the availability of new organizational forms such as limited liability, enabled these traditional institutions to evolve and pave the way for primitive accumulation required for economic modernization. Yet political restrictions persisted, creating barriers to access to these new forms, which not only undermined the potential for sustained growth but also weakened the co-existence of diverse ethnic and religious communities. Furthermore, while the reformers emphasized "national interests" and legitimized Muslims' pursuit of wealth, there was little effort for building an indigenous discourse on business ethics. As a result, neither the indigenous nor the borrowed institutions were able to align business interests with long-term welfare concerns.

2.1 Institutional Pillars of Ottoman Economic Activity: Guilds and *Waqfs*

There is a significant body of literature that investigates the evolution and impact of business organizations. Yet the history of business in the Middle East in general and in Turkey, in particular, is meager. The few studies on business history in the Middle East have focused on the period since the modern corporate form emerged in the region, and have concentrated on the local impact of foreign and multinational companies. Research on the earlier history of business institutions, on the other hand, has emphasized the drawbacks of the Islamic/Ottoman law in enabling long-term and sizeable capital pooling.[3] As such, the question as to why modernization, and in particular modernization of business and business law, did not bring about the intended consequences, remains unanswered. This chapter explores the peculiarities of Ottoman political economy, and their impact on later development of business law and culture. To this end, it focuses on two pillars of Ottoman economy—guilds and *waqfs*—during the classical age and how the institutional framework that supported these seemingly "archaic" forms of business continued to shape business culture and law during the period of modernization.

Ottoman historians, in general, have been unwilling to adopt the notion of "business" as an autonomous, profit-seeking agent within the context of the Ottoman economy. This is mostly due to the conventional portrayals of Ottoman political economy. The dominant paradigm assumes that the Ottoman state in its "classical age" conducted what may be loosely termed a "command economy": The nature and degree of government intervention in the economy was different from that of the European political ruling classes. Decisions by the Empire's ruling elite on economic issues were based on the priority given to fiscal well-being and equitable welfare.[4] The regulatory policies (such as the trade privileges granted to foreign merchants, internal customs hindering domestic circulation, regulations suppressing luxury consumption, and interventions in the price mechanism) were generally attributed to a distinctive Ottoman mentality:[5]

> It is obvious that the best interest of the Ottoman economy did not lie behind the protective measures given to all Ottoman *millets* and foreign nationalities, regardless of whether they lived within or without the realm or whether they were attached to the land or not. The fact that the Ottomans were ridiculing/belittling the economic activities outside the established normative economic frame may be behind this

attitude. This was complemented by a non-economic material viewpoint, tightly bound to the belief that the world order (*nizâm-ı alem*) could be sustained by freedom and justice.[6]

Despite these portrayals of an "anti-capitalistic" Ottoman political economy, recent studies have demonstrated that moneymaking activities in the form of tax-farming, long-distance trade, and financial investments were widespread in the Empire. Ottomans, like their counterparts in other parts of the world, sought for channels to transfer their savings into income. The moral economy within which they acted might have been different from what is perceived to be the norm in modern Western capitalism. Yet what is pertinent is how these differences manifest themselves in economic institutions—the institutions that enabled exchange, partnership and investment. This part focuses on two institutions that prevailed in the Ottoman economy up until the late nineteenth century: guilds and *waqfs*.

2.1.1 *Ottoman Guilds: Beneficial or Detrimental?*

Guilds (known as *esnaf* in Ottoman Turkish) could be broadly defined as groups of tradesmen and craftsmen that act collectively to preserve their interests.[7] In the pre-industrial world, guilds and guild-like institutions played a central role in regulating access to factors of production in urban centers.[8] Under the supervision of the state, albeit with varying degrees of independence, guilds were in charge of setting prices, ensuring quality standards, and controlling distribution of inputs and outputs. Did these regulations serve to further private interests of the guild members or to ensure some socially beneficial outcomes? Were guilds rent-seeking institutions with adverse implications for efficiency?

Did they play any welfare-enhancing role? These are the issues on which no academic consensus has formed yet.[9] Yet the fact that the craft and trade guilds continued to dominate economic activity, at least in major urban centers up until the late nineteenth century, points to one of the peculiar characteristics of the Ottoman economy.

The recent literature has shown that urban economic activity in the Ottoman Empire—prior to the arrival of modern forms of business—was mostly organized around guilds. Barriers to entry were central to the functioning of the guild system: in order to open a shop or operate an itinerant business in any sector, one needed to become a member of the relevant guild. Membership was restricted through various means, such as the requirement of formal apprenticeship, the imposition of an entry fee, and the existence of a *numerus fixus* (a fixed membership size). In this sense, guild membership functioned like the license needed for practice in some professions today, such as admission to the bar, acquisition of a taxi medallion, or a pharmacist's degree, which aim to ensure not only quality standards but also stable earnings in these professions. There is, however, a significant difference between the modern forms of licensing and process of admission into the guild: while today most barriers to entry are impersonal (barriers are set by objective criteria such as passing an exam, paying a certain fee, or a "first come, first served" rule) in traditional guild system the barriers faced by potential entrants were determined as much by their personal qualifications as impersonal criteria. In gaining admission to a guild, family ties, ethno-religious affiliation, and gender played as important a role as the payment of an entrance fee or the requirement to be a resident of the town. When legal barriers distinguish potential entrants with respect to their personal characteristics and ties, transferability is limited at the outset. Guild membership, unlike a taxi medallion, was not conceived as a property to be bought, sold, or transferred.

In the Ottoman Empire, the most obvious tool for restricting entry was a legal code that limited the number of individuals or stalls that were allowed to operate in a certain branch of business and in a certain district. This legal code, known as *inhisar-ı bey ü şira* (or *inhisar*),[10] was in effect in all sectors until the last decade of the eighteenth century and prevented people outside the guilds from legally pursuing any trade or craft in urban areas. In retail sectors, *inhisar* served to regulate demand for inputs and supply of outputs, thus enabling control over prices and profits. Taking an active role in the allocation of factors of production and intermediate goods, guild administration had both monopsonistic and monopolistic power, which it was authorized to use for setting the price of final commodities at just levels, ensuring both the subsistence of the guild members and the well-being of the consumers.

While in retailing sectors, entitlement to one's daily bread was the main point on which the rules against the opening of new shops was based,[11] in craft guilds, especially those regulating the production of necessities, restrictions were justified with reference to the consumers' welfare. Limiting the number of suppliers in such sectors was considered a way to control demand for inputs and thereby input and output prices. In guilds regulating skill-intensive crafts, only skilled journeymen, upon approval of the guild administration, were allowed to acquire the status of master and to practice alone. The requisite of in-guild training aimed to guarantee the quality of work. Through regulations governing apprenticeship, guilds facilitated technical training—and thus served to sustain pre-industrial crafts—but also "potentially restricted legal entitlements to work in the industry."[12] Since access to in-guild training and the consequent privileges associated with mastership would require first and foremost one's acceptance as an apprentice by a master, relations established through social networks (such as family, neighborhood, and religious community) played a crucial role in access to work and workplace.

Another social function of traditional guild regulations originates from the nature of pre-modern credit relations. The sustenance of business depended on the long-term credit relations between suppliers—long-distance traders—and local shopkeepers, which required either formal credit institutions or "community responsibility systems." In the absence of the former, guilds functioned as community responsibility systems by creating mutual liability schemes that reduced the risks for suppliers and wholesalers dealing with urban shopkeepers mostly on a credit basis. In these mutual liability schemes (*müteselsil kefalet*), guild members stood surety for each other for the purchases they made on credit and therefore personal knowledge and social ties through which this knowledge was acquired played an important role in one's admission into the guild.

Of course, it is questionable whether the guilds were ever able to regulate handicraft production and retail shop keeping as effectively in practice as their charters called for. There was considerable variation as to the extent of autonomy and profit-making capacities of the individual members.[13] There can, however, be no doubt that there were barriers to entry that rendered production and trade in certain sectors more costly for potential entrants. Otherwise, urban craftsmen and tradesmen in guilds would not have rigorously organized and claimed the right of exclusive dealing in their sector prior to the nineteenth century.[14] In the Ottoman Empire, guild members' efforts to prevent entry are documented to have surged especially in times of economic contraction, as was the case in the seventeenth and eighteenth centuries.[15] During this period, organized craftsmen and tradesmen solicited charters limiting the number of legitimate businesses in their respective sectors, prohibiting potential entrants within a certain geographical area.[16]

Whether through entry barriers guilds furthered only private interests of its members or also served to ensure some socially beneficial outcomes depended on the overall framework of regulations.[17] Many Ottoman guilds were not legally allowed to set output prices above the "fair price" imposed by the government authorities.[18] Towards the end of the eighteenth century, however, central authorities considered the entry barriers as the main cause of high prices in the marketplace.[19] Indeed, the fact that many craftsmen and tradesmen appealed to the authorities to obtain and defend guild privileges suggests strongly that the guilds delivered some real economic gains to their members. The private gains associated with occupational licensing (such as access to a risk-free, stable stream of income or monopoly profits) were accompanied by social returns obtained through guild regulations, such as quality standards, in-guild training, and transmission of technology and know-how. As such, Ottoman guilds can be conceptualized as pillars of a market welfare system "that partially stifled competition and efficiency for the sake of economic stability and equity for those established within its boundaries."[20] In other words, the guilds had two functions: (1) creating entry barriers that stifled competition and created rents—including access to a risk-free, stable stream of income; (2) generating social benefits such as facilitating access-to-credit, technical training, and quality standards.

Another issue related to the Ottoman guilds concerns what they implied for financialization and capital accumulation. Recent research shows that the rents generated by the guilds gradually transformed into tradable assets in a wide variety of sectors during the late eighteenth century.[21] The entitlement to workplace and capital goods acquired through guild membership (known as *gedik*), in response to the needs of the economic actors, became—albeit with some restrictions—tradable in a wide variety of sectors at the end of the eighteenth century. Through sale of *gedik*s and *gedik* shares, guild members could raise funds from investors who were not directly involved with guilds. These tradable assets also enabled diversified investment and speculation. *Gedik* markets, however, failed to mobilize savings for large commercial and industrial ventures. *Gedik*s emerged within the confines of small-scale economic activity supplying domestic markets, whereas the instruments that emerged in Western Europe were adopted by capital-intensive, large enterprises oriented towards overseas markets. While the latter gradually evolved into forms that standardized credit and provided higher ease of transfer, the former disappeared after a century of vibrant existence.

The tradability emerged in response to financial needs of the small actors operating within the confines of a domestic economy (the guild members' need for using collateral to sustain trade)[22] and was conditional upon guilds' prerogatives. Depending on the sector in which they operated, guilds imposed limitations on outsiders' access to *gedik* markets. Due to these restrictions, *gedik*s' tradability was far from perfect, and thus the asset value of *gedik*s as financial instruments was not optimal. More importantly, the same institutions that ensured the emergence and sustainability of *gedik* markets prevented them from responding to welfare-enhancing opportunities: It was guild-imposed entry restrictions that made *gedik*s valuable in the first place. These very restrictions, however, prevented use of *gedik*s to reallocate capital towards more productive uses. Unlike negotiable instruments that emerged in Western Europe, *gedik*s could not be put into use to expand production and therefore could not contribute to the financing of growth-promoting, large-scale capital investments. While the emergence of *gedik* markets reveals the flexibility in the Ottoman institutional framework, it also attests to its limitations: Restricted access to factors of production embedded in the Ottoman political economy enabled emergence of a financial instrument stripped of growth-promoting qualities.

The case of guilds and *gedik*s attest to the institutional potentials and limitations of the Ottoman economy for business initiatives: Guilds fulfilled some significant social and economic functions within the moral economy context of the Ottoman Empire. They solved collective-action problems among urban tradesmen, balanced interests of consumers and producers, and shaped standards of production. Yet they also institutionalized state-business relations in a way that restricted entry into business, stifled competition and limited opportunities for capital accumulation.

2.1.2 Ottoman Waqfs: Uses and Limitations

Waqfs, like guilds, served some significant social and economic functions, yet at the same time had some shortcomings in terms of enabling investment and promoting growth. *Waqf* is defined as a trust, founded under Islamic law by a person for the provision of a designated social service in perpetuity. Endowing a property as *waqf* provided it a substantial immunity against expropriation.[23] Furthermore, like a corporation, *waqf* had the capacity to outlive its founder, employees, and beneficiaries. But it had also some limitations in terms of enabling directing funds for investment:

> First, whereas an association could turn itself into a corporation through the collective will of its members, ordinarily the founder of a waqf had to be an individual. Second, whereas a corporation was meant to be controlled by a changing membership, a waqf was supposed to be controlled forever by its founder, through directions enunciated in the founding deed (*waqfiyya*). Accordingly, a waqfs mission was irrevocable; not even its founder was authorized to alter its declared purpose retroactively. A third difference concerned self-governance. Unlike a corporation, which could remake its own rules, a waqf's rules of operation were meant to be fixed; the founder's instructions were enforced through judges and, where the deed was silent, according to local custom.[24]

While *waqf*, as the main vehicle for financing both commercial and public ventures in the Ottoman Empire, could serve as a model for social entrepreneurship, help relieve problems such as poverty, and provide a protection against expropriation, it did not allow emergence of innovative instruments such as securitization. Furthermore, by design, the *waqf* had little capacity to solve collective action problems and therefore not able to serve as a tool for representing "business interests" vis-à-vis the state. Ultimately, *waqfs* were unable to substitute for autonomous business organizations that might have generated an effective demand for innovations in business law and protection of property rights.

Guilds and w*aqfs* point to two aspects of Ottoman political economy that render it relatively less conducive to business creation vis-à-vis Western European economies in retrospect: First, the political and social restrictions on entry were not to be challenged from within the Ottoman economy. Non-Muslims, who had access to certain legal privileges, dominated the large-scale commercial and financial activity and had access to certain legal privileges (such as access to foreign jurisdiction and exemption from custom duties) but had little political sway. Proto-industrialization that might have undermined guild-imposed regulations, on the other hand, was restricted to rural regions in the Balkans. Furthermore, the Janissaries, originally an elite section of the infantry corps, came to integrate into the urban commercial life during the seventeenth and eighteenth centuries.[25] This was another historical contingency that led to the persistence of entry barriers and state-business networks oriented towards rent-seeking.

The persistence of guilds and *waqfs* should be understood within the broader context of Ottoman economy. Integration into the world economy might have undermined these traditional institutions and eventually they did so. But foreign trade constituted a minimal fraction of Ottoman economic activity up until the mid-nineteenth century.[26] At that time, the opening of trade led to the demise of political and social restrictions, but at the same time distorted terms of trade with adverse impact on domestic industry and indigenous businesses that could have played a role in industrialization and modernization.

2.2 Modernization of Corporation Law in the Ottoman Empire

Most countries received Western law by way of colonization. Ottoman Turkey is one of two major exceptions, along with Japan. As the military and fiscal challenges of the Ottoman state became obvious in the late eighteenth century, Ottoman bureaucrats developed a willingness to recognize and adopt the successful policies and institutions of rival nations. Yet legal borrowing was also contingent upon the preexisting political economy context and institutional heritage. In other words, the will to adapt Western law did not translate into a legal framework analogous to the one in Western countries. In this sense, the Japanese and the Ottoman cases stand as two strikingly different yet informative examples of the nature of institutional borrowing.

In line with their increasing access to foreign ideas and practices, Western corporate law became of interest to the Ottoman reformers as early as the 1830s. Sadık Rıfat Paşa, who played a prominent role in the drafting of the Gülhane Edict (1839), which initiated the series of major political and social reforms known as the Tanzimat, wrote on the role of corporations in capital formation and economic development in his treatise on Europe (*Avrupa Ahvaline Dair Risale*) in 1837. Thirteen years later, in July 1850, an Ottoman commercial law was codified based on the translation of the French *Code de Commerce* of 1807.[27] This law introduced corporations (*anonim şirket*) along with unlimited and limited partnerships (*kollektif* and *komandit*) as legal forms of business.

Prior to 1850, Ottoman entrepreneurs were able to form partnerships according to Islamic law, which allowed limited partnerships in the form of *mudaraba*.[28] In Islamic law, there was no concept of corporation as a separate legal entity. Foreigners and foreign-protected Ottoman subjects, on the other hand, could establish corporations since the Capitulations enabled them to operate according to the foreign jurisdiction in the

Ottoman lands.[29] There is, however, little information on the formation and activity of these corporations established prior to 1850. After the transplantation of the French commercial code in 1850, Ottoman entrepreneurs, along with foreigners, were able to use the corporate form as a vehicle to raise capital, either to expand production or to start new ventures. Except for a few flawed tabulations of the numbers of Ottoman corporations incorporated during this period, however, little is known about these corporations and more specifically about their legal characteristics.

We have surveyed the Ottoman Archives, contemporary primary and secondary sources, to estimate the number of corporations established during this period (1850–1918). Data on the corporations established during 1914–1918 come from special folders in the Ottoman Archives (*İ.DUİT*s) designed solely for keeping records of corporate charters and seem to be more comprehensive. There was no such source or registry for the previous period. Therefore, we had to build our estimate for the number of corporations established prior to 1914 on a variety of sources that were created for different purposes, and hence the numbers may not add up to a definitive account of the corporate sector. Our survey indicates that 221 "Ottoman" corporations (corporations established according to the Ottoman jurisdiction) were established in the core Ottoman lands (Balkans and Anatolia) prior to 1914.[30] While this number may be flawed, it is the most reliable estimate at the moment, given available sources. If we make an unrealistic assumption and suppose all these corporations have survived until 1914, the number would still indicate a very small corporate sector in the Empire.[31] Furthermore, more than half of these 221 corporations were public utility corporations (providing services such as electricity, gas, water, railroads) and banks established mostly by foreign capital. In other words, between 1850—when the corporate form was introduced—and 1914, use of the corporate form by the Ottoman subjects was extremely limited.

This is in striking contrast with Japan, which allowed general incorporation (corporations could be established without prior permission from the government) in 1899. In Japan, there were 5,253 registered joint-stock companies, making up more than one third of multi-owner enterprises in 1911.[32] Later, in the 1920s, joint stock companies came to account for the largest share of all enterprises in Japan.[33] The prevalence of the joint stock form in Japan is striking in itself and has been examined with comparison to European cases. But the sources of its success are also worth examining in comparison to the diametrically opposite case of Turkey, which had seemingly similar motivations such as modernization and development in transplanting the Western law.

Apart from the low level of savings and capital accumulation given the underdeveloped state of Ottoman economy, there are two major factors embedded in Ottoman legal framework that might account for the low level of incorporation prior to 1914. The first one concerns the nature of legal transplantation and change. Until well into the second half of the nineteenth century, in all countries recognizing corporation as a legal business form, incorporation was a privilege granted only by a special act of the legislature for purposes deemed to be in the public interest.[34] This was also true for the French commercial code of 1807 transplanted into the Ottoman legal system in 1850, in which the charters of corporations were still granted upon concession. In the second half the nineteenth century, however, the laws governing incorporation evolved rapidly, allowing general incorporation—a registration system that does not require state approval prior to the establishment of the company—to take hold and spread in Western Europe and the United States. In France, the shift from the concession to the free registration system took place in 1867.[35] In the Ottoman Empire, however, the transplanted law of 1850 did not change for decades.

The late Ottoman Empire and early Republic retained the French commercial law, albeit with some minor alterations and additions, for more than seventy years, up until 1926 when a new commercial code was introduced based primarily on the French code of commerce of 1925. While the new code introduced private limited liability firm (limited *şirket*) as a new legal form of business, it also diverged from the new French commercial code in some significant aspects. Most importantly, it retained the concession system, which had eroded in France many decades ago, and as a result incorporation continued to be a highly difficult and costly process in the Turkish Republic. Under these circumstances, it was understandable that the corporate form was used almost exclusively in very large enterprises, such as public utility enterprises with high capital needs and high prospects of return guaranteed through monopolistic regulation that allowed these companies to pass on the costs to their customers. The possible reasons for the persistence of the concession system will be discussed further in the last section.

Second, up until 1914, there was an asymmetry between foreigners and the Ottoman subjects in terms of their access to the corporate form. In the concession system, the state had control rights and veto power over incorporation. Ottoman entrepreneurs aiming to incorporate firms had to go through a process through which their proposed charters were examined by the concerned departments of the state before a concession was granted. The documents that record official correspondence between applicants and the state bureaus indicate a very lengthy and cumbersome process that might last up to 24 months.[36]

In short, an Ottoman entrepreneur hoping to form a corporation had to petition the state legislature for a charter and go through a process that was accessible only to wealthy and well-connected businessmen. The foreigners and foreign-protected non-Muslims (*Beratlıs*), on the other hand, were exempt from such procedures in accordance with the extraterritorial privileges granted by the capitulations. In other words, capitulations restricted the judicial power of the Ottoman state, which made the incorporation process so cumbersome for Ottoman (non-protected) subjects of the Empire. There is not much evidence on the use of corporate form (or limited liability form) by the *Beratlı* merchants. In fact, non-Muslim Ottomans could access foreign jurisdiction through purchase of *Berat*s prior to the general incorporation laws, and when general incorporation laws were introduced in Europe, *Berat* sales had already stopped. Hence, as long as they were not naturalized by the government that protected them, the Ottoman non-Muslims did not have an advantage over Ottoman Muslims in having access to the corporate form. After the general incorporation laws, however, foreigners were able to establish corporations in the Ottoman Empire without going through the concession process. Because of capitulations, foreign companies could operate as if they were operating in their own country, which means they were operating according to the "general incorporation laws." For instance, even though private limited liability company was not yet legally recognized, there were British PLLC companies operating in the Empire. Indeed, there were various newspaper articles about the relative ease with which foreigners established firms in the Empire and the problems associated with the absence of supervision over these firms.[37]

The concession system along with foreigners' exemption from it rendered the corporate form a means of capital pooling available primarily for foreign entrepreneurs in the Ottoman Empire. In 1887 and 1906, the Ottoman government attempted to subject foreign companies to the Ottoman legislation by enacting statutes requiring foreign corporations to acquire an official permission from the Ministry of Commerce to operate in the Empire.[38] Yet neither of these statutes could be put into effect due to the objections that foreign ambassadors and consuls raised on the grounds of concessions obtained through the Capitulations. Eventually, in December 1914, the Committee of Union and Progress (CUP) was able to enact a new statute aiming to level the playing ground for foreigners and Ottomans.[39] The new statute required foreign corporations operating in the Ottoman Empire to acquire permission from the Ministry of Commerce by submitting the documents pertaining to their registration and activity in their home country. Unlike its predecessors, this statute on foreign corporations could be put into effect since the outbreak of World War I offered the CUP, the authoritarian party in power, a chance to abolish the Capitulations.[40]

The unilateral abrogation of the Capitulations in October 1914 enabled the Ottoman Empire to exercise unrestricted sovereignty in domestic affairs, including commercial activity. The 1914 Statute, enacted two months later, was an outcome of this authority implemented in the realm of business activity and helped eliminate the gap between foreigners and Ottomans in terms of their access to corporate form. Incorporation was still subject to concession for Ottoman subjects, and the legal process through which foreigners could establish corporations, as it was specified in the 1914 statute, seems to have been simpler and shorter than the one Ottoman subjects had to go through.[41] Yet the conditions created by the war and the policies favoring Muslim over non-Muslim Ottomans, coupled with this legal transformation, paved the way for the emergence and spread of the Muslim-owned corporations in late Ottoman Empire and early Turkish Republic. These corporations, however, did not exhibit certain characteristics associated with the corporate form in the modern literature (i.e., the secondary markets for shares).

2.3 The Rise of the Muslim/Turkish Corporation (1914–1919)

To understand the emergence and spread of Muslim-owned corporations during the late Ottoman period, it is important to understand the political economy of the Empire's last decade. In the last decade of the nineteenth century, a group of young intellectuals known as the *Young Turks* in the West formed an organization called the CUP, which restored the constitutional rule in 1908. The Young Turk revolution, which started as a liberal reform movement, claimed to represent all the ethnic groups of the Empire. However, the regime change did not stop the unrest among the different nationalities. After the Balkan Wars of 1912–13, the Empire lost most of its European territories, including places such as Macedonia, Albania, and Thrace, which had been the heart of the Empire for centuries. After 1913, the CUP rather than the parliament came to dominate politics in the Ottoman Empire based on its members' power and influence in the military.

During World War I, the CUP government undertook some legislative and political actions favoring Muslims/Turks in the economic sphere. As mentioned earlier, unilateral abrogation of the Capitulations provided the government with unrestricted sovereignty. In December 1914, the government enacted the law concerning foreign corporations in the Ottoman Empire. Customs were increased first in October 1914 (from 8 percent to 15 percent) and then in May 1915 (to 30 percent). In 1916, ad valorem tax structure was annihilated and replaced by a protectionist one based on a specific tariff structure to support domestic industry. At the same time, there was an Empire-wide policy of "Turkification" that included harassment, boycott, and exclusion from employment, especially targeting Armenian and Greek subjects of the Empire.

The 1914 Act, along with the "national economy" policies of the CUP government within the context of World War I[42] led to a substantial increase in the number of corporations incorporated by the Ottoman Muslims vis-à-vis corporations established by non-Muslims and foreigners.[43]

While the share of corporations established by non-Muslims and foreigners decreased significantly (from 18 percent to 4.8 percent and from 31.3 percent to 6.3 percent respectively), there was a substantial increase in the share of corporations established by Muslim subjects (from 40.6 percent to 78.6 percent). The sectoral distribution of these corporations indicates that it was not the "industrial support" programs that caused an increase in the number of corporations. As Table 2.2 shows, the Ottoman corporations mainly did business related to trade and banking, followed by construction and transportation sectors. There was no significant change in terms of the sectoral distribution of corporations established after 1914.

Table 2.1 Corporations' Founders, 1908–1918 (254 Companies)

Origin	*Number*			*Percentage*		
	1908–1914	*1915–1918*	*Total*	*1908–1914*	*1915–1918*	*Total*
Muslim	52	99	**151**	40.6	78.6	**59.4**
Foreign	40	8	**48**	31.3	6.3	**18.9**
Non-Muslim	23	6	**29**	18	4.8	**11.4**
Non-Muslim-Muslim	7	7	**14**	5.5	5.6	**5.5**
Muslim-Foreign	1	4	**5**	0.8	3.2	**2**
Foreign-Muslim-Non-Muslim	2	2	**4**	1.6	1.6	**1.6**
Foreign-Non-Muslim	3	0	**3**	2.3	0	**1.2**
Total	**128**	**126**	**254**	**100**	**100**	**100**

Source: Gökatalay, "Corporations in the Late Ottoman Empire," p. 31

Table 2.2 Sectoral Distribution, 1908–1918 (254 Companies)

Sectors	*1908–1914*		*1915–1918*		*Total*
	Number	*%*	*Number*	*%*	*Number*
Trade	48	37.5	61	52.5862	119
Manufacture	27	21.09375	27	23.2759	54
Banking	19	14.84375	12	10.3448	31
Construction	9	7.03125	6	5.17241	15
Transportation	13	10.15625	2	1.72414	15
Mining	6	4.6875	2	1.72414	8
Public Utilities	6	4.6875	2	1.72414	8
Insurance		0	4	3.44828	4
Total	128	100	116	100	254

Source: Ağır ve Gökatalay, "Hukuk ve İktisat"

How did the Ottoman Muslims finance the corporations established during this period? Did tradable shares, considered one of the most significant advantages on the corporate form, enable capital pooling? Were there other means through which these corporations financed themselves? The charters of the Ottoman corporations established by Muslims help us answer this question by providing us with the information on the identity of the founders and the rules concerning ownership, voting, and share transferability. Along with supporting evidence from other archival sources on how these corporations were financed, these charters reveal an idiosyncratic characteristic of the Ottoman corporate activity: The Ottoman government, non-profit associations supported by the government, and the traditional organizations of *waqfs* and guilds played a significant role in financing these corporations. As a result, corporate ownership, even widely dispersed, reflected personal networks dependent on political and social affiliations.

In 1909, the Ottoman government enacted the Law of Associations (*Cemiyetler Kanunu*),[44] which obviated the need to get official permission from the Ottoman government before establishing an association, unlike corporations.[45] Accordingly, the years following the introduction of the Law of Associations witnessed the emergence of many associations all around the Empire. Here, we will focus on one of these associations, the Artisans' League (*Esnaf Cemiyeti*), which played a crucial role in establishing connections between political authorities and potential investors and enabled capital pooling in spite of the absence of capital markets. The Artisans' League was an association created with the direct support and involvement of the Ottoman political authorities, which was a modified version of the traditional guild organization of the Muslim-Turkish merchants, artisans, and shopkeepers.

With the abolishment of the traditional guild system, the CUP tried to bring the organization of the Ottoman urban craftsmen and tradesmen (*esnaf*) in line with the modern business practices. Indeed, the Ottoman government had attempted to encourage re-organization of Muslim tradesmen before the second constitutional era. For example, the Industrial Reform Commission (*Islah-i Sanayi Komisyonu*) was founded in 1864 in order to increase the custom tariffs and offer support to Muslim businessmen who wanted to establish new factories. One of the objectives of the Commission was to encourage the traditional urban craftsmen and tradesmen to create corporations. The Artisans' League represented the culmination of these efforts during the CUP period and indicated that there was a persistent need on behalf of the Ottoman reformers to merge the remnants of the traditional institutions of the Ottoman economy, such as guilds, with modern institutions borrowed from the West, such as corporations.

The League contributed to the financing of the three largest "national" corporations established during the World War in the Ottoman Empire:[46]

Table 2.3 Corporations Supported by the Artisans' League

Company	*Year*	*Initial Capital (OL)*
Anadolu Milli Mahsulat Osmanlı Anonim Şirketi	1915	200,000
Milli İthalat Kantariye Anonim Şirketi	1916	200,000
Milli Ekmekçiler Anonim Şirketi	1917	100,000

Source: Ağır and Gökatalay, "Hukuk ve İktisat"

All three corporations were established, as defined in their charters, with the aim of provisioning food within the Empire. They had relatively higher amounts of initial capital compared to other corporations of the period thanks to the Artisans' League, which helped raise the capital by obliging its members to purchase company shares.

Anadolu Milli Mahsulat Osmanlı Anonim Şirketi was founded in 1915. Half of the initial capital (100,000 Ottoman Liras) was provided by the Council of Trade (Heyet-i Mahsusa-i Ticariyye)—a governmental organization in charge of provisioning Istanbul. The rest of the capital was collected from the Muslim traders and merchants living in both Anatolia and Istanbul. The shares of these companies were not sold in the stock exchange; rather, the local officials of the CUP gathered capital through its networks. The second company, Milli İthalat Kantariye Anonim Şirketi, was founded in 1916. Again, the Council provided half of the capital and the CUP collected the rest from the grocers in Istanbul through the League, by distributing shares of the company to the League members in exchange for sugar. All founders of this company were Muslims and most were artisans. The third corporation, Milli Ekmekçiler Anonim Şirketi, was founded in 1917. Once more, half of the capital was paid by Heyet-i Mahsusa-i Ticariyye, while the other half was collected from the bakers who were members of the League in Istanbul.

The Artisans' League was an example of how government-supported non-profit associations played a role in the establishment of the Muslim/Turkish corporations. There were other associations involved in raising revenue for the corporations established during this period.[47] The fact that most of these corporations restricted the transferability of the shares (either through restricting share transferability to foreigners or non-Muslims or just assigning a significant percentage of shares as *titres nominatifs*) also indicates that the capital pooling in these corporations was not enabled through impersonal share markets. The role of political networks in the emergence of the Muslim/Turkish corporations during this period is also corroborated by the data on the founders' identity. Of 151 Muslim corporations established during this period, we were able to identify more than 40 percent that had at least one politically affiliated person[48] among its founders.[49]

Table 2.4 Identity of the Founders/Managers

Founder	*Number of Companies*	*Percentage (%)*
Merchant	47	31.1
Political Authorities	40	26.5
Political Authorities and Local Notables	17	11.3
Local Notables	28	18.5
Unknown	18	11.9
Women	1	0.7
Total	151	100

Source: Ağır and Gökatalay, "Hukuk ve İktisat"

In short, the Muslim/Turkish corporations that emerged during the World War were based on the deliberate attempts of the government to create a "national economy." The local Muslim interest groups, such as small town gentry and rural landlords (*eşraf* and *ayan*), that had already infiltrated the ranks of the local government branches to some extent, collaborated with the government in these efforts to build a Muslim business class. Yet the fact that most of these corporations disappeared during the transition to the Republic indicates the importance of political alliances and the limitations imposed by the state legislation. The post-war period (including the Independence War) presented significant economic obstacles to the survival of these corporations, in addition to the political turmoil that made such alliances highly risky.

To understand the institutional context within which these early Muslim corporations emerged, we can also look at ideas on business ethics during this period. Late Ottoman intellectuals' writings on the reasons for economic backwardness refer to Muslims' attitudes on business as a problem: lack of striving for profit through trade, asceticism, and laziness are considered prevailing characteristics of Muslims that have prevented them from succeeding in business activities.[50] These writers claimed that the governmental policies trying to fill the institutional void to promote industry and trade failed because of the cultural attributes of the "Ottoman man." It was also during this period that the notion of "economic formation/*Bildung*" (*iktisadi terbiye*)[51] was first used to refer to the shortcomings of Ottoman/Muslim economic culture.[52] As we will see in the next section, this concept of "economic formation" was also used to justify restrictions on access to corporate form. But this concern seems to have targeted only foreigners and non-Muslims in the later period of nationalist government. In fact, the leading political actors explicitly justified "illicit gains" acquired through political favors such as corporate concessions by claiming that the Muslims should first "get the taste of trade."[53]

The Ottoman reformers' attempts to promote corporations through legal reform and political involvement were not a unique case. In Japan, another latecomer, the reformers transplanted the Western law and used various means to support the formation and expansion of business in order to facilitate economic development. The fact that both countries were politically independent and striving to catch up, yet had an institutional heritage that was obviously different from the cases they borrowed from, makes them similar enough to compare their unique paths. How does the introduction and spread of corporate form in Turkey stand in relation to the Japanese case?

The literature on Japanese business history demonstrates that the business leadership of reformers such as Eiichi Shibusawa (1840–1931) played an important role in promoting corporations as a tool for modernization and industrialization.[54] Shibusawa stated: "To make the nation truly prosperous, we must enrich the country, we must make scientific progress and help commerce and industry thrive; to help commerce and industry thrive, we must establish joint-stock corporate organizations" (Shimada 2012, p. 9). While we find a similar discourse on the importance of joint-stock companies for industrialization and development among Ottoman reformers (see the first section), the way company law was transplanted and applied in Turkey indicates a significant difference between the two cases. While both countries derived their commercial laws from same sources (France and Germany), in Japan, general incorporation was adapted quite early, while in Turkey it was delayed until 1957. Two factors were important in this reluctance: First is the apprehension of the political elites, Muslim Turks, that the corporate form could be a vehicle for the already-existing dominance of foreigners and non-Muslims over Muslims in the economic realm. We should keep in mind that the large infrastructural investments that required the use of joint stock form was realized through national companies in Japan, while foreign capital—which came to enter the country through special concessions—played a crucial role in Turkey. In the latter, there would not be any need or pressure for developing the corporate law to enable capital pooling from indigenous resources.

Second, the already-existing means of enabling collective action and capital pooling to form the limited number of corporations in the late Ottoman context (i.e., guilds and *waqfs*) depended on and sustained a political economy pattern that precluded emergence of relatively autonomous business interests. In other words, state-business relations continued to depend on competition-stifling and rent-seeking norms. As a result, the state, reluctant to release its extensive control on access to finance, was not to be pressured by Muslim and Turkish business interests, whose power also depended first and foremost on their relationship to the state. Non-Muslims, who held more human and physical capital and who would be probably more willing and able to use corporate form in an extensive way, on the other hand, were stripped of any political influence within the context of late nation-state building.[55] As such, there was no reason for the emergence of widespread demand for new organizational forms in the Ottoman-Turkish context. Consequently, familiarity with the benefits and risks of these new forms as well as public pressures to deal with them, which seem to have played an important role in the development of stock exchange and the accompanying governance structures in Japan,[56] were largely absent. The later development in the Turkish commercial law and enterprise activity, examined in the next section, attest to these observations.

2.4 The Emergence of the Limited Liability Company in Turkey

The 1850 Commercial Code defined the legal framework within which Ottoman corporations were established. The law, with very minor changes and modifications, survived until after the Independence War. Both the Turkish and foreign corporations were subject to a concession process. Turkish firms had to acquire the Council of Ministers' approval by a special decree, and there was no specification as to how much time the approval process could take. The process was more clearly defined for the foreigners. In 1926, American Consul in Istanbul, Bie Ravdal, described the procedure that foreign corporations had to go through in detail:

> Corporations and Stock Companies, desiring to do business in Turkey, must register with the Ministry of Commerce. Registration consists of filing a declaration as to a firm's proposed activities, its capital and financial resources, and its estimated volume of business, accompanied by a copy of its charter authenticated by the diplomatic representative in charge of Turkish interests in the country in which the home office is located. . . . These formalities usually consume about six weeks, and the cost in fees, stamp taxes, etc., amounts to approximately £T125, plus attorney's and other expenses. . . . There is no registration for partnerships and individual businesses; these are merely required to obey the laws and pay the taxes provided for by the law.[57]

In 1926, a new commercial code was introduced based primarily on the French code of commerce of 1925. While the new code introduced private limited liability firm (limited *şirket*) as a new legal form of business, it also diverged from the new French commercial code in some significant aspects. Most importantly, it retained the concession system, which had ended in France in 1867. Incorporation required a governmental decision signed by the Council of Ministers, the highest executive authority, and as such continued to be a very cumbersome process until the new commercial code of 1957.

The aversion of the Turkish authorities towards general incorporation can be traced back to the late Ottoman period. In 1918, Mehmet Asım, editor-in-chief of the Ottoman newspaper *Vakit*, who also became a member of the parliament during the Republican era, writes the following about the corporations:

> In order to understand the actual (or "true") economic development of a country, one must first examine the quantity and worth of the corporations in that country. Corporations are an important means of bolstering the economic prosperity of a country. Yet if these corporations are not kept under strict control, especially in countries such as ours whose inhabitants generally lack a good economic education, they can provide an opportunity for a group of crooked men to swindle away the wealth of the nation. In particular, if foreign investors are allowed to mingle among these crooked men, it is not difficult to guess how much harm they would do.[58]

While in the late Ottoman period and early Turkish republic, the concession system was justified with reference to potential risks (pertaining especially to the activities of the foreigners), in the 1930s the concession system came to be justified with reference to the *étatist* (statist) outlook of the Turkish state. Ernst Hirsch, a German Jewish legal scholar and specialist in commercial law who immigrated to Turkey and trained a whole generation of legal scholars in the Istanbul Faculty of Law in the 1930s and 40s, defended the concession system in following words:

> In a country ruled by a statist (*étatist*) government, the legal license of any legal entity cannot be unrestricted. That is why the formation of corporations are subject to concession by the legislator in Turkey.[59]

Halil Arslanlı, Hirsch's student and later collaborator who became one of the most important legal scholars of the 1940s and 1950s in Turkey, wrote his thesis on the "The Effect of Statism on Corporations" and argued that a corporate entity cannot hold unlimited legal license in an *étatist* state, explaining the Turkish commercial code's article regarding the concession system (Article 280) according to this principle.[60] Furthermore, Arslanlı points to some contradictions in the law due to its hybridity, in particular inserting the "concession system" and related articles into the French legal code, which was prepared according to the general incorporation principles.[61]

While the 1926 code still required the legislature's concession for incorporation, its insertion of the private limited liability form might be considered a significant novelty that made limited liability more accessible for small and medium enterprises. According to the 1926 law, PLLC could be established by a minimum of two persons and 1,000 Turkish

Lira as initial capital. These requirements were considered as the primary advantage of the PLLCs. Furthermore, there was no official requirement of general meeting and auditor assignment for PLLCs that had less than 20 partners. These were also considered as a source of convenience provided by the PLLCs.[62]

There were, however, two issues that restricted the use of the limited liability form in the Turkish Republic. First, the provisions on the limited liability were taken from the French code in a condensed form. The reasons for this condensation is not clear,[63] but seven years after the code was enacted, Mehmed Ali, the Undersecretary of Trade, wrote a 200-page book on the legal features of the limited companies to clarify ambiguous elements in the Turkish commercial code and help illustrate the benefits of the form to the Turkish potential entrepreneurs.[64]

Second, in order to establish a limited liability firm, one needed to acquire permission from the Ministry of Trade. While this requirement was easier to meet compared to the Council of Ministers' approval needed for incorporation, it still made the Turkish law significantly more cumbersome compared to the French law, where a simple registration was sufficient for the firm to exist. In Ali's book, written to encourage spread of limited liability form, the author underlines the easy registration process as one of the advantages of the limited liability firms in other countries such as France and Germany. Yet he also justifies the requirement on two grounds: First, the corporations in Turkey also required concession. In other words, Turkey was different from other countries in this respect as well, and the reasons that require concession for corporations—without explaining what they were—would also justify a concession process, albeit a less demanding one, for the PLLCs as well. Second, as mentioned previously, the legal provisions about the PLLC in the Turkish commercial code were incomplete/deficient and, therefore, most rules concerning the company had to be incorporated into the contract. This, according to Mehmet Ali, implied too much freedom that might lead to creation of companies that would not fit into the "limited" form and could harm stakeholders, most importantly the creditors of the firm.[65]

Both the problems in the transplantation process (especially for parts concerning the limited form) and the aversion to adapting easier registration processes for the establishment of the private limited liability company might indicate a certain reluctance or ignorance on behalf of the policy makers about the introduction of this form in the country. Actually, it took 14 years after the Code of Commerce that introduced PLLC, for serious critiques of the concession system (for PLLC) to be raised by Turkish legal scholars. In 1940, the chief editor of *Hukuk Gazetesi* (The Law Journal), Cevat Hakkı Özbey, published an article titled "There is a need for altering the legal provisions to promote limited companies and small scale enterprises."[66] Özbey argued for abolition of the official permission requirement for the establishment of the private limited liability company. Yet he also emphasized that he disagreed with the scholars who suggested, along with removal of the concession requirement, the abolition of official auditing for PLLCs. He considered the "official audit" requirement as a legal provision in line with the two main principles of the Turkish state, statism (*devletçilik*) and populism (*halkçılık*). Legal scholars used the ideological underpinnings of the Turkish state as a justification for the strict state control. Whether this discourse reflected an actual ideological resistance to free incorporation and free registration (for PLLCs) inherited from the late Ottoman national economy or based on any observed threats to the so-called statist objectives of the Turkish government in the 1940s is not clear.

Yet even in the 1940s, the number of private limited liability companies established in Istanbul seems to have been relatively small compared to partnership forms. In the late 1920s, 97 percent of all multi-owner firms were corporation or limited liability in France, whereas only 32 percent of all multi-owner firms were limited liability private companies or corporations in Turkey. Furthermore, the limited liability firms were mostly restricted to the very large firms, which are considered in the highest initial capital range (*fevkalade*) according to the Istanbul Chamber of Commerce.

2.5 Conclusion

Ottoman statesmen legitimized corporations as a means of technical borrowing and catch-up; but the institutional framework within which these corporations were adopted exhibit some features peculiar to the political economic structure of the Ottoman Empire. The introduction of General Incorporation Acts was very late (1957) in the Ottoman/Turkish case. Furthermore, the private limited liability company, which was introduced as a more flexible, convenient form for small and medium enterprises, was also subject to a burdensome bureaucratic procedure. The transplantation process was incomplete and contained serious contradictions that legal scholars acknowledged and tried to solve for many decades. The law, however, barely changed in response to these problems.

This legal stagnation cannot be explained solely with reference to a lack of legal experience and a bureaucratic learning gap. The preexisting institutions based on competition-restricting regulations (such as guilds) survived into the later period of incorporation into the world economy, the late nineteenth and early twentieth centuries, with little capacity to industrialize but with socio-political power base to participate in a nationalist agenda that worked mostly along the lines of primitive accumulation and wealth transfer from non-Muslim businesses. Within this context, the capital-pooling depended mostly on traditional political and social networks inherited from *waqf*- and guild-like institutions, rather than modern instruments such as stock exchange. The Muslim entrepreneurs—with sufficient means and political/economic capital—did probably benefit from the political support and evolution of traditional institutions into "corporate" practices, but had no incentive to demand further reduction of barriers to entry (to demand easy access to corporate and limited liability form), or to demand legal innovations or governance structures that would improve investor rights.

As outlined in this chapter, the late Ottoman and the Turkish governments pursued a specific developmental agenda that identified national interests with Muslim/Turkish economic involvement. In line with these political concerns, they imposed restrictions on corporate activity and engaged in practices that helped transfer wealth from non-Muslims to Muslims. This was also justified through a discourse that underlined the need to create a striving among Muslims for trade and profit, but which undermined the development of business ethics. While businesses that were politically connected and supported probably benefited from this privileged position due to restricted access to corporate form, those who had the ability to use these novel forms of organization—without much political support—lacked access to it and were not in a position to demand change.

Recent research has shown that institutions matter for the structure of business enterprise and economic progress. Yet while there has been extensive research on what type of institutions are more conducive to business activity, few studies have examined where these institutions have come from. Having examined how the commercial law was modernized and early corporations were established in Turkey, we show that the particular features of political economy were decisive. Turkey, unlike Japan or some other "late-comers" in the European context, did not exhibit "flexibility" in transplanting the law. Rather, the legal context was markedly rigid and reflected the "political" priorities of the recently emerging nation-state. The political discourse also legitimized rent-seeking and illicit gains as the creation of a national bourgeoisie was deemed a priority. The late nation-building process, the peculiar nature of Ottoman ethno-religious heterogeneity, and the previous institutional set-up shaped the unique characteristics of the Turkish business environment.

Notes

1. Fridenson and Kikkawa demonstrated the significance of Shibusawa Eiichi's thinking and business activities in creating such a successful model in Japan. P. Fridenson and K. Takeo (eds.), *Ethical Capitalism: Shibusawa Eiichi and Business Leadership in Global Perspective*, Toronto: University of Toronto Press, 2017.
2. For a comparative analysis of the state-business relations underlying business environment and development policy, see J. Biddle and V. Milor, "Economic Governance in Turkey: Bureaucratic Capacity, Policy Networks, and Business Associations," *Business and the State in Developing Countries*, 1997, pp. 277–311.

3. Timur Kuran maintains that an aversion to the corporation in Islamic law held back the Middle East. "The Absence of the Corporation in Islamic Law: Origins and Persistence," *American Journal of Comparative Law*, v.53, n. 4, 2005, pp. 785–834.
4. See M. Genç, *Devlet ve Ekonomi*, Istanbul: Ötüken, 2000; H. İnalcık, "The Ottoman State: Economy and Society, 1300–1600," in H. İnalcık and D. Quataert (eds.) *An Economic and Social History of the Ottoman Empire*, Cambridge: Cambridge University Press, 1994, pp. 44–53. İnalcık maintained that "state interventions in the Ottoman Empire, namely regulations for customs and guild manufacture, fixing maxima in prices, market inspection on the quality and measures of goods, monopolies on the manufacture and sale of certain necessities, were different in essence and in intention from the regulation of a mercantilist state." "The Ottoman State," p. 51.
5. A.G. Sayar, *Osmanlı İktisat Düşüncesinin Çağdaşlaşması*, İstanbul: Ötüken, 2000, 1986; S. Ülgener, *İktisadi Çözülmenin Ahlak ve Zihniyet Dünyası*, İstanbul: Der Yayınları, 1981.
6. Sayar, *Osmanlı İktisat Düşüncesinin Çağdaşlaşması*, p. 115. The main actor of this mental world was the Ottoman man, defined by Sayar as a kind of "homo Ottomanicus" who was characteristically obedient to the state, religion, and customs and had poor consumption patterns.
7. While the literature has differentiated the European and non-European guilds, the recent focus on the role of guilds as institutions of "corporate collective action" has brought forward more generalizable aspects of the guilds. Tine de Moor uses the concept of "corporate collective action" to describe "the exclusive, self-governed autonomous institutions" that depended on the idea that a group of people could form a legal body, a *universitas*, a core idea that developed during the legal revolution of the twelfth and thirteenth centuries. Explaining European guilds' capacity to act as corporate institutions able to take collective action, de Moor underlines that guilds, like commons, "differentiate insiders from outsiders, to set boundaries to the group and to the use of its resources by means of a set of rules that could be expanded or reduced according to the needs of the moment." "The Silent Revolution: A New Perspective on the Emergence of Commons, Guilds, and Other Forms of Corporate Collective Action in Western Europe," *International Review of Social History*, v.53, 2008, Supplement, pp. 179–212. See pp. 192, 195.
8. J. Lucassen, T. De Moor, and J. Van Zanden, "The Return of the Guilds: Towards a Global History of the Guilds in Pre-industrial Times," *International Review of Social History*, v.53, 2008, Supplement, pp. 5–18. "The Return of the Guilds" Conference and the resulting publications aim to assess the role guilds and guild-like institutions played in the pre-industrial economy from a comparative perspective and constitute an excellent source to take stock of recent advances in the field.
9. S.R. Epstein, "Craft Guilds in the Pre-Modern Economy: A Discussion," *Economic History Review*, v.61, n. 1, 2008, pp. 155–174; C.R. Hickson and E.A. Thompson, "A New Theory of Guilds and European Economic Development," *Explorations in Economic History*, v.28, n. 1, 1991, 127–168; S. Ogilvie, "Guilds, Efficiency and Social Capital: Evidence from German Proto-Industry," *The Economic History Review*, v.57, n. 2, 2004, pp. 286–333.
10. For a brief definition of *inhisar*, see G. Baer, "Inḥiṣār," in P. Bearman et al. (eds.) *Encyclopaedia of Islam*, 2nd ed., http://dx.doi.org/10.1163/1573-3912_islam_SIM_8702, accessed April 23, 2019.

11. E. Yi, *Guild Dynamics in Seventeenth-Century Istanbul: Fluidity and Leverage*, Leiden: Brill, 2004. See p. 157 where Yi refers to the arguments made by guilds with reference to their rightful entitlement to legitimate gain.
12. Ogilvie, "Guilds," p. 302. Minns and Wallis also argue that the guilds restricted the number of apprentices in order to secure payment in the form of labor from apprentices. "Rules and Reality: Quantifying the Practice of Apprenticeship in Early Modern England," *Economic History Review*, v.65, n. 2, 2012, pp. 556–579.
13. S. Faroqhi, "Ottoman Craftsmen: Problematic and Sources with Special Emphasis on the Eighteenth Century," in S. Faroqhi and R. Deguilhem (eds.) *Crafts and Craftsmen of the Middle East: Fashioning the Individual in the Muslim Mediterranean*, London: IB Tauris, 2005, pp. 84–118.
14. Yi, *Guild Dynamics,* pp. 146–147.
15. Yi, *Guild Dynamics*, p. 150; S. Faroqhi, *Artisans of Empire: Crafts and Craftspeople Under the Ottomans*, London: IB Tauris, 2009, p. 120; M. Kütükoğlu, "Osmanlı Esnafında Oto-Kontrol Müessesesi," in *Ahilik ve Esnaf: Konferanslar ve Seminer; Metinler, Tartışmalar*, İstanbul: İstanbul Esnaf ve Sanatkarlar Dernekleri Birliği Yayınları, 1986, p. 60; O. Yıldırım, "Ottoman Guilds in the Early Modern Era," *International Review of Social History*, 2008, pp. 73–93.
16. C. BLD. 1698 (1764), IM 76/17 (1797), IM 76/23 (1792), IM 98/12 (1805), C. BLD. 15 (1808). C. BLD. refers to the "Cevdet Belediye" collection in the Turkish Presidency of the State Archives-Department of Ottoman Archives. and IM refers to Istanbul Mahkemesi (The Court of Istanbul) registers located in the Center for Islamic Studies.
17. For a recent and heated debate on the efficiency and social benefits of the European guilds, see Epstein, "Craft Guilds"; Ogilvie, "Guilds"; S. Ogilvie, "'Whatever Is, Is Right'? Economic Institutions in Pre-Industrial Europe," *Economic History Review*, v.60, n. 4, 2007, pp. 649–684.
18. The archival evidence of price supervision and sanctions exists only for products such as bread, meat, and candles.
19. HAT 192/9342 (1791), HAT 180/8133 (1791), C. IKT. 34/1867 (1797).
20. For this conceptualization of Ottoman economy, see R. Shechter, "Market Welfare in the Early-Modern Ottoman Economy—A Historiographic Overview with Many Questions," *Journal of the Economic and Social History of the Orient*, v.48, n. 2, 2005, pp. 253–276.
21. S. Ağır, "The Rise and Demise of Gedik Markets in Istanbul, 1750–1860," *Economic History Review*, v.71, n. 1, 2018.
22. In the second half of the eighteenth century, the political and military difficulties of the empire had disrupted the traditional supply networks of Istanbul, raising the price of inputs and thereby creating payment difficulties, especially in sectors that depended primarily on these networks. Traditionally, long-term credit relations between suppliers and local shopkeepers were sustained by mutual liability schemes that reduced the risks for merchants dealing with urban shopkeepers mostly on a credit basis. As the defaults on debt increased, the merchants' unwillingness to extend further credit placed all guild members under pressure. As a result, the guilds and merchants agreed to recognize *gediks* as collateralizable property in those sectors. Accordingly, the earliest *gedik* transactions were the resale of *gediks* expropriated by the guild officials aiming to pay the debts of guild members to various actors, including the suppliers. See S. Ağır and O. Yıldırım, "Gedik: What's in a Name," in S. Faroqhi (ed.) *Bread from the Lion's Mouth: Artisans Struggling for a Livelihood in Ottoman Cities*, 2015, pp. 217–236.

23. T. Kuran, "The Provision of Public Goods Under Islamic Law: Origins, Impact, and Limitations of the Waqf System," *Law and Society Review*, v.35, n. 4, 2001, pp. 841–898.
24. Kuran, "Absence of the Corporation," p. 800.
25. There were many examples in which Janissaries employed coercive methods to circumvent existing rules and regulations in the commercial life for their advantage. In other words, the corps had become "an institutional base by which various urban elements tried to protect their privileges and interests against the ruling elite." This integration of the Janissaries with urban elements enabled the guilds to enjoy more autonomy, limiting the central administration's efforts to reorganize the economy. In fact, the guild members played a significant role in the popular riots of the eighteenth century, including the one that led to the dethronement and death of Sultan Selim III, who attempted to abolish Janissary corps and remove entry barriers during his tumultuous reign.
26. E. Eldem, *French Trade in Istanbul in the Eighteenth Century*, Leiden: Brill, 1999.
27. Between 1840–1879, other components of French law, such as penal law and procedure law, were translated and put into effect in the Ottoman Empire.
28. This is a partnership in profit, but—for the passive partner—not in liability. In terms of the concept of liability, the Islamic *mudaraba* was very similar to *commenda*. Indeed, A.L. Udovitch traces the origins of *commenda* to Islamic *mudaraba*. See Udovitch, *Partnership and Profit in Medieval Islam*, Princeton, NJ: Princeton University Press, 2011.
29. Capitulations allowed Europeans to use consular jurisdiction in any dispute not involving Muslims. Capitulations also allowed foreign merchants to be exempt from various taxes levied on non-Muslims and also let them enjoy lower tariffs (for instance, in most of the nineteenth century, they only needed to pay 3 percent duty on customs, unlike all other non-Muslim Ottomans, who were subject to a 5 percent tariff). In the 18th century, these privileges acquired through capitulations became accessible to non-Muslims through the sale of foreign protection by the consulates (*Berats*).
30. This archival research is presented in detail in two studies: S. Gökatalay, "The Political Economy of Corporations in the Late Ottoman Empire and Early Turkish Republic (1908–1929)," unpublished PhD dissertation, Ankara, Middle East Technical University, 2015; S. Ağır and S. Gökatalay, "Hukuk ve İktisat Perspektifinden Milli İktisat Mirasını Yeniden Düşünmek," in M. Koyuncu, H. Mıhçı, and A.E. Yeldan (eds.) *Geçmişten Geleceğe Türkiye Ekonomisi*, İstanbul: İletişim Yayınları, 2017, pp. 193–223.
31. On the eve of the World War I, there were 250,000 corporations in the US (about 2.5 corporations for every 1000 people); 5,100 in Germany (less than 0.1 per 1000); 13,000 in France (more than 0.3 per 1000), and 63,000 in the UK (more than 1.3 per 1000). See T. Guinnane et al., "Putting the Corporation in Its Place," *Enterprise & Society*, v.8, n. 3, 2007, pp. 687–729, 9.
32. Statistical Yearbook of Japan. I am grateful to Professor Takashi Shimizu for providing me with the information on Japan.
33. T. Nicholas, "The Organization of Enterprise in Japan," *The Journal of Economic History*, v.75, n. 2, 2015, pp. 333–363, p. 341.
34. In Lamoreaux and Rosenthal's words (2006: 127), "at the beginning of the nineteenth century, corporations were still regarded as quasi-governmental institutions." "Corporate Governance and the Plight of Minority Shareholders in the United States before the Great Depression," in E.L. Glaeser and C. Goldin (eds.) *Corruption and Reform: Lessons from America's Economic History*, Chicago: University of Chicago Press, 2006, pp. 125–152.

35. By the late nineteenth century, Germany (1860s), the United Kingdom (1855–56), and the United States (1860s-70s, depending on the state) had all introduced general incorporation. See Guinnane et al., "Corporation," p. 692, Table 2.1.
36. Ağır and Gökatalay, "Hukuk ve İktisat." For instance, it took 24 months to receive the charter for Konya Osmanlı Anonim Şirketi. For most corporations, the approval process lasted at least 6 months.
37. B. Nazır and U. Gülsoy, *Türkiye'de Ticaretin Öncü Kuruluşu: Dersaadet Ticaret Odası, 1882–1923*, Istanbul: ITO Yayınları, 2009, p. 183.
38. "*Memalik-i Ecnebiyede Teşekkül eden Anonim Şirketlerin Memalik-i Devlet-i Aliyye'de Icra-yı Muamelat için Kuşad ve yahud Tayin Edecekleri Acenteler Hakkında Nizamname*" (1887) and "*Memalik-i Mahruse-i Şahane'de İfa-yı Muamele Etmekte Olan Ecnebi Anonim Şirketleriyle Sigorta Kumpanyaları Hakkında Nizamname*" (1906).
39. "*Ecnebi Anonim ve Sermayesi Eshama Münkasim Şirketler ile Ecnebi Sigorta Şirketleri Hakkında Kanun-ı Muvakkat*" (December 1914).
40. Towards the end of the nineteenth century, the Capitulations came to be seen not only as a yoke on the Imperial sovereignty but also the foremost barrier to the development of the Empire, and all previous efforts of the Ottoman government to weaken the capitulatory system were undermined by the European powers.
41. According to the 1914 statute, the ministry had to respond to the foreigners' application in three months. There was no such time limit for the grant of Ottoman corporate charters.
42. When the World War began, France and Britain, major foreign investor states up until then, withdrew from the Empire while Germany and Austria continued to invest. See N. Geyikdağı, *Foreign Investment in the Ottoman Empire: International Trade and Relations 1854–1914*, London: IB Tauris, 2011, p. 526.
43. Ethnic restructuring in the Empire should have also contributed to the decreasing number of new corporations established by the non-Muslims. By 1914, 150000 Greeks were already expelled from the Empire.
44. In the literature, the word "*Cemiyet*" is translated as league, community, society, association, or union. Kuran (2012: 127) considers this law the first corporate law in the Middle East. However, the law explicitly refers to "non-profit" organizations. *The Long Divergence: How Islamic Law Held Back the Middle East*, Princeton, NJ: Princeton University Press, 2012; Z. Toprak, "1909 Cemiyetler Kanunu," in *Tanzimat'tan Cumhuriyete Türkiye Ansiklopedisi*, Istanbul: İletişim, 1983, pp. 205–208.
45. Toprak, "1909 Cemiyetler Kanunu," see Article-2.
46. Sources: İ.DUİT, 120–6; İ.DUİT,120–21; İ.DUİT,122–2. İ. DUİT. refers to "Dosya Usulü İradeler Tasnifi" Collection located in the Turkish Presidency of the State Archives-Department of Ottoman Archives.
47. Another association, which played an important role in the establishment of national corporations was the Navy Association (*Donanma Cemiyeti*), which is examined in detail in Gökatalay, "Corporations in the Late Ottoman Empire," Chapter 3.
48. "Politically affiliated person" refers to the CUP members, bureaucrats, Pashas, and the military.
49. Many corporate charters identified their founders as the original administrative board, with a tenure of five years after the establishment.
50. S. Ağır, "Osmanlı İktisat Düşüncesinde Bir Kalkınma Stratejisi Olarak Örnek Alma," in Alp Yücel Kaya, Erdem Özgür, Alper Duman (eds.) *Türkiye'de İktisadi Düşünce*, Istanbul: İletişim, 2017, pp. 49–92.

51. The term *iktisadi terbiye* is hard to translate; it seems to refer to both education and moral qualities associated with "right" economic behavior.
52. Although the writers (all of whom were Muslim) who refer to lack of "economic formation" did not explicitly distinguish among Muslim and non-Muslim economic actors, their generalizations about "Ottoman man" seem to have depended on an identification of the "Ottoman" with the Muslim (and later Turkish) identity.
53. T. Çavdar, *Türkiye'de Liberalizm (1860–1990)*, Ankara: İmge Kitabevi, 1992, p. 161.
54. Please see Chapter 1 in this book.
55. For the differences in non-Muslims' and Muslims' firms in performance in the early Turkish Republic, see S. Ağır and C. Artunç, "The Wealth Tax of 1942 and the Disappearance of Non-Muslim Enterprises in Turkey," *Journal of Economic History*, v.79, n. 1, 2019, pp. 201–243.
56. Nicholas, "The Organization of Enterprise in Japan."
57. G.B. Ravndal, *Turkey: A Commercial and Industrial Handbook* (No. 28). US Government Printing Office, 1926, pp. 203–204.
58. The article appeared in *Vakit* in 1918. The original text is transcribed in C. Yılmaz, *Osmanlı Anonim Şirketleri*, Istanbul: Scale Yayıncılık, 2011, pp. 437–441.
59. E. Hirsch, *Ticaret Hukuku Dersleri*, Istanbul: Istanbul Universitesi, 1938.
60. "*Etatist bir devlette hükmi şahsın hukuki ehliyeti gayri mahdut olamaz*". See H. Arslanlı, "Türk hukukunda devletçiliğin anonim şirketlerin ehliyeti üzerine tesiri," unpublished dissertation, İstanbul Universitesi Hukuk Fakultesi, 1938.
61. Arslanlı, "Türk hukukunda devletçiliğin," referring to Articles 280, 300, 301, and 385.
62. C. H. Özbey, "Küçük sermayeli teşebbüsleri teşvik, mahdut mes'uliyetli limited şirketleri tezyit için kanuni hükümlerin tadili gerektir," Hukuk Gazetesi, vol. 42/43, 1940, pp. 10–11.
63. Mehmet Ali mentions that part of the law was taken from Germany, which had a separate act for the limited firms and part was taken from France. He says that the part that specifies contractual requirements for the limited firm were forgotten ("*her nasılsa unutulmuş*") in the process of the transplantation. In another part, he says that lack of provisions concerning limited liability firms resulted from "absence of mind" ("*zuhul eseridir*"). See M. Ali, *Limitet Şirketler*, Istanbul: Sanayii Nefise Matbaası, 1933, pp. 68–73.
64. Ibid.
65. Ibid, pp. 64–65.
66. Özbey, "Kucuk sermayeli."

3 Politics and the Development of Capitalism in Turkey[1]

Ayşe Buğra

In an essay written in the 1920s, J.M. Keynes wrote that "Modern capitalism is absolutely irreligious, without internal union, without much public spirit, often, though not always a mere congeries of possessors and pursuers."[2] This observation has been challenged by a wide body of literature, from the early work of Alexander Gerschenkron[3] where he discussed ideologies and institutions of late industrialization, to more recent studies on the "Varieties of Capitalism,"[4] which have shown, in different ways, that capitalism is not a socioeconomic order with universally given, unchanging characteristics, but one that varies from society to society and is historically transformed under the impact of changing domestic and international factors. Capitalist development proceeds in society-specific environments that inform the way economic actors define and pursue their interests as social beings by adapting to and acting upon the cultural, political and institutional contexts in which they operate. That is why business history often provides important insights for the investigation of the nature of capitalism and capitalist development in a given country.

In his chapter on Japanese government-business relations in *The Oxford Handbook of Government and Business*, the political scientist Yukihiko Hamada refers to "the extensive use of informal political activities by firms, which integrate their business interests into the policy making process and make the boundary of public and private spheres blur."[5] The phrase "blurring of the boundaries" is very useful in an analysis of government-business relations, and it could be used in a much wider sense than Hamada uses it to compare the types of boundary blurring in different countries or to investigate the historical changes in business environment in the same country. In this chapter, two sets of factors will be considered to explore the nature of government business relations in Turkey as an important aspect of capitalist development in the country.

One set of factors pertain to the formation and the composition of the business community. The questions which emerge in relation to this factor include the following: Has the modern capitalist development in the country proceeded in the presence of a business community with a basis of social legitimacy derived from a prior process of capital accumulation in land ownership, commerce or a tradition of craftsmanship later developed in industrial activity? Or do we see, instead, the emergence of a new business community taking advantage of politically supported mechanisms of capital accumulation through the modern development process? Does the composition of the business community remain stable over time or has it been subjected to changes with new actors replacing the old? Finally, what is the nature of the relations between different segments of the business community, between big and small businesses in particular? How is the character of these relations reflected in the associational environment?

The second set of factors has to do with the nature of the economic development strategy pursued by the government. Do we see the implementation of a coherent and consistent development strategy in the presence of a strong, autonomous bureaucracy? A related question emerges concerning the moral norms with which business compliance is expected. Are these norms defined in relation to loyalty to the political power or with economic efficiency considerations in mind? What is understood by "socially responsible business behavior" and to what extent is this understanding conducive to economic development?

These questions will guide the discussion of government-business relations in Turkey presented in this chapter. Through the historical changes in the political context of business activity, it has always remained difficult to make a clear demarcation between business and politics, but the fluidity of the boundaries between the two spheres has appeared in different forms in different periods of the Republican history. The first four sections of this chapter will cover three stages in the development of the private sector and government-business relations in Turkey. The final section will then present some suggestions for the development of a comparative frame of analysis of government-business relations in the development of capitalism in late industrializing countries. Following Gerschenkron's discussion of the late industrialization experiences of Germany and Russia, the case of Japan could be considered along with the later capitalist industrialization in other countries of East Asia, Latin America or Turkey. The discussion in the final section will be pursued with particular reference to the cases of Japan and Turkey.

3.1 Formative Years: The Emergence of the Turkish Bourgeoisie as Part of a Nation State Building Project

In Turkey, under the Union and Progress Party rule in the early 20th century and after the foundation of the Republic in 1923, the building of a modern nation state appeared as an objective with inseparable political and economic aspects. The emergence of a modern nation state required the development of a national economy in which the private sector was to have an important role, albeit with a significant change in its composition. The creation of a "national bourgeoisie" to replace the non-Muslim minorities who had dominated the 19th century Ottoman economy was part of a political agenda which shaped the initial phase of boundary blurring in the Turkish context.

The modern nation building project in the Republican period took shape against the background of World War I and the following War of Liberation mainly with the Greek forces, and it was marked by fear of decimation of the country and distrust of the non-Muslim minorities seen to have pursued their own territorial claims in collaboration with imperialist forces. First the Armenian tragedy of 1915 and later the population exchange with Greece led to a massive demographic change in the country. A new business community then emerged in a politically led process whereby business actors relied on the political authority not only economically but also to assure the social legitimacy of private property and freedom of economic enterprise.

When we look at the socioeconomic backgrounds of the founders of the most important business groups that established TÜSİAD (Turkish Industrialists and Business Association in English) in 1971, we see that most of these entrepreneurs did not command important economic resources to be invested in modern industry; nor did they enjoy a social status derived from big landownership or a well-established family crafts tradition. For example, the founder of the Koç Holding Company, the oldest of the large private corporations in the country, was a small merchant in Ankara when the Republic was founded. The Sabancı Group, another one of the oldest and the largest family holding companies, was founded by Hacı Ömer Sabancı, a simple villager from Central Anatolia. Since the emergence of big entrepreneurs was not part of a gradual process of institutional and ideological development in a capitalist economy, the political authority also appeared as the main source of legitimacy of their business ventures.

The provisions of the Law for the Encouragement of Industry, first enacted in 1913, was replaced by a similar law in 1927, which remained in application until 1942, were very important for the young business community of Turkey. Business enterprises benefitted from tax exemptions and credit facilities, free allocation of land and buildings, as well as provisions for the purchase of domestically produced rather than imported goods. The beneficiaries were mainly Muslim Turkish entrepreneurs who replaced the non-Muslim business actors, and the transfer of non-Muslim property to the emerging Muslim entrepreneurs has been an important aspect of new business development.

During the 1930s tariff protection was also added to the instruments of politically supported capital accumulation. Import controls were of course beneficial for domestic producers. However, the Law for the Protection of Turkish Currency, which formed the basis for policy implementation in this area, gave the state extensive control over the allocation of foreign currency and issuing of import licenses, and ambiguities in the text of law made the importers of raw material and intermediary goods dependent on the discretionary decisions of authorities for every single imported item. In this "etatist" period between 1930 and the end of World War II, business people were not bothered by the extent of government intervention. The form of intervention, however, was a constant source of complaint. The National Union of Industrialists kept asking the government to define the instruments of intervention more clearly and to avoid frequent changes in the economic policy orientation. It is not possible to say that these demands received a sympathetic hearing, and government-business relations acquired an increasingly hostile character in this period.[6]

Etatism formally entered the constitution in 1937 as a constituent part of the country's political regime. This constitutional amendment caused uneasiness among some members of the parliament who asked whether it would constitute a violation of the constitution to profess one's belief in liberalism or socialism, and the radical *etatists* who had pushed for the constitutional change answered in the affirmative. In fact, it was not at all clear what the concept meant and different interpretations of *etatism* were offered. Less radical ones suggested that "the state does what the private sector cannot do," and the most radical ones implied that public enterprise would be more desirable regardless of the ability of the private sector to operate in these areas. While both approaches were characterized by a strong element of pragmatism and none involved a doctrinaire position that could be associated with Soviet socialism, they were both unable to clearly define the boundaries between state intervention and the area where private property and freedom of enterprise would be protected. Businessmen were thus uncertain about the coordinates of their position in society, and they did not know the possible direction state intervention could take. As a politician of the era later stated in 1945, the problem with *etatism* in Turkey was the failure of the government authorities to clarify the boundaries of the public sector and to specify the area left to the private sector.[7]

With little power and influence on the policy process, the business community had little choice other than adapting to the requirements of operating under the double uncertainty created by an imperfectly specified economic regime and the absence of a stable strategy of economic development. Although Turkey did not enter World War II, the 1940s were very difficult years for the country. There were acute shortages of basic necessities, and the inflationary pressures, with which the government tried to deal by establishing price controls, could not be reduced. These wartime difficulties, which also affected many other countries, marked the formative years of the Turkish business class and had a determining impact on government-business relations. Public hostility toward the business community increased and government authorities increasingly blamed businessmen for speculative activity and illicit profiteering.

Some of the accusations were indeed well-founded, and some people were really getting rich in the midst of widespread poverty. Given the inability of the government to punish those engaged in activities of dubious legality and its reluctance to accuse the business community at large, as well as the absence of influential business leaders who could collaborate with the government to alleviate the problems of the economy, the atmosphere of distrust and hostility continued until the end of the war and the transition to a multi-party system. With the feelings of insecurity fostered by this environment, business people both refrained from criticizing government policy and attempted to strengthen the social legitimacy of profit-making behavior by engaging in philanthropic activities. During the 1930s and 1940s, the contrast between rampant poverty and increasing wealth was a recurrent theme in the media, which often appealed to the rich to provide charity to those in need. Nevertheless, "conspicuous giving" by the rich for purposes other than poverty alleviation could often be more fruitful in its impact on government-business relations. The contributions made by prominent government contractors to an organization such as the Turkish Aviation Association could, for example, well exceed voluntary assistance to the poor through Red Crescent or the Society for the Protection of Children.[8] Under the first elected government of Turkey formed by the newly established Democratic Party, which was pro-business, the fear of regime change largely disappeared. But a coherent economic development strategy remained absent. The business community continued to complain about discretionary policy intervention, and it was not possible to establish an effective policy community including political and economic actors. At the end of the 1950s, not only Turkish businessmen but also international financial institutions such as the IMF and the OECD were expressing concern about a government policy orientation that totally dismissed the idea of strategic planning in an economic situation that was increasingly unstable.[9]

Democratic Party government ended with a military intervention that, somewhat paradoxically, introduced a liberal constitution. The impact of this change was first observed in the emergence of strong labor union organizations and left-wing political movements, which became influential in the increasingly radical atmosphere of the 1960s and 1970s, where anti-business sentiments could be freely expressed. Once again, economic regime change was on the agenda, but the big business community was now in a position to respond to the challenge. It was now at a much more advanced stage of capital accumulation and organizational development and, at the same time, the freedoms introduced by the liberal constitution of 1962 could also be used for business interest articulation and representation.

3.2 Coming of Age of a State-Created Bourgeoisie?

Until the 1960s, chambers of commerce and industry with compulsory membership were the only business organizations in Turkey. The chambers were and still are important actors in the political environment. After the transition to the multi-party system in 1946, they became a dynamic site for political debate. Ruling governments have always tried to control the chamber administrations to gain their support in the elections, but political consent and consensus was not automatically assured. Notwithstanding their political significance, given their regional- rather than sectoral- organizational structure and compulsory membership base, the chambers have been in a position to represent a myriad enterprises of different sizes in different sectors and hence they were not very effective mechanisms of intermediation. The tensions in industrial relations that have emerged with a newly significant labor union movement, as well as the enterprise size and sector related cleavages within the business community, have led some entrepreneurs to explore alternative types of organizational development. An early step in this direction was taken in 1962 with the establishment of TİSK (in English, Turkish Confederation of Employers' Unions) which had a highly confrontational position in industrial relations.

Istanbul-led large business enterprises did not share TİSK's confrontational position against organized labor. While they were also concerned with left-wing political hostility against private business that the radical labor unions amply manifested, for them the challenge was situated beyond the realm of industrial relations. The problem that they found necessary to address was the broader terms of the private sector's position in society. Hence, TÜSİAD was established in 1971 with the objective of consolidating and strengthening the socioeconomic status of big business.

At the time of the foundation of TÜSİAD, the founders of the Association were economically strong businessmen who had no difficulty promoting their own economic interests through informal relations with political authorities. The associations could contribute little to these relations; they could even have a negative impact by introducing political tension in the dialogue between business and government actors who were used to informal channels of negotiation. One could, therefore, think of a certain trade-off between short term economic interest representation and longer term objectives pertaining to the consolidation of status.

With the insights derived from Michael Useem's study *The Inner Circle*, one could interpret this development as led by a small group of corporate leaders who could convince the rest of the community to accept this trade-off.[10] One could suggest that with the establishment of TÜSİAD, ideas about the moral dimension of business activity were explicitly incorporated in an entrepreneurial vision. As in the earlier stages of

Republican history, the emphasis of this moral dimension extended to the importance attached to philanthropy, and the big business community in Turkey has been increasingly engaged in different philanthropic activities taking traditional or modern forms. Voluntary contribution to education, in particular, has been an important aspect of business philanthropy. As will be discussed later, business philanthropy has currently become an important component of the neoliberal social policy environment and contributed to the networks forming the constituency of political Islam.

This observation does not, however, conflict with an approach according to which TÜSİAD could be seen as a class organization, an organization prioritizing long-term and not-only-economic interests of the business class over the short-term economic interests of individual business people. Approaching TÜSİAD as a class organization introduces a new way of looking at the fluidity of the boundaries between the realms of government and business. If, in the earlier stages of Turkish Republican history, strong ties of dependency binding business to politics were the main reason it was difficult to separate the domain of private sector activity from politics, the difficulty now had to do more with the quasi-political character of a class project concerning strategies and institutions of development.

What the founders of TÜSİAD demanded was to have an important big business influence on policy orientation. The association problematized the previous absence of a coherent strategy of development and advocated a set of economic reforms that would enable the economy to follow a stable growth path. The strategy that the association proposed could incorporate both government intervention and labor organizations, but would nevertheless allow the private sector to act as an important partner in the policy environment. The association was not against a "private sector friendly interventionism." In fact, a few months before the foundation of TÜSİAD, one of the most prominent founders, Vehbi Koç, pointed, in a public statement critical of the then ruling Justice Party government, to the urgent need for economic reform and rational planning.[11] Even in the economically liberal atmosphere of the 1980s, the association remained faithful to the principle of strategic planning both to realize rapid economic growth and to bring about a better distribution of income to prevent the rise of radical movements that would be more detrimental to the business community than to any other group.

Although the class project in question was carefully formulated in a way to accommodate the interests of the society at large, it was not able to gain a strong support even from the very constituency of TÜSİAD. Against the historical background of state-dependent development of the big business community and the rather weak foundations of the social legitimacy of profit making activity, the rise of a group of big entrepreneurs demanding to be included in the realm of political decision making was interpreted by the holders of economic power as a trespassing of boundaries. Small and medium enterprises and the chambers that represented them, government authorities who were not used to being overtly criticized by private sector actors, and labor unions whose legitimacy was defended by TÜSİAD did not have much sympathy for the association. In the political atmosphere of the 1970s, marked by leftwing activism, the association was labeled the "club of the rich" and attracted widespread hostility. Even the association's own constituency was not convinced of a strategy that involved criticizing the government in a way that harmed the economic interests that had been so far pursued informally and without much difficulty. In fact, such informal relations have continued; TÜSİAD or business associations in general have never become central to interest mediation in government-business relations.

Nevertheless, TÜSİAD has become increasingly vocal in the advocacy of an economically and politically liberal strategy of development. It has been particularly active in promoting Turkey's relations with European countries and trying to contribute to the country's EU accession process. In fact, foreign economic relations were one area where business involvement in the policy environment has appeared acceptable to governments before the Justice and Development Party (AKP) rule. For example, already in the 1960s the Economic Development Foundation (IKV) was formed with the initiative of the Istanbul Chamber of Industry and Istanbul Chamber of Trade to facilitate Turkey's relations with the (then) European Economic Cooperation, and its associational members later included TÜSİAD and TİSK. At a later stage The Foreign Economic Relations Council (DEİK) was founded in 1987 with the initiative of the Union of Chambers and Stock Exchanges, and it has become a key organizational actor in Turkey's foreign economic relations.

Even beyond foreign economic relations, the position of private business in the economy and politics seemed to be well consolidated in the post-1980 period, with Turkey's insertion in the global market economy and in the ideological atmosphere of the nearly complete demise of leftwing politics. The uncertainties about a possible regime change were no longer present, and the business community was gradually having more of a presence in the policy environment in spite of occasionally visible tensions with the government. It therefore did not appear unjustified to think that the state-created bourgeoisie of Turkey was finally coming of age in a market economy where government-business relations would necessarily assume a different, less unequal character. This prediction has not, however, been fulfilled by the developments to come.

3.3 Changing Form of Government Intervention and the Rise of Political Islam

In Turkey the period between 1980 and 2000 was a time of unregulated market economy, a period when there was a rather unrealistic faith in the possibility of a market-led economic development without the regulatory framework of market institutions in place. This unregulated market economy nevertheless functioned with continued government intervention of a discretionary character inimical to stable growth and has been marked by a series of crises, the last of which came in 2001 and had a truly devastating impact on the economy. After this crisis, the ruling coalition government invited a leading World Bank bureaucrat of Turkish origin, Kemal Derviş, to stabilize the economy and put in place a series of independent regulatory institutions that would assure a healthy process of development by preventing, especially, the discretionary intervention of political authorities. This attempt at "good governance" assigned an important role to the state in assuring the stable functioning of the market economy without compromising the principles of economic rationality by prioritizing political concerns. As such, it was enthusiastically welcomed by TÜSİAD, whose members were now at a stage of capital accumulation where they no longer relied on state favors and found the post-crisis reforms in conformity with the objective of consolidating the position of big business in its relations with the political authority. The AKP, which came to power after the general elections of 2002, too, seemed to be committed to the market reforms put in place after the crisis. Hence, TÜSİAD was in general favorable to the AKP during the party's initial years in power.

Nevertheless, the expected turn in government-business relations could not be taken because of a new element in Turkish politics that has led to a radical transformation of the political coordinates of the business environment. This new element was the rise of political Islam, which formed the background to the establishment of the first AKP government in 2002. Islamic politics was in many ways in conformity with the global changes whereby economic class relations had become less important than culturally informed identity claims in shaping the dynamics of political development. In the society-specific context of Turkey, Islamic references have proven to be very effective in mobilizing a wide variety of social groups ranging from the economically disadvantaged to the upwardly mobile around a social project addressing the limitations of the past Republican regime and aiming to transform it in conformity with the country's religious culture.

In Turkey, religion had always been an element in party politics and all right-wing parties had in different ways manipulated the religious sentiments of voters for electoral purposes. Yet until the 1980s, and especially in the 1990s, when the Welfare Party (RP), then representing political Islam, had significant success in municipal and national elections, religious references in political ideology had not been translated into attempts at redesigning economic and social institutions. In the post-1980 period, Islam was also used as a network resource to establish bonds of trust and solidarity among devout Muslims and to bind them in a coherent community within the constituency of political Islam. This Islamic networking strategy was pursued in a language of social disadvantage to present devout Muslims as a group marginalized by secular Republican elites who controlled both politics and the economy. This very polarizing strategy has extended to the realm of business and introduced a divide between old established business actors and the emerging ones situated in the constituency of political Islam. The establishment of MÜSİAD (Association of Independent Industrialists and Businessmen) in 1990 was an initial step in this direction. MÜSİAD has presented itself as the representative of those entrepreneurs excluded not only by TÜSİAD but also by DEİK.[12] The role of networking and other factors in the growth of pious capitalism are explored in Chapter 5 by Fabbe, Özlale, and Balıkçıoğlu

In the literature on the recent capitalist development in Turkey, the divide in the business community was often interpreted with reference to the changing character of government- business relations in the current market economy, where the competitive potential of small and medium provincial entrepreneurs was unleashed. The contributions to this literature often presented the conservative outlook of these new entrepreneurs who have acquired economic power without government support as a crucial factor explaining the rise of political Islam represented by the AKP. However, a serious empirical investigation of the recent developments in Turkey does not lend support to this narrative. Government intervention in the economy, although it has surely changed form with the insertion in the global market economy, has remained important and continued to affect patterns of capital accumulation and business development. Previous mechanisms of government support such as tariff protection, allocation of foreign exchange and import quotas, and subsidized prices for inputs produced by the State Owned Enterprises have no longer been available. However, public-private partnerships in infrastructure building or the provision of social services, as well as the regulation and license granting operations in the energy sector, have provided important opportunities for state-supported capital accumulation.[13]

3.4 Government-Business Relations in a Politically Divided Business Community

The market reforms of the early 2000s aimed, first and foremost, to introduce, by means of independent regulatory agencies, a rules-based, non-discretionary character to government intervention through the consolidation of an autonomous bureaucracy. During the AKP rule, this regulatory framework has been gradually but systematically transformed through a series of legislative changes which have created business opportunities and also generated concerns about the policy makers' partial treatment of entrepreneurs.

Discretionary government intervention has continued to be important, and it has been accompanied by the spectacular rise of a new group of entrepreneurs who, until recently, had no significant presence in the business environment. The nature of the trajectories of business development of these entrepreneurs, which have been discussed extensively elsewhere, constitutes a challenge to the received views about the relationship between local business development and political change.[14] Rather than representing a contrast to the state-dependent development of big business people established at earlier stages of Republican history, newly emerging entrepreneurs have also benefitted from their position within the constituency of political Islam, and their business expansion has taken place not at the local but the national level in a setting where privatization and the expansion of the market take place without the retreat of the state.

Particularism, an important characteristic of the relations between these new entrepreneurs and the government, was also an important feature of business development in the past. Yet, particularism is now shaped more than ever by the entrepreneurs' background in political activity, which they share with the politicians now in power, their involvement in party politics, and their position in political networks formed by foundations or faith-based movements. What we see today is a new type of relationship where economic and political interests are jointly pursued by politicians and business people. Media acquisitions by some of the big entrepreneurs close to the ruling AKP constitute an important example of business involvement in politics, which has culminated in a quasi-total control of the government over the media.[15]

Apart from the big entrepreneurs, the business constituency of political Islam also includes the owners of provincial small and medium enterprises. What seems doubtful is the validity of presenting these small and medium business people as a "conservative bourgeoisie" which existed prior to the emergence of the Islamist movement and determined its rise to power. This direction of causality could indeed be challenged with reference to the political role played by an association like MÜSİAD, which, rather than representing the interests of a given group of business people with a particular religious outlook, aimed at organizing them in a coherent community around common interests and a shared outlook defined for them in a particular way. This association aimed to define and put in a codified form the place of religion in business life and the type of behavior proper to a Muslim businessman.[16] MÜSİAD has in fact taken an active part in the establishment and activities of a foundation called the Foundation of Voluntary Associations (TGTV), which brings together over a hundred philanthropic associations and other voluntary organizations with an Islamic outlook. In this context, business philanthropy has become a particularly important factor in the changing welfare regime of the country where government, business and civil initiatives collaborate in the provision of social services and assistance to the poor.[17]

MÜSİAD, therefore, appears in many ways as an actor in the development of Islamic politics and a partner to the RP in the 1990s and the AKP in the 2000s. The same observation could also be made with regard to the newly emerging big entrepreneurs, some of whom are MÜSİAD members. Here, we again find an example of the blurring of the boundaries between politics and business and the joint pursuit of economic and political interests. Yet, this new manifestation of an old phenomenon takes place in a highly polarized society and is accompanied with the co-existence of two rival projects of capitalist development, which is explained in the paragraphs the follow.

TÜSİAD and its members have never enjoyed a relationship with political authority as close (one might even call it "organic") as the relationship of the new business actors with the Islamist politics in which they have emerged. In fact, while TÜSİAD's critical stand in its relations with all governments have created tensions between the association's administration and its membership, MÜSİAD's warm relations first with the RP and then the AKP, have been particularly useful in representing the economic interests of its members and significantly contributed to the expansion of its membership.

While the membership of MÜSİAD has expanded, in both provincial towns and big cities,[18] and by including large enterprises as well as small and medium ones, TÜSİAD, often called the club of the secularist big business elite, has also been actively developing closer relations with provincial businessmen of all sizes. The regional and sectoral platforms organized with the initiative of TÜSİAD have been active since the 1990s, and in 2004 they were unified under the umbrella organization of TÜRKONFED, which now incorporates around 190 local and sectoral business associations and has around 24 000 individual members.[19] Members of TÜRKONFED, too, significantly include small and medium business people, and most would consider themselves devout Muslims in spite of their distance from Islamist politics.

It is, therefore, not the differences of economic interest or even religious identity that have shaped the current, severely polarized business community. TÜSİAD and TÜRKONFED clearly stand for a secular society and against the increasing salience of religion in the realm of public relations. However, their position in the associational universe can not be explained with reference to exogenously given differences of religious belief with other associational actors. The divide in the business community rather stems from the way Islamic tenets of behavior are interpreted to serve network formation in a political process in which TÜSİAD and TÜRKONFED were excluded from the ranks of business actors placed within the constituency of first the RP and then the AKP. Hence, the key to analysis of the cleavages in the world of business is the position of different business actors vis-a-vis the ruling government.

While these cleavages cannot be explained with reference to economic interests related to the size, sector and the geographic location of the enterprises, they are not unrelated to the rival strategies of capitalist development found to be conducive to the pursuit of economic interest by different segments of the business community. There are, in fact, differences related to the stage of business development that inform the way entrepreneurs evaluate the desirability of different forms of government intervention for their business interests. The interests of the well-established business enterprises represented by TÜSİAD, which are at an advanced stage of capital accumulation and organizational development, lie in the respect for the rules put in place for the protection of private property and free enterprise. Although these enterprises have been formed and grown by amply benefitting from government support, they now stand in favor of a regulated market economy where government intervention is not excluded but is expected to take place in an institutional setting with formal rules defining its scope and nature. What would not be allowed in this context is the discretionary involvement of the government in the economic process to support politically privileged entrepreneurs.

The possibility of discretionary government action is precisely what the emerging entrepreneurs situated within the constituency of political Islam demand. Since these entrepreneurs derive crucially significant benefits from their privileged relations with the ruling government, they adhere to a notion of flexibility incompatible with bureaucratic control over taxation and government spending on infrastructure investments, over government-business relations in general. This approach is clearly revealed, for example, in MÜSİAD's assessment of the advantages and the disadvantages of the independent regulatory agencies and in its evaluation of the proposals to the government made by the IMF after the global crisis of 2008.[20]

The approaches to foreign economic relations of the new business actors in good standing with the ruling AKP government are not unrelated to their preferences concerning the institutional environment of economic policy. Since respect for the rule of law and bureaucratic autonomy do not figure in their vision of capitalist development, these business actors are also not very enthusiastic about closer economic relations with developed capitalist countries that would necessarily require conformity to these principles. Hence, unlike the established enterprises represented by TÜSİAD, this particular segment of the business community has continued to take a skeptical view of Turkey-EU relations since the 1995 Customs Union membership agreement and endorsed a foreign economic relations strategy basically geared toward non-OECD countries. This strategic choice can also be seen as better suited to the economic interests of the entrepreneurs at an early stage of development where they rarely have the potential to compete in developed country markets. It is in fact possible to observe that during the AKP rule there has been an increase in the share of non-OECD countries in Turkey's foreign economic relations.

This brief overview of the current business environment in Turkey could be interesting in showing that government-business relations can take highly complex forms in politically polarized societies. In light of this complexity, analysis of the role of business in capitalist development requires an investigation that looks beyond the society-specific characteristics of business outlook and behavior to the cleavages shaped by the nature of the relations with the political authority. In the context of economic globalization, the Turkish economy's insertion in the global market economy has not led to the retreat of the state but continued with a new type of politically-supported capital accumulation and an accompanying transformation of the configuration of business interests with significant, politically-shaped cleavages within the business community. These cleavages result from the emergence of new business actors close to the AKP, with these actors and the ruling government acting in tandem for the joint pursuit of economic and political interests which are in harmony with a capitalist development model different from the one endorsed by the big business enterprises established at an earlier stage of Republican history.

Although this chapter does not specifically address approaches to corporate social responsibility and business ethics, it could be suggested that the business actors' different perspectives on economic regulation and foreign economic relations are also likely to be reflected in these approaches. For example, the large family groups established at the earlier stages of Republican history and which are affiliated with TÜSİAD, such as Koç, Sabancı and Eczacıbaşı, have extensive philanthropic activities in the realm of education or arts and culture, which are formally organized and professionally managed. Organized philanthropy of such dimensions can hardly be found among new enterprises, although those, too, contribute to socially useful initiatives by building schools and student residences or engaging in diverse forms of charity. It might be possible to suggest that the difference lies in the way these philanthropic activities articulate with government action in the areas where they are undertaken. While TÜSİAD-affiliated big business philanthropy is often independent of or constitutes an alternative to what the government does, the new business philanthropy is situated in areas prioritized by the government, and is in line with and supportive of the objectives set by the government. This general observation might be useful to further explore with empirical research.

3.5 Concluding Remarks

In this overview of government-business relations through the capitalist development process in Republican Turkey, it was argued, first, that studies of business history need to be sensitive to complex patterns of interaction that challenge the approaches that conceptualize politics and business as neatly separated fields with distinct boundaries between them. "The blurring of the boundaries" was thus presented as a central concept that was explored in an analysis of continuity and change in government-business relations. Through this analysis, it was also argued that the fluidity of the boundaries between politics and business has manifested itself in different ways and acquired new meanings in different historical periods of Turkey's capitalist development. In this chapter, a three-stage periodization was proposed to discuss the historical changes in government-business relations. The first covers the emergence and formative years of a "state-created bourgeoisie" in the Republican period. The developments in the second stage involve the steps taken by big enterprises to have more influence on the policy environment and to consolidate the position of the private sector in the economy and society. The last stage is marked by the changes in government- business relations through the rise of political Islam in a market economy inserted in the global economic order. In this stage, the attempts made to put in place an institutional frame of market regulation were situated in the same context in which a new group of state-created entrepreneurs were emerging, a development that led to the polarization in the business community under the AKP rule.

This evaluation of the Turkish case could perhaps be useful for the development of a comparative frame of analysis of government-business relations in shaping the patterns of capitalist development in late industrializing countries. It could be suggested, for example, that the idea that business should serve national interests is more salient in East Asian countries such as Japan or South Korea than in Latin American countries where state autonomy appears to be historically more limited.[21] In this regard, the case of Turkey appears to be more similar to the East Asian cases. Yet, as will be briefly discussed in the following, certain important features of the Japanese *gappon* capitalism are surely absent in the Turkish pattern of capitalist development. In the Turkish case, unlike the case of Japan, we find politically-supported capital accumulation (or the emergence of a "state-created bourgeoisie") as a salient feature. It might also be possible to talk about a state created bourgeoisie in South Korea. Although one could suggest that in all three countries government and business appear as partners in development, what we see in the cases of South Korea and Turkey is not an equal partnership, but a relationship in which the government appears as the stronger partner.

The cases of Turkey and Korea, however, are different in several respects. In Turkey, politics of economic policy has always been marked by electoral concerns, which have created an obstacle to bureaucratic autonomy and the stable pursuit of a coherent economic development strategy. This, along with the ever-present tensions in government-business relations, constitutes a factor that might be useful to consider in a comparative analysis of the successful Korean and much less successful Turkish patterns of industrialization and development. Although such an analysis would need to address many different factors that clearly lie outside the scope of this chapter, one could nevertheless mention another difference in government-business relations that might have affected the economic development performance of these two countries.

As the political economist Alice Amsden put it, "No firm in South Korea could succeed if it openly criticized the government. No firm could flourish if it was not a staunch government supporter. Nevertheless, despite pervasive corruption surrounding the allocation of subsidies to specific companies, discipline has still been effective: generally only good performers have been rewarded and poor performers have been punished."[22] In Turkey, on the other hand, it would be possible to observe that loyalty to the ruling government has often taken priority over efficiency and competitiveness in business performance. This observation is not unrelated to the changes in the composition of the business community, which has undergone two major transformations: first in the early Republican era, and later under the AKP rule since 2002, where established business actors were faced with politically generated challenges and politically-supported new actors emerged. The likely impact of these transformations on accumulation of capital or entrepreneurial skill development might be important to consider in a comparative analysis of Turkish economic development performance.

In a parallel vein, the current divide within the business community could be analyzed as an obstacle to the effective mobilization of the entrepreneurial potential of the country in a stable strategy of economic development. Although it was not explored in any detail in this chapter, the nature of the private sector's political expectations is also likely to affect the moral context of business activity in a way that shapes society-specific evaluations of corruption or the extent and form of business philanthropy in different societies. Where business actors are called upon to collaborate with the government and to contribute to the latter's politically-set agenda, business philanthropy might lose its voluntary character and appear as part of a reciprocal relationship between business people and the government that legitimates deviations from legal provisions and formal rules. In such a context, business ethics acquires a different meaning than they do in a setting where the market economy operates on stable legal foundations that help to foster trust and alleviate uncertainty. Chapter 10 by Hunter and Jones, explores the issue of corruption further, comparing Turkey with India and Japan.

As to the Turkish and Japanese patterns of capitalist development, they are surely different in many respects, including the timing and the level of industrialization or the way economic and political institutions are designed to operate. Yet these are also countries where the relationship between politics and business has been crucial in its impact on the economy and society. With such differences and similarities in mind, it might be interesting to depict certain elements of a comparative inquiry along four axes. The history of business development constitutes the first axis. Here we see a clear difference between the two countries given the long history of big Japanese corporations such as Mitsui or Mitsubishi, which effectively began operations in the 17th and the 19th centuries, respectively. In his article "Fifty Years of Business History in Japan," Takeo Kikkawa refers to the importance of political contacts in the power and influence acquired by these corporations, but also mentions that the instability introduced by heavy reliance on government support was recognized at a relatively early stage, and the companies abandoned "their old political influence-centric strategies" through a series of structural reforms.[23]

While the close ties between government and business have been widely documented by historians of Japanese business, in these accounts economic and political actors appear to be in an interdependent and equal partnership, unlike the situation in Turkey where complex ties of dependency binding big business actors to the political authority have remained important for a long time. This relationship is closely reflected in the second axis constituted by business presence in politics. In an analysis of the equal partnership between Japanese business and the government, we read, for example, that "The armed revolt of Satsuma in 1877 was put down by a conscript army, transported by Mitsubishi ships, supplied by the Mitsui Bussan and paid by the Mitsui Bank."[24] At a later stage, during the Cold War period, the challenge of a socialist change in the country is said to have led the big business association Keidanren to mobilize corporate funds for political donations to support the LDP in an effort to preserve the capitalist system.[25]

Such examples of business contributions to political objectives have been rare in Turkish business history, at least until recent developments brought about by political Islam's rise to power. Turkish business operated for a long time under the threat of regime change—first in the etatist period in the 1930s and 1940s, and then in the 1960s and 1970s because of the radical leftwing movements—without much influence on the political environment. In fact, the political uncertainty surrounding business life was closely related to government-business relations, which were characterized by tension rather than harmony.

Yukihiko Hamada writes that "in the Japanese political setting, where business and government are closely intertwined, the concept of harmony (*Wa*) is essential to maintain their relationship."[26] In stark contrast to this, in Turkey tension appears as the essential concept in an investigation of not only government-business relations, but also the relations among business actors. As was discussed in this paper, big business association TÜSİAD never had the political clout of Keidanren, not only because it often lacked government support and sympathy but also because its relations with other business organizations or even its own membership have not been totally harmonious. This brings us to the third possible axis of comparison, which has to do with the associational environment and relations within the business community. Here, too, the Turkish and Japanese cases differ. The Japanese business community is said to be hierarchically organized, with close relations between different associations that engage in business activism in conformity with an accepted division of roles in their approach to bureaucrats and politicians at different levels.[27]

Especially since the publication of Chalmers Johnson's seminal work,[28] the role of bureaucratic autonomy has been the main point of emphasis in most studies of government-business relations in Japan. A strong bureaucracy that could pursue a systematic policy of economic development unhampered by political concerns of governments and profit- oriented behavior of business people is the central element in Japanese business history. This is the fourth and final axis of comparison, and it is here that we find probably the most striking contrast between the cases of Japan and Turkey. Political intervention in the functioning of bureaucracy has been an ever-present element of Turkey's policy environment, and it has taken a truly alarming form since 2002 under the AKP government, as was argued in this paper. No comparison between Turkish and Japanese government-business relations can avoid addressing this issue.

It is nevertheless important to note that the elements of these four axes of comparison are both interdependent outcomes and determinants of the political situation prevailing in Turkey. The frame of analysis suggested here might be useful for a comparative static investigation but it needs to be further developed by taking into account the elements of continuity and change in the determinants of government- business relations. Government-business relations have always been tense in Turkey, but both the extent of this tension and the way it manifested itself in the economy and politics have changed in different periods. While the contested legitimacy of profit making activity and the policy-related uncertainties affecting business life constituted the main source of tension in earlier periods, what seems to be particularly significant in the current context is the divide within the business community, which is situated in a highly polarized society. It might be useful to ask whether in Japan business development has always proceeded in the same stable political environment dominated by an autonomous bureaucracy and whether this will always be the case in spite of the new challenges such as the ones presented by economic globalization. Drawing on studies of Japanese business history in the pre-World War II period and examining the new types of tension ushered in by economic globalization might open new avenues beyond the familiar narratives on Japan Inc.[29] It might then be possible to situate comparative analysis in a dynamic setting and trace the historical trajectories followed by government- business relations in Japan and Turkey in their differences and similarities. Such a dynamic analysis would also be useful in a study of the historical transformations in other country contexts such as the Korean one mentioned in this chapter.

Notes

1. The analysis of government-business relations in Turkey presented in this chapter draws on the previous work of Ayşe Buğra on the subject. See, especially, *State and Business in Modern Turkey: A Comparative Study*, New York: State University of New York Press, 1994; A. Buğra and O. Savaşkan, *New Capitalism in Turkey: The Relationship Between Politics, Religion and Business*, Cheltenham, UK: Edward Elgar Publishers, 2014.
2. J.M. Keynes, *Essays in Persuasion*, New York: W.W. Norton and Co., 1963, pp. 306–307.
3. A. Gerschenkron, *Economic Backwardness in Historical Perspective*, Cambridge, MA: Belknap Press of Harvard University Press, 1962.
4. P.A. Hall and D. Soskice (eds.), *Varieties of Capitalism: The Institutional Foundations of Comparative Advantage*, Oxford and New York: Oxford University Press, 2001.
5. Y. Hamada, "Japanese Business-Government Relations," in D. Coen, W. Grant, and G. Wilson (eds.), *The Oxford Handbook of Government and Business*, Oxford: Oxford University Press, 2010, p. 333.
6. For a discussion of government-business relations in this period, see Buğra, *State and Business*, pp. 101–119.
7. *Akşam*, 16 December 1945. Also quoted by F. Ahmad, *Turkish Experiment in Democracy: 1950–1975*, London: C. Hurst and Company, 1977, p. 123.
8. See A. Buğra, *Kapitalizm, Yoksulluk ve Türkiye'de Sosyal Politika (Capitalism, Poverty and Social Policy in Turkey)*, Istanbul: Iletisim, 2008, pp. 146–147.
9. *Forum*, 1 September 1959.
10. M. Useem, *The Inner Circle: Large Corporations and the Rise of Business Political Activity in the U.S. and the U.K.*, Oxford: Oxford University Press, 1984.
11. *Cumhuriyet*, 10 April 1971.
12. For a discussion of the official MÜSİAD narrative on the foundation of the association, see A. Buğra, "Class, Culture and the State: An Analysis of Interest Representation by Two Turkish Business Associations," *International Journal of Middle East Studies*, v.30, n. 4, 1998.
13. For a discussion of these developments, see Buğra and Savaskan, *New Capitalism*, pp. 76–108.
14. Buğra and Savaskan, *New Capitalism*.
15. Ibid., pp. 95–101.
16. On this, see, for example, MÜSİAD, *Homo Islamicus: İş Hayatında İslam İnsanı*, Istanbul: MÜSİAD, 1994.
17. On this, see also A. Buğra, "Philanthropy and the New Politics of Social Policy," in B. Morvaridi (ed.) *New Philanthropy and Social Justice*, Bristol: Policy Press, 2015, pp. 117–136.

18. In fact, MÜSİAD's membership in Istanbul has been larger than in any other city.
19. "Türkonfed: Hakkımızda," http://turkonfed.org/tr/hakkimizda
20. For example, in a report on the Turkish economy prepared by MÜSİAD in 2002 the independent regulatory institutions introduced by Derviş reforms could at times prevent politicians from fulfilling their responsibilities to the electorate and could develop into unaccountable and non-transparent bureaucratic institutions, which would counterbalance their expected positive contribution to the eradication of corruption and the limitation of populist tendencies. In a parallel vein, the IMF proposals of 2008 warmly welcomed by TÜSİAD are criticized by MÜSİAD for neglecting the requirements of the "real sector" and national economic development with their emphasis on financial discipline and good governance. See, on this, MÜSIAD, *Türkiye Ekonomisi 2002*, Istanbul: MÜSİAD, 2002, p. 82; "MÜSİAD: İMF Yerine Reform Gerek," *Milliyet*, June 9, 2009; "MÜSİAD: Türkiye' nin İhtiyacı Stand-by Değil, Reformalar ve Yeni Anayasa," *Radikal*, June 9, 2009.
21. For a more extensive comparison of the Turkish case with East Asian and Latin American cases, see Buğra, *State and Business*.
22. A. Amsden, "Third World Industrialization: Global Fordism or A New Model?" *New Left Review*, v.182, July–August 1990, p. 22.
23. T. Kikkawa, "Fifty Years of Business History in Japan," *Japanese Research in Business History*, v.30, 2013.
24. R. Boyd, "Government-Industry Relations in Japan: Access, Communication, and Competitive Collaboration," in S. Wilks and M. Wright (eds.) *Comparative Government-Industry Relations*, Oxford: Clarendon Press, 1987.
25. M. Kazuo, "How Corporate Japan Lost Its 'Voice' ": The Plight of Keidanren in the Post-Japan Inc. Area," October 03, 2014, www.nippon.com/en/currents/d00111/, accessed April 20, 2016.
26. Hamada, "Japanese Business," p. 352.
27. Hamada presents a very useful discussion of how this type of business activism through associations is made compatible with the significance of informal networking activity, something which appears to be quite intriguing to outsiders. See Hamada, "Japanese Business," p. 333.
28. C. Johnson, *MITI and the Japanese Miracle: The Growth of Industrial Policy 1925–1975*, Stanford, CA: University of California Press, 1997.
29. In this regard, compelling insights are presented by Peter von Staden, who discusses the historical background to the emergence of the post-World War II context of government-business relations that inform Chalmers Johnson's analysis of the Japanese "developmental state." See Peter von Staden, "Business Shaping Political Decision Making? An Examination of the Iron and Steel Promotion Law of 1917," Discussion Paper, Suntory Centre, Suntory and Toyota Centres for Economics and Related Disciplines, London School of Economics and Political Science, 2002. See also M. Kazuo, "How Corporate Japan Lost Its 'Voice': The Plight of Keidanren in the Post-Japan Inc. Area.

4 Development of Business Groups and Entrepreneurship

The Koç Group in Global Perspective[1]

Asli M. Colpan and Geoffrey Jones

While Chapter 3 surveyed the evolution of the Turkish business system within the broad political economy context, this chapter will provide a detailed analysis of the development of the largest of the Turkish business groups that played a leading role in the Republic of Turkey's economy before the rise of the religious-conservative groups discussed in Chapter 5. As Chapter 1 identified, the dominance of business groups is typical rather than atypical of emerging markets. Indeed, they are a prevalent form of business enterprise across much of contemporary Asia, Latin America and the Middle East, although they are also highly heterogeneous.[2]

There remain differences between academic disciplines in the dominant theoretical explanations for the growth of business groups. The market imperfections theory favored by many economists and in the discipline of strategy has explained them as responses to the institutional voids that are often found in developing countries.[3] Political scientists have emphasized the role of government policies in targeting particular industries and sectors for growth through selective policies and giving special privileges to selected business groups.[4] Some management researchers have identified the importance of the "contact capabilities" of business groups, both with their home government and with the multinational enterprises that supplied advanced technology.[5]

A much less-well developed insight concerns the role of entrepreneurship. In 2001, Kock and Guillen, employing an evolutionary perspective on the growth of business groups, suggested that the development of their "contact capabilities" was an entrepreneurial response to the environment of late industrializing countries. These authors argued that the protectionist environment in developing economies after World War II encouraged entrepreneurs not to innovate new products, but rather to leverage local and foreign contacts to combine international knowledge with local markets. They also predicted that as economies liberalized and reduced tariff barriers, entrepreneurs would shift to building organizational and technological capabilities.[6] In 2006, in a study of the evolution of Taiwanese business groups, Chung also emphasized the role of entrepreneurial founders in diversification strategies. He suggested that the personal relationships of entrepreneurial founders, more especially networks in politics, shaped early diversification strategies, although over time the business groups developed their own capabilities that shaped later growth patterns.[7]

The business history literature on business groups has provided empirical support for all of the dominant theories of business group formation and growth. This research has shown that business groups were a vibrant form of business enterprise for a century before World War II, and found no evidence to support a view that they declined as economies liberalized. This literature has also supported Chung's emphasis on the importance of entrepreneurial founders in the initial phases of business group formation. Indeed, by identifying the role of successive generations of family owners and managers, business historians have pointed to a continuing and important role for families in the growth and resilience of business groups. This appears to be as true for the families behind the long-established business groups owned in the developed economies of Britain and Sweden, such as the Swire's, Keswick's and Wallenberg's, as for their counterparts in Latin America, India and other emerging markets.[8]

In the case of Turkey, the importance of business groups in the emergence of modern industry is well established. As Table 4.1 shows, out of the 50 largest enterprises by employment in Turkey in 2005, 28 were diversified business groups. These groups accounted for 57% of the total workforce of Turkey's top 50 business enterprises.

Table 4.2 traces the origins of the 28 business groups listed in Table 4.1 in Turkey by employees in 2005. The table shows that five of these large businesses originated in the interwar years, including Koç as well as

Table 4.1 50 Largest Turkish Business Enterprises by Employment, 2005

Business enterprise	*Number of employees*	
	Total number	*Ratio (%)*
Largest (Koç Group)	81,926	10.72
5 largest units	249,172	32.62
10 largest units	367,016	48.04
Family business groups (26 units)	389,124	50.94
All business groups (28 units)	436,235	57.10
State-owned enterprise	260,091	34.05
Foreign-owned enterprise	61,237	8.02
Total 50 units	763,946	100.00

Source: Adapted from A.M. Colpan, "'Business Groups in Turkey," in A.M. Colpan, T. Hikino and J.R. Lincoln, eds., *Oxford Handbook of Business Groups*, Oxford: Oxford University Press, 2010, p 495

Table 4.2 Years of Foundation of the Largest Turkish Business Groups in 2005

1920s	*1930s*	*1940s*	*1950s*	*1960s*	*1970s*	*1980s*
Koç	Sabancı	Ülker	Zorlu	Oyak	Ciner	Şahinler
Çukurova	STFA	Anadolu	Doğuş	Sanko	Kibar	Fiba
İş Bankası		Eczacıbaşı	Tekfen	Nergis		
		Yaşar	Doğan			
		Borusan	Boydak			
			Alarko			
			Profilo			
			Enka			
			Güriş			
			Kale			
			Çelebi			

Source: Compiled from A.M. Colpan, "'Business Groups in Turkey," in A.M. Colpan, T. Hikino and J. R. Lincoln, eds., Oxford Handbook of Business Groups, Oxford: Oxford University Press, 2010, p 491–494

Note: Company names are listed in terms of their size (in employee count) as of 2005

Çukurova and Sabancı. This was not the norm. Of the largest business groups in 2005, Koç, Çukurova and İş Bankası emerged in the 1920s, Sabancı and STFA in the 1930s; four emerged in the 1940s.[9] However, Table 4.2 shows that majority of them emerged in the 1950s and seven of them after the 1960s.[10]

This chapter aims to go beyond broad mapping of the chronological growth of Turkish business groups by exploring the dynamics of that growth through the case of the Koç Group. The Koç Group has been the largest business group in Turkey, which was ranked the ninth largest (following Samsung, Tata and others) among the *private* enterprises in late-industrializing economies in 2007 (see Table 4.3). It is also the only Turkish enterprise in that table. A closer look at the table also shows that the private large enterprises in emerging economies share strikingly similar characteristics. They consist of business groups with unrelated diversified product portfolio often controlled by families.

Drawing on the entrepreneurship theories associated with Kirzner and Schumpeter,[11] the detailed examination of Koç Group in this chapter especially underlines the significance of the entrepreneurial process, which goes beyond the rudimentary contact capabilities and personal relationships argued in the previous literature. The chapter also points to a continuing and important role for entrepreneurship in the growth and resilience of the business group organization well after the initial formation stages. It draws on the Koç corporate archives, interviews with the Koç family and retired and current managers, and published autobiographies of Vehbi Koç, other Koç family members, and executives in the Koç Group.

Table 4.3 The Largest Private Enterprises in Emerging Markets, 2007

Rank	*Name*	*Country*	*Revenues (US$ million)*	*Control*	*Industry*
1	Samsung	161,780	S.Korea	family	unrelated diversified
2	Hyundai Motor	83,392	S.Korea	family	unrelated diversified
3	SK	75,784	S.Korea	family	unrelated diversified
4	LG	71,498	S.Korea	family	unrelated diversified
5	Tata Group	62,500	India	family	unrelated diversified
6	Carso	51,199	Mexico	family	unrelated diversified
7	Formosa Plastics	49,519	Taiwan	family	unrelated diversified
8	Hon Hai	47,571	Taiwan	family	unrelated diversified
9	Koç Holding	39,392	Turkey	family	unrelated diversified
10	Bradesco	38,264	Brazil	family	unrelated diversified
11	Reliance Group	35,915	India	family	unrelated diversified
12	Vale (CVRD)	34,080	Brazil	pension funds	unrelated diversified
13	GS	33,478	S.Korea	family	unrelated diversified
14	Posco	31,163	S.Korea	institutional shareholders	steel
15	Lotte	31,070	S.Korea	family	unrelated diversified
16	Anglo American	29,532	South Africa/ UK	institutional shareholders	unrelated diversified
17	Aditya Birla Group	29,200	India	family	unrelated diversified
18	Itausa	28,961	Brazil	family	unrelated diversified
19	Hutchison Whampoa	28,035	Hong Kong	family	unrelated diversified
20	Flextronics International	27,558	Singapore	institutional shareholders	electronics
21	Quanta Computer	23,665	Taiwan	family	computer
22	Noble Group	23,497	Hong Kong	family	unrelated diversified
23	Asustek	22,993	Taiwan	family	computer
24	Hanwha	22,496	S.Korea	family	unrelated diversified
25	Techint	22,000	Argentina	family	unrelated diversified

Source: Compiled (with minor changes) from A.M. Colpan and T. Hikino, "Foundations of Business Groups: Towards an Integrated Framework," in A.M. Colpan, T. Hikino and J.R. Lincoln (eds.), *The Oxford Handbook of Business Groups*. Oxford: Oxford University Press, 2010, pp 39–40

Section 4.1 discusses the origins of the Koç Group before 1945. Section 4.2 examines the expansion of the Koç business group after World War II until the late 1950s. Section 4.3 analyzes the reorganization and further expansion of the Koç Group between the 1960s and 1980s. Section 4.4 examines the development of the Group after the passing of Vebhi Koç. Section 4.5 provides conclusions.

4.1 Vehbi Koç and the Origins of the Koç Group

Vehbi Koç was born in 1901 in Ankara, at the time an impoverished city in the middle of Anatolia. At the time Koç was born, his father was living on the rent he obtained from the stores left by his own father. In 1916, Koç's father together with three Muslim friends decided to found a partnership to trade wheat. When his father's business failed, Koç decided to enter into business himself and dropped out of school. Together with his father, in 1917 he opened a small grocery shop selling shoe rubber, sugar, olives and pasta below their own house. After two years, Vehbi started to investigate new opportunities by looking at the businesses of his Greek, Armenian and Jewish neighbors. As a result, he decided to enter into leather trading, and offered a high salary to an ethnic Greek salesperson to provide the necessary expertise.[12]

As he succeeded in the leather business, Koç looked for new opportunities. He entered the hardware store business, which was largely controlled by ethnic Jewish merchants, and recruited a leading salesperson from one of these enterprises. Over time, the initial hardware business was expanded to include textiles, glassware and other products. He also sought to enter the large business of selling kerosene for gas lamps, and attempted to become the Ankara agent of an international company. After working successfully for the Anglo Persian Oil Company, a small petroleum business, he secured the Istanbul agency of Turkey's largest importer, Standard Oil.[13]

When Ankara became the capital of the Republic of Turkey, new business opportunities emerged, such as development and construction work in the city. Given the increasing demand for such services, Koç entered into the sale of construction materials and exited grocery and leather sales. He worked with Nafiz Kotan, a politically well-connected building contractor in the construction materials business who was able to secure multiple government contracts. As Koç's business grew, he also built a contracting business, undertaking projects in partnership with other firms.[14] In 1926, his father passed the ownership of their firm to Vehbi, changing the enterprise's name to Koçzade Ahmet Vehbi.

Ankara's new prosperity provided other opportunities. During the 1920s, US firms including Ford and Chevrolet began their automotive sales in Turkey by using local agents primarily based in Istanbul. Koç observed that the representative of Chevrolet in Ankara had a profitable business bringing in automobiles from Istanbul. Thanks to his established reputation in Ankara, when Ford was searching for an agent in that city in 1928, they gave Koç an agency agreement.[15] In order to build the automotive business, Koç later hired an ethnic Jewish manager, Bernar Nahum, who at the time was working at an automobile and parts company in Ankara. With the assistance of a government agreement not to charge customs duties on imported parts, Ford started its own local assembly facility in Istanbul in 1929. Nevertheless, Ford closed the plant in 1934, in the wake of the Great Depression, as hopes to develop an export business collapsed, and Turkish workers, fearing for their jobs, emptied boxes of automotive parts into the sea.[16] Koç, however, retained the sales agency, Otokoç.

As his success in Ankara grew, in 1937 Koç opened an Istanbul construction materials venture, organized as a partnership. Koç owned 70% of the company, and gave the remaining shares to two partners who would manage the branch. As none of the partners spoke foreign languages, Koç recruited İsak Atabef, an ethnic Jewish banker who had been educated and worked in Germany, and at the time was working for a firm that was successful in winning contracts from the Turkish government. He gave Atabef 15% of the equity out of his own shares to make him a partner. He then took as a partner another competitor who was known as a good salesperson to lead the sales department of his Istanbul business, and convinced executives from two-state-owned banks to join him by offering them high salaries.[17]

In 1938 Koç turned his unincorporated company Ankara-based "Koçzade Ahmet Vehbi" into an incorporated firm, "Koç Ticaret Anonim Şirketi" (Koç Trade Corporation), with 300,000 lira ($238,095) of capital. His two stores—one dealing with construction and electricity, the other with automobiles—were organized as branches of Koç Trade Corporation. The partnership in Istanbul also became an incorporated company that served as a branch of the Koç Trade Corp. in Ankara. Koç Trade Corp. was also being utilized as the financing vehicle of the various Koç businesses.

A key constraint on the growth of the business was a shortage of capital. The country lacked both a capital market and banks willing to make loans to promote industrial growth. With the outbreak of World War II, however, Koç decided to move into the truck importing business, for which there was a massive demand because of wartime shortages. A huge black market for vehicles emerged, as a result of which huge profits were made. Koç later lamented in public that in this venture the "morality" of his organization "deteriorated." However, there had also been significant capital accumulation.[18]

The evidence on the formative stages of Koç's group, then, confirms that all three leading theories have empirical support. Interwar Turkey had plentiful institutional voids. The policy regime was clearly favorable to the emergence of domestic business groups. The importance of contact capabilities was clear, as evidenced by Koç's alliance with Nafiz Kotan in securing government contracts.

However, the role of entrepreneurship seems especially important in explaining the success of Koç. The story is partly one of a Kirzner-type entrepreneur who was alert to opportunities. Koç was at a disadvantage by not being located in Istanbul, but he successfully identified the new opportunities arising from Ankara's becoming the new capital. He also identified that the ethnic minorities in the city, especially Jews, were knowledgeable about business, knew foreign languages, and were vulnerable because of their ethnicity in the highly charged nationalist climate. He offered them high salaries and, more importantly, made them partners in his companies.

However, Koç was also a Schumpeterian entrepreneur. This was most evident in Koç's assembly as well as mobilization of financial resources. Capital scarcity was a huge constraint on the development of modern entrepreneurship. Koç accumulated capital in the Koç Trade Corporation, which used it to fund diverse businesses, from construction to automobile agencies, and to create an internal capital market. A large proportion of capital accumulation came from the commissions in import deals, especially during the distinctive circumstances of World War II.[19] In a country that was short of capital and, especially, efficient financial institutions and markets, the effective assembling and mobilization of financial resources was an act of Schumpeterian entrepreneurship.

4.2 Making a Diversified Business Group 1940s-1960s

This section now turns to the growth of Koç as a diversified business group between the 1940s and the 1960s. The policy regime of import protection and obstacles to foreign firms provided the key exogenous context for the emergence and growth of multiple business groups. However, it would be misleading to describe Vehbi Koç's business strategy in functional terms as a passive response to policy and market conditions. The strategy was proactive and Schumpeterian.

In particular, he began a lengthy and single-minded pursuit of alliances with highly skeptical foreign multinationals. In 1943, Koç became convinced that the Allies would win the war, and there would be many business opportunities with American firms. Accordingly, he sent Vecihi Karabayoğlu, a young engineer with an American undergraduate degree, to the United States. Karabayoğlu returned to Turkey with the agencies of several firms, including General Electric (GE) and US Rubber.[20] In 1945, Koç established the first Turkish company in the US—New York-based "Ram (Koç in Turkish) Commercial Corporation"—with a capital investment of $25,000. Until the company was closed in 1954, its primary business was to provide consulting to official Turkish delegations visiting the US.[21]

In 1946, Koç himself went to the United States to meet the executives of the firms that he represented in Turkey, and to persuade them to invest in manufacturing in the country. He persuaded GE to establish a light bulb factory. In 1948 GE Lighting was founded as the first joint venture with a foreign company in Turkey. Negotiations with US Rubber to build a tire factory, though, were unsuccessful. Koç also met with Ford executives in Detroit to discuss the creation of a joint venture assembly operation. However, Ford, which had serious problems in its Western

European business, had no interest in investing in developing countries, especially Turkey, where its prior experience had ended in disaster.[22]

Because imports were restricted by high tariffs, Koç remained in dogged pursuit of a Ford assembly plant.[23] In 1956 he found an opportunity to meet Henry Ford II, President of the Ford Motor Company, after his automotive agency won a dealership contest among Ford's 34 agencies in the Near East. Koç carried a letter from Prime Minister Menderes introducing Koç, encouraging Ford to invest in Turkey jointly with him, and offering to support the joint venture through incentives.[24] Ford eventually agreed to support the establishment of a truck assembly factory by providing up to $300,000 in credit, although this came with highly demanding guarantee conditions, and the proviso that the name Ford was not to be used. However, this time it was the Democratic Party government under Menderes that declined to support the initiative, which floundered amidst lengthy administrative delays—Koç waited eight and a half months for a meeting with the Prime Minister to approve the agreement.[25]

The Ford agreement had become entangled in the conflicted politics of postwar Turkey. Koç had been loosely associated with the ruling political elite during the interwar years. In 1920, at his father's request, he became a member of Müdafaa-i Hukuk Cemiyeti (Association for Defense of National Rights), the predecessor to the CHP (the Republican People's Party). Later he regularly met with the CHP and government officials, including the second President of Turkey, İsmet İnönü. He was even invited to become the Representative for Ankara in the Turkish Parliament for the CHP in 1943, an offer he declined. The Democrat Party's advent to power in 1950, therefore, was a problematic development. Koç's businesses' tax records were checked, and his business dealings were investigated in Parliament. Even though no allegations of corruption or other transgressions by Koç were made, government ministries stopped buying gasoline and other goods from his companies, and he was also removed from his position as the Ankara Chamber of Commerce President.[26]

During the late 1950s, the Democrat Party increased pressure on Koç to join their ranks, as it wanted powerful business leaders on their side. But Koç did not want to leave CHP, not least because he felt any move would be interpreted as an attempt to win special favors or cover illegal business dealings.[27] The delay in the approval of the agreement with Ford was one of the casualties of this period. Eventually, in 1960 pressure from the Democrat Party became so strong that Koç had to resign from the CHP, though without joining the Democrat Party.[28] This was a shrewd move as within months the Army had seized power, executing Prime Minister Menderes despite international uproar. For the next four decades, the Turkish Army remained the country's power broker. Koç never re-joined a political party, although he did seek to maintain good relations with new governments as well as the Army. In 1974 he donated, through Koç Group companies and the Vehbi Koç Foundation, a total of 10 million TL ($740,000) to the foundations established to support the Armed Forces and the Turkish Red Crescent Society.[29]

Despite his political travails, Koç continued to seek a path into automobile assembly. In 1958 he finally secured an agreement with the government under which an assembly plant could be established with Ford, though under strict conditions. Ford executives considered this venture, which involved no equity investment by the company and continued avoidance of the American company's name, as a temporary project that would be unnecessary when import restrictions were relaxed. In 1959 the Otosan company was launched, and was initially engaged in the knock-down assembly of Ford trucks. Koç group companies and other Ford dealers in Turkey became shareholders in the new business.[30] This was a modest venture, certainly, for example, compared to the automobile manufacturing facilities that Volkswagen had begun to construct in Brazil in response to market closure policies.[31] However, it was Turkey's first automotive assembly plant. In 1963 Koç explicitly noted the first mover advantages he believed would accrue to the first company to start an automotive industry.[32]

Koç became involved in domestic assembly and manufacturing more broadly from the mid-1950s onwards. Policy incentives to private enterprises to move into manufacturing, as well as growing protectionism, provided the exogenous context, yet Koç was creative and ambitious in his pursuit of partners. He sought to enter steel furniture manufacturing in 1954 with the Burla family, ethnic Jews who owned an established steel trading business. As incomes rose in the country and the demand for white goods expanded, there was an insufficient supply of goods such as washing machines and refrigerators; accordingly, in 1959 Koç and his partners decided to make an agreement with a Belgian company for technical assistance. They bought motors, gearboxes and other parts to manufacture washing machines. In the same year, after initial attempts at licensing and know-how agreements with US and European firms including GE and Siemens failed, as those companies considered the local Turkish market too small, the company, then named "Arçelik," was able to conclude an agreement with Amcor, an Israeli company, to receive technical assistance and purchase parts for the manufacturing of refrigerators.[33]

Difficulties in importing key components prompted Arçelik to look for ways to produce components for the white-goods business within Turkey. The company initially began to manufacture plastic plates and gearboxes itself, as it found there were no qualified domestic suppliers that could provide these products to Koç. For more sophisticated parts, Arçelik made agreements with multinational firms, including technology licenses from GE and German-based Bosch-Siemens. Arçelik soon diversified. Due to fluctuations in the domestic market for home appliances, the company used their steel plates to make other products, including harvesters and steel bathtubs.[34]

On one level, then, Koç's growth in diversified assembly and manufacturing businesses can be explained by policies that provided incentives for profitable entry into such activities. Rising incomes generated demand that the low-level industrialization of the country could not meet. On another level, the way such opportunities were seized needs to be seen as Schumpeter-style entrepreneurship. Koç was not so much alert to taking advantage of new opportunities, as to creating them. Koç perceived how to capture value by acquiring knowledge from the multinational firms who were shut out of the market, but were not especially interested in entering it, as it was considered small, marginal and risky. He was relentless in pursuing and negotiating with those international firms. When Koç could not persuade such firms to partner with him, he pursued the innovative gambit of seeking knowledge from innovative firms in the newly created state of Israel. Koç also did not appear to be a rent-seeker benefiting from political contacts. Indeed, he suffered from being affiliated with the political party that had lost power, and subsequently carefully avoided explicit political affiliation whilst remaining on good terms with the power brokers in the regime.

4.3 Reorganization and Expansion: 1960s to 1980s

The rapid growth of the Koç Group between the 1960s and the 1980s saw attempts to build organizational capabilities, although the search for an ideal organizational model to manage such a diversified business proved challenging. This section highlights Vehbi Koç's efforts to change laws that stood in the way of the organizational form he envisioned. It also shows his role in searching for the best administrative mechanism and instituting organizational innovations within the Group. Now owner and manager of a large business enterprise, Koç continued to function as a disruptor of established legal norms and organizational methods while still continuing to play critical roles in the strategies of his companies.

The number of Koç companies increased from the early 1960s. They were nominally independent firms in which Vehbi Koç personally was the dominant voice in strategic decisions.[35] However, the managerial diseconomies of this strategy soon became apparent as he struggled to manage unrelated businesses, including preventing duplication of service functions. Koç, who was sixty-four in 1965, also began to consider his legacy. He was concerned that his successors might struggle to manage his personal creation, which had become a complex business entity involving multiple outside shareholders.[36]

These challenges were hardly unique to Turkey. Indeed, they had been faced decades previously as firms in the United States and Europe had begun to grow. By this period there was a substantial body of management theory addressing the issues, especially in the United States. In 1960 Filiz Ofluoğlu, a human resources manager in Koç companies, who held an MBA from Wharton and a doctorate from Columbia University, suggested the creation of a holding company.[37] Koç asked the American consulting firm of George Fry and Associates to prepare a report on the concept, and it suggested a similar plan—to incorporate Koç's companies within a central holding company.[38]

By the time of the consultancy report, there was already an embryonic headquarters structure in place in the form of the Koç Trade Corp, which had evolved as a management and monitoring center—the building that housed the company was appropriately named the "Central Inn." An initial idea was to change this company into one that would hold the shares of several other Koç companies.[39] The Koç family would transfer their shares in the several operating companies to the newly established holding company, which would then become the shareholder of the operating companies. Koç also planned to allocate shares to senior managers in the holding company. To balance the family's majority ownership in management, Koç also wanted to give certain shares of the holding company to a foundation under his name.[40]

The creation of such a holding company, however, faced considerable challenges from the Turkish legal system. Turkey had a multiple taxation law, which taxed corporate income when a firm transferred profits to a parent firm. This meant that when an affiliate transferred profits to a holding company, the same profit would be taxed twice. In addition, Turkish Civil Law did not appear to allow the establishment of the kind of foundation that Koç envisioned. The upshot was that Koç needed to lobby to get laws either changed or clarified. In 1961 the government legislated to remove the obstacle of double taxation, and six years later a law was passed permitting the establishment of foundations.[41]

As changes to the law were pursued, it was eventually decided that Koç Trade Corp. would remain as it was, and that another company, "Koç Holding," would be established. In November 1963 Koç Holding became the first such holding company established in the country, although in time other business groups also adopted this structure.[42] Vehbi Koç himself was the largest shareholder with 73.7% of the equity, with the remaining majority held by his wife, and each of his four children. With the passing of the law on foundations in 1967, Koç established the Koç Holding Foundation, a pension fund for employees, which also invested in the holding company.[43] In 1969 the Vehbi Koç Foundation was established to handle the philanthropic contributions of the Koç family. This also took equity in the holding company.[44]

In 1965 the new Holding Company assumed ownership of 28 Koç companies, organized into an automotive group, an industry group, a trading group, and an LPG group.[45] Subsequently, the Group mainly grew organically, but also by means of acquisitions. It engaged in both related diversification to produce components necessary for manufacturing operations, such as the creation of an alloy steel plant and a foundry to cast engine blocks, as well as technologically unrelated areas, including canned food, supermarket chains, foreign trade, banking and insurance, and meat processing. While decisions about related diversification mainly hinged on the Group's resources, decisions about technologically unrelated areas were dependent on Vehbi Koç's entrepreneurship. For example, when Koç visited Japan in 1969 and saw the role of large trading companies, he thought that a similar export and import company would be a significant asset for the Koç Group. He established Ram Dış Ticaret (Ram Foreign Trade) in 1970.[46] In 1975 Koç also decided to acquire the majority of the shares of the supermarket chain Migros Turk, established as a joint venture between the Swiss co-operative Migros and the municipality of Istanbul twenty years previously. The acquisition was promoted by news that Migros Turk had decided to exit the market due to economic and political instability.[47] Koç's decision came despite the opposition of his executives, who were alarmed that price controls would cause losses.[48]

In his autobiography, published in 1983, Koç drew particular attention to the nature of the domestic market in order to justify such diversification:

> Turkey is a small country relative to the world's developed countries. Here, it was difficult to grow [business] by focusing in one industry as it is done in large countries. Our economic and political status has continuously shown ups and downs. If one business made a deficit, the other would make a profit, and as such I acted in thinking that I would make a balance[d portfolio].[49]

The number of companies in the Koç Group increased from 28 in 1965 to 92 in 1988, while the product groups also increased from four to seven. The three automotive-related businesses, Tofaş, Otosan and automotive supplies, stood as the largest of the Koç businesses in terms of total sales before 1990. Table 4.4 shows sales ratios by activity.[50]

Koç used the earnings from individual group companies to provide equity capital for newly established companies in new business fields. Koç family members would also personally invest in such businesses, which served as a signaling device to outside investors.[51] A complex web of cross- ownership structures emerged as a result. The provision of capital for new ventures was another classic example of a business group filling an institutional void. The country continued to lack a modern organized stock exchange market until 1985, when the Istanbul Stock Exchange was established after a major scandal concerning brokerage firms.[52] The banking system before the mid-1980s also focused on short-term credit finance rather than longer-term industrial investment.[53]

Table 4.4 Koç Consolidated Sales by Activities, 1972–90 (% of total)

	1972	*1975*	*1980*	*1985*	*1990*
Automotive	57.2	52.4	53	44	45
Industry	27.1	28.6	31		
Commerce	8.1	8.4	6	45	45
LPG	7.6	7.1	9		
Koç Investment and Marketing Company	-	3.6	1	-	
Financial and Foreign Trade Companies	-	-	-	11	10

Source: Compiled and calculated from Koç Holding Annual Reports, 1976–90 and reports provided by Koç Holding, Koç Holding Archives

Note: The table shows figures from year 1972, the first year consolidated data became available.

When the Holding company was established in 1963, its initial function was seen as assisting in the formulation of the corporate strategies and execution of the operating companies, as well as controlling and monitoring their budgets. Vehbi Koç and two key managers were at the core of decision making in the Management Council (later renamed the Board of Directors) of the Holding.[54] A retiree from Sümerbank, a state-owned enterprise established in 1933 to create and manage diverse industrial businesses, including weaving, mining, cellulose, ceramics, and chemistry, was brought in as a lateral hire to be General Coordinator (later renamed President and then CEO) to assist in administrative matters.[55] The Holding's top management was involved in key strategic decisions of the operating companies. Vehbi Koç continued to have the last say in critical decisions.[56]

The following decade saw a search for structures that would systematize the chain of command, and clarify the authority of each "commanding member" across the entire Group. In 1970 an Executive Committee was formed to mark the first formal operational division of labor within the Holding. The task of the Executive Committee was to execute the decisions that the Management Council had made and to follow up on the consequences of such decisions. It also coordinated the relationships between the Holding Company and operating affiliates.[57] Rahmi Koç, the only son of Vehbi, became the first President of the Executive Committee. He had started working in the business in 1958, when he joined Otokoç. In 1971, Koç formed an office of planning coordination for establishing long-term (five year) plans for the whole group.[58] The following year Vehbi set up a "Family Council," an administrative mechanism he developed that included both himself and his four children. This council was established to discuss the strategies of the Koç group at the family level on a weekly basis.[59]

The first organization chart of the Koç Holding, which was drawn in 1973, omitted the Family Council by design.[60] The organization chart was clearer than the reality. For instance, while the Industry Group (or division) was responsible for the production of white goods together with other industrial activities of Koç, the Trade Group (or division) was responsible for the marketing of some of the white goods and other goods as well as international trade. On the other hand, the Automotive Group included auto manufacturing and marketing companies under its own Group, but Koç Investment and Marketing Company under the Trade Group also marketed the Automotive Group's products.[61]

Two further organizational developments followed. First was the establishment of Group-wise Research and Development (R&D) Center, pioneered by Bernar Nahum, then Vice-Chairman of Koç Holding, in 1973. This was the first private sector R&D Center in Turkey, which engaged in incremental technological innovation to adapt foreign technologies to local circumstances. Its main task was to support the automotive and industry groups in design, engineering, technical consulting, optimization, knowledge sharing and future research directions. In practice, it mostly worked for the Automotive group, due to Nahum's expertise in that business.[62]

In 1982 the Koç Holding Training and Development Center was founded, at the suggestion of one of the human resource managers in the Holding. This Center, whose function was to develop managers in different Koç companies, was the first attempt in Turkey to provide executive education within a business. Again, it was a classic example of filling an institutional void—the teaching of management education had begun in Turkish universities by the 1970s, although primarily at the undergraduate level, and graduate level training, or executive education, was minimal.[63]

Koç's investment in research and development and management education was pioneering in Turkey, and over time the other large business groups followed suit. However there was no rapid Americanization of the management system, even as policy liberalization took hold. Vehbi Koç remained firmly in control as the final authority for the whole group in the 1980s, with key strategy-formulation processes and decision-making mechanisms left in the hands of the family.[64]

Koç was interested in the management of the family-owned businesses of his partners, including Siemens, Ford and Fiat, and by the late 1980s had begun to believe that professional salaried managers could play an important role in a family business, which they did not in his own firm. In 1988 he hired another American management consultancy, Bain & Company, to advise on the changes in organization and strategy that would be required if the Koç Group were to flourish during

Table 4.5 Financial Performance of the Koç Group at Benchmark Years, 1972–1990

	1972	*1975*	*1980*	*1985*	*1990*
Return on sales	0.12	0.10	0.06	0.06	0.11
Return on assets	0.12	0.10	0.10	0.15	0.32
Return on equity	n.a.	0.44	0.70	1.02	1.49
Current assets-current liabilities ratio	n.a.	1.40	1.27	1.20	1.49
Debt-equity ratio	n.a.	2.81	5.54	4.83	2.81

Source: Compiled and calculated from Koç Holding Annual Reports, 1976–1990 and reports provided by Koç Holding, Koç Holding Archives

Turkey's potential transition to a more open economy.[65] Given that the need to focus on core competences and avoid unrelated diversifications had become the mantra of American management thought during the 1980s, Koç received advice that was both predictable and predicted when the firm was hired: Bain recommended reducing the range of businesses in which Koç was involved, further restructuring of the organization—especially clearly defining roles and responsibilities from the Board down to the operating company managers—and empowering individual product divisions and business units. Bain also predictably suggested the appointment of a professional CEO.[66]

The Bain report was not acted upon, however. Few businesses had been sold by the time Vehbi Koç died in 1996. There was little progress in the professionalization of top management. The family continued to take active roles in decision-making about the strategies of the Holding and its operating companies, as well as the execution.[67] Koç was evidently better at creating a diversified business group than dealing with the considerable resulting organizational challenges. Whatever the merits or flaws of the Group's existing management structure, however, the performance of the business was quite good. Table 4.5 shows that while return on sales and return on assets fluctuated between 1972 and 1990, the return on equity steadily improved.

Table 4.5 reveals a business that was conservatively managed and operated with low debt levels. Evidently, there were no pressing financial incentives for Koç to rush to follow the recommendations of Bain and then-fashionable American management theory.

4.4 The Group after Vehbi Koç

The Group continued to be led by family members. Rahmi Koç was appointed chairman of the Holding management committee in 1980. Vehbi Koç transferred his chairmanship to his son in March 1984. Rahmi Koç himself retired in 2003, and transferred his chair to his eldest son,

Mustafa, who had joined the automotive affiliate Tofaş after graduating from the George Washington University School of Business, in the United States. He remained chairman until his early death in 2016. He was succeeded by Ömer Koç, Rahmi's second son.

During the 1990s, in order to improve corporate governance, the Koç family started looking for ways to include independent directors on the Board of the Holding company, even though they continued to hold the majority of the shares in the Holding company. This move was a first among Turkish companies. The number of outside independent board members increased over time. John McArthur, who had served as dean of the Harvard Business School between 1980 and 1995, joined the board in 1999. Vehbi's daughter Suna argued, unsuccessfully, for more radical progress. She told the Family Council in 1998: "Our age has come to a certain point. . . . Our capabilities are obvious. For the well-being of our businesses the only way is for us, the family members, to stay entirely out of execution. Every minute that we extend this, it is to the harm, not to the advantage, of our company."[68] In 2000 a non-family professional manager was appointed CEO. This represented a further step towards the professionalization of management or, as it was called in Turkey, "institutionalization."

The Koç Group was slow in following the recommendations of Bain and Co. to focus its business portfolio, despite—once more—admonitions from Suna. In a strategy meeting at Koç Holding in 1992, she noted: "It is not possible for us to successfully compete and increase our market share in an open competitive market in 14 different business lines. . . . Before difficult decisions come in front of us and catch us in testing circumstances, we have to make bold decisions and get out of some sectors."[69]

It took a further decade for the Group to undertake a radical restructuring of its portfolio. By 2005 consumer durables and automotives accounted for 28% and 21% of total sales respectively, but the Group remained active in many other sectors. Mustafa resolved to focus on five core sectors: energy, automotive, consumer durables, finance and retailing.

In 2005 Koç Holding undertook three major acquisitions. In energy, a Koç-Shell consortium acquired 51% of the state-owned refining and petrochemicals company Tüpraş, the largest industrial company in Turkey and the seventh largest refiner in Europe. Koç Holding held 75% of shares; 23% belonged to other Koç energy companies. Shell, the Anglo-Dutch oil company, partnered with Koç in the acquisition with 2% partnership in the consortium. In banking, the Group acquired Yapı Kredi Bank, fourth in asset size among the country's private sector banks, in a 50%-50% partnership with UniCredit of Italy. In retailing, Tansaş, a large supermarket chain, was acquired from Doğuş Group, another family-owned business Group in Turkey. It was hoped that this acquisition would create operational synergies with Koç's own supermarket chain, Migros.[70]

In 2008 Mustafa decided to exit retailing gradually, as it was considered a low-profitability business.[71] Koç Holding needed cash to finance the large debts from its recent acquisition of Tüpraş.[72] Between 2005 and 2008, total acquisitions amounted to $6.6 billion, while divestitures were $3.0 billion. Insulation materials, heating appliances, automotive supplies, industrial gas, and insurance were all sold. Still, because of emotional attachments the family declined to exit some businesses they had held for a long period. These included the tomato processing company that Vehbi had nurtured from scratch, and Setur and Divan, the tourism companies in which Vehbi's daughter Semahat had a particular interest.[73]

Among the core businesses, the automotive business remained, based on 50–50% joint ventures with Ford and Fiat. Koç remained dependent on the global strategies of their partners for manufacturing in Turkey. The vehicles produced, most of which were designed for light commercial use, were basically Ford and Fiat models that were in line with the two international companies' global operations. Ford Otosan and Tofaş controlled a vast dealership network for their own vehicles in Turkey and had extensive knowledge of the local market. Ford enjoyed the highest market share in Turkey among all European markets. Fiat sold the largest number of vehicles in Turkey (after Italy) in all its European markets.[74] Ford Otosan and Tofaş had begun to invest in R&D from the late 1980s and early 1990s, respectively. Ford Otosan was the largest investor in R&D in the Turkish automotive sector by 2012, while Tofaş was home to one of Fiat's three main R&D centers globally.[75] The two companies became international manufacturing hubs for new vehicle models and thus contributed to the exports of the Group thanks to their low-cost, high-quality production expertise.[76]

Consumer durables were another long-established business for the Group. In 1991 Arçelik began investing in in-house R&D. Arçelik developed its own designs to circumvent restrictions attached to technology licensing contracts and to survive increasing competition at home.[77] By 2012 Arçelik had 850 researchers in its central and operational R&D department. In the same year the company submitted around 130 patent applications, the highest number in Turkey. It spent 2% of its total sales on R&D, which made Arçelik among the top ten in terms of R&D investing companies in the country.[78] Arçelik held market leadership with about 50% of market share in Turkey.[79]

Mustafa Koç was also eager to invest in energy as demand for electricity in Turkey was estimated to grow rapidly.[80] The liberalization of the formerly state-owned and highly regulated electricity, natural gas and petroleum markets began in the 2000s. The Group already owned Aygaz, which engaged in cylinder LPG gas manufacturing and distribution, and had a large distribution network in Turkey. It then undertook a series of acquisitions. In 2002 Koç acquired a 50% stake of Opet, a fuel distribution company. Following Koç's acquisition of Tüpraş in 2005, energy became the largest industry in terms of the Group's total sales. In 2012, energy represented 63% of the Group's total revenues, and 44% of operating profits.[81]

Banking was also identified as a sector in which the Group sought a larger presence. Loans and deposits in total GDP were much lower in Turkey compared to the Eurozone, and the number of bank branches per total population was also relatively low in Turkey.[82] Koç already owned Koçbank, which concentrated on private banking, corporate banking and asset management, but it was a small venture. After the acquisition of Yapı Kredi Bank in partnership with UniCredit in 2006, Koçbank merged into Yapı Kredi. The new bank secured prominent positions in credit cards, asset management, leasing and factoring, and had a widespread network with 922 branches and 2,742 ATMs in 2012.[83]

Meanwhile, international expansion became a growing concern under Rahmi's Chairmanship. While only a few of the Group companies exported to neighboring countries in the Middle East and North Africa during the 1970s, foreign markets began to become a greater priority after Turkey abandoned the import substitution regime during the following decade. The government began to provide financial incentives to exporting companies. Nonetheless, exporting was not an easy path. Rahmi was told by some of his executives that "To make a $500,000 export revenue, we will make a deficit of $500,000."[84]

After 1988, when Turkey reached an agreement with the EU to reduce customs tariffs to create a free trade area in manufacturing goods by 1996, there was growing urgency about globalization. One Koç manager later noted that

> we needed to find out more about our future likely competitors. One way to do so was to sell. . . [our] products in the tough developed markets. . . . We thought we would learn a great deal by competing against the best in the world on their home turf and better prepare ourselves to defend our domestic market share against. . . [those foreign companies].[85]

The Group also held large market shares in its domestic market, which left little room for further domestic expansion.[86]

Arçelik became a pioneer of expansion in foreign markets by adopting a two-pronged strategy. The first was organic growth through exports; the second was acquisitions of new companies. Arçelik initially started its export activities in the 1970s on an opportunistic basis to use its surplus production. Thanks to a shortage of foreign exchange in the country, the company was also in great need of foreign exchange to pay for imported components. The company targeted neighboring countries including

Iran, Pakistan, Iraq, Syria and Tunisia, for exports. In collaboration with the foreign trade company RAM which had been established in 1970, government institutions were the major buyers of Arçelik's goods in those nations.[87]

Arçelik established its own export division in 1983 to search for potential markets, bid in foreign government tenders and find foreign contract builders.[88] Through this division, in 1988 Arçelik got its first contract for original equipment manufacturing (OEM) from Sears Roebuck, the US retail chain store, to supply the company with refrigerators under the Kenmore brand for distribution in the Caribbean and Latin America. In 1996 a European OEM deal was struck with Whirlpool, the US home appliance manufacturer, to supply the company with dishwashers for the next five years.[89]

At the same time Arçelik invested in R&D to overcome the potential challenges of the opening of the domestic market to competition after the EU customs union. This enabled the firm to enter the markets of the UK, France and Germany, in 1989, 1993 and 1994, respectively, to sell its own branded products.[90] The UK was selected first as it was believed to be more price-sensitive and might accept a low-cost new entrant.[91] Arçelik scaled up its global growth after the 2001 financial crisis in Turkey, which caused home demand for consumer durables to contract. It lost its first bid in Europe to acquire France's Brandt to Israel's white goods producer Elco, which offered the government better employment conditions. In 2002 Arçelik acquired five foreign companies: Blomberg in Germany, Elektra Bregenz in Austria, Arctic in Romania, and the Leisure (cookers) and Flavel (appliances and TV sets) brands in Britain. With these acquisitions, Arçelik aimed to build on these brands in international markets as it was lacking a strong global brand itself.[92]

In 2004 Arçelik acquired Grundig (a German electronics maker), which at the time suffered financially. The following year the firm's large European manufacturing business, primarily in Austria, was closed and production was moved to Turkey. Ali Sümerval, the general manager of the Beko Elektronik subsidiary, which handled the transaction, noted: "Instead of having the manufacturing facilities in Europe, we would rather keep the brand name, the sales organization and all patents. Creating a brand name could be a strategy, but it would be very costly. . . . We didn't want to emphasize the company that was acquiring Grundig as a Turkish company, because the brands have a flavor of the country they belong to. We didn't want to lose the feeling of Grundig being a German brand; solid, long life and a little bit conservative, maybe."[93] While the initial acquisition was done together with Alba Plc., a UK based electronics firm, Beko Elektronik acquired shares from Alba in 2008 to wholly own Grundig (Beko Elektronik merged into Arçelik in 2009).

In 2005 Arçelik began construction of a refrigerator and washing machine greenfield plant in Russia. In 2007 Arçelik acquired

Shanghai-based Changzhou Casa Shinco Electrical Appliances to operate a washing-machine factory in China.[94] Four years later Arçelik acquired the leading appliances company in the Republic of South Africa, Defy Appliances. This acquisition was the single largest Turkish investment ever made in Africa's industrial sector. In 2012 Arçelik opened a sales subsidiary in Egypt and achieved significant sales growth in West, Central and East Africa.

By 2012 Arçelik held the largest market share in home appliances in Romania and South Africa. It also held the second largest position in the UK (accounting for 18% market share) and was within the top five in Europe as a whole in home appliances. It owned sales and marketing companies in 19 countries in addition to its manufacturing plants in China, Romania, Russia, and South Africa, as well as Turkey.[95]

In 1990 exports formed only 7% of total revenues for the Koç Group.[96] It had sales offices in nine countries and no production facilities abroad. By 2012 international sales had reached 28.6% of the Group's total combined revenues, of which 24.3% were exports and 4.3% were sales from overseas operations. Only Arçelik, which made up 18.5% of total international sales, had manufacturing operations overseas. While Ford Otosan and Tofaş contributed 30.3% to the Group's international sales, this was in the form of exports, mostly to the respective partners' global networks.

The Group remained cautious and incremental about global expansion. Banking had domestic focus, with insignificant international activity. Similar to automotive, the partnership with Unicredit restricted the Group's ability to pursue an independent international expansion strategy in banking. The energy business, which was mostly the newly acquired Tüpraş, contributed a 46.3% share to international sales, consisting of exports from surplus gasoline output of the refineries, and marine and aviation fuels.[97] "It is not easy in this global world," Rahmi Koç observed in 2015. "Competition is very, very tough, even merciless. The companies in other markets are very strong. They can afford to lose ten years in order to get control of one market. We do not have that kind of financial muscle, so have to count our pennies very carefully and take the next step forward extremely diligently."[98]

By 2018 the Group owned businesses in 24 countries, which accounted for about 55 percent of the Group's combined sales, but the majority of the operations were in nearby regions of former Soviet republics, the Middle East, North Africa as well as Europe.[99]

4.5 Conclusion

This chapter has examined the growth of the Koç business group in Turkey. The empirical evidence presented here confirms many of the prevailing theories explaining the growth of business groups. As noted in earlier chapters, twentieth century Turkey has been a textbook case of institutional voids in an emerging market. There were weakly developed capital markets, banks focused on short-term credit, and a scarcity of skilled management. Government policies provided a broadly favorable context for the growth of domestic business groups. State construction contracts were important for the initial growth of the Koç business, and Koç was one of the recipients of the import exemptions and other incentives designed to nurture indigenous business. The new Republic of Turkey's restrictions on non-Muslim communities also put Koç in a favorable position alongside other Muslim entrepreneurs. In addition, protectionism and bureaucratic obstacles on inward FDI meant that foreign multinationals wishing to sell in Turkey had to form licensing and other agreements with local companies. However, the case of the Koç does challenge assumptions that government policies were always supportive. Governments are not homogeneous, and in the case of Koç, there were periods when they were as much an obstacle as a benefit.

The story of the growth of the Koç Group can be told in conventional terms of building contact and organizational capabilities. Administrative mechanisms were developed over time. However such terms hardly capture the reality of developing a large business in a volatile environment. Indeed, this study builds on the insights of Kock and Guillen and Chung that entrepreneurship needs to be incorporated into the determinants of business group growth, especially to account for why particular entrepreneurs built such groups while others, faced with similar exogenous conditions, did not. Moving beyond the personal networks and contact capability functions in the entrepreneurial process, this chapter finds evidence both of Kirzner-style entrepreneurship of being alert to the new opportunities offered by the Republic, and Schumpeterian-style disruption and creation of new opportunities.

In the founding stages of the group, Vebhi Koç showed himself alert to the new opportunities created by government policies, and to his location in Ankara. He extensively reached out to ethnic minorities to build managerial expertise. His assembly and mobilization of financial resources was Schumpeterian. However, and departing from previous work that emphasized the role of the entrepreneurial process in the initial phases of group formation, the continued growth of the Koç Group demonstrated the continued importance of entrepreneurship during the postwar decades. Koç proactively sought to attract technological expertise from established businesses in the United States and Europe that had little motivation to invest in Turkey, and when he could not entice such firms, he sought other partners in Israel. It is superficial to label Koç's search for, and negotiation of, such diverse partnerships solely as "contact capabilities." As he sought to make desired organizational innovations, Koç lobbied to change the legal framework of Turkish business. Koç also took the lead in Turkey in disrupting and changing traditional organizational methods.

The period after Vehbi Koç saw the liberalization of the Turkish economy and an increasingly competitive market, accompanied by consecutive financial crises. While this resulted in moves to achieve greater focus of the product portfolio, the strategy of the Group remained expansive, thanks to new opportunities such as privatization. The Group continued to enter into new business fields when there were profit-making opportunities, while exiting some other less profitable activities. This period also saw a new energy behind internationalization, especially from the 1990s. More than half of Koç's sales eventually came from international markets, though the Group remained heavily dependent on geographically proximate markets in the Middle East and Europe. In terms of governance, professional managers increased their presence in top management positions, including the CEO position, although the extent of authority they gained is debatable, as Chapter 8 will show.

The example of Koç and Turkey was not different from other emerging economies in the twentieth century in many respects. As in Turkey, the largest business groups in East Asia and Latin America also stayed resilient, and even increased their standing, despite the liberalization and financial crises in those economies, even though individual groups might have suffered. However, in contrast to some of the Asian groups, especially those based in South Korea and India, the Turkish groups had limited global presence, and this even applied to the Koç Group, which was amongst the most internationalized business groups in the country. Possibly this was the result of the pervasive import substitution regime and the limited presence of foreign competitors in the domestic market. The low competitiveness of Turkish products and businesses in international markets was a factor, too, reflecting an excessive reliance on licensing foreign technology rather than building in-house innovation capabilities. Perhaps the cautious and subdued international strategies simply reflected the decades of domestic political and economic turbulence that Koç and other groups successfully navigated, but which left limited resources and bandwidth for the global world.

Notes

1. This chapter draws extensively on, and is a variant of, A.M. Colpan and G. Jones, "Entrepreneurship and Business Groups: An Evolutionary Perspective on the Growth of the Koç Group in Turkey," *Harvard Business School Working Paper*, n. 15–035, November 2014. A revised version of that working paper was published as A.M. Colpan and G. Jones, "Business Groups, Entrepreneurship and the Growth of the Koç Group in Turkey," *Business History*, v.58, n. 1, 2016, pp. 69–88. Section 4.4. also draws extensively on A.M. Colpan and G. Jones, "Vehbi Koç and the Making of Turkey's Largest Business Group (B)," *Harvard Business School Case*, No. 9–815–078 (revised January 13, 2015).
2. See also A.M. Colpan, T. Hikino, and J.R. Lincoln (eds.), *The Oxford Handbook of Business Groups*, Oxford: Oxford University Press, 2010.

3. T. Khanna and Y. Yafeh, "Business Groups in Emerging Markets: Paragons or Parasites?" *Journal of Economic Literature*, v.45, n. 2, 2007, pp. 331–372.
4. B.R. Schneider, "Business Groups and the State: The Politics of Expansion, Restructuring, and Collapse," in Colpan, Hikino, and Lincoln (eds.) *Oxford Handbook*.
5. M.F. Guillén, "Business Groups in Emerging Economies: A Resource-Based View," *Academy of Management Journal*, v.43, n. 3, 2000, pp. 362–380.
6. C. Kock and M.F. Guillén, "Strategy and Structure in Developing Countries: Business Groups as an Evolutionary Response to Opportunities for Unrelated Diversification," *Industrial & Corporate Change*, v.10, n. 1, 2001, pp. 1–37.
7. C-N. Chung, "'Beyond Guanxi': Network Contingencies in Taiwanese Business Groups," *Organization Studies*, v.27, n. 4, 2006, pp. 461–489.
8. A.M. Colpan and T. Hikino (eds.), *Business Groups in the West: The Evolutionary Dynamics of Big Business*, Oxford: Oxford University Press, 2018.
9. See also A. Buğra, *State and Business in Modern Turkey: A Comparative Study*, New York: State University of New York Press, 1994, p. 56.
10. Decades denote the period during which the business groups started their original businesses.
11. M. Casson, B. Yeung, A. Basu, and N. Wadeson (eds.), *The Oxford Handbook of Entrepreneurship*, Oxford: Oxford University Press, 2008.
12. V. Koç, *Hayat Hikayem*, Istanbul: Otokoç A.Ş., 1983, pp. 11–23.
13. Ibid., pp. 39–42.
14. Ibid.
15. L. Duruiz, "Ford in Turkey: From Imports to Partnership," in H. Bonin, Y. Lung, and S. Tolliday (eds.) *Ford: The European History 1903–2003*, vol. 2, Paris: Editions PIAGE, 2003, p. 486; Koç, *Hayat*, pp. 50–51.
16. Ibid., p. 487.
17. Koç, *Hayat*, pp. 38–39; Interview by A.M. Colpan with Hasan Bengü, March 19, 2010, Istanbul, Turkey.
18. Koç, *Hayat*, pp. 53, 62.
19. Buğra, *State*, pp. 77–79.
20. Email from Rahmi M. Koç to A.M. Colpan, June 13, 2013. *Hayat*, pp. 69–73.
21. S. Brynildssen, *International Directory of Company Histories*. "Koç Holding A.S.," 2003, pp. 195–198, www.biyografi.info/kisi/vehbi-koc
22. "Ford Otosan, 50: Yıl Projesi Kitap Metni," unpublished book draft, 28 January 2010 Version, 2010, p. 50. *Yıl Projesi*, pp. 9–12; Koç, *Hayat*, pp. 69–74, 81–84.
23. "Ford Otosan, 50: Yıl Projesi," pp. 8–12.
24. Koç, *Hayat*, pp. 136–137.
25. M.A Birand, *Vehbi Koç Belgeseli*, DVD, Koç Holding Archives, 1993; "Ford Otosan, 50: Yıl Projesi," p. 10.
26. Koç, *Hayat*, pp. 129, 132–134.
27. Ibid., p. 139.
28. Ibid., pp. 139–148.
29. C. Dündar, *Özel Arşivinden Belgeler ve Anılarıyla Vehbi Koç, 1961–1976*, Istanbul: Yapı Kredi Yayınları, 2008, pp. 166–167.
30. "Ford Otosan, 50: Yıl Projesi," pp. 11–12.
31. H. Shapiro, *Engines of Growth: The State and Transnational Auto Companies in Brazil*, Cambridge: Cambridge University Press, 1994.
32. Tofaş interactive history at http://english.tofas.com.tr/Tarihce.aspx; Koç, *Hayat*, p. 87.
33. A.Ş. Arçelik, *Mamulattan Markaya: Arçelik Kurum Tarihi 1955–2000*, Istanbul: Nurol Matbaacılık, 2001.p. 41; Koç, *Hayat*, p. 75.

34. Arçelik, *Mamulattan Markaya*, pp. 74, 108–109.
35. Interview by A.M. Colpan with Rahmi M. Koç, March 26, 2010, Istanbul, Turkey.
36. B. Nahum, *Koç'ta 44 yılım*, Istanbul: Milliyet Yayın A.S., 1992, p. 263; C. Kıraç, *Anılarımla Patronum Vehbi Koç*, Istanbul: Doğan Yayın Holding A. Ş., 1995, p. 146; Koç, *Hayat*, pp. 94–95.
37. *Nahum, Koç'ta* 44 yılım, p. 265.
38. Email from Rahmi M. Koç; *Hayat*, p. 96.
39. Email from Rahmi M. Koç; Interview with Rahmi M. Koç.
40. Koç, *Hayat*, pp. 95–96.
41. Kıraç, *Anılarımla*, p. 146; Koç, *Hayat*, p. 96; Email from Rahmi M. Koç; Interview with Rahmi M. Koç.
42. Email from Rahmi M. Koç.
43. Koç's establishment of a pension fund followed a conversation with the chief executive of Siemens in Germany, who had advised him that the step would make his employees more loyal to their employer. See İnfini İçerik İnternet İletisim Çözümleri, *Dünden Yarına Siemens Türkiye*, Istanbul: Omsan Ofset Matbaacılık San. Ve Tic. AŞ, 2007.
44. Shareholding structure of Koç Holding in 1963; Koç Holding Archives; Koç Holding Annual Report, 1970.
45. Koç Holding Annual Report, 1965.
46. Information received by A.M. Colpan from Koç Holding.
47. Ş. Karlıklı (ed.), "Migros Türk'te Koç İmzası," in *Migros: 45 Yılın Öyküsü*, Istanbul: CamEv Yayıncılık, 1999.
48. Ibid.
49. Koç, *Hayat*, pp. 93–94.
50. Koç Holding Annual Report, 1988.
51. Email from Rahmi M. Koç; Interview by A.M. Colpan with Temel Atay, March 16, 2010, Istanbul, Turkey.
52. Istanbul Stock Exchange Historical developments at www.imkb.gov.tr/25yil/index.html; Capital Markets Board of Turkey at www.spk.gov.tr; M. Celasun and D. Rodrik, "Turkish Experience with Debt: Macroeconomic Policy and Performance," in J.D. Sachs (ed.) *Developing Country Debt and the World Economy*, Chicago: University of Chicago Press, 1989.
53. K. Balkaş, "Kredi Kavramı ve Sektör Kredilerine Göre Türkiye'deki Belli Başlı Sektörlerin Analizi," Ankara Üniversitesi Sosyal Bilimler Enstitüsü İşletme Anabilim Dalı, unpublished Thesis, 2004.
54. The two managers were Bernar Nahum (responsible for the automotive businesses) and Isak de Eskinazis (responsible for finance). Can Kıraç website at www.cankirac.com/yazidetay.asp?id=177&kat=10; Koç Holding Annual Report, 1965, Koç Holding Archives.
55. This was Hulki Alisbah. He drafted the initial Koç Holding project and became especially influential in financial and legal matters during the initial establishment process.
56. Interview with Rahmi M. Koç; Koç Holding Annual Report, 1965, Koç Holding Archives.
57. Nahum, Koç'ta 44 *yılım*; Email from Rahmi M. Koç; Interview with Rahmi M. Koç.
58. Email from Rahmi M. Koç.
59. Interview with Temel Atay; Interview with Rahmi M. Koç.
60. Nahum, *Koç'ta 44 yılım*, Suna Kıraç, *Ömrümden Uzun İdeallerim*, Var. Istanbul: Suna ve İnan Kıraç Vakfı Yayını, 2006, p. 104; Koç Holding Annual Report, 1973, Koç Holding Archives.

61. Koç Holding Annual Report, 1973; Interview by A.M. Colpan with Samim Şeren, March 22, 2010, Istanbul, Turkey; Beko History at www.beko.com.tr/tarihce.html.
62. Email from Rahmi M. Koç; Interview with Rahmi M. Koç; Koç Holding R&D Center Report, Koç Holding Archives.
63. B. Üsdiken and D. Çetin, "From Betriebswirtschaftslehre to Human Relations: Turkish Management Literature before and After the Second World War," *Business History*, v.43, n. 2, 2001, pp. 99–124; M. Kipping, B. Üsdiken, and N. Puig, "Imitation, Tension, and Hybridization: Multiple 'Americanizations' of Management Education in Mediterranean Europe," *Journal of Management Inquiry*, v.13, n. 2, 2004, pp. 98–108. Email from Rahmi M. Koç.
64. Kıraç, *Ömrümden.*
65. Ibid., pp. 137–138.
66. Bain Report, Koç Holding Archives, December 22, 1988.
67. Kıraç, *Ömrümden*, pp. 144–147.
68. Ibid., p. 147.
69. Ibid., pp. 142–144.
70. Koç Holding Annual Report, 2005.
71. Interview by A.M. Colpan with Mustafa V. Koç, March 18, 2010, Istanbul, Turkey.
72. Interview with Rahmi M. Koç; "Migros Satisi En Buyuk Pismanligim" at http://ekonomi.haberturk.com/makro-ekonomi/haber/751366-migros-satisi-en-buyuk-pismanligim
73. Interview with Mustafa V. Koç.
74. Koç Holding Annual Report, 2011, pp. 40–42.
75. Koç Holding, Investor Presentation, 2012.
76. Koç Holding, Annual Report, 2003.
77. F. Bonaglia, A.M. Colpan, and A. Goldstein, "Innovation and Internationalization in the White Goods GVC: The Case of Arçelik," *International Journal of Technological Learning, Innovation and Development*, v.1, n. 4, 2008, pp. 520–535.
78. Ar-Ge Liginin Sampiyonlari at www.capital.com.tr/arge-liginin-sampiyonlari-haberler/16984.aspx
79. Koç Holding, Investor Presentation, 2012.
80. Ibid.
81. Koç Holding, Annual Report, 2011; Koç Holding, Investor Presentation, 2012.
82. Koç Holding, Investor Presentation, 2012.
83. Yapı Kredi, Our History at www.yapikredi.com.tr/en-US/investorRelations/corporate_information/our_history.aspx; Koç Holding, Investor Presentation, 2012.
84. Interview with Rahmi M. Koç.
85. Robin Root and John Quelch, "Koç Holding: Arçelik White Goods," *Harvard Business School Case*, No. 598–033, p. 8.
86. Interview with Rahmi M. Koç, interviewed by Felix Oberholzer-Gee, February 12, 2015, Creating Emerging Markets Project, Baker Library Historical Collections, *Harvard Business School*, www.hbs.edu/creating-emerging-markets.
87. Arçelik, *Mamulattan Markaya*, pp. 240–253.
88. Root and Quelch, "Koç," p. 8.
89. Bonoglia, Colpan, and Goldstein, "Innovation."
90. Ibid.
91. Root and Quelch, "Koç," p. 9.

92. Colpan and Jones, "Vehbi Koç."
93. "Turkey switches on to TV market," January 17, 2005, www.cnn.com/2005/BUSINESS/01/17/turkey.beko/index.html
94. A.M. Colpan, "Business Groups in Turkey," in A.M. Colpan, T. Hikino, and J.R. Lincoln (eds.), *The Oxford Handbook of Business Groups,* Oxford: Oxford University Press, 2010.
95. Colpan and Jones, "Vehbi Koç."
96. Calculated from data provided by Koç Holding.
97. Based on data provided by Koç Holding.
98. Interview with Rahmi M. Koç by Felix Oberholzer-Gee.
99. Portfolio structure at www.koc.com.tr/en-us/investor-relations/presentations-and-bulletins/Koc%20company%20bulten/KocHoldingIRpres%20Apr19.pdf

5 Islamic Capitalism and the Rise of Religious-Conservative Big Business

Kristin Fabbe, Ümit Özlale, and Efe Murat Balıkçıoğlu

Discussing the role of politics in the development of Turkish capitalism in Chapter 3, Buğra begins her analysis with Gerschenkron's argument, which postulated that capitalism should be viewed as a system that varies across societies and transforms itself in accordance with changing domestic and international factors.[1] Equally important, however, is the other side of the equation—that is, the ways in which capitalist systems transform economic and political elites. The success of economic and political elites may critically depend on their responsiveness to the different stages of capitalist development, rendering the study of their beliefs and actions critical to understanding any particular capitalist transformation. This chapter examines how conservative economic and political actors in Turkey have positioned themselves, from the late 1960s until the present, with respect to capitalist development while simultaneously accruing political, social, cultural and economic power.

This chapter argues that the rise of "Islamic capitalism" and the country's so-called "conservative bourgeoisie" owes much to the pragmatism and agility of Islamic actors who are quick to seize upon new economic and political opportunities by leveraging religious identity markers, religious discourse, and religious networks. By revealing their pragmatic approach to introducing the idea of Islamic capitalism in Turkey, and especially their efforts to distinguish it from capitalism more generally, the chapter sheds light on how religious and cultural values *both shape and are shaped by* the economic imperatives of participation in the global economic system. We find that Islamist political actors and pious business elites have molded business culture in ways that are mutually beneficial, selectively drawing upon ethical norms and religious networks in an adaptive fashion. We find that over the last fifty years, as they constantly shift and adapt Islamic values to justify economic positions and policymaking, the country's political Islamists and the emergent pious bourgeoisie alike have consistently sought to increase their power and influence vis-à-vis the coastal big-business elite and their traditional political allies.

Section 5.1 starts with an analysis of Turkey's business history before 1980 that focuses on two interrelated themes in the Islamist movement: first, its ideological responsiveness and practical flexibility and, secondly, its insistence on erecting boundaries around concepts such as "Islamic capitalism" and the "pious bourgeoisie," so as to distinguish conservative businessmen from the traditionally dominant players in Turkey's economy, despite the fact that they too were predominantly Muslim (although many held secular worldviews).[2] Curiously then, common tropes that depict tensions between "secular business" and "Muslim business" obfuscate the fact that the salient cleavages in Turkey's business community probably have less to do with nominal religious identity and more to do with class and region—what Buğra calls the first generation of "state-created bourgeoisie," located primarily in Western coastal regions, vs. the second generation of "state-created bourgeoisie," located in Anatolia and the periphery.[3]

Next, we analyze the emergence of a distinctly pious business community in Turkey during the formative period between 1980 to 2002, when Turkey began liberalizing its economy, embracing globalization and ceding ground to Islamist politics. A grievance-based discourse, around which this business community formed itself, decried the exclusion of conservative entrepreneurs in the provincial towns of Anatolia from the economic benefits doled out to large holding firms during the etatist and import substitution periods.[4] Whether such exclusion was real or imagined, intentional or unintentional, Islamist politicians seized upon the narrative with vigor and used it as a justification for founding voluntary organizations, banking systems and business associations of their own, including MÜSİAD (Independent Industrialists' and Businessmen's Association), the leading business association representing the pious business community.[5]

The final section of the chapter focuses on the AKP era and the increasing dominance of the conservative bourgeoisie. We argue that as the boundaries between business and politics became further blurred, Islam was leveraged as a network and ideational resource with increasing effectiveness. Initially, the AKP used the prospect of EU accession and neoliberal policies to secure its place on the political scene and to facilitate capital accumulation within the pious business community. As the first decade of the twenty-first century progressed, AKP-friendly holding companies and conglomerates gained power as the state granted resources to these large enterprises through patronage strategies rooted in privatization schemes and changes to public procurement laws.[6]

5.1 Capitalism from an Islamist Perspective: Erbakan's "Millî Görüş," 1969–1980

From the end of one-party rule in 1945 to the 1960 military intervention, the balance of political and economic power in Turkey skewed heavily in favor of state elites. Although the DP, which ruled between 1950 and 1961, demonstrated a commitment to private sector expansion, it proved unwilling to relinquish the advantages that could be reaped through direct, ad hoc government intervention into the economy. It was therefore only after 1960, when the DP's poor economic performance and authoritarian tendencies led to the party's ouster in a coup, that the Turkish business community was able to begin asserting influence over economic policies as well as garner political power of its own. As Buğra and Savaşkan have outlined in their authoritative work on Turkish capitalism, chambers of industry and commerce had become fora for political debate in the multi-party era, yet they also hindered private-sector interests from collectively organizing around particular issues.[7] The chambers were (and still are) organized by region, as opposed to sector, and had compulsory membership, which meant that under the umbrella of each regional chamber sat a wide variety of enterprises. Big business in particular became increasingly disenchanted with this organizational structure, as it struggled to exert its prerogatives in the face of resistance from each chamber's multitude of smaller firms.

In this environment, the first voluntary big-business association, TÜSİAD (Turkish Industry and Business Association), was established in 1971, with the objective of strengthening the political clout of its members. TÜSİAD developed into a significant actor in Turkish politics, and it was not until nearly two decades later that other associations with overtly religious prerogatives and discourse—namely MÜSİAD, AKSON, and TUSKON, described later in this chapter—emerged as counterweights to TÜSİAD. Still, Islamists began cultivating influence in Turkey's political-economy long before the formation of business associations with pious leanings. A case in point is Necmettin Erbakan's Islamist National Outlook (*Millî Görüş*) movement, an influential political faction that evolved in tandem with Erbakan's own involvement in Turkey's business community. Erbakan's contested role in Turkey's business associations, as well as his political pronouncements and maneuvering, provide a window into the early discursive and political strategies used to mobilize Turkey's Islamic capitalists.

Erbakan's involvement in the Turkish business community began in 1956, when he founded a motor factory in Turkey, *Gümüş Motor*, which he launched together with twenty other partners and the support of the influential Naqshbandī shaykh Mehmed Zahit Kotku.[8] Erbakan, who had received his doctorate prior to the founding of *Gümüş Motor*, later became a professor at Istanbul Technical University in 1965. Drawing on his business experience, Erbakan believed that the country urgently required more heavy industry and manufacturing initiatives so that the economy could shed its dependence on Western technology and know-how.[9] Eventually, Erbakan's efforts to establish motor factories in under-developed regions of Anatolia led him to become the General Secretary of the Union of Chambers and Commodity Exchanges of Turkey (*Türkiye Odalar ve Borsalar Birliği*, TOBB) in 1967.[10] In 1968, Erbakan set his sights on politics, resigning from his position as General Secretary of TOBB and declaring his intention to run for parliament on the ticket of Süleyman Demirel's center-right AP party in the conservative district of Konya. His application to the party was denied, leading him to return to TOBB as part of the Executive Committee, a position that eventually allowed him to win election to TOBB Chairman in May 1969.[11]

Erbakan's second stint at TOBB also did not last long. The İzmir branch of TOBB soon claimed that Erbakan's election to the chairmanship of the association was dubious and the branch refused to cooperate with his office.[12] Then, some three months after his tenure began, the government and police intervened to force him out of the position. During this period, secular-minded industrialists often referred to Erbakan as a *takunyalı* ("a clog-wearer"), a slur that emphasized his religiosity and "backwardness."[13] Nonetheless, over the course of his tenure at TOBB Erbakan gained a reputation for opposing the hegemony of Turkey's urban, cosmopolitan, large-scale businessmen, many of whom had close ties with the Western world. In contrast, he supported policies in favor of provincial small businesses that traditionally lacked a direct say in TOBB decision-making and policy. According to Ruşen Çakır, Erbakan also increasingly worked to broaden his political appeal among middle-class Anatolian businessmen, lower-class provincial Sunnis and affluent conservative families with a secular upbringing, shaping a core support base for his future political parties. Erbakan's Islamist discourse appealed to these groups as it emphasized business ethics, social values and a conservative worldview.[14]

Erbakan's ouster from TOBB became part of an emerging narrative about how Turkey's first-generation capitalists were working with the state to repress the pious Muslim majority and their enterprises. And with this narrative now at hand, Erbakan shifted his attention back to politics. He again applied to Demirel's AP to become a candidate in the conservative Konya district. Demirel, however, had already been criticized for allowing other pro-Islamist cadres into the party, and had no intention of admitting Erbakan, vetoing his candidacy. In part, this decision stemmed from a fear that Erbakan's Islamist cadres would throw their support behind Demirel's political rival within the party, Sadettin Bilgiç, in an effort to remove Demirel from the party leadership.[15] Shunned from the AP, Erbakan entered into the general election as an independent. After winning a seat in Turkish Parliament, he next set about forming what was to become one of the most influential conservative Islamist parties in Turkey, the National Order Party (*Millî Nizam Partisi*, MNP), along with eighteen like-minded right-wing politicians in January 1970.

The booklet published by the MNP's first party congress in 1971 outlined its political vision in great detail. The document is laced with sweeping generalizations about the world as well as numerous *ad hominem* attacks against rival political leaders and parties. Ideologically, Erbakan followed the prevailing Cold War sentiments of the era and divided the developed world into two blocs, the capitalist and the Soviet. He accused Turkey's then-dominant parties—Demirel's AP and Bülent Ecevit's CHP (Republican People's Party)—of conforming to this divide, with the AP serving capitalist interests and the CHP favoring the Soviet camp.[16] According to Erbakan, the Communist system infringed upon basic human rights and the capitalist system caused moral and social degeneration. As an alternative, his proposed system, the so-called National Order (*Millî Nizâm*), was based on "national" values and placed the imperatives of religious moral development above financial growth.[17] The National Order Party's founding charter promised to respect the "democratic legal rights" of its citizens, yet the discourse the party embraced as "national" had a pronounced Islamic bent.[18] Erbakan envisioned a political ideology in accordance with God, who was referred to in the party's texts as *Hakk* (the Truth), and he allowed little room for heterodox religious (i.e., non-Sunni Muslim) and political orientations. The National Order concept came under criticism almost immediately. For example, a Kemalist Professor of Law, Hıfzı Veldet Velidedeoğlu, argued that Erbakan's ideas would give rise to a grey zone for illegal practices and that the declaration of National Order was tantamount to a declaration of "*millî menfaat*" (vested interest in a national disguise).[19] Several years later Erbakan would rethink his strategy and summarize his views under the banner of National Outlook (*Millî Görüş*), a more politically neutral term.[20]

5.2 Erbakan, European Economic Integration and the Turkish Political Establishment

Turkey applied to join the European Economic Community (EEC), then consisting of six western and southern European nations, on July 31, 1959, soon after it had been formed. Turkey's application was welcomed but presented problems, as it was abundantly clear that the Turkish economy could not yet handle the market competition with European countries that accession would bring. Negotiators on both sides thus settled for a compromise: Turkey would begin a gradual process of integration into a customs union, with the idea of full Turkish membership to be revisited at a later date. The 1963 Ankara Agreement laid out the basic framework for eventual Turkish integration into the EEC.[21] Accession to the EEC was a hot topic in Turkey in the late 1960s, especially after 1967 when Demirel announced that there would be additional protocols required for full accession. A wide spectrum of political parties, including Alparslan Türkeş' Nationalist Movement Party (*Milliyetçi Hareket Partisi*, MHP), the socialist Workers' Party of

Turkey (*Türkiye İşçi Partisi*, TİP) and Erbakan's Islamist MNP, came out in opposition to the accession process.[22]

Interestingly, the booklet produced at the MNP's first party congress did not provide any alternative to accession or even substantial economic analysis. Instead, it cast blame on Turkey's incumbent politicians and made sweeping anti-Western generalizations about the nature of European institutions. For example, Erbakan quipped that, despite Turkey's abundance of resources, incapable AP politicians and the country's resultant lag in heavy industry had led to poor economic performance.[23] Similarly, he condemned future economic collaboration with Europe as a flimsy cover-up for a secret agenda intended to preserve a Zionist Israel, maintain European economic hegemony, and make way for the future colonization of Muslim countries by Western powers.[24] In another booklet published during the first MNP congress in January 1971, however, Erbakan did offer an alternative, proposing a common market between Turkey and Muslim states with which it shared common cultural and religious values, such as Pakistan and the Arab world. He also claimed that an international cabal of freemasons had impeded any such process.[25]

Erbakan's most controversial move regarding the EEC came in the form of a provocative resolution presented to parliament after the formation of the MNP. The resolution alleged that the accession process was anti-constitutional and Demirel's politics were a crime against the national interest.[26] Like this resolution and the MNP party booklets, Erbakan's later speeches about the EEC followed a similar pattern, brimming with anti-Western invective and accusations that Demirel had sold out to Western interests.[27] He argued that Turkey's economy would be reduced to the production of agricultural commodities, such as cotton and tobacco, and would never develop a strong national military or industrial complex.[28] He also railed against Turkey's urban elite, accusing them of being cosmopolitan Zionist masons and Rotary members who worked in the service of Western powers.[29] In short, the "ethics" and "values" espoused by Erbakan and the MNP in this period were relatively vague, defined primarily in opposition to the interests of perceived domestic and international rivals. Still, when combined with Erbakan's ouster from TOBB and the alleged economic injustices perpetrated by the state in favor of first-generation capitalists, these ideas laid the foundation for a powerful narrative of economic (not to mention political) victimhood and repression—a narrative that would come to unite many conservatives under the banner of Islam.

5.3 From National Order to National Outlook: Islamists Adapt

In March 1971 the Turkish military delivered a memorandum and removed Demirel from power. As part of this "coup by memorandum" (often referred to as the *12 Mart Muhtırası* or March 12th Memorandum), the military took control of the political domain and began to curb parties it considered radical, including Erbakan's MNP.[30] Within less than a year, the party was officially closed by the Republic's Office of the Chief Public Prosecutor (*Cumhuriyet Başsavcılığı*) on the basis of statements made in various MNP speeches. Most of the speeches had been secretly recorded and transcribed by state prosecutors between 1970 and 1971, and there were twenty-four statements held against Erbakan and other MNP delegates.[31] Illuminating just how deeply intertwined economic, political and religious issues had become, one of the key statements used in the case against the MNP came from Erbakan's parliamentary speech about the EEC: the prosecution referenced a section of the speech in which Erbakan promised that the MNP would establish God's "just way" and eradicate the colonial (*müstemleke*) mentality of the Republic.[32]

By the time of the next general election, in 1973, Erbakan had already started a new party with Islamist leanings: the National Salvation Party (*Millî Selâmet Partisi*, MSP). The concept of National Outlook now took center stage, and the MSP received 11 percent of the vote, becoming the third biggest party in parliament and eventually forming a brief coalition government with Bülent Ecevit's leftist CHP. For our purposes here, it is noteworthy that the years between the coup-by-memorandum and the 1973 elections had produced a marked turn in Erbakan's political discourse, which now included an even heavier emphasis on Turkish nationalism. Indeed, when the MSP-CHP coalition government collapsed after just 10 months, the MSP joined with nationalist parties, including the MHP, to form right-wing coalitionist governments in both 1975 and 1977.

The MSP election booklets from 1973, 1975 and 1977 were notably different from the MNP's first party congress charter issued in 1971. Erbakan's previous references to certain Islamic theologians (e.g., al-Ghazālī) and past Naqshbandī Sufi masters (e.g., Imām Rabbānī), which had been used as evidence in the MSP closure case, were conspicuously absent.[33] The MSP's 1973 General Election Manifesto used *Allah* only once in the preface.[34] Likewise, the 1977 General Election Manifesto mentioned God only once[35] and certain key Arabic words that connote Islamic piety, such as *mü'minler* (believers),[36] were replaced with more "neutral" Turkish translations (e.g., *inananlar*).[37] Furthermore, by 1977 Islamic references had largely been replaced with mentions of early Seljuq and Ottoman rulers and educators such as Alparslan, Nizamülmülk, Orhan Gazi, Mehmed II the Conqueror and Akşemseddin.[38] This later party literature also deployed historical narratives that did not start with the early days of the Prophet Muhammad's life but rather with the battle of Manzikert in 1071.[39]

In terms of economic policies, the MSP's 1973 Election Manifesto had little in common with the parochial economic vision presented by MNP in 1971. The 1973 manifesto included detailed sections on Erbakan's proposed policies regarding foreign trade, heavy industry, the working class and the agriculture and fishing industries.[40] It also promised to lower taxes—and even waive them for the poor—and to fight against unreasonable interest rates (*fahiş faiz*) and wasteful government spending (*israf*).[41] The 1973 manifesto did criticize the EEC accession process; however, this time the discourse was not dominated entirely by anti-Western rallying calls or *ad hominem* accusations against Erbakan's political opponents.[42] The MSP's strategy for the 1973 general elections was to position itself as party that was going to strike a balance between social conservatism promoted via religious education and technologically minded innovation promoted via state planning and heavy industrialization.[43]

The most detailed account of the MSP's economic policies, replete with data and figures, can be found in the party's 1977 General Election Manifesto. Again, the MSP had shifted, this time embracing a new vision of economic development (*kalkınma*)[44] based on the mobilization of energy resources and heavy industry. The 1977 Manifesto also led with a distinctly nationalist and populist slogan: "Make Turkey Great Again" (*Yeniden Büyük Türkiye*). This iteration of Erbakan's economic thinking did exhibit some continuity with past ideas—for example, he retained his moral stance against usury through interest rates, leaned into nationalist tropes and criticized cosmopolitan values—but there were also notable departures.

First, he emphasized a need for absolute transparency in government spending and proposed a special loan (*tam teşvik*) system to benefit the entrepreneurial working class,[45] especially for cooperative associations and local initiatives.[46] Touting its concrete results, the MSP claimed that in 1976, it helped open more than one hundred heavy industry factories from Edirne to Kars, with another hundred such initiatives in the works.[47] Instead of focusing purely on business interests from the provinces, the 1977 Manifesto underscored that the party was seeking a nationwide revitalization of the private sector, which it would begin facilitating by introducing incentive funds (*teşvik fonları*) via the Ministry of Industry and Trade.[48] Perhaps the most significant aspect of the 1977 Manifesto, however, was what it did not include—the MSP's previous antipathy towards the EEC was not mentioned even once. It is unlikely that this omission was coincidental, for opening to global markets was one of the central promises of the Party's new economic vision,[49] a policy the MSP continued to implement during the Nationalistic Front governments of the late 1970s.[50]

In sum, we see gradual but notable changes in Islamists' economic views in the short period between the late 1960s and the end of the 1970s. First, their discourse softened, especially when it came to economics and business, and they appeared to imitate a more centrist right-wing model, with a particular emphasis on policies of "nationalization" (*millîleşme*). Indeed, the movement's religious discourse was largely restricted to discussions regarding educational and social reform.[51] By 1977, Erbakan and his Islamist cadres had also toned down their anti-European rhetoric and come to tacitly support more open markets, export-driven development and direct assistance to Turkey's private sector via government grants and loans. Above all, however, the chaotic international and domestic politics of the 1970s had created new opportunity structures that served to benefit both political Islamists like Erbakan and eventually Turkey's pious business community, regardless of the appeal of religious morals, values or ethics. Internationally, Turkey was the heart of the so-called Islamic "green-belt"—a geographic zone that the United States and the Gulf monarchies hoped would act as bulwark against communism—and thus Turkish Islamist organizations became the beneficiaries of external funding.[52] Domestically, it was hoped that the political cooperation between conservative Islamist and right-wing nationalists that had occurred between 1975 and 1980 could be spun into a more general model for enhancing social cohesion at a time when left-right violence seriously threatened Turkey's stability.

5.4 Globalization, the Emergence of a Conservative Bourgeoisie and the Role of MÜSİAD, 1980–2002

The industrialization wave that ushered in a structural transformation of the Turkish economy in the beginning of the 1980s has accurately been described as the emergence of industrial capitalism in a predominantly rural and mercantile society.[53] Generous structural adjustment loans from the World Bank helped the Turkish economy capitalize on trends towards globalization and financial liberalization. International organizations soon began touting Turkey as a model for the rest of the developing world.[54] At the same time, global post-Fordist production systems in labor-intensive sectors helped small and medium-sized enterprises in Turkey to become globally competitive in low-cost, low-tech sectors such as textiles, garments and furniture. However, it would be naïve to claim that these structural reforms would have gone as smoothly had it not been for the 1980 coup that installed a military government that quelled almost all potential domestic threats to globalization and financial liberalization. Between 1980 and 1983 the military regime banned labor unions and also largely turned a blind eye to social security violations.[55]

The military government did not, however, seek to expunge religious ideas, institutions or actors from the political or economic realm. Rather, it made instrumental use of religious networks and values through the promulgation of the "Turkish-Islamic Synthesis" as national policy and the expansion of the role of the Presidency of Religious Affairs (*Diyanet İşleri Başkanlığı*, the Diyanet), an arm of the state bureaucracy charged with supervising the appointment and payment of religious functionaries to all mosques, and monitoring the production of religious knowledge through state-sanctioned channels.[56] Developed by a small anti-communist,

Islamist-conservative-nationalist organization called the Hearth of the Enlightened (*Aydınlar Ocağı*, AO), the Turkish-Islamic Synthesis was an Islamisation program designed to placate the social and political upheaval of the 1970s.[57] In 1983, Turkey's State Planning Organization (*Devlet Planlama Teşkilatı*)—which included members from the AO—prepared a National Culture Report on the basis of the Turkish-Islamic Synthesis in an effort to unify society around "the mosque, barracks and the family." The report contained

> a comprehensive strategy of cultural engineering . . . including the creation of a 'model human' and a pious (*dindâr*) Turkish nation through the expansion of religious education (including compulsory lessons) in schools, hospitals, prisons and worker's associations, and the promotion of Islam by the Diyanet . . . and the state public broadcasting agency.[58]

The program both tapped into and reinforced what White has described as Turkish society's tendency to pursue its aspirations within powerful collective frameworks that glorify family and nation.[59]

Taken together, these factors combined with the previous political maneuverings of Erbakan to help propel the emergence of a new industrial class—the devout bourgeoisie (or so-called Anatolian Tigers)—especially in the provincial towns of Anatolia. As Lord has shown in her definitive work on religion in modern Turkey, the number of Istanbul Chamber of Industry top 500 companies located in Anatolian Tiger regions grew in tandem with the vote-share of Islamist parties throughout the 1980s.[60] These Anatolian-based firms—many, but certainly not all, of which began as or remained SMEs[61]—gradually became integrated into the world economy, first by operating as sub-contractors for major Turkish firms and later by exporting directly, especially to the Middle East and North Africa (MENA) and former Soviet countries (see later in this chapter).

Although these firms realized that they had a vested interest in economic liberalization and globalization, they faced numerous obstacles to competing in world markets and raising capital for investment. Thus, they relied on a variety of faith-based resources: voluntary organizations, private institutions, business associations, religious networks and concepts of "religious proximity" and religious values. First, because a large number of these firms had limited funds for investing and access to capital, the pious business community sought to leverage faith-based voluntary organizations for capital-raising purposes as well as introduce new forms of banking. Second, Turkish SMEs had to develop and position new "pious" business associations to effectively lobby for state resources. Third, Turkish SMEs had to secure their export markets for low-tech goods, which was a challenge given that their Asian counterparts enjoyed comparatively low production costs while their European counterparts produced higher quality goods, and thus they homed in on export destinations that were religiously proximate (i.e., Muslim-majority countries).

5.5 Leveraging Faith-Based Institutions to Access Finance

As military rule came to an end in 1983, the Motherland Party (*Anavatan Partisi*, ANAP), a coalition of conservative and Islamist politicians, won the first post-coup elections. Its leader, Turgut Özal, had already played a critical role in the first round of liberalization attempts made in 1980, and he planned to continue economic and financial reforms backed by international organizations including the World Bank and the IMF. Within this context, both the Turkish government and Anatolian companies deemed it important to attract the remittances of Turkish workers in Europe to help solve the balance of payment problems that characterized the first stages of structural reform. Generally speaking, these workers had migrated to Europe from conservative regions in Turkey and they tended to be pious Muslims.

According to Özcan and Çokgezen, a certain "euphoria around Islamic economics" developed around Erbakan's new Islamist Welfare Party (*Refah Partisi*, RP) and its affiliated organizations as they started Anatolian holding companies, in part with funds repatriated from Turkish workers in Germany. Capitalizing successfully on Islamic prohibitions against collecting interest, many of the pious businessmen who established these Anatolian holding companies followed Islamic finance principles "of profit and loss sharing or partnership finance through selling issued bonds of companies and investors to individuals, families and businesses."[62] In a short period of time these big Anatolian holding companies began actively supporting a wave of Islamic industrialization with what they called "Just Order" (*Adil Düzen*). The concept was central to the Welfare Party's political platform, which called for social and economic security, the protection of state property, an end to corruption, a fight against poverty and an end to excessive Western influence in Turkey.[63] Eventually, eleven of the large Anatolian holding companies attracted over 80,000 shareholders, most of whom were Turkish workers in Germany, "through the use of a wide range of Islamic associations, mosques and coffee houses, family and kinship networks" and without the use of intermediary financial institutions.[64]

The conservative bourgeoisie also enacted other policies that sought to leverage Islam as a network resource. For example, Hoşgör finds that religious networks based on Islamic values and trust served many functions: sect members made joint investments, obtained loans from one another, established mutual assistance networks to purchase inputs, and distributed their products more widely by creating a religiously-attuned consumer base.[65] These practices helped to solve SMEs' scaling problems and reduced transaction costs within an increasingly broad network. Meanwhile, the private schools, universities and dormitories founded by religious networks provided a ready source of labor. Silverman similarly provides numerous examples that illustrate the importance of personal relationships to devout capitalists, whether it be friendships dating back to student days or strategic marriage choices in establishing Turkey's Islamic business networks.[66]

Additionally, two types of faith-based organizations became increasingly important venues for aggregating interests, raising capital and providing alternative sources of welfare. The first was the foundation (*vakıf*), a type of charitable endowment with roots in Islamic and Ottoman history. The second was the association (*dernek*), a type of voluntary organization, some of which receive state funding and privileges. During the period in question, the number of these organizations with religious leanings proliferated. For example, the number of *vakıf*s doubled from less than 1,000 in the early 1980s to just under 2,000 by the early 1990s, and the number of religious associations granted state privileges (e.g., public benefits status and tax exemption) grew markedly during the 1980s and 1990s (and especially after 2001, see section 5.7).[67]

Furthermore, in a matter of days after assuming power in 1983, the ANAP (Motherland Party) government opened Turkey to Islamic banking under the banner of Special Finance Organizations through a prime ministerial decree. Turkey's two first Islamic banks were established with the assistance of Gulf capital in 1985. Islamic banks were exempted from the national banking regulatory framework, including reserve requirements. Anatolian SMEs that had struggled to secure financing from conventional banks could now leverage this new banking system. Islamic banks also eventually built vertical and horizontal alliance networks as well as established their own Islamic associations and foundations. The spread of Islamic banking in Turkey, however, remained relatively limited when compared to other Muslim-majority countries. Nonetheless, for our purposes here it is notable that the system emerged and grew as a result of direct state support, again revealing the web of linkages between state, society and business that propelled Turkey's pious business community into prominence.[68]

5.6 Creating New Business Associations to Lobby the State: The Advent of MÜSİAD

Given the obvious benefits that could be derived from state support in the Turkish business environment, it was only a matter of time before the country's pious business community sought to create its own business associations to rival the dominance of TÜSİAD. The most important in this respect was the aforementioned MÜSİAD, which was established in

1990. Interestingly, in its early years, MÜSİAD successfully positioned itself as independent from the state. The association heavily criticized the large holding companies that had emerged in the etatist and import substitution period (and were primarily represented by TÜSİAD) for growing with government support.[69] Several studies, including MÜSİAD's reports, support this argument. In 1993, the year that the association's online archives start, MÜSİAD published two important reports. The first criticized the government bureaucracy and explicitly stated the need to protect SMEs and to prevent large holding companies from monopolizing the economy. The second report, which summarized a panel on privatization, argued that state-driven economic enterprises are burdensome.[70] Similarly, in its 1994 annual report on the Turkish economy, MÜSİAD focused on the need to strengthen industry outside the Marmara region. Finally, in its annual report in 2000, MÜSİAD advocated privatization as a means for reducing public debt.

The 2000 report also emphasized the importance of empowering local governments to design policies that would benefit their respective local business communities.[71] It should also be noted, however, that MÜSİAD favored a decentralized approach to economic—not political—decision-making. Indeed, nationalistic views have permeated MÜSİAD (as well as other Islamic business associations, especially TUSKON—the Turkish Confederation of Businessmen and Industrialists). Any policy that could be construed as "separationist," including certain solutions to the "Kurdish problem," it vociferously opposed. In addition, MÜSİAD expressed reservations towards granting more rights to minorities in Turkey, a critical issue in the European Union (EU) negotiation process. (With the formation of the EU in 1993, EEC was renamed the European Community and eventually fully absorbed into the wider EU framework in 2009.) Put simply, a pronounced emphasis on Turkishness became a salient feature of MÜSİAD's collective politics and preferences.[72]

As MÜSİAD's nationalist proclivities suggest, the question of just *how* independent the Anatolian Tigers and MÜSİAD were from the state is debatable. Silverman has argued that the Anatolian Tigers did not depend on state assistance and achieved success by utilizing social and financial networks that were largely separate from the state and oriented around a shared sense of Islamic piety.[73] Similarly, research by Uygur provides evidence that pious businessmen have regarded the state and its bureaucracy as a barrier to entrepreneurship and thus favor a minimal role for the state.[74] Still, at the very least, it is improbable that the official state policies rooted in the Turkish-Islamic synthesis that sought to instrumentally leverage religion to enhance social cohesion throughout the 1980s hampered groups like MÜSİAD. Rather, such policies, when combined with structural factors and the willingness of the pious business community to adapt to neo-liberal principles, were likely advantageous to them. Therefore, MÜSİAD's early insistence that pious businesses succeeded despite the state, not because of it, is perhaps better understood in the context of long-standing political grievances against Turkey's first-generation capitalists. For example, according to Adaş, MÜSİAD was the collective voice of Islamic-oriented SMEs and their political, economic and cultural grievances against established secular big business groups.[75] Similarly, Özcan and Turunç have drawn attention to the Muslim business community's pronounced antipathy towards the family cartels (or so-called disingenuous cosmopolitan Istanbul capitalists) that controlled the Turkish economy.[76] In addition, as the following section reveals, MÜSİAD notably stopped advocating for a minimal role for the state once the AKP came to power and the association's access to state resources grew undeniably stronger.

Regardless of the question of state support, MÜSİAD's role became pivotal in the 1990s, and the association grew to include over 3,000 firms by 1997.[77] MÜSİAD not only helped to organize pious business networks but also attempted to safeguard the role of its member firms and of Islamic values in the economic system through acts of self-regulation, which included penalizing firms for corrupt practices. For example, citing several severe cases of corruption and the rampant abuse of Islamic values, MÜSİAD invited eighteen multi-ownership companies to come together to address these problems in March 2000. The upshot of this meeting was that several holding companies, including Jet-Pa and GAP, were expelled from the association entirely and Endüstri Holding was forced to resign after it failed to comply with the association's guidelines.[78]

As will be shown in the next section, MÜSİAD ultimately failed to stamp out corruption, but the pious business community did largely succeed in improving access to finance and investment funding as well as in building a religiously sensitive consumer base and a competent labor force, all by leveraging trust-based networks built upon shared religious and culture values and institutions.

5.7 Capturing Export Markets Through Religious Proximity

The conservative bourgeoisie did achieve low-cost production and eventually became competitive in export markets. The Turkish government's reluctance to crack down on informal practices—such as employing unregistered workers, violating safety regulations and avoiding tax payments—definitely helped conservative enterprises. At the same time, these firms appealed to the common values of Islam to penetrate further into markets in Muslim countries, and they benefited disproportionately from trade to non-OECD and MENA countries. For example, Turco and Maggioni have found that firms from religiously conservative regions are more likely to enter export destinations with a higher share of Muslims and argue that religious proximity eases export entry for producers of "trust intensive" (i.e. differentiated and advertising-intensive) goods.[79]

MÜSİAD's preferences and initiatives weighed heavily on Turkey's foreign trade relations. For example, during the 1990s MÜSİAD opposed a customs union between Turkey and the EU and instead promoted the establishment of closer relations with MENA and/or CIS countries, where it was believed that Turkey had a competitive edge.[80] As evidenced by MÜSİAD's 1997 annual report, the association criticized and lobbied intensively against the embargos imposed on Iraq in an effort to stop the severe trade losses that its members faced as a result, especially MÜSİAD representatives from southeastern Turkey.[81] Exports from the Central Anatolian region, where a sizable portion of the Anatolian Tigers operated, grew 13.5 percent between 2002 and 2015, while exports from Turkey's traditional industrial heartland—sometimes referred to as the "developed west"—grew only 10.5 percent over the same period. Furthermore, by 2015, 53 percent of exports from Central Anatolia went to MENA countries, as opposed to 24 percent of the exports from the Western region. If we include Gaziantep, another Anatolian Tiger hub located in Turkey's southeast, the share of exports going to the MENA increases even further.[82]

The Anatolian Tigers largely produced low- or mid-tech products, whereas Turkey's traditional industrial heartland exported products of a significantly higher technological grade. In 2003 more than 60 percent of exports from Central Anatolia were low tech, adding merit to the argument that the region gained its competitive edge in low-wage, low-productivity segments. In addition, despite these firms' growing clout and access to state resources, the technological sophistication of their exports improved only slightly: the share of Central Anatolian exports in the high-tech category increased from 12.5 to 17.8 percent between 2002 and 2015, whereas the share of high-tech exports from the traditional industrial region grew from 32 to 38.8 percent over the same period.[83]

Taking a "courageous step," a number of MÜSİAD members eventually criticized the economic outlook and export strategy of past Islamist parties.[84] Several MÜSİAD members openly expressed their concerns about adherence to a "false" Islam. For example, the founding president, Erol Yarar, blamed the mystical frugality inherent in Sufi Islam as the main factor contributing to the backwardness of the Muslim world. Thus, while criticizing and thereby putting distance between itself and the Welfare Party's concept of a "Just Order," MÜSİAD also came to realize it had a vested interest in partnering with a party that was pro-liberalization and friendly to the secular and Western world. Tuğal describes this ideational shift as the marriage of formal democracy, free market capitalism and conservative Islam.[85] Consequently, as Gümüşçü and Sert have argued, support for a pact between MÜSİAD and a nascent reformist wing of the Welfare Party began gaining ground prior to 1997.[86]

After the 1997 Turkish Military Memorandum (also referred to as *28 Şubat* or the *Postmodern Darbe*), during which Erbakan was forced out of power and banned from politics, his Welfare Party shut down, and many other conservative or Islamist-leaning scholars and bureaucrats were purged from government offices and universities. A substantial faction of reform-minded political Islamists, however, regrouped under the Virtue Party in 1998, and this short-lived successor to the Welfare Party offered a softer version of Islam and full integration with the West.[87] The Virtue Party became staunch supporters of the European Union accession process due to the EU's emphasis on freedom of speech and human rights. In little over twenty years, a reversal of the Islamists' stance on Europe, first encapsulated in the virulent anti-EU rhetoric of Erbakan's National Outlook Movement, had occurred.[88]

As their views towards Europe softened and European export markets and integration looked increasingly attractive, the conservative bourgeoisie felt obliged to justify their reluctance to pay taxes and their criticisms of the distributive role of the state and of labor unions.[89] Here, and for their own purposes, they again relied on religious legitimization, and were quick to seize upon the romanticized concept of "Medina Society" or "Medina Market," which endowed capitalist activities "with a sort of sacredness that an ideal Islamic society and economy should be based on. . . [with the main characteristics] of this historical marketplace . . . defined as non-interventionist, non-monopolistic and tax-free to attract merchants and stimulate higher profits."[90] Since *zakat*, the main form of Islamic philanthropy, was an obligatory charitable contribution or tax used to help the poor, the "Medina Society" archetype could conveniently dismiss the moral duty of paying an extra tax to the state, and arguments about rights-based social policy were also successfully muted. The conservative bourgeoisie's approach to the labor movement should also be assessed in this context. Trade organizations and unions are depicted "as disturbing harmony and order in the workplace by inculcating conflict and animosity between employers and employees," which ran counter to the harmony proffered by the ideal "Medina Market."[91]

5.8 The Era of the AKP: Using Neoliberal Tools for Political Empowerment

Since MÜSİAD already hoped by the end of 1990s to ally with a conservative party that would be open to the forces of globalization, it was no surprise that the association put its support behind the AKP in the 2002 elections. The Turkish economy faced a deep economic crisis at the beginning of 2001. Problems brought on by fiscal irresponsibility, an underregulated banking system and political uncertainty could not be overcome with a stabilization program based on a fixed exchange rate regime. Capital fled the country. From the very start of the election period, the AKP emphasized that it would commit to the IMF-backed stabilization program and structural reforms. The party also expended significant effort to position itself as "pro-business" and signal its willingness to form broad alliances with global financial actors. At the same time, the AKP emphasized the importance of Turkey's EU membership and democratization more than did its political rivals. Voters heavily penalized the parties in the incumbent ruling coalition as a result of the 2001 crisis and the new parliament formed in 2002 contained only two parties: the ruling AKP and the opposing CHP (Republican People's Party).

A great many of the suggestions put forward in MÜSİAD's 2002 annual report were reflected in the AKP's first strategy documents.[92] Nonetheless, the AKP anticipated pressure from the first-generation "secular" business community as well as international financial actors, and thus it positioned itself accordingly. Indeed, the AKP's success in securing a place for itself in Turkish politics is an excellent example of an Islamist party's ideological flexibility in response to changing conditions. This was no small feat for several reasons. First, in terms of economic policies, the IMF stabilization program and 2001 structural reforms necessitated the establishment of independent regulatory authorities who would, by definition, reduce the state's discretionary power. This was inherently risky, as it threatened to undercut the state's ability to grant access to the resources that the devout bourgeoisie needed to further expand their market power. In addition, the new reform agenda threatened to take away some of the important competitive advantages enjoyed by the Anatolian Tigers, including tax avoidance, the employment of informal labor and lax oversight of compliance with safety regulations. Moreover, MÜSİAD resisted both banking reform and the advent of regulatory bodies.

The AKP established some regulatory institutions while simultaneously making it possible for the business community to continue to operate under relatively loose conditions in its early years. Öniş defines this pragmatic approach as "regulatory neo-liberalism" and "controlled neo-populism."[93] Buğra and Savaşkan take a slightly different stance and define this first period of AKP rule as one of mutual dependence between the government and the broader business community.[94] As both the first-generation and second-generation business communities relied on government support to secure their economic interests and associational power, they tacitly lent support to the AKP, which thereby further bolstered the rise of political Islam. Indeed, during this period the AKP used privatization as an effective tool to establish its pro-business credentials and the party did not always favor the second-generation pious business community in the process. The privatization of Tüpraş, the state-owned petroleum refining company, to Koç Holding, the largest holding company in Turkey and a primary representative of the traditional secular business community, offers a good example for understanding the AKP's early approach, which initially sought to appeal to a broad business base.

The AKP's landslide victory in the 2007 and 2011 elections earned the party an almost uncontested position in Turkey's political arena. With each political victory, the AKP's pragmatic approach of forming a broad alliance between different business organizations gave way to a more discretionary and authoritarian policy framework. Neoliberal tools including public-private partnership models, especially for the provision of social services and infrastructure projects, were used extensively in an effort to feed state contracts to new big businesses operating on a national scale. Many of these new big businesses preferred to make investments in energy (both generation and distribution) and/or construction, sectors in which the ability to secure permits from local or central government authorities was critical. MÜSİAD's increasing interest in the construction sector starting in 2009 is therefore fitting. For example, in its 2009 annual report MÜSİAD characterized the construction sector as the locomotive of the Turkish economy. Similarly, in its 2011 annual report, MÜSİAD emphasized the need for a broader urban transformation and more investment in the construction sector.[95] It is perhaps also not surprising then that one of the members of the consortium that won the massive third Bosporus bridge construction procurement in 2016 was the president of MÜSİAD at the time.[96]

Indeed, as the AKP strengthened its grip on power, it began circumventing regulatory mechanisms with increasing frequency and with less regard for the consequences. Accusations of favoritism and patronage also began to abound. Corruption seeped into the political economy, as an analysis of the frequent changes to procurement laws makes evident. Between 2003 and 2013, 29 changes were made to procurement laws. And, as Gürakar and Meyersson show, a limited number of firms with close ties to the AKP began winning a disproportionately large share of construction procurement contracts. After the 2008 amendment to procurement laws, the likelihood for AKP-connected firms to win procurements rose from 40 percent to 70 percent.[97] The government-fueled construction boom also made Turkey's Public Housing Development Association (*Toplu Konut İdaresi Başkanlığı*, TOKİ) a key player in the AKP's strategy to enhance its grip on power in key urban municipalities through the handout of urban renewal projects. Marshal, Aydogan and Bulut, for example, find that TOKİ investments (in the form of housing units and associated expenditures) were a significant determinant of the number of times the AKP won mayoral elections in period from 2004 to 2014.[98] As shown in Chapter 10 in this volume, corruption has a long lineage in Turkey and was likely exacerbated by AKP policies.[99]

Indeed, the party fused its economic development programs and patronage networks into a formidable political machine that served to enhance its grip on power, especially in urban centers, as long as the economy was growing.

Theoretically, this process of capital accumulation by a few big firms could have been problematic for the AKP had it hurt smaller actors in the pious business community. To avoid such a fate, the AKP pursued a number of measures. First, it leveraged Islamic business networks and Islamic culture to come up with effective subcontracting practices, mainly through dividing tenders and limiting subcontracting firms to domestic business.[100] By doing so, smaller and local firms that were close to the AKP's network could also benefit from the success of pious big business.[101] The AKP therefore was able to maintain its support for the economic activities of government-friendly SMEs without losing the support of big business. In yet another about-face, the Muslim business community had thus adopted a dramatically different approach towards the role of the state in the economy, as it established a closer relationship with the ruling government.[102]

5.9 Conclusion

The argument developed in this chapter reveals that Turkey's pious business community has shown a remarkable degree of responsiveness to shifts in the economic and political environment and were not inhibited by religious institutions, scripture or ethics. Instead, they leveraged and transformed a repertoire of religious and cultural frameworks in the service of both political power and capitalist development. This strategy has strengthened their ability to accumulate influence over the traditional stewards of Turkey's economy. These findings are consistent with Adaş, who has argued that Islamic entrepreneurs reinterpret Islam in ways that comport with current and anticipated economic conditions and are thus able to navigate potential conflicts between capitalism and Islamic norms, such as the prohibition of interest (*ribā*).[103] Similarly, this chapter complements work by Tuğal, who has compared Islamist and Kemalist actors' ability to respond to the values promoted by globalization, and claimed that the Islamists have been more successful.[104]

The responsiveness of Islamic actors in Turkey has taken several forms. First, Islamist political actors—and the conservative bourgeoisie class they have sought to cultivate—have been quick to adapt, demonstrating that they can effectively use the policy tools and dominant economic and political frameworks of the time, even if these frameworks deviate from their immediate preferences and assumed religious proclivities. Islamists' increasing willingness to adopt neo-liberal policies—including the private-sector provision of social services and the devolution of authority to local municipalities, which reached its apex with Justice and Development Party rule—in a discretionary fashion is a case in point. Adherence to these policies gradually fastened the capital accumulation process to a government-friendly conservative bourgeoisie.[105]

Second, both Islamic political actors and business associations exhibit a high degree of cultural and ideological flexibility: they can and do successfully reference different Islamic moral codes with respect to business culture at different periods to give religious legitimacy to their actions. Such flexibility is evidenced by the fact that the moral codes emphasized by MSP at the end of 1970s—and also those derived from Sufi philosophy—are markedly different from the "Medina market" business culture that Muslim business associations began to romanticize with increasing vigor in the mid-1990s.[106]

Although the adaptivity and ideological flexibility of Turkey's conservative business and political elite is remarkable, one factor—the use of religion as a *network resource*—has remained relatively constant over the period studied here. Throughout the recent history of Islamic capitalism—and, in fact, in an effort to create this very category—Islamist political actors and the Muslim business community leveraged religious networks, associations and organizations to build trust and thereby reduce transaction costs between market participants, to access various sources of financing and support and to ensure close proximity to the Turkish government. As a result, this chapter makes a case for the bidirectional nature of the transformation that has dramatically changed business–state–society relations in Turkey. While the capitalist system and composition of the business community in Turkey has changed as a result of exogenous factors, such as globalization and demographic realities, we also observe a transformation of Islamist actors themselves as they have strategized how best to utilize new opportunities, both locally and globally.

Notes

1. See Chapter 3, this volume.
2. Several prominent Jewish businessmen also established holding companies in the 1950s that came to be associated with first generation business elite in Turkey. These holding companies include Alarko Holding and Profilo Holding.
3. A. Buğra, "Class, Culture and State: An Analysis of Interest Representation by Two Turkish Business Associations," *International Journal of Middle East Studies*, v.30, n. 4, 1998, pp. 521–539.
4. Ş. Gümüşçü, "Class, Status and Party: The Changing Face of Political Islam in Turkey and Egypt," *Comparative Political Studies*, v.43, n. 7, 2010, pp. 835–861; Chapters 2 and 3, this volume.
5. For a convincing account of how this narrative ignores the fact that the state had indeed worked to develop industrial capacity in key parts of the periphery starting in the early years of the Republic see K. Cengiz, "*Yav İşte Fabrikalaşak": Anadolu Sermayesi'nin Oluşumu: Kayseri Hacılar Örneği*, Istanbul: İletişim, 2013.
6. Gürakar and Meyersson show that increased government discretion in public procurement increases the likelihood of the winning firm being politically connected to the AKP (E.Ç. Gürakar and E. Meyersson, "State Discretion,

Political Connections and Public Procurement: Evidence from Turkey," *Economic Research Forum Working Paper Series* No. 1053, 2016.

7. See A. Buğra and O. Savaşkan, *New Capitalism in Turkey*, Northampton, MA: Edward Elgar Publishing, 2014.
8. *Gümüş Motor* later took the name *Pancar Motor*. The daily newspaper *Hürriyet* mentions that the initiative was supported by the Turkish Naqshbandī community ("Erbakan Hoca'nın Gümüş Motor'u sustu," *Hürriyet*, February 3, 2012, www.hurriyet.com.tr/ekonomi/erbakan-hoca-nin-gumus-motor-u-sustu-19838676, accessed November 20, 2018.
9. Interestingly, it was around the same time that the influential Istanbul-based Koç family, an emerging pillar of "secular big business," made similar moves in the automotive industry.
10. TOBB is best described as the umbrella organization for Turkey's other business associations, including the regional chambers of commerce and industry.
11. Serkan Yorgancılar, *Milli Görüş 1969–1980*, Istanbul: Pınar, 2012, pp. 28–35.
12. Ibid.
13. Ibid.
14. R. Çakır, "Milli Görüş Hareketi," in *İslamcılık*, vol. 6, Istanbul: İletişim, 2004, pp. 545–546.
15. T.S. Halman, "AP'den Sapmalar ve Kopmalar," *Milliyet*, December 08, 1969 (also quoted in Yorgancılar, *Milli Görüş 1969–1980*, 51).
16. *MNP 1inci Büyük Kongresi 24 Ocak 1971*, Ankara: As, 1971, pp. 34–38. Also see the 1975 local elections propaganda booklet that cited the main reasons why people should not vote for any political party other than the MSP: Zafer Karib, *1975 Türkiyesinde Niçin MSP De?* Istanbul: İhya Yayınları, 1975, pp. 13–76.
17. Ibid., p. 40.
18. Ibid., p. 43.
19. Velidedeoğlu likened the term *nizâm* to the way in which Sultan Mehmed II justified fratricide within the fifteenth-century legal framework (Hıfzı Veldet Velidedeoğlu, *Türkiye'de Üç Devir*, Ankara: Sinan, 1972, pp. 355–356).
20. Although the National Order Party's foundational charter made no mention of *Millî Görüş*, it did reference all the terms that Erbakan's subsequent parties would adopt as names, including *selâmet* (salvation), *refah* (virture) and *saadet* (felicity).
21. Mehmet Döşemeci, "Turkish Opposition to the Common Market: An Archaeology of Nationalist Thought, 1967–1980," *South European Society and Politics*, v.17, n. 1, March 2012, pp. 88–89.
22. Necmettin Erbakan, *Mecliste Ortak Pazar*, İzmir: Gençlik Teşkilâtları Genel Başkanlığı, 1971, pp. 38–39.
23. *MNP 1inci Büyük Kongresi*, pp. 62–63.
24. Ibid., pp. 54–55.
25. Erbakan, *Mecliste Ortak Pazar*, pp. 38–39.
26. See the section on "Ortak Pazar" in a booklet about Erbakan's new five year plan published after the closing of the MNP (Necmettin Erbakan, *Millî Görüş ve 3. Beş Yıllık Plan*, Ankara: Furkan, 1973, pp. 86–89).
27. Erbakan, *Mecliste Ortak Pazar*, pp. 68–71, 85–89.
28. Ibid., pp. 107–111.
29. Ibid., pp. 94–95.
30. It is important to note that the MNP was not only the party closed down during this time. The socialist TİP (*Türkiye İşçi Partisi*), was also closed down due to its radical leftist proclamations during the election campaign (Yorgancılar, *Milli Görüş 1969–1980*, p. 164).

31. For the full text of the various pieces of evidence see: *Millî Nizam Partisi Niçin Kapatıldı?* Ankara: Vesika, 1990.
32. Erbakan, *Mecliste Ortak Pazar*, p. 114.
33. Sufism (*taṣavvuf*) and Sufi orders, also sometimes referred to in the literature as religious orders, brotherhoods, cemaats, or tarikat (*tarīḳāts*, literally meaning "way" or "path"), began to rise sometime in the twelfth and thirteenth centuries. In the Ottoman period Sufi orders congregated around building compounds known as a *tekke* or *dergāh/dargāh (zāwiyya* in Arabic), which were essentially hostels that provided a space for rituals and social gatherings. The Sufi orders fulfilled a variety of functions: religious, social, charitable, intellectual, psychological and sometimes political. Above all, the Sufi orders' diverse functions and malleable institutional structure also allowed them to develop closeness with common subjects and to adapt to very different social environments. See Kristin E. Fabbe, *Disciples of the State? Religion and State-Building in the Former Ottoman World*, New York: Cambridge University Press, 2019, pp. 41–42. Also see *Millî Nizam Partisi Niçin Kapatıldı?* 17.
34. *Millî Selamet Partisi 1973 Seçim Beyannamesi*, Istanbul: Fatih Matbaası, 1973, p. 4.
35. The 1977 General Election Manifesto employed the term *Cenâb-ı Hakk* for Allah, though also only once in the preface (*Millî Selâmet Partisi 5 Haziran 1977 Seçimleri Seçim Beyannamesi*, Ankara: Basın-Yayın Genel Müdürlüğü, Başbakanlık Basımevi, 1977, p. 12).
36. See *MNP 1inci Büyük Kongresi 24 Ocak 1971. Hakk* or *Cenab-ı Hakk* was used many times and the believers were referred to as *mü'minler*.
37. *İnananlar* potentially served as a double entendre here. It could both refer to Muslims and/or the supporters of Erbakan's political vision of *Millî Görüş*. See *Millî Selâmet Partisi 5 Haziran 1977 Seçimleri Seçim Beyannamesi*.
38. *Millî Selâmet Partisi 5 Haziran 1977 Seçimleri Seçim Beyannamesi*, p. 33.
39. Ibid., pp. 12 and 32.
40. *Millî Selamet Partisi 1973*, p. 82.
41. Ibid., p. 42.
42. Ibid., pp. 34–38.
43. J.M. Landau, *Politics and Islam: The National Salvation Party in Turkey*, Salt Lake City: The University of Utah's Research Monographs, 1976, p. 17.
44. The expression *kalkınma* will later become the AKP's central vision and concept.
45. *Millî Selâmet Partisi 5 Haziran 1977 Seçimleri Seçim Beyannamesi*, pp. 51–52.
46. Ibid., p. 57. *Milli Selamet Partisi 3: Büyük Kongresi*, Ankara: Elif, 1976, pp. 64–67.
47. *Millî Selâmet Partisi 5 Haziran 1977 Seçimleri Seçim Beyannamesi*, pp. 57–65. Again the MSP also promised to lower taxes and increase the number of factories for manufacturing motors, planes, heavy machinery and electronics. See Ibid., pp. 43–44.
48. Ibid., 49. This push for private-sector mobilization (*Özel Sektör Seferberliği*) also included proposals to develop industrial sites (*sanayii siteleri*), create regional industry directorates (*bölge sanayi müdürlükleri*), build organized industrial zones (*organize sanayi bölgeleri*) and found a State Industry and Laborer Investment Bank (*Devlet Sanayi ve İşçi Yatırım Bankası, DESİYAB*).
49. Ibid., p. 53. The manifesto made no distinction between the West and the Muslim East with respect to its trade liberalization policies and the party

simply promised to increase export volumes without mentioning their destination.

50. M.A. Birand, *Türkiye'nin Ortak Pazar Macerası*, Istanbul: Milliyet, 1986, pp. 359–406. For Demirel's political stance see 388–406; and for Ecevit's see 364–387.
51. *Millî Selâmet Partisi 5 Haziran 1977 Seçimleri Seçim Beyannamesi*, pp. 33–37; *Milli Selamet Partisi 3. Büyük Kongresi*, 49. Erbakan promised to increase the number of theological seminaries and Qur'anic day schools along with the number of personnel working for the Presidency of Religious Affairs (*Diyanet İşleri Başkanlığı*).
52. C. Lord, *Religious Politics in Turkey: From the Birth of the Republic to the AKP*, New York: Cambridge University Press, 2018, p. 66.
53. Ş. Pamuk, "Globalization, Industrialization and Changing Politics in Turkey," *New Perspectives on Turkey*, v.38, 2008, pp. 267–273.
54. R. Owen and Ş. Pamuk, *A History of Middle East Economies in the Twentieth Century*, Cambridge, MA: Harvard Universit Press, 1998, p. 119.
55. For the effects of the military regime on the labor unions and wages, see E. Taymaz, E. Voyvoda, and K. Yılmaz, *Demokrasiye Geçiş, Reel Ücretler ve Verimlilik: Türk İmalat Sanayiinden Bulgular*, St. Louis: Federal Reserve Bank of St Louis, 2014; Pamuk, "Globalization, Industrialization and Changing Politics in Turkey," p. 207.
56. Fabbe, *Disciples of the State?* pp. 10, 179.
57. See B. Güvenç, G. Şaylan, İ. Tekeli, and Ş. Turan, *Dosya: Türk-İslam Sentezi*, Istanbul: Sarmal, 1991.
58. Lord, *Religious Politics in Turkey*, pp. 66–67.
59. See J. White, *Muslim Nationalism and the New Turks*, Princeton, NJ: Princeton University Press, 2012. As İlhan argues, the Turkish business community from the early Republican period overemphasized their service to the nation as the motive in their profit-making activities (E. İlhan, "Turkey's State-Business Relations Revisited: Islamic Business Associations and Policymaking in the AKP Era," PhD Thesis, King's College, London, 2014).
60. Lord, *Religious Politics in Turkey*, p. 167.
61. Many of these firms would join MÜSİAD when it formed a decade later; however, Buğra and Savaşkan correctly caution that it is misleading to conclude that MÜSİAD only represents SMEs (See Buğra and Savaşkan's *New Capitalism in Turkey*).
62. G.B. Özcan and M. Çokgezen, "Limits to Alternative Forms of Capitalization: The Case of Anatolian Holding Companies," *World Development*, v.31, n. 12, 2003, pp. 2061–2084.
63. Z. Öniş, "The Political Economy of Islamic Resurgence in Turkey: The Rise of the Welfare Party in Perspective," *Third World Quarterly*, v.18, n. 4, 1997, pp. 743–766.
64. See Özcan and Çokgezen's "Limits to Alternative Forms of Capitalization" as mentioned in Note 62.
65. E. Hoşgör, "Islamic Capital/Anatolian Tigers: Past and Present," *Middle Eastern Studies*, v.47, n. 2, 2001, pp. 343–360.
66. R. Silverman, "Dogan Versus Erdogan: Business and Politics in AKP Era Turkey," *Mediterranean Quarterly*, v.25, n. 2, 2004, pp. 131–151.
67. Lord, *Religious Politics in Turkey*, pp. 199–200.
68. Ibid., pp. 203–206; F. Başkan, "The Political Economy of Islamic Finance in Turkey: The Role of Fetullah Gülen and Asya Finans," in Clement M. Henry and Rodney Wilson (eds.) *The Politics of Islamic Finance*, Edinburgh: Edinburgh University Press, 2004, pp. 216–239.

69. When Erol Yarar, the founding president of MÜSİAD, said in an interview that "We Are the Real Bourgeoisie!" he implicitly meant that the conservative bourgeoisie that he represented emerged without any state support while TÜSİAD owed much of its capital accumulation to state support and protectionist policies ("'Asıl Burjuva Biziz'," *Sol Haber*, July 9, 2008, http://haber.sol.org.tr/devlet-ve-siyaset/asil-burjuva-biziz-haberi-15982, accessed March 30, 2019.
70. These reports can be found at www.MÜSİAD.org.tr/F/Root/burcu2014/Ara%C5%9Ft%C4%B1rmalar%20Yay%C4%B1n/Pdf/Ara%C5%9Ft%C4%B1rma%20Raporlar%C4%B1/Orta_Buyuklukteki_isletmeler_ve_Burokrasi.pdf and www.MÜSİAD.org.tr/F/Root/burcu2014/Ara%C5%9Ft%C4%B1rmalar%20Yay%C4%B1n/Pdf/Ara%C5%9Ft%C4%B1rma%20Raporlar%C4%B1/Ozellestirme_Paneli.pdf, respectively, accessed March 28, 2019.
71. See www.MÜSİAD.org.tr/F/Root/burcu2014/Ara%C5%9Ft%C4%B1rmalar%20Yay%C4%B1n/Pdf/Ekonomi%20Raporu/Turkiye_Ekonomisi_2000.pdf, accessed March 28, 2019.
72. See İlhan's, "Turkey's State-Business Relations Revisited."
73. See Silverman's, "Dogan Versus Erdogan: Business and Politics in AKP Era Turkey."
74. S. Uygur, "The Islamic Work Ethic and the Emergence of Turkish SME Owner-Managers," *Journal of Business Ethics*, v.88, 2009, pp. 211–225.
75. E.B. Adaş, "The Making of Entrepreneurial Islam and the Islamic Spirit of Capitalism," *Journal for Cultural Research*, v.10, n. 2, 2006, pp. 113–137. In fact, one of the incidents that created resentment among the Muslim business community and was said to lead to the foundation of MÜSİAD was the removal of some conservative businessmen from a business trip to Soviet Republic, which was organized by DEİK (Foreign Economic Relations Board).
76. G.B. Özcan and H. Turunç, "Economic Liberalization and Class Dynamics in Turkey: New Business Groups and Islamic Mobilization," *Insight Turkey*, v.13, n. 3, 2011, pp. 63–86.
77. M. Çokgezen, "New fragmentations and Co-Operations of the Turkish Bourgeoisie," *Government and Policy*, v.18, 2000, pp. 525–544.
78. See Özcan and Çokgezen's, "Limits to Alternative Forms of Capitalization."
79. A. Lo Turco and D. Maggioni, "Effects of Islamic Religiosity on Bilateral Trust in Trade: The Case of Turkish Exports," *Journal of Comparative Economics*, v.46, n. 4, 2018, pp. 947–965.
80. MÜSİAD's preference towards the destination of the export markets can be seen in its reports that summarize the business trips of its representatives. A good example can be seen at www.MÜSİAD.org.tr/F/Root/burcu2014/Ara%C5%9Ft%C4%B1rmalar%20Yay%C4%B1n/Pdf/Ara%C5%9Ft%C4%B1rma%20Raporlar%C4%B1/Afrika_ve_ingiltere_is_Gezileri.pdf, accessed March 28, 2019.
81. Vannetzel and Yankaya analyze MÜSİAD clout as a role model for other Islamic business associations and find that MÜSİAD actively supported the creation of Islamic business associations in the broader region by exporting its own organizational model. M. Vannetzel and D. Yankaya, "Crafting a Business Umma? Transnational Networks of 'Islamic Businessmen' After the Arab Spring," *Mediterranean Politics*, November 2017, pp. 1–21.
82. From another point of view, these new intensified trade relations with the countries in the MENA also increased the importance of the Kurdish business community for the overall economy. The invasion of Iraq had already opened up new profit opportunities in Northern Iraq and led to the emergence of a new Kurdish entrepreneurial class.

83. Analysis based on data from OECD (2003) and Turkstat.
84. For example, in its 1999 report, MÜSİAD openly criticized the Refah-Yol coalition, within which the Islamist Welfare Party (*Refah Partisi*, RP) was the bigger partner.
85. C. Tuğal, *The Fall of the Turkish Model*, New York: Verso Publishing, 2016.
86. Ş. Gümüşçü and D.Ş. Sert, "The Power of the Devout Bourgeoisie: The Case of the Justice and Development Party in Turkey," *Middle Eastern Studies*, v.45, n. 6, 2009, pp. 953–968.
87. Ji-Hyang also finds that regions with more MÜSİAD members provided greater support for this reformist wing in the Virtue party (see his "Taming Political Islamists by Islamic Capital: The Passions and the Interests in Turkish Islamic Society").
88. R. Çakır, "İslamcıların Batıcılaşma Süreci," *Birikim*, v.129, December 1999.
89. The "Turkish Economy" report in 1999 is a very good example of where MÜSİAD heavily opposes the new tax law on the grounds that it will create an incentive, especially for small firms, to engage more in informal activities, www.MÜSİAD.org.tr/F/Root/burcu2014/Ara%C5%9Ft%C4%B1rmalar%20Yay%C4%B1n/Pdf/Ekonomi%20Raporu/Turkiye_Ekonomisi_1999.pdf, accessed March 28, 2019.
90. Adaş, "The Making of Entrepreneurial Islam and the Islamic Spirit of Capitalism," p. 133. It is also ironic to see that, to control the inflation that peaked after the dramatic depreciation of the Turkish Lira in the second half of 2018, the AKP did not hesitate to apply strict price controls, which received critical support from MÜSİAD.
91. Ibid., p. 122.
92. www.MÜSİAD.org.tr/F/Root/burcu2014/Ara%C5%9Ft%C4%B1rmalar%20Yay%C4%B1n/Pdf/Ekonomi%20Raporu/Turkiye_Ekonomisi_2002.pdf, accessed March 28, 2019.
93. Z. Oniş, *The Political Economy of Turkey's Justice and Development Party: The Emergence of a New Turkey and the AK Parti*. Edited by H.M. Yavuz, Salt Lake City: The University of Utah Press, 2006.
94. Buğra and Savaşkan, *New Capitalism in Turkey*, 2014.
95. www.MÜSİAD.org.tr/F/Root/burcu2014/Ara%C5%9Ft%C4%B1rmalar%20Yay%C4%B1n/Pdf/Sekt%C3%B6r%20Kurullar%C4%B1/insaat_Sektor_Raporu_2009.pdf, accessed March 28, 2019.
96. www.hurriyet.com.tr/ekonomi/hasen-yapi-dev-ihalenin-surpriz-firmasi-40105508, accessed March 28, 2019.
97. E.Ç. Gürakar and E. Meyersson. "State Discretion, Political Connections and Public Procurement: Evidence from Turkey," *Economic Research Forum Working Paper Series*, No:1053, 2016. Another strategy for circumventing regulatory mechanisms was to allow municipalities and local authorities to form their own companies, which, with the necessary legislative changes, were then freed from having to undergo inspection.
98. M. Marschall, A. Aydogan, and A. Bulut, "Does Housing Create Votes? Explaining the Electoral Success of the AKP in Turkey," *Electoral Studies*, v.42, 2016, pp. 201–212.
99. As Chapter 9 in this volume shows, public perceptions of corruption originally declined under the AKP but then spiked in 2013, which likely had much to do with media coverage patterns. Also, evidence from the early 2000s suggests that the business sector administrators' emphasis on and experience of corruption was reportedly greater than that of the general public.
100. See Silverman's, "Dogan Versus Erdogan: Business and Politics in AKP Era Turkey," which characterizes business politics under the AKP as leveraging

a vast class of Turks connected with each other through either a shared sense of Islamic values or through family ties.

101. On the other hand, with a change in the law, the AKP government could demand a subcontractor change, which stands as yet another example of its political discretion.
102. This argument is also supported by Ji-Hyang, who finds that Islamist capitalists were more independent and critical of the state compared to their secular counterparts until the mid-1990s. He adds that Islamic business interests later developed a taming effect on the political Islamists (See J. Ji-Hyang, "Taming Political Islamists by Islamic Capital."
103. See Adaş's, "The Making of Entrepreneurial Islam and the Islamic Spirit of Capitalism."
104. See Tuğal, *The Fall of the Turkish Model*. It is, however, an open question whether the responsiveness of Turkish Islamist actors is peculiar to Turkey or can be generalized to other Muslim countries as well. See I. Saif and M. Abu Rumman, "The Economic Agenda of the Islamist Parties," *The Carnegie Papers*, May 2012, pp. 1–26.
105. See Buğra and Savaşkan's *New Capitalism in Turkey*; E.C. Gürakar, *Kayırma Ekonomisi*, Ankara: İletişim, 2018, for a detailed analysis of how neo-liberal policies have been used extensively to preserve the economic and political hierarchy during the AKP era.
106. A clarification about Muslim business associations is necessary. As İlhan mentions, a Muslim business association does not mean a sharia-compliant association. Nor are we arguing that all the members of such business associations are Islamists or even pious (see İlhan's, "Turkey's State-Business Relations Revisited."). Instead, these associations can be characterized as conservative agents that are willing and able to negotiate the terms of their faith with policy actors.

6 Reciprocity in Business-Government Relations

A Comparative Perspective

Patrick Fridenson

Government has been at the center of three of the previous chapters of this book. Indeed, in Chapter 1 Colpan and Jones, as they explore the coevolution of business enterprises with political and social institutions in order to locate the long-term evolution of Turkish capitalism in global history, often return to the role of government. Furthermore, in Chapter 3, Buğra focuses on government-business relations in Turkey and sees politics at the origins not only of the earlier bourgeoisie but also of the new business community. In Chapter 5, Fabbe, Özlale and Balıkçıoğlu connect the rise of religious-conservative big business during the past fifty years in Anatolia and in the periphery to the increasingly blurred boundaries between business and politics, and to the state granting resources to their large enterprises.

The purpose of this comparative chapter is to stand back from detailed engagement with the empirical evidence on Turkey. It looks not just at policy and business, but also at the interaction between them. The chapter also addresses the heterogeneous nature of the business sector, both in Turkey and elsewhere. The goal is that the comparative evidence at the core of the chapter will help to deepen our understanding of Turkey.

Since the 1960s a number of scholars have framed an approach to the role of the state in economic growth for emerging markets that offers a theory of the developmental state as a major source of growth for "latecomers," described more often today as emerging countries. This now conventional wisdom was developed by economic historians like Alexander Gerschenkron on the basis of the case of Tsarist Russia, and political scientists like Chalmers Johnson on the basis of the case of Japan during the postwar economic miracle. It was generalized by Johnson and others to most similar countries.[1] It was endorsed by the Harvard Business School business historian Thomas K. McCraw in the influential edited volume entitled *America versus Japan.* (1986).[2]

A body of scholarship has developed in the social sciences that locates the coordination of industrial development inside government or its specialized agencies. A recent study has noted that "developmental states tend to have coherent Weberian bureaucracies that are autonomous but embedded within society." They ideally "allow state actors to implement a development project without political influence or capture from social groups and classes. They are characterized by individuals driven by collective goals and tied to state agencies as well as their constituents. A bureaucracy's *esprit de corps* allows it to transcend individual interests in order to achieve national goals, and its embeddedness allows the state to negotiate goals, monitor activities, and receive feedback to ensure the success of a project." This display of state capacity is more fruitful when, the study argues, "the industrial development bureaucracies, the industrial elite, and the state are in agreement" about policies like "protection of domestic industries through high tariffs on foreign imports, guiding investments into priority sectors, and promotion of joint public/private research organizations to build indigenous technical capacity."[3]

Obviously, this approach works to some extent. It stresses the role of institutions in markets: governments (national, but also in some matters local, regional, and more recently supranational) may enact market rules on competition, pricing, intellectual property, quality, safety, financing, or foreign exchanges and capital controls; promote technologies, industries and regions; supply public orders; allocate funding; create, nationalize or privatize firms; and finance their action by taxes. It applies to different geographical areas and stages of development. In "old Europe," it makes sense of France's policies from Colbertism in the second half of the 17th century guiding business to sell abroad and buy domestically, to post-World War II economic planning and support to larger firms considered as national champions.[4] In major emerging countries, it covers a combination of promotion of sectors and control of firms in order to foster economic development. The governments of emerging countries are in unequal relations to developed countries, and generally pursue catch up strategies. Yet the former may have a power of their own when they move to attract foreign capital and firms, when they award armament contracts, as for surface-to-air missiles Saudi Arabia did in 1974 and 1984 to the French electronics company Thomson,[5] or when they can reverse their dependence on resource-based exports by raising the prices or limiting quantities of major materials like oil, although without necessarily generating development.

This power can also be a negative one, when these countries ban the entry of foreign multinationals, as in the case of China under Mao, and such rejections were by no means limited to Communist countries. In capitalist countries, however, outcomes were sometimes unexpected, as when Mexico's nationalist government in the 1970s blocked a joint venture in steel, which prompted the construction company Acindar to diversify into a wholly owned integrated steel company. In Turkey itself, the regulatory environment which forbade private companies from importing foreign goods led Murat Vargi to become a representative of foreign companies in 1993, work as an intermediary with the Turkish state, and then found Turkcell, which became Turkey's largest mobile provider.[6]

Last, but certainly not least, the role of states always matters in macroeconomic management. This includes control of inflation and other monetary policies, and the part played by central banks in their definition and enforcement. It may in addition include, as between the end of World War II and the 1970s, economic planning. Planning is then, in principle, a tool designed to supply firms with perspectives beyond the short term, to enforce a growth policy, and to coordinate business, government and other actors of society. The central bank may become an ally of planning, as the French central bank was between 1948 and 1973: contrary to both its traditional doctrine and international wisdom, the bank successfully moved to support planning by selectively distributing credit.[7]

It has been generally believed that the two oil shocks of the 1970s and the widening of globalization began to put planning, wherever it was practiced, and developmental states in emerging markets, to test. Moreover, "it is broadly understood that since the early 1990s it has become more difficult for nations to implement developmental state policies. Developing countries are now incorporating a global economic integration strategy whereby they are conforming to rules put forward by the World Bank, the International Monetary Fund and the World Trade Organization. These policy strategies typically include privatization of state-owned industries, reduction or elimination of trade barriers, and relaxation of state control over the markets through deregulation."[8]

New research has introduced several qualifications to the theory of developmental state. It has drawn attention to intermediate states, which can register some success in development when these states have industries where "key actors in the state apparatus have carved out an 'island' or pocket of industrial efficiency. It is however fragile."[9] More recent scholarship on the "developmental network state" has suggested that states should support innovation from below and facilitate connections between local and global networks—in short, use these ties to motivate the private sector to make long-term commitments to development.[10]

This chapter attempts, on several grounds, to move developmental state analysis in another direction, particularly for the more recent period. This revision adopts a comparative perspective in order to illuminate the Turkish case,[11] but also to suggest that some of its apparently most specific characteristics may be part of broader trends. Agreeing with two Turkish scholars that "the privatization of natural monopolies and the commercialization of social services create market opportunities without necessarily leading to a retreat of the state,"[12] this chapter sketches the divisions within business, the agency of firms, and the importance of morality and religion in the economy. It argues that between public and private there are reciprocal influences.

6.1 Dealing With Divisions Among Business Enterprises

The question here is twofold: what is the extent of divisions among business firms? Do governments attempt to reduce them, tinker with or shape them?

Beyond the usual differentiations between firms (created by size, competition, economic branches, geographical location and resources), beyond the distinctive position of international merchants, comprador businesses[13] and trading companies, the relation to government itself may be another source of differences among enterprises. In this respect there is a constant division within business of capitalist economies between two groups of firms. The first consists of firms that find their interest or the basis of their strategy in supplying the state and/or are dependent on loans and subsidies supporting its policies: infrastructure companies such as public works, water, gas, electricity, telecommunications, armament companies generally feature in this category. The second group consists of firms which, because of their markets, resources or managerial ideologies, behave in a much more autonomous way. In the case of postwar Japan, examples might include such start-ups as the motorcycle, and subsequently auto, company Honda (1948), and Kyocera in industrial ceramics (1959), which diversified into electronic components, photovoltaic cells, document solutions and cell phones.[14] Their CEOs used to make statements stressing the expertise of the companies, the usefulness of competition, and the inefficacy of government guidance of the economy. Similarly, in 1966 Suresh Krishna founded the Chennai, India-based high precision component supplier Sundram Fasteners because he wanted to "stay away from any industry which is under the control of the government."[15]

A source of further divisions is the growing frequency of multinationals active in foreign markets as they attempt to make agreements with state banks or the state itself, but keep pursuing their own interests. They may be rejected or accepted by the national firms of their sector, which in turn may try to shape relevant public policies. Let us take two opposite examples from the history of the French automobile multinational Renault. In 1969 the company was allowed by the Turkish government to build a large production plant because Renault granted the pension fund of Turkish military officers 49 percent of the capital.[16] In contrast, in India, which has been a moderately open economy since the liberal reforms began in 1991, most domestic car producers lobbied for, and in 2013 secured, the creation of a tax on cars longer than four meters, which was designed to block the entry of multinationals planning to produce a low-cost car. However, the Franco-Japanese Renault-Nissan group managed to design a car adapted to that tight constraint.[17]

The ability of local firms to lobby their national government to oppose or encourage foreign investment has been previously observed at great length by Mark Mason in his study of foreign multinationals in twentieth century Japan. Indeed, in his 1992 survey of 10 case studies of US multinationals and their efforts to build a manufacturing base in Japan, Mason emphasized the central influence not of government, but business:

> Domestic business largely initiated foreign investment policies, and greatly influenced their timing and substance. . . . Japanese business officials often played the critical role even during the decades of the 1950s and 1960s-a period often referred to as the high tide of postwar government power in Japan.[18]

Then foreign companies could create leverage by splitting the united front of Japanese business.

Two examples of such practices are relevant here. One comes from a printed source. By the late 1950s all the Japanese companies refused to pay the standard royalty for the painting of their bike fenders and tanks to the American electrostatic paint company Ransburg. It appealed to the Ministry of Industry and International Trade but was rebuffed: MITI was eager to see the practice of "price fixing and market share allotment" continue. Ransburg contacted Soichiro Honda, a warm supporter of open competition. They won Honda's acceptance. When it became obvious that MITI would not allow Honda to make the payments, Honda further agreed with Ransburg to go into an astute judiciary scheme that would leave MITI "no choice but to accept it."[19]

The second example, in consumer goods, concerns a much larger multinational: Coca-Cola. It comes from Mason's book and shows how the company could get rid of the remaining controls after the Japanese government had been led by Western powers to initiate the first "liberalization" of the soft-drink industry in the late 1950s. By 1959 strict limits were placed on the amount that could be produced and this could only be sold at designated outlets and no advertising was permitted. The price could not drop below 35 yen per bottle (domestic soft drinks cost 20 yen per bottle) and each case sold was subject to a stiff luxury tax. The force behind this official measure was the domestic soft drink industry. Coca-Cola found a crack in the system. Shin-Mitsubishi Heavy Industries made bottling equipment and, as a supplier to Coca-Cola, stood to gain as the latter's market expanded. Mitsubishi pressed Kirin Beer, "the single most influential member of the Coke opposition, but a relatively weak member of the Mitsubishi keiretsu," to cooperate with Coca-Cola. Kirin and Coca-Cola then formed a joint venture. The two Japanese firms brought pressure to bear on the government. Within a month, the authorities announced the repeal of controls on sales outlets and advertising and Coca-Cola was on its way to establishing the presence it commands in Japan today."[20]

These examples drawn from business-government foreign investment cases raise a question of general significance: What does a government do in the face of divisions within the business community? It may yield to a dissident, when an across-the-board agreement with business is undermined, as we have just seen. On the contrary, it may utilize the divisions to enforce a public policy—in other words, to maintain or increase its authority over leading forces within society.[21] From 1949 to 1951, for example, French governments relied on the support of consumer industries, such as the mechanical and automobile industries, against the majority of steel companies in order to gain support for the project for a West European Coal and Steel Community.[22] Or governments may reverse their support of private entrepreneurship, as China did with respect to rural business after the 1980s, and become stronger, more intrusive and hence more effective, as in state-led development in the urban region of Shanghai in the 1990s.[23]

What about Turkey then? In 1963 Turkey, over a decade later than some other countries including Iran and India, created a State Planning Organization and launched its first Five Year Development Plan.[24] This was initially focused on heavy industry, but from 1989 onward there was a greater emphasis on small and medium enterprises, which was reinforced during the Seventh Plan, from 1996 to 2000, under pressure from both these firms and Islamic political movements.[25] This coordination by the state was no longer the main feature after 1991. The Turkish case, as examined in both Chapters 3 and 5, shows a deliberate action by the AKP party in power since 2002, to exacerbate the divisions between the two leading trade associations, TÜSİAD and MÜSİAD, in order to support the new political, economic and religious order. Less frequently, governments try to reduce such divisions. Thus, they may use "economic nationalism as a tool to exhort social groups to engage in economic advancement."[26]

Conversely, research has shown that "if a capitalist business class significantly weakens the power of the "nodal" development bureaucracy, a country will not have the capacity to become a developmental state. For instance, the lack of institutional power of India's planning commission industrial agency was predicated on the presence of strong business associations that undermined its autonomy. Due to various domestic and external factors, this capitalist check on autonomy was more or less absent in Korea."[27] This raises the question of the agency of firms.

6.2 The Resilient Agency of Firms

Political scientists and business historians have shown in detail the increasing levels of influence of business on politicians and high ranking civil servants worldwide. Business was extensively and continuously involved in shaping legislation in the formation of the European Union.[28] In particular, research has documented the growth of lobbying. By 2014, there were 30,000 lobbyists in Brussels "allegedly shaping 75 percent of European legislation in some form." At the same time 12,000 lobbyists were working in Washington, DC, with a total annual spending of $US 3.3 billion.[29]

Since the 1995 customs union agreement between Turkey and the European Union, the three main Turkish trade associations have had permanent representatives in Brussels, supported by internal committees and divisions. They have become members of the two pan-European trade associations: Eurochambres and BusinessEurope, both founded in 1958. They try to influence the European institutions, but at the same time they are entangled in their complex relations with the Turkish government.[30]

Such lobbying is only the tip of the iceberg. If it is generally agreed that it is the role of states to shape part of the rules that make market exchanges viable, firms do not content themselves with lobbying or with finding tax loopholes or favorable tax regimes. In every sort of regime, from capitalist to socialist, and in every stage of development, there are a wide range of possibilities for agency by firms. Regulations enacted by governments may be understood by business leaders as either a deterrent or a promoter of growth. In Sri Lanka, Abkar Brothers, which would in time become Sri Lanka's largest tea exporter, profited from the high tax barriers that undermined foreign firms after the mid-1970s, and the company was able to diversify into new activities to fill the gap. In Latin America the political and financial stability of Chile attracted South American investors who were often put off by the turbulence in Argentina.[31]

Firms may display their agency in relation to the state, even to a strong state, for various reasons. The simplest usually is asymmetry of information: firms may know better markets, customers, prices, trends in technology or in fashion, suppliers and distributors. One example, as Jones and Spadafora have shown, is how from the 1970s small entrepreneurs in Costa Rica, rather than the government, were central in preserving the areas devoted to national parks, because the government was hindered by budget restrictions and bureaucracy, and firms were also able to establish a symbiotic relationship between tour operators and eco-lodge proprietors.[32] But this notion does not give a unilateral privilege to firms as it also recognizes the power of other market stakeholders:

> the buyer of insurance may know more about his prospects of having an accident (such as how he drives) than the seller; a worker may know more about his ability than a prospective employer; a borrower may know more about his prospects for repaying a loan than the lender.[33]

Still, it is generally true that a number of business actors have more or better information than states do. As a result, many postwar capitalist states in Western Europe, Japan and elsewhere that opted for some sort of economic planning chose to work through agencies rather than directly. These agencies in turn employed management consultancies and investment banks for advice.[34]

This trend was carried further when states, then assisted by legal firms, had to deal with such economic maneuvers as privatizations, nationalizations, mergers and acquisitions. Second, firms may develop specific or unprecedented technological, commercial or financial expertise. Third, firms may be more sensitive to opportunities or constraints deriving from globalization than states, which keep to their own national domain. Finally, most firms become members of associations that increase both their information and their reach. This is the case with chambers of commerce, mostly at the local level, but also at the national level, and true even of the World Chambers Federation, created under another name in 1951.[35]

Turkey has two different institutions at the local level: chambers of commerce and chambers of industry, who created their national associations in 1950. Like in most other countries, they express the voice of small and medium-size enterprises. Moreover, firms gather in trade associations that behave as semi-political or even political actors.[36] These trade associations have attracted a lot of recent research, which simultaneously underlines their importance and the variety of national structures. Germany has been unified for more than a century, with a division of labor between the Federation of German Industries and the Confederation of German Employers' Associations. Both try to maintain the autonomy of the enterprise sphere and circumscribe government intervention· although the rules finally are enforced.[37] France has been characterized since 1944 by a recurring tension between a general employers' association and one or two associations of small and medium-size employers.[38]

As previous chapters by Buğra and Fabbe et al. have shown, Turkey has experienced fragmentations of another type. Like other nations, for a long time it has had chambers of industry and commerce, but, contrary to practices elsewhere, major relations between government and business in Turkey long existed in an institutional void, without organized interest representation, a state of affairs that disappeared in 1971 with the birth of the big business association TÜSİAD, which was less dependent on the state than chambers, and more willing to criticize vocal government policy. Chapters 3 and 5 highlight that the rise of political Islam since the 1990s has brought about three alternative trade associations. In contrast with TÜSİAD, which they oppose, these associations positioned themselves within the constituency of political Islam and as political allies of the new governments. Indeed, the old elite large business enterprises were very different when compared to the new pious large business enterprises. This development could be compared to counterparts in Islamic developing countries such as Iran and Indonesia, and perhaps placed in a broader comparative perspective (including Central and Eastern Europe, or the role of the Chinese diaspora's minority entrepreneurs in non-Chinese nations).

Among government actors, some ministries or agencies may be captured by the industries that they are supervising and become their advocates or spokesmen.[39] This may be even true of state-owned enterprises, which quite often may influence their stakeholder, or in a handful of cases constitute a state within the state, like, in emerging countries, the national oil companies in Algeria, Venezuela or Indonesia, which periodically lead governments to reassert control over these SOEs.[40]

In the international arena, many multinationals are successful in enlisting the support of their home governments when competing for a foreign contract, bargaining to open a foreign regulated market like Japan (telecommunications), or expressing their views on an economic treaty. Beyond the voice of large corporations in the Business and Industry Advisory Committee to the OECD (BIAC), OECD's growing commitment to manage both the international and national economies and to cope with "socio-ecological challenges" have made it an important locus for reciprocal influences between governments and business—and Turkey has been a member of OECD since 1961.[41] A similar characterization applies to their relations with the institutions of continental market zones (EU, NAFTA, Mercosur). Economic diplomacy accordingly both develops and diversifies: "commercial diplomacy, trade diplomacy, finance diplomacy, and consular visa services in relation to increased immigration flows."[42] Yet there are limits or contradictions, and governments may have their own (political, military or environmental) agenda in this respect.

Do such elements of agency also exist in an economy dominated by a strong state? The case of the contemporary People's Republic of China is quite revealing, even though it lends itself to different interpretations. Recent research has shown that in socialist China under Mao's rule (1949–1976) adaptive networks emerged "beneath the veneer of China's formal socialist economy," and promoted "illicit entrepreneurship." Actors consisted of "innumerable entrepreneurs—from the farmer who bought and sold ration coupons to the engineer who worked part-time in an underground factory, to the state official who helped domestic smugglers circulate goods throughout the economy—[who] identified opportunities to profit from inefficiencies in the planned economy and, more generally, made things work." Their voluntary networks "subsumed the ordinary functions of markets (ex. coordination, information aggregation, risk sharing, lending) and enabled the productive assemblage of capital, labor, and knowledge in an otherwise stultifying system." In the short run, it can be argued that without these initiatives the Chinese socialist economy would have performed very badly, and they thus paved the way for subsequent structural reforms. In other words, the Chinese economy led the state, not the other way around."[43] Also, even within the formal socialist economy, shortages, failures, and learning may foster pockets of adaptation in socialist enterprises themselves.[44]

6.3 Drawing Upon Religions

Religions can supplement these elements of agency. In Turkey since 1991 this has taken a specific form in the quasi-partnership between the successive leading parties with Islamic orientation: the Welfare Party, followed by the AKP and a new segment of the business world sharing the same values.

As early as 1953 Alexander Gerschenkron stressed in a pioneering study the need to study "the significance for a country's economic development of popular evaluations of entrepreneurs and entrepreneurial activities; that is to say, of the general climate of opinion within which entrepreneurial action takes place." This study discusses religion (the Orthodox Catholic Church) during "the second half of the 19th century" as part of "the dominant system of values, which remained determined by the traditional agrarian pattern," and was "at variance" with entrepreneurship.[45]

It took only a few years after Gerschenkron to see a revival of Max Weber's analysis of the relationship between religion and capitalism, while Asian scholars began to ask similar questions. Anyway, scholars of various fields over the world have studied the new role of religion since the 1980s both "in economic transactions between market participants and in their dealings with the government."[46] However, Fabbe et al. in Chapter 5 have shown that for Turkey the use of Islam as a network and ideational resource "remained relatively constant" over the period. It is Islamic business actors who transformed themselves as they found ways to use new opportunities.

The role of religion when deeply influencing either leading employers or small entrepreneurs in their choices is therefore relevant in our approach to public-private mutual influences. Not only does it add a level of complexity to the understanding of their daily practices and decisions, it also informs or frames their own vision of morality or ethics in a number of domains: market transactions, to be sure, which may include their relations to suppliers and subcontractors, human resource management, welfare. Moreover, it reinforces the possibility of autonomy of some businesspeople when in dialogue with public administration or government.

A recent issue of the French business history journal *Entreprises et Histoire* devoted to businesses and religion included two relevant articles. One, by a Chinese sociologist, begged to differ with most scholarship arguing that "contemporary Chinese cities are secular, national, and capitalist projects," and introduced an alternative—and provocative—view by presenting an "ethnography on the development of religious communities in manufacturing plants" of Shanghai "started by capital-linked immigrant entrepreneurs since the 1990s." These Buddhist practices in the workplace, relayed by a charity foundation, promote a model of "benevolent enterprise," bent on "sustainable development." They might be taken into account as "a new way of understanding the changes of morality in modern China."[47] The other article, by two management scholars, dealt with a minority of religious businessmen in Madagascar: Adventist entrepreneurs. A study involving 40 entrepreneurs of the Adventist sect was carried out to analyze the influence of religion on their behavior in business. It highlights that the foundations of this religion promote entrepreneurship, the involvement in the activities of the Adventist church builds a network, and the emphasis on the control of company resources is responsible for the low level of debt. Yet it qualifies the homogeneity of this group, as "the intention and motivation to undertake such efforts are not always the same."[48]

There are other examples. The first is the influence of Catholicism on entrepreneurs. The very oldest national federations of Catholic employers were those formed in Western Europe countries, such as the Netherlands in 1915, Belgium in 1921, and France in 1926. In 1931 an international federation of such associations was created in Europe. Later called UNIAPAC, and having become an ecumenical organization, it "gathers today Christian business leaders associations in 38 countries in Europe, Latin America, Africa and Asia." It "represents more than 30,000 very active business executives around the world, working in various leading sectors of the world economy." This number is not large, nor does it even represent the totality of Christian economic elites in its member countries, but it is enough to create a significant minority in the world of organized business leaders. It pledges "to promote amongst business leaders the vision and implementation of an economy serving the human person and the Common Good of humanity at large."[49]

This Catholic association is significant for our purpose in two ways. In most of its member countries it has had an impact on the deepening of businesspeople's reflections on business ethics. Its French branch has taken public-private relations as one of its favorite topics: it led the organization to stage an unprecedented and powerful campaign against corruption in the early 1990s.[50] Yet its position towards the role of government oscillated over the postwar years between gradual acceptance of economic planning and today the largest possible independence from government intervention.

Another example of the influence of religion can be found in contemporary Japanese company Kyocera, one of the most striking examples of independence from the state. In recent decades Kyocera has been one of the most profitable and innovative companies in Japan. The company's motto is "Respect the Divine and Love People." The company's founder and longtime CEO, Kazuo Inamori, was a strong believer in Buddhism, and in the application of its ethical principles to management; as "a natural conclusion," he himself was ordained a Buddhist monk in 1997. He has expressed his views in several books, which by 2018 had reached 15 million copies, as well as in oral history interviews. He has advocated a set of principles:

> recognizing your deepest desires and using them to create a better reality, informing all decisions with simple truths and principles, elevating your mind and practicing humility, living your life steered by an attitude of selfless service, [and] controlling the trajectory of your life by accepting the "will of the universe."[51]

There are comparisons to make between Kazuo Inamori's contemporary precepts and the views of Eiichi Shibusawa, whose pioneering role in Meiji Japan is discussed in Chapter 1. One of the leading early Japanese businessmen, both banker and industrialist, he reconsidered Confucian values and campaigned for the primacy of the private sector in Japanese economy and society while espousing a doctrine of inseparability of morality and economy, based on his belief that in business public interest and private profit are "absolutely compatible."[52] According to a thorough comparative essay, "there has been a move towards reassessing" Shibusawa's "doctrine in Japan since the global economic crisis in 2008. It has increasingly been attracting attention overseas too. This trend has been prompted by a sense of mistrust towards global capitalism and market economics, driven by the increasingly excessive pursuit of private profit, and a mounting sense of crisis."[53]

Both Inamori and Shibusawa share the view that "when engaging in activities in pursuit of private profit, companies should intentionally set out to pursue public interest, and should adopt the position 'public interest first, private profit second.'"[54] Inamori's philosophy of management—advocating that "the primary mission" of a company "is to maximize total profits" while simultaneously targeting beneficence and justice—is perhaps more altruistic, aiming to "contribute to the advancement of society and humankind." On the other side, Shibusawa in the beginning "firmly believed that it was quite enough to rely on Confucian teachings without depending on religion" and thought critically that "Religion only comes to life when applied to the political and business worlds," thus putting greater emphasis on norms of morality "for the real world, including business." In other words, neither business leader equates public interest with politics, although at a "lower" level both embrace the notion of "politics for the benefit of the private sector," and can suggest policies "necessary for the self-reliance and independence of the private sector."[55]

From this brief survey of Catholicism, Confucianism and Buddhism in business, it appears that the development of the values of Islamic religion in Turkey, both in business and politics, at the local and central levels is very different. To be sure, as Fabbe et al. have shown in Chapter 5, as elsewhere it bears the mark of the new era of globalization, which modified institutions and regulations, increased the participation of late industrializing countries in the world economy, brought about the relocation of production to less-developed areas, and "the reform of the existing state structure" came "to the agenda." In Turkey, however, the end of the "protectionist economic system, where business development relied heavily on state intervention," coincided with "the rise of Islamic politics." Here a global trend, not limited to emerging countries, which made religion "a fundamental source of political tension as well as an important element of economic and social solidarity among different groups and a rationale for philanthropic activities," took specific forms. In the turmoil that followed both the defeat of the secularist republican regime, "the transition from national developmentalism to economic liberalism in an open economy" and the setting of "increased economic prerogatives of the local branches of the central government and the municipalities," Islam was turned into not only a network resource, but an actual cornerstone for an alliance between the new ruling party's governments and the pious business sector. As a result, the independent regulatory agencies created in 2002 to avoid discretionary political intervention lost influence after a few years. The affirmation of religious identity stabilized new economic and political networks, while largely excluding the previously dominant secular business elite.[56] A parallel might be established between the French Catholic employers' campaign of the early 1990s against corruption and MÜSİAD's campaign against corruption in Turkey in 2000, but the latter largely failed.[57]

Finally, it may be argued that some of the modern views on corporate social responsibility or on sustainable development find some of their roots in religion as interpreted by business or management. This certainly needs to be approached with much caution. For instance, the view of Buddhism as a naturally "green" or "eco-friendly" religion that prevailed in the 1990s, and led to the hypothesis of an alliance between Buddhism and radical ecology, has been abandoned. It underestimated the different traditions and practices within Buddhism and, symmetrically, the diversity of environmental concerns and of their advocates. Yet it appears on the whole that Buddhism is "in certain respects amenable to environmental concerns."[58] For instance, in Thailand during the 2010s some Buddhist entrepreneurs greened their agricultural businesses in line with a government program. Moreover, the preoccupation with climate change led to new forms of Buddhist practice from below—about trees, work and re-inhabitation: projects which attempted to meet "the moral challenge of climate change." Such activities may become sources of inspiration for pioneering Buddhist entrepreneurs, provided they "evolve towards greater efficacy."[59]

In France, it can easily be argued that several of the large businesses that changed their strategies and began to move ahead in terms of greener products and/or of corporate social responsibility, like Danone in food, Lafarge in cement and concrete or Michelin in tires, were led by openly Catholic entrepreneurs. The association of Christian entrepreneurs mentioned earlier formed in 2011 a working group on sustainable development and social and environmental responsibility; in 2015 they issued a joint statement with UNIAPAC against climate change. It is therefore not surprising to find them among the signatories of the "Business Proposals in view of a 2015 international climate change agreement at COP 21 in Paris" alongside much larger secular French and international business organizations, the latter being the Global Compact, the World Business for Climate and Sustainable Development (WBCSD), Business Europe.[60] In parallel, the most vocal ministers of Environment in French governments since 1970 belonged to the Catholic tradition and maintained good relations with like-minded business leaders, while being also influenced by experiments led by a few smaller businesses.

As for Islam, it "has a rich tradition of highlighting the importance of environmental protection and conservation of natural resources."[61] The same caveats as for other religions should be taken into consideration when looking at the policies of the majority of Islamic entrepreneurs or political parties.

On these environmental matters, our general argument needs to be qualified. Here also firms are divided. They move towards greening business under pressure from NGOs, often relying on religious sources, and from scientists.[62] Meanwhile, government intervention develops nationally and internationally under the same pressure. But up to now it is often characterized by inconsistency and frequently shifting policies.

6.4 Concluding Remarks

Studying the transformations of public-private relationships worldwide, of which the waves of privatizations since the 1980s are the most obvious part, has now become familiar to historians, political scientists, and economists. Some of this research has shown the changing importance of these two sectors, or of their power relations. Others have stressed their porosity or complementarity, as I have argued in *Ethical Capitalism*.[63] By 2003 business historian Matthias Kipping believed that, in industrialized countries, "the borderline between the public and private spheres is largely imaginary and artificial" and that "neither governments nor businesses can be seen as unitary and/or all-powerful actors."[64] This is not enough. This chapter has made the case for another point: the continuous existence of reciprocal influences. The work of American political scientist Gerald Berk is relevant here. It contains powerful suggestions to "trace the mutual constitution of state and enterprise" and to turn "our attention on the relational *processes* that mediate state and enterprise—because it is in those processes that the nature of meaning of both entities are forged."[65]

The chapter also highlights that such a reciprocity in business-government relations is partly framed by the divisions on each side. Contrary to its own claims and to a number of current assessments, the state itself is not a homogeneous strategist and regulator. In several countries conflicts over financial resources and policies are frequent between the Ministry of Commerce and Industry and the Ministry of Finance.[66] The Ministry of Foreign Affairs is not simply the synthesizer in the global arena of other ministries and of trade associations or large firms. It may have its own views. This is even truer of specialized ministries. The Ministry of Railways and Transportation in Mao's Communist China fulfilled its agenda to restore, maintain and expand its bureaucratic, technological and economic system in the context of shifting political and economic priorities. Its most recent historian argues that it thus "provided a blueprint for the past forty years of ambitious, semipublic business development."[67] The Ministry of Defense usually fights for its expenses and for its vision of the world. When all is said and done, the state is either waging internal battles or making compromises internally or with Parliament (when the latter is able to play a role). Countries where Islam is the predominant religion are not so different. In Turkey and Iran, power may shift within the state, although successive governments adhere to similar religious and political orientations.[68]

On the other side, we have seen the divisions between companies that are economically or financially dependent on government, those which are more autonomous, and foreign multinationals. These three categories try to influence government for their own purposes or to weaken their opponents in government.

On the whole, the usual statements by social scientists about developmental states, such as "a strong nodal organization" within government "leads to a growth-oriented alliance between state and capital,"[69] only describe results. These statements do not explain the interplay between these two sets of influencers nor the exclusion or defeat of some of the actors.

Still, the evolution of the balance of power in these influences remains a major issue. How does it account for Turkey's evolution in comparative perspective?

First, the role of foreign capital and multinationals in the Turkish economy has remained modest. In descending order, Ford, Toyota, Renault, Hyundai, Daimler, Unilever, Bosch, Philip Morris, and Coca-Cola are the key industrial foreign players today—a ranking which illustrates the major role of automobile multinationals in Turkey.[70] But, as suggested in Chapter 1 in this volume, if these multinationals may be more influential than they were in India before 1991 or in most branches of the Iranian economy today, their influence is still limited. Therefore, the question is to what extent the model of firm-level innovation that had been previously "strongly influenced by capabilities built up in a relatively closed environment" will be replaced by a model of innovative firms "in interaction with international business," according to the pattern for emerging market economies that Edmund Amann and John Cantwell et al. have outlined for Asia and Latin America.[71]

Second, there has been a change in the place of state-owned enterprises in the post-1980 economy. As in other countries, privatizations began in Turkey during the 1980s, in particular for companies manufacturing consumer goods, and they expanded in the 2000s (mining, energy, tourism, health, public land) after the AKP came to power. These privatizations were, like everywhere, desired by part of the private sector, and also by portion of the public managers themselves. But the result of our comparative approach is striking. On one side, the combination of the political situation and the limited penetration of foreign capital allows us to think that these privatizations amount to a recasting of state power by a combination of various means, not to its weakening. On the other, the difference with another major developmental state such as China is twofold. China has been much more open to foreign capital than Turkey, and the remaining SOEs in Turkey do not play the same major role as in China. Also, it has been argued that for quite a while "the high levels of foreign investment in China arose, in part, from the failure of the Chinese state to allocate domestic savings efficiently" as it distributed "broad economic resources to the least efficient firms—state-owned enterprises—while denying them to China's most efficient firms, that is, private firms."[72]

Yet our comparative approach confirms that these reciprocal influences are asymmetrical both before and after 1980. Before 1980, as highlighted in Chapters 2, 3 and 5, the state prevailed for lack of a sufficiently broad business community and because of the interest of the established big business in international economic relations. After 1980, political action relying on the Islamic religion has shaped "the configuration of the business community" itself, and informed "the emergence of rival models of capitalist development and political change" among groups of entrepreneurs:[73] firms that aligned their strategy with the government; firms that display their agency in relation to the state, especially due to trade associations; and a role of religion that is used by particular firms.

At the same time another model is emerging outside reciprocal influences between business and national government: the global compact launched by the United Nations in 2000. It is a "call to companies to align strategies and operations with universal principles on human rights, labor, environment and anti-corruption, and take actions that advance societal goals"—in other words, "a voluntary initiative based on CEO commitments to implement universal sustainability principles and to take steps to support UN goals." It has been acknowledged by UN member states and is thus gaining government recognition. In Turkey it has won the support of 222 large enterprises, out of 8,000 worldwide.[74] A number of scholars, after initially thinking that such a practice was useless, now consider that such micro-devices may be a significant step to meet "pressing people and planet challenges."[75]

Notes

1. C. Johnson, "The Developmental State: The Odyssey of a Concept," in M. Woo-Cummings (ed.), *The Developmental State*, Ithaca: Cornell University Press, 1999, pp. 32–60.
2. T.K. McCraw, *America Versus Japan: A Comparative Study of Business-Government Relations Conducted at the Harvard Business School*, Boston: Harvard Business School Press, 1986.
3. D. Mehri, *Iran Auto: Building a Global Industry in an Islamic State*, Cambridge: Cambridge University Press, 2017, pp. 4–5.
4. For a standard summary, J.-P. Dormois, *The French Economy in the Twentieth Century*, Cambridge: Cambridge University Press, 2004, pp. 43–62. Not every historian agrees with such views today.
5. M. Lévy-Leboyer, P. Fridenson, and V. Rostas, *Thomson's First Century*, Jouy-en-Josas: Campus Thomson, 1995, pp. 98, 125.
6. Interview with Murat Vargı, by Felix Oberholzer-Gee, September 17, 2014, Creating Emerging Markets Project, Baker Library Historical Collections, *Harvard Business School*, www.hbs.edu/creating-emerging-markets
7. E. Monnet, *Controlling Credit: Central Banking and the Planned Economy in Postwar France, 1948–1973*, Cambridge: Cambridge University Press, 2018.
8. Mehri, *Iran Auto*, p. 11.
9. Ibid., pp. 4–5.
10. Ibid., p. 11.
11. S. Maxfield and B.R. Schneider (eds.), *Business and the State in Developing Countries*, Ithaca: Cornell University Press, 1997, divided these countries in two categories: strong States and weak ones. Their chapter on Turkey is in the second category. Things have certainly changed since 1997.
12. A. Buğra and O. Savaskan, *New Capitalism in Turkey: The Relationship Between Politics, Religion and Business*, Cheltenham, UK: Edward Elgar Publishers, 2014, p. 170.
13. R. Murphey, *The Outsiders: The Western Experience in India and China*, Ann Arbor: University of Michigan Press, 1977.
14. On Honda, see H. Oshima (ed.), *Top Talks. Honda's Origin*, Tokyo: Honda Motor, 2006. J. Rothfeder, *Driving Honda: Inside the World's Most Innovative Car Company*, New York: Random House, 2014. "Launching the S360 and T360 1962 Paving the Way for Auto Production," http://world.honda.com/history/challenge/1962autoproduction/page06.html. On Kyocera, see the two unpublished oral history interviews of Kazuo Inamori by Professor Takeshi Abe, Seiji Okada and Ryuta Nanao, November 22, 2001 and January 21, 2002 (my thanks to the Museum of Entrepreneurs in Osaka for sharing them with me); R.W. Adler and T. Hiromoto, "Amoeba Management: Lessons From Japan's Kyocera," *Sloan Management Review*, v.54, n. 1, Fall 2012, pp. 83–89.
15. Interview with Suresh Krishna, by Tarun Khanna, Chennai, India, December 19, 2012, Creating Emerging Markets Project, Baker Library Historical Collections, *Harvard Business School*, www.hbs.edu/creating-emerging-markets. Cited in G. Jones and R. Comunale, "Business, Governments and Political Risk in South Asia and Latin America Since 1970," *Australian Economic History Review*, v.58, n. 3, 2018, p. 257.

16. "Les quarante ans d'Oyak-Renault," *Renault Histoire*, special issue, July 2009.
17. C. Midler, B. Jullien, and Y. Lung, *Rethinking Innovation and Design for Emerging Markets: Inside the Renault Kwid Project*, Boca Raton, FL: CRC Press, 2017.
18. M. Mason, *American Multinationals and Japan. The Political Economy of Japanese Capital Controls, 1899–1980*, Cambridge, MA: Harvard University Press, 1992, p. 249.
19. Robert Whiting, *Tokyo Underworld: The Fast Times and Hard Life of an American Gangster in Japan*, New York: Pantheon Books, 1999.
20. This is taken from the summary provided by the American expert Brad Glosserman in *The Japan Times*, January 13, 1993. Mason, *American Multinationals*, pp. 166–170.
21. R. Abdelal, "The State," *Harvard Business School Industry and Background Note*, No. 9–701–077 (rev. May 24, 2001).
22. For the context, see M. Kipping, "Les relations gouvernement-monde des affaires dans la France de l'après-guerre: Adaptations et adaptabilité d'un système original," *Histoire, économie et société*, v.20, December 2001, pp. 577–596.
23. Y. Huang, *Capitalism with Chinese Characteristics. Entrepreneurship and the State*, Cambridge: Cambridge University Press, 2008. For this characterization of the State, see Abdelal, "The State."
24. J. Perry, C. Carey, and A.G. Carey, "Turkish Industry and the Five Year Plans," *Middle East Journal*, v.25, n. 3, Summer 1971, pp. 337–354. For Iran, see F. Bostock and G. Jones, *Planning and Power in Iran: Ebtehaj and Economic Development under the Shah*, London: Frank Cass, 1989, chapter 5.
25. Buğra and Savaskan, *New Capitalism*, pp. 35, 67.
26. Mehri, *Iran Auto*, p. 10. On MÜSIAD, see D. Yankaya, *La nouvelle bourgeoisie islamique: le modèle turc*, Paris: PUF, 2013.
27. Ibid.
28. G. Jones and P. Miskell, "European Integration and Corporate Restructuring: The Strategy of Unilever, 1957-c1990," *Economic History Review*, v.58, n. 1, February 2005, pp. 113–139.
29. A. Crane and D. Matten, "Engagement Required: The Changing Role of the Corporation in Society," in D. Barton, D. Horvath, and M. Kipping (eds.), *Re-imagining Capitalism*, Oxford: Oxford University Press, 2016, p. 120.
30. H. Sevim, "Les organisations patronales turques et l'Union Européenne: Ressources et modes d'action," in D. Fraboulet, C. Druelle-Korn, and P. Vernus (eds.), *Les organisations patronales et la sphère publique*, Rennes: Presses Universitaires de Rennes, 2013, pp. 307–318. Hélène Michel (ed.), *Représenter le patronat européen. Formes d'organisation patronale et modes d'action européenne*, Brussels: Peter Lang, 2013. BusinessEurope originated from two earlier, more informal networks: The Council of European Industrial Federations (CEIF) and the Council of the Directors of European Industrial Federations (CDEIF). On the shifting attitude of MÜSIAD to the European Union, Yankaya, *La nouvelle*, pp. 118–121.
31. G. Jones and R. Comunale, "Oral History and the Business History of Emerging Markets," *Enterprise & Society*, v.20, n. 1, March 2019, pp. 26–27.
32. G. Jones and A. Spadafora, "Creating Ecotourism in Costa Rica, 1970–2000," *Enterprise & Society*, v.18, n. 1, March 2017, pp. 146–183.
33. For a short survey see J.E. Stiglitz, "Asymmetries of Information and Economic Policy," Project Syndicate, 4 December 2001; idem, "Information and the Change in the Paradigm in Economics," *American Economic Review*, v.92, n. 3, 2002, pp. 460–501.

34. C. McKenna, *The World's Newest Profession: Management Consulting in the Twentieth Century*, Cambridge: Cambridge University Press, 2006; M. Kipping and T. Clark (eds.), *The Oxford Handbook of Management Consulting*, Oxford: Oxford University Press, 2012.
35. R.J. Bennett, *Local Business Voice: The History of Chambers of Commerce in Britain, Ireland and Revolutionary America, 1760-2011*, Oxford: Oxford University Press, 2011. The International Chamber of Commerce, created in 1919, has a different function and history, being specialized in international trade.
36. P. Eichenberger and A. Mach, "Organized Capital and Coordinated Market Economy: Swiss Business Interest Associations Between Socio-Economic Regulation and Political Influence," in C. Trampusch and A. Mach (eds.) *Switzerland in Europe: Continuity and Change in the Swiss Political Economy*, London: Routledge, 2011, pp. 63–81.
37. W. Bührer, *Der Bundesverband der deutschen Industrie, 1949–1999*, Paderborn: Schöningh, 2003; Idem, "Genèse et développement des syndicats patronaux en Allemagne (XIXe-début XXe siècle)," in D. Fraboulet and P. Vernus (eds.), *Genèse des organisations patronales en Europe*, Rennes: Presses Universitaires de Rennes, 2012, pp. 111–121. Idem, "Les organisations patronales et la régulation de la concurrence en République fédérale d'Allemagne (1945–1957)," in D. Fraboulet, M. Margairaz, and P. Vernus (eds.), *Réguler l'économie. L'apport des organisations patronales*, Rennes: Presses Universitaires de Rennes, 2016, pp. 129–139; Idem, "Syndicats patronaux, politique de communication et tournant néo-libéral en République fédérale d'Allemagne (RFA) (1970–1980)," in D. Fraboulet, C. Druelle-Korn, and P. Vernus (eds.), *Les organisations patronales et la sphère publique*, Rennes: Presses Universitaires de Rennes, 2013, pp. 77–88.
38. M. Offerlé, *Les patrons des patrons: Histoire du Medef*, Paris: Odile Jacob, 2013.
39. G.J. Stigler, "The Theory of Economic Regulation," *The Bell Journal of Economics and Management Science*, v.2, n. 1, Spring 1971, pp. 3–21. J.-J. Laffont and J. Tirole, "The Politics of Government Decision Making: A Theory of Regulatory Capture," *Quarterly Journal of Economics*, v. CVI, n. 4, 1991, pp. 1091–1127.
40. P. van der Eng, "Pertamina Crisis (1975–1976)," in Ooi Keat Gin (ed.) *Southeast Asia: A Historical Encyclopedia, from Angkor Wat to East Timor*, Santa Barbara: ABC-Clio, 2004, pp. 1064–1065. D. Felisini (ed.), *Reassessing the Role of Management in the Golden Age. An International Comparison of Public Sector Managers 1945–1975*, Cham: Palgrave Macmillan, 2017.
41. M. Leimgruber and M. Schmelzer (eds.), *The OECD and the International Political Economy Since 1948*, Cham: Palgrave Macmillan, 2017.
42. L. Badel, *Diplomatie et grands contrats: L'État français et les marchés extérieurs au XXe siècle*, Paris: Publications de la Sorbonne, 2010; D. Lee and B. Hocking, "Economic Diplomacy," in *Oxford Research Encyclopedia of International Studies*, Oxford: Oxford University Press, 2010, www.oxfordre.com/internationalstudies/view/10.1093/acrefore/9780190846626.001.0001/acrefore-9780190846626-e-384
43. A.K. Frost, "Illicit Entrepreneurship in Socialist China," Conference paper at the 2019 Business History Conference, Cartagena, March 2019.
44. P. Scranton, *Enterprise, Organization and Technology in China. A Socialist Experiment, 1950–1971*, Cham: Palgrave Macmillan, 2019.
45. A. Gerschenkron, "Social Attitudes, Entrepreneurship, and Economic Development," reprinted in W. Friedman and G. Jones (eds.), *Business History*, Northampton, MA: Edward Elgar, 2013, pp. 54–72.

46. Buğra-Savaskan, *New Capitalism*, pp. 14, 17.
47. W. Wuang, "The Blissful Enterprise: Buddhist Cultural Turns in the Workplace in Contemporary Shanghai," *Entreprises et Histoire*, n. 81, December 2015, pp. 73–91.
48. C. Ratsimbazafy and L. Ranaivoarisoa, "Entrepreneurs adventistes à madagascar," *Entreprises et Histoire*, n. 81, December 2015, pp. 92–110.
49. On MÜSIAD's views on ethics and morality, see also Yankaya, *La nouvelle*, pp. 165–196 and on finance pp. 197–203. M.E. Chessel, N. de Brémond d'Ars, and A. Grelon, *L'entreprise et l'Evangile. Une histoire des patrons chrétiens*, Paris: Presses de Sciences Po, 2018, pp. 79–83.
50. Ibid., pp. 254–263. On the relative acceptance of corruption among many members of French elites at the time, see P. Lascoumes and C. Nagels, *Sociologie des élites délinquantes: De la criminalité en col blanc à la corruption politique*, Paris: Armand Colin, 2014. See also Chapter 10 in this volume.
51. Unpublished oral history interviews of Kazuo Inamori, November 22, 2001 and January 21, 2002, quoted in note 13. K. Inamori, *A Passion for Success: Practical, Inspirational, and Spiritual Insight from Japan's Leading Entrepreneur*, 1995, Singapore: McGraw-Hill, 2007. Idem, *A Compass to Fulfillment: Passion and Spirituality in Life and Business*, Singapore: McGraw-Hill, 2009, pp. xxii–xxiv.
52. M. Shimada, *The Entrepreneur Who Built Modern Japan: Shibusawa Eiichi*, Tokyo: Japan Publishing Industry Foundation for Culture, 2017.
53. K. Tanaka, "Shibusawa Eiichi no Dotoku Keizai Goitsu-setsu kara Mita Philosophy to Amoeba Keiei—Koeki to Shici no Ryoritsu wo Megutte-" [Philosophy and Amoeba Management from the Point of View of Shibusawa Eiichi's Doctrine of Inseparability of Morality and Economy—Serving a Double Purpose: Public Interest and Private Profit-], in Amoeba Management Academic Community (ed.), *Amoeba Keiei no Shinka—Riron to Jissen-* [The Evolution of Amoeba Management: Theory and Practice], Tokyo: Chuo Keizai Sha, 2017.
54. Tanaka, typewritten English translation, 2017.
55. Shimada, pp. 101–102, 145 (the statement on religion dates back to January 17, 1928).
56. Y. Uyarci, "http://www.sudoc.abes.fr/xslt/DB=2.1/SET=1/TTL=1/CLK?IKT=1016&TRM=Les+dynamiques+des+PME+en+Turquie" Les dynamiques des PME en Turquie: structuration et développement régional étudiés à partir de la confédération TUSKON," PhD in Sociology, University of Strasbourg, 2014. See also Chapters 3 and 5.
57. See Chapters 5 and 10.
58. S.P. James and D.E. Cooper, "Buddhism and the Environment," *Contemporary Buddhism*, v.8, n. 2, 2007, pp. 93–96 (introduction to a special issue on this theme).
59. C.R. Strain, "Reinventing Buddhist Practices to Meet the Challenge of Climate Change," *Contemporary Buddhism*, v.17, n. 1, 2016, pp. 138–156.
60. Joint statement by the French Christian entrepreneurs and UNIAPAC, October 26, 2015, www.lesedc.org/wp-content/uploads/2015/10/cpcop21-engagements_edc_uniapac_26102015.pdf
61. F.M. Khalid, "Islam and the Environment," in P. Timmerman (ed.), *Encyclopedia of Global Environmental Change*, vol. 5: *Social and economic dimensions of global environmental change*, New York: Wiley, 2003, pp. 332–339.
62. G. Jones, *Profits and Sustainability: A History of Green Entrepreneurship*, Oxford: Oxford University Press, 2017. G. Jones, *Varieties of Green Business: Industries, Nations and Time*, Northampton, MA: Edward Elgar Publishers, 2018.

63. P. Fridenson, "Public-Private Connections and Boundaries: From Shibusawa Eiichi's Experience to a Global Historical Perspective," in P. Fridenson and T. Kikkawa (eds.), *Ethical Capitalism: Shibusawa Eiichi and Business Leadership in Global Perspective*, Toronto: University of Toronto Press, 2017, pp. 60, 64–66, 71.
64. M. Kipping, "Business-Government Relations: Beyond Performance Issues," in F. Amatori and G. Jones (eds.), *Business History Around the World*, Cambridge: Cambridge University Press, 2003, p. 391.
65. G. Berk, "The Magnetron and the State: Practicing Technological Rivalry in World War II," unpublished article, 2015; Idem, "State Building Through Mediation: The U.S. Anti-Submarine Warfare Operations Research Group in World War II," *Polity*, v.51, n. 3, July 2019, pp. 466–497.
66. S. Fukukawa, F. Amatori, and C. Molteni, "Industrial Policy and the Role of MITI in Japan," in Felisini (ed.), *Reassessing*, pp. 150–151.
67. E. Köll, *Railroads and the Transformation of China*, Cambridge, MA: Harvard University Press, 2019.
68. Mehri, *Iran Auto*, Chapters 1–3.
69. Ibid., p. 10.
70. From the ranking of the 500 largest industrial enterprises in Turkey for 2017 provided by the Istanbul Chamber of Commerce, www.iso500.org.tr/500-buyuk-sanayikurulusu/2017/
71. E. Amann and J. Cantwell, "Conclusions," in E. Amann and J. Cantwell (eds.), *Innovative Firms in Emerging Market Economies*, Oxford: Oxford University Press, 2012, pp. 355–371.
72. Y. Huang, *Selling China. Foreign Direct Investment During the Reform Era*, Cambridge: Cambridge University Press, 2003.
73. Quoted from chapter 5 in this volume.
74. Turkey UN Global Compact 2019, www.unglobalcompact.org/engage-locally/europe/turkey
75. J.G. Ruggie, "Foreword," in J.-P. Robé, A. Lyon-Caen, and S. Vernac (eds.) *Multinationals and the Constitutionalization of the World Power System*, Abingdon: Routledge, 2016, p. 11.

Part II

Corporate Actors and Public Interest

7 Governance and Social Responsibility in Large Turkish Firms

B. Burçin Yurtoğlu

Corporate governance and corporate social responsibility, phrases that two decades ago meant little outside academia, have become mainstream concerns around the globe. In the late 1990s, a wave of financial crises in Russia, East Asia, and Latin America demonstrated that the behavior of the corporate sector can affect entire economies and even endanger global financial stability. A couple of years later, corporate scandals at large European and US corporations suggested that such events are not unique to economies in the developing world. These developments are driven largely by the increasing globalization process and the rising importance of market-led allocation of capital. With corporations growing in size and scope, and the increase in the importance of financial intermediaries and institutional investors, the financing of investments has become more complex. Moreover, the increasing economic integration of the world's economies strengthens the competitive process and exposes companies to a much wider set of market risks. These developments necessitate a more sophisticated monitoring of the use of capital and enhance the need for good governance.

Corporate governance is often defined as the set of legal mechanisms that enable outside investors to protect themselves against expropriation by corporate insiders.[1] A broader perspective extends the definition to include both the determination of value added by firms and its allocation among all stakeholders that transact with the firm.[2] Under this definition, corporate governance would include the relationship between shareholders, creditors, and corporations; between financial markets, institutions, and corporations; and between employees and corporations. Corporate governance would also encompass the issue of corporate social responsibility, including such aspects as the dealings of the firm with respect to culture and the environment. Consistent with this definition of corporate governance, the last decade has also witnessed a growing emphasis on issues related to corporate social responsibility (CSR). Since the early 2000s, companies have increasingly integrated environmental, social, and governance (ESG) aspects into their market and non-market strategies, reflecting the high priority they attach to CSR activities.

Most research on corporate governance focuses on conflicts of interest between owners and managers. Under a dispersed ownership structure, managers can pursue goals that do not necessarily coincide with those of the shareholders. A potential correction is to introduce a less dispersed share ownership structure. Shareholders with a large stake in the company have greater incentives to monitor and discipline the managers because the former can internalize the benefits from their monitoring effort in proportion to the size of their ownership stakes. This type of agency problem is prevalent in countries with a legal system based on common law, where the corporate governance system is characterized by a large number of listed companies with dispersed ownership, a liquid capital market facilitating the frequent trade of ownership and control rights, and very few inter-corporate shareholdings.

In most countries with an alternative legal system, share ownership is much more concentrated. Most companies remain private, and even when they are listed on stock exchanges, a single large shareholder or a small group of shareholders retains a controlling share in the company. Since concentrated ownership structure makes companies impervious to takeovers, the controlling stake commonly remains with the founder of the company and his descendants, even when the company is large and publicly listed. The controlling shareholder generally takes an active interest in running the company by appointing the management or directly taking executive positions. In such circumstances a different type of agency problem arises: between the controlling shareholder and the minority shareholders. Conflicts can materialize, for instance, as rent extraction in the form of diversion of company earnings or assets to the controlling shareholder. Such systems are often characterized by (1) few listed companies, (2) a high concentration of ownership, and (3) large inter-corporate shareholdings. Outside investors, while able and encouraged to participate in equity returns through the stock market, are not able to exert much control.

This chapter describes the Turkish case and examines the extant research on governance and corporate social responsibility practices. Another objective of the chapter is to link these practices to the behavior and performance of Turkish companies. The characteristics of the Turkish corporate governance system can be summarized as follows: First, few Turkish companies are traded. Even though the number of traded companies increased from 80 in 1986 to 405 by the end of 2016, the market capitalization fluctuated around 25% of the GDP over the last decade, which is quite low even in comparison to other emerging markets and developing economies.[3] Second, Turkish traded companies exhibit highly concentrated and centralized ownership structures. Families, directly or indirectly, own more than 75% of all listed companies and keep the majority control. They achieve the separation of ownership from control through pyramidal or more complex ownership structures within business groups. Third, an active market for corporate control does not exist given the limited openness and concentrated ownership of the typical listed company. There are also no signs that a market for large stakes operates in a way that disciplines poor performance. Critically related to these factors is that the Turkish economy is dominated, as shown by earlier chapters, by a strong presence of diversified family-controlled business groups and the important role of founding families in defining business group strategies.

Section 7.1 summarizes the macroeconomic background and the institutional framework surrounding corporate governance in Turkey from the 1930s to the late 2010s. Section 7.2 turns to firm-level corporate governance practices and their effects. Section 7.3 provides a background and a summary of the CSR practices. Section 7.4 discusses the implications of these findings and offers some concluding remarks.

7.1 The Context of Turkish Corporate Governance

The nature of corporate governance challenges is determined in a general way by countries' overall development and institutional environment. This section therefore provides a brief overview of Turkey's macroeconomic background and its financial environment as well as key aspects of its institutional environments, including the ease of contracting and the degree of legal and judicial efficiency. The measures and their relations with good corporate governance are discussed in more detail in the next sections.

Table 7.1 presents basic background data on the institutional and structural characteristics of the Turkish economy, using 13 contextual indicators between the 1930s and 2017.

The main contours of the economic history of the Republic of Turkey have been outlined in earlier chapters. After a long era of protectionism between the late 1950s and 1970s Turkey began to gradually open up to global competition, deregulated the domestic markets, and reduced the role of the state. However, this was accompanied by severe political instability.

A more comprehensive liberalization program and fundamental changes in market institutions were not fully undertaken until after the far-reaching financial crisis that Turkey experienced in 2001 and the advent of the new single party government the year after. The year 2001 also marks the starting point of a series of reforms that have changed the institutional framework of the Turkish economy in several ways.

Fueled by the requirements to comply with the EU integration process, the most significant component of these reforms was the change in the legal and regulatory framework of the financial sector. A series of newly established institutions and new laws laid a strong foundation for the emergence of a robust banking industry overseen by an

Table 7.1 Overview of the Macroeconomic and Institutional Environment in Turkey

	1930–1940	*1941–1950*	*1951–1960*	*1961–1970*	*1971–1980*	*1981–1990*	*1991–2000*	*2001–2010*	*2011–2017*
Macroeconomic Environment									
Population	16	19.2	24.6	31.8	41.3	49.7	59.3	68.6	77.0
GDP	19.54	22.03	34.57	58.76	108.45	149.15	228.1	328.92	402.11
GDP Growth	5.01	0.52	6.38	5.41	3.58	5.27	3.73	3.99	6.60
Inflation	-2.1	13.78	9.94	4.05	41.94	46.29	76.7	18.99	8.32
Product Market									
Trade	15.67	10.19	11.34	9.92	14.34	31.1	40.9	49.13	50.99
FDI (% of GDP)	~0	~0	~0	~0	0.099	0.238	0.424	1.738	1.609
Privatization	~0	~0	~0	~0	~0	0.52	4.21	34.31	26.33
Capital Market									
MC	0	0	0	0	0	6.75	19.87	28.92	24.63
Interest rate	5.5	4	3.85	7.36	6.48	44.31	72.57	30.76	15.41
Domestic Credit	na	na	9.06	16.29	17.77	18.2	18.84	25.25	61.34
Contracting Environment									
Legal System & Property Rights Index	na	na	na	na	4.2	5.3	4.9	5.8	5.0
Regulation of Credit, Labor, and Business Index	na	na	na	na	4.5	4.8	5.6	5.7	6.5
Economic Freedom Index	na	na	na	na	3.9	4.5	5.4	6.3	6.9

Sources: All data starting from 1960 are from the World Development Indicators, 2012, The World Bank. The data covering the 1930s to 1960 come from "Statistical Indicators 1923–2010" published by the Turkish Statistical Institute (2011). The three indicators of the *Contracting Environment* are measured on a scale of 0 to 10 with higher values indicating a freer environment. These indices are compiled from data provided by *The Fraser Institute*. *Legal System & Property Rights Index*: the key ingredients of this variable are rule of law, security of property rights, an independent judiciary, and an impartial court system. *Regulation of Credit, Labor, and Business Index*: an index of regulatory restraints in credit, labor, and product markets. *Economic Freedom Index* is based on forty-two data items and measures the degree of economic freedom in five broad areas (Size of Government, Legal Structure and Security of Property Rights, Access to Sound Money, Freedom to Trade Internationally, and Regulation of Credit, Labor, and Business). 2015 is the most recent year of data from the Fraser Institute so that 2011–2017 values reflect averages from 2011–2015.

Note: All variables represent the average values by decade, except when indicated. *Population*: Population, total; *GDP*: GDP (constant 2000 US$ Bn.), *GDP Growth*: GDP growth (annual %); *Inflation*: Inflation in consumer prices (annual %); *Trade*: The sum of exports and imports of goods and services (% of GDP); *FDI*: Foreign direct investment (net inflows of investment to acquire a lasting management interest in a domestic enterprise (current US$ Bn.); *Privatization*: Total revenues generated from privatized entities (current US$ Bn.); *MC*: Market capitalization of listed companies (% of GDP); *Interest rate*: Deposit interest rate paid by commercial banks for demand, time, or savings deposits (%); *Domestic Credit*: Domestic credit to private sector (% of GDP).

independent central bank. For the non-banking sector, the Foreign Direct Investments Law, which was enacted in 2003, removed all restrictions on foreign direct investment (FDI). Accordingly, measures of openness to trade have improved substantially, from around 30% of GDP in the 1980s to over 50% in the late 2010s. Corporate Governance guidelines were issued in the same year, and the accounting and auditing standards were improved by conforming to International Financial Reporting Standards (IFRS) starting in 2005. These measures reduced the opacity in the corporate sector and facilitated financial development and stability, thereby improving firms' access to finance. The market capitalization of domestic firms increased from an average of about 7% of the GDP in the 1980s to around 25% in the last decade. Domestic credit to the private sector increased from 18% in the 1980s to 25% in the 2000s, and to much higher levels in the last decade. Adoption of EU competition policies and rules on the protection of intellectual and industrial property rights along with the establishment of a Competition Authority further strengthened the competitiveness of the corporate sector. Furthermore, IMF induced stabilization reforms that resulted in fiscal discipline, and inflation dropped to single digits for the first time in 40 years. The reforms accelerated the transition to a free-market regime through policies of privatization and deregulation in major industries, such as energy and telecommunications.

With the IMF conditionality and the EU as an anchor of the institutionalization process, the government, which had been a major actor in the Turkish economy as the main resource allocator and creator of both opportunities and uncertainties for decades, started to assume its important new major role in the economy as the "regulator of markets."[4] The decade following these developments witnessed a significant reduction in uncertainty surrounding the investment climate, and lower transaction costs of doing business in Turkey. At the same time, entry barriers that had inhibited foreign firms from competing in domestic markets were removed, exposing the Turkish corporate sector to intensified foreign competition. As a result, these macroeconomic and institutional changes have been accompanied by significant investment opportunities and increased competition in the Turkish business environment.

Table 7.2 presents salient institutional elements that matter for corporate governance, compares Turkey to the group of developed countries, emerging markets and transitional countries. Crucial for corporate governance and financial markets development in general are properly functioning legal and judicial systems. This involves a number of dimensions: the general definition and legal protection of property rights; the formal definition and protection of creditor and shareholder rights, specifically; the enforcement of legal rights in the judicial system; the lack of corruption in general; and the overall disclosure regime and the transparency of matters specifically related to corporate governance. Many of these

Table 7.2 Governance Indicators

	Legal Rights Strength	*Creditor Rights*	*Legal Protection of Minority Shareholders*	*Case A Efficiency*	*Anti Corruption*	*Disclosure Requirements*	*Corporate Governance Opacity*
Turkey	4.0	2	43	6.6	–18.0	50	11
Developed Countries	6.7	2.0	46.9	80.0	173.1	60.7	13.1
Emerging Markets	5.5	2.0	47.3	47.1	–11.0	58.9	9.5
Transition Countries	6.8	2.0	35.4	42.7	–13.8	-	8.0

Sources: Strength of legal rights index: World Development Indicators, 2000–2010; Creditor rights: Djankov et al., 2007; Anti-self-dealing index and Disclosure requirements index: La Porta et al., 2006; Case A Efficiency: Djankov et al., 2006; Average corruption score: Worldwide Governance Indicators; Corporate governance opacity: Laeven et al., 2008.

Note: Table compares Turkey with developed countries, emerging markets, and transitional countries based on the following country-level governance indicators: Strength of legal rights index (0=weak, 10=strong); Creditor rights aggregate score (0=weak, 4=strong,); Anti-self-dealing index (0=weak, 100=strong); Case A Efficiency (0=weak, 100=strong); Average corruption score (higher numbers indicate "less corrupt"); Disclosure requirements index (0=weak, 100=strong), and Corporate governance opacity (higher numbers mean "less opacity").

aspects are of a qualitative nature and consequently not easily captured and codified. The comparisons nevertheless show some clear differences between countries.[5]

The starting point for understanding the corporate governance institutions of a country is often the origin of its legal system: Common Law (British) or Civil Law (French or German). A smaller category is the Scandinavian legal system. Legal foundations include clearly defined and enforced property rights and other key rules (e.g., disclosure, accounting, regulation, and supervision). In terms of the overall strength of (formal) property rights protection, the Common Law system is generally considered to be stronger than the Civil Law system. As a result of past colonization, emerging markets do not differ much from advanced countries in this area. Transitional economies differ in that they all have a Civil Law origin. Turkey, with its Civil Law (French) background, does not score particularly well in terms of the various elements reflected in the following indicators.

The strength of countries' formal legal rights is often captured using an index based on various features of the countries' legal system (column 1). This index shows little difference between the averages for advanced countries versus transitional economies, but emerging markets tend to have less strongly defined rights. The formal definition of property rights is particularly weak in Turkey, consistent with its French legal system background.

The specific property rights of creditors and shareholders in Turkey (columns 2 and 3) are on average equally strong as the average of advanced countries and emerging and transition economies. However, the legal protection of shareholder rights is less strongly defined in Turkey than in both developed countries and emerging markets.

What matters at least as much as the formal definition of property rights is the degree of enforcement of these rights. This aspect, while hard to codify, is captured to some extent in the efficiency of enforcement index (column 4) and the lack of corruption index (column 5). These indices show differences much larger than the formal rights between advanced countries on one hand and emerging markets and transitional economies on the other. The efficiency of enforcement in Turkey is below the averages for all three groups of countries, substantially lower than the average of emerging markets. There is a considerably higher incidence of corruption in Turkey compared to developed countries.

Next is an index of the degrees to which corporations listed on local stock exchanges have to disclose relevant financial and other information (column 6). Differences between advanced countries and emerging markets are not large on average (these data do not cover the transition economies). There is also much variation buried in the average figure for emerging markets. Some emerging markets countries like Malaysia, Thailand and South Africa, impose disclosure requirements on their stock exchanges that equal or exceed those of most advanced countries. Others, such as Brazil, Ecuador, Uruguay, and Venezuela, though, have disclosure requirements that are very weak. Turkey scores below the average value observed for emerging markets.

The last comparison is a de facto quality of corporate governance index, based on actual corporations' behavior (column 7). It reflects how accounting statements are being provided, how earnings are being smoothed, and how stock prices behave and reflect information about the firm. It shows Turkey to score below the developed countries as a group and somewhat above the group of emerging markets and transition economies.

The role of legal foundations and other governance institutions for financial and general development is well understood and documented.[6] Legal foundations matter crucially for a variety of factors that lead to higher growth, including financial market development, external financing, and the quality of investment. A strong legal and judicial system is also important for assuring that the benefits of economic development are shared by many actors in the economy.[7] This evidence has been overwhelmingly cross-national. A rapidly expanding literature has shown that corporate governance institutions can also affect company performance *within* a country.[8] Gompers et al. (2003) constructed an index of the strength of shareholder rights and showed that shareholders of companies in the highest decile of shareholder rights earned significantly higher returns on their shares than did shareholders of companies with weak shareholder rights. Among the institutional elements that were measured in this index are provisions in state laws governing corporate governance, and provisions in corporate charters governing things like the existence of golden parachutes and poison pills, voting rules, compensation plans and the like. Thus, the Gompers *et al.* results pointed to some firm-specific corporate governance institutions that affect company performance and could affect firms' ability to raise capital in the equity market.

One way to combine country- and company-specific governance characteristics is to think about country characteristics, such as legal protections for minority investors, and the level of economic and financial development, as factors that influence firms' costs and benefits in implementing measures to improve their own governance and transparency.[9]

7.2 Firm-Level Corporate Governance

This section turns to firm-level governance characteristics and practices of Turkish listed firms. As the prior section suggests, historically, Turkish legal rules and institutions have been weak. From a firm-level perspective, such weaknesses change the costs and benefits in adopting governance mechanisms. They also offer firms flexibility to choose governance arrangements beyond the minimum required by law and regulation. The next subsection provides a background for firm-level differences in governance practices and an overview of the literature that documented such differences for Turkish listed firms. The last subsection assesses the evidence on the effects of firm-level governance practices.

Access to finance has been a persistently important constraint on growth at the macroeconomic level, and for many Turkish firms since the inception of the Turkish Republic.[10] While growth could be financed with moderate reliance on foreign funding until the end of 1960s, reliance on foreign assistance gained increasing importance starting from early 1970s. Foreign investment, both in form of direct and portfolio investment, is extremely important; foreign investors own around 63% of the market capitalization of the Turkey stock market, Borsa Istanbul.[11] Better governance can help firms to meet their capital needs at lower cost by making them attractive to investors. Moreover, good firm-level governance complements the traditional functions of various legal institutions, builds and maintains public confidence in the corporate and financial sector, and ultimately contributes to its integrity and credibility.

Corporate governance initially became a concern in Turkey for banks, in the aftermath of the banking crisis of 2000, in which banks suffered large losses on loans to related parties.[12] In the aftermath of this crisis period, the greater macroeconomic stability underpinned by public governance reforms encouraged corporate governance reforms in Turkey.[13] The Turkish securities regulator, the Capital Markets Board of Turkey (CMBT), initially followed a "soft law" approach, issuing Corporate Governance Guidelines largely following the OECD's corporate governance guidelines. As of 2004, listed companies are mandated to include a CG compliance statement in their annual reports. Moreover, financial reporting based on IFRS became mandatory in 2005. These changes pushed Turkish listed companies towards more disclosure and improved their transparency. At the same time, they highlighted common corporate governance issues in Turkey. A concurrent restructuring process in the banking sector with a new legal and regulatory framework for financial institutions provided stimulus for further improvements.[14]

Most of the guidelines were recommended and not mandatory. Banks were subject to stricter governance rules imposed by the banking regulatory agency. Starting in 2006, firms were required to include a "Corporate Governance Compliance Report" in their annual report, indicating which guidelines they met or, if not, explaining why not.[15]

Another significant development since 2010 has been the enactment of the New Turkish Commercial Code (TCC), which governs company law in Turkey. TCC laid the foundations for the New Capital Markets Law (CML, 2012), which brought capital market regulations into full compliance with EU directives, and introduced various changes that matter to investors. One key legal aspect of the TCC is the superiority of the company; directors owe their duty to the company, not to the shareholders. The former may be liable for their actions even when they simply implement general assembly decisions that turn out to be harmful to the company.[16]

The nature of the corporate governance problems varies by ownership structures. For an individual firm, ownership structure defines the nature of principal—agent problems and the resulting governance issues. Thus, this section starts with an overview of the studies that have analyzed ownership structures. A related factor is business group affiliation, especially important in emerging markets, where business groups can dominate economic activity. While rarely studied, ownership and group-affiliation structures vary over time and are likely to be endogenous to country-level factors, such as economic and financial conditions, and institutional foundations.[17] As such, ownership structures and business group affiliation both are affected by and affect legal and regulatory infrastructures. The last part of this section reports on other governance aspects such as board structure, board procedures, and transparency and disclosure.

7.2.1 Ownership Structures

Due to limited and inconsistent disclosure of other aspects of governance, early studies of the governance characteristics of Turkish listed firms focused predominantly on ownership structures and rights attached to shares. These studies, which consider the late 1990s and early 2000s, document that, similar to other emerging markets, Turkish companies exhibit highly concentrated ownership structures.[18] Families, directly or indirectly, own about 80% of all companies and keep majority control. Table 7.3 documents that the separation of ownership and control is mainly achieved through pyramidal and, to a lesser extent, complex ownership structures. Also, dual-class shares are used to separate the voting and cash flow rights. In a substantial fraction of companies, the management coincides with the family of the controlling owner. Holding companies are the most frequently observed direct shareholders followed by financial and non-financial companies, and families.

At the direct ownership level, the average stake of the largest shareholder is around 45% (Table 7.3, Panel A). This number understates, however, the true control potential of large shareholders. The controlling shareholders usually have more than a single direct ownership stake. When all ownership stakes under the control of the ultimate shareholders are combined, the true fraction of control rights amount to 65 % of the outstanding shares, and they are controlled in the overwhelming majority of cases by families. The cash-flow rights are, however, substantially lower than this figure (Table 7.3, Panel B). The cash-flow rights of families average 54%. In more than half of the companies controlled by families there are substantial deviations of cash-flow rights from control rights leading to an average discrepancy of 7.47 (the ratio of voting rights to cash-flow rights).

Table 7.3 Ownership and Control Structures of Turkish Listed Companies

Panel A: Direct Ownership

Ownership Identity	N	*Largest Shareholder*		*Three Largest Shareholders*		*Dispersed Ownership*	
		Mean	*Std. Dev.*	*Mean*	*Std. Dev.*	*Mean*	*Std. Dev.*
Holding company	96	47.62	17.66	65.8	15.31	30.59	14.35
Non-financial companies	47	47.84	17.2	67.31	14.6	28.85	13.71
Financial companies	5	49.25	13.09	58.62	11.81	39.2	14.07
Families	42	34.11	22.64	52.22	24.2	38.33	25.96
Foreign companies	20	67.77	19.22	81.2	13.38	17.5	13.45
State	5	67.25	29.93	70.02	26.27	22.98	20.29
Miscellaneous	3	63.87	34.02	68.42	27.37	31.22	27.68
Total	218	47.63	21.07	64.89	18.85	30.54	17.96

Panel B: Ultimate Ownership

Ownership Identity	*Voting Rights (VR)*		*Cash Flow Rights (CFR)*		*VR/CFR*		
	N	Mean	Std. Dev.	Mean	Std. Dev.	Mean	Std. Dev.
Families	173	66.1	21.54	54.04	22.84	7.47	49.84
Foreign companies	21	67.3	20.73	65.31	19.67	1.04	0.16
State	7	65.83	22.57	65.83	22.57	1	0
Miscellaneous	17	65.35	19.42	42.56	22.84	2.18	1.95
Total	218	66.15	21.2	54.61	22.98	6.23	44.44

Panel C: The Frequency of Dual Class Shares and Corporate Charter Arrangements

Number of Companies With	*N*
One share one vote	125
Two types of shares with different voting rights	66
More than two types of shares with different voting rights	19
Special treatment in the distribution of earnings	24
Special treatment in the election of the board of directors	82
Special treatment in the election of the audit committee	41
Preemptive right to buy new issues of stock	13

Source: Yurtoğlu (2000).

Note: Table presents summary statistics on ownership and control structures of 218 Turkish companies listed on Borsa Istanbul (former name: Istanbul Stock Exchange) by the end of 2001.

While these observations stem from the late 1990s[19] and early 2000s,[20] later studies[21] report similar empirical regularities, suggesting that ownership structures were relatively stable over the last two decades with two exceptions: first, the number of listed firms with the state as the controlling shareholder has gone down; and, second, foreign ownership has increased.

7.2.2 *Business Groups*

Many of the largest corporations in Turkey are affiliated with each other within a business group structure. These highly diversified groups are organized around a holding company and are the outcome of investments by a single family or a small number of allied families who, once having established the core of the group, keep the constituents together as a single entity within which resources can be shifted.

Given their indisputable significance, the documentation of the activities of business groups in Turkey remains fragmentary. A major reason for this circumstance is that official data are reported at the company instead of the group level. A longitudinal study of 51 business groups over their life cycle spanning the period 1925–2012 reports that as of 2012 these groups collectively employed more than 500,000 employees, with the biggest ones controlling over 150 affiliated firms.[22]

The firms affiliated with a business group can be linked to one another either through a complicated web of inter-corporate shareholdings, or by means of a pyramidal structure.[23] In the latter structure, the voting rights of outside shareholders are spread out over a large number of firms and those of the ultimate owner are concentrated at the top of the pyramid. Thus, several companies can be controlled by the same legal entity at the apex (an individual, a family, or more often a holding company) through a series of ownership relations. The length of this chain and the size of the ownership stakes determine the deviation of voting rights from cash flow rights and thereby lead to agency problems between inside and outside shareholders of the group firms. The ultimate controlling owners are able to use their position to derive private benefits at the expense of minority shareholders. Families hold the majority control of a holding company, which in turn has shareholdings in several other companies, giving rise to a pyramidal structure. Hence, while some of their affiliated companies can be listed on the stock exchange, the typical business group remains an organization that is ultimately controlled by the founding families—a condition that creates its own agency problems.[24]

Furthermore, the governing bodies—boards and to some extent the top management teams—of business groups are directed by family members.[25] These governance structures exhibit little variation with respect to the size and age of business groups.[26] There is also evidence that the size and scope of Turkish business groups are in part driven by the structural characteristics of the controlling families.[27]

7.2.3 Other Aspects of Corporate Governance

In 2007 Borsa Istanbul (BIST) introduced a "Corporate Governance Index" (BIST CG Index; XKUR) comprising firms that meet at least 70% of the Guidelines based on a voluntary assessment of their compliance. The BIST CG Index started with five firms, but its coverage has increased over time, and by June 2018 included 51. The institutional interest in corporate governance practices also led S&P to conduct annual transparency and disclosure surveys of roughly 50 of the largest Turkish firms between 2005 and 2008.[28] These surveys documented sizeable improvements in transparency and disclosure scores from 2005 to 2006 largely due to mandatory adoption of IFRS, but little change over 2006–2008, and limited between-firm variation from 2006 on. Most firms met the legal requirements, but did little more to go above the legal minimum. A study of the determinants of S&P transparency and disclosure scores reports that firm size, financial performance, and market-to-book ratios were positively associated with these scores.[29]

Changes in the Turkish Commercial Code, the Capital Markets Law and regulations issued by the Capital Markets Board in 2011 and 2012 increased disclosure standards and introduced stricter board independence requirements, including a provision, effective in 2012, that public companies have at least one-third independent directors.

There is limited research that seeks to capture the variety of governance mechanisms that Turkish companies display. Many studies use a specific corporate governance construct, which measures only a limited number of governance practices. However, different aspects of governance are often correlated. A firm with a high performance in one of these aspects, for instance, by having a highly independent board, or by abstaining from deviations from one-share-one-vote, is likely also to perform well in others, for example, by offering high quality disclosure. A study that analyzes the impact of only one of these aspects may document a relationship between the included aspect and a measure of performance; however, the true driver of superior performance is likely to be an omitted dimension of governance. This raises concerns both for studies that use a broad measure of governance and for studies that employ a specific measure. Using a broad measure of governance raises the concern that the true driver(s) would remain hidden in the definition of the broad measure, and using a specific measure might suggest a link between this measure and firm performance due its correlation with other aspects omitted from the analysis. Both approaches can potentially deliver misleading policy recommendations.

One study that seeks to overcome such concerns in the Turkish context analyzed the corporate governance practices of Turkish public firms from 2006 to 2012.[30] This study relies on hand-collected data covering the vast majority of listed firms, excluding those that are foreign-owned, and builds a Turkey Corporate Governance Index (TCGI). TCGI is composed of 46 governance elements that seek to capture five important aspects of firm-level governance: board structure, board procedures, disclosure, ownership structure, and shareholder rights. Prior research suggests that the overwhelming majority of these 46 governance elements are potential indicators of good governance, while some of them reflect characteristics that are specific to Turkey. Most elements are coded as "1" if a firm has the attribute and "0" otherwise. The exceptions are fractional ownership by the control group and the "wedge" between voting rights and economic ownership, which are coded as continuous variables with values from 0 to 1.

The first aspect of governance is related to board structure. Board independence is a key factor in corporate governance.[31] One element of the Board Structure Subindex asks whether a firm has *one or more* independent directors; a second element asks whether a firm has *more than one* independent director. While in many countries such questions would be irrelevant, due to either custom or a legal requirement for a minimum number or percentage of independent directors, in Turkey these elements matter. Indeed, in 66% of firm-years, Turkish listed companies have no independent directors at all. Only a negligibly small fraction of firms (1% of firm-years) have boards with a majority of independent directors. These elements are affected by 2012 Turkish legal rules that require that the boards include at least one-third independent directors.

Board Structure includes three elements related to the CEO. They involve the flow of information from management to the board and the division of authority within the firm. The first element asks whether the CEO is a member of the board of directors. The second whether the CEO and board chair are different people. Having one person hold both positions is often thought to signal weak board checks on the CEO's power. The third element asks whether the CEO is from outside the controlling family.

Functioning audit committees can improve disclosure quality and reduce cost of capital. Turkish firms are required to have audit committees.[32] Board Structure Subindex includes two questions related to audit committee independence: does the audit committee have an independent *member*, and does the committee have a non-executive or independent *chair*? The Board Structure Subindex also includes an element for existence of a Corporate Governance Committee. New rules, effective for 2012, require firms to have fully independent audit committees and a corporate governance committee.

Measures of board procedures constitute the second major aspect of corporate governance. In Turkey, however, the availability of such measures is limited. There is no reliable and systematic information on how often the board or the audit committee meets, how well attended the meetings are, or whether formal board or committee minutes are kept. Hence, the absence of a relationship between the Board Procedure Index and firm value (or other outcome measures) may indicate that board procedures do not matter, or that our subindex fails to capture relevant aspects of board procedure.

The Board Procedure Subindex includes elements that assess whether there is a corporate governance charter or board charter that governs the board's activities; whether the firm has a code of ethics; and whether the firm discloses the audit committee members and the committee charter, as proxies for effective functioning of this committee. The final element is whether the firm has an internal control or audit function.

The third aspect of governance is disclosure. A reliable disclosure regime that ensures transparency is a key factor of market-based monitoring of companies and forms the basis of shareholders' ability to exercise their ownership rights on an informed basis. Investors require access to regular and reliable information to assess the quality of managerial decisions and make informed decisions about the valuation, ownership and voting of shares. Prior research provides evidence of an association between the extent and quality of corporate disclosure and firm market value.[33] There is also evidence that disclosure predicts lower cost of equity capital by reducing the potential for appropriation of cash flows by insiders and the cost to investors of monitoring insiders.[34] The elements of the Disclosure Subindex cover a number of aspects of both financial and nonfinancial disclosure, including companies' financial and operating results; their noncommercial objectives relevant to investors and other stakeholders; ownership and voting rights; compensation policies, information about managers and board members; and related party transactions. For financial disclosure, Turkey adopted IFRS in 2005; thus, the financial items that firms disclose are reasonably standardized, and hence do not have a large weight in the Disclosure Subindex.

The fourth aspect of governance is related to ownership structures of firms. A disparity between the control group's voting rights and cash flow rights can provide incentives for self-dealing, and is associated with lower firm value.[35] Many companies in Turkey create such a disparity by using pyramids and dual-class shares.[36] The Ownership Structure Subindex includes the control group's fractional ownership of voting shares; the disparity between this group's voting and economic rights; whether the firm has a class of shares with special nomination rights for directors or special cash flow rights; whether the firm has an outside blockholder with more than 5% of shares (who can potentially monitor the controlling shareholder); and whether there exist founder certificates which give the holders special cash flow rights.

The fifth and last aspect of governance reflects the various rights of shareholders. Minority shareholder rights are often seen as central elements in corporate governance.[37] The Shareholder Rights Index is, however, a less than ideal measure of these rights, due to lack of data. Instead, it includes several governance elements that do not fit in other subindices: whether directors are elected annually; whether the firm has an insider trading policy; whether it has made loans to directors; and whether it has an investor relations officer/department.

Table 7.4 provides summary statistics for *TCGI* over time. *TCGI* ranges from 10.22 to 82.97, with a mean of 46.73, and shows a slight upward trend between 2006 and 2011. The table also reports the development of the five subindices that constitute the *TCGI* and suggests that this upward trend is driven principally by higher Disclosure Subindex scores, and a larger increase in 2012, driven by Board Structure and Board Procedures Subindices Four elements of Board Structure (firm has

Table 7.4 Turkey Corporate Governance Index (TCGI)

Panel A. Summary Statistics for TCGI

Year	*Obs.*	*Mean*	*Median*	*Std. Dev.*	*Min*	*Max*
2006	172	42.97	41.64	13.30	14.04	79.29
2007	175	44.18	42.57	13.33	15.67	79.29
2008	168	45.32	43.54	13.76	15.67	79.29
2009	183	41.67	40.04	12.41	10.22	73.40
2010	192	45.12	45.29	12.99	11.61	78.22
2011	193	46.60	46.75	13.27	14.33	78.22
2012	175	61.55	62.56	10.92	25.43	82.97
2006–2012	1,258	46.73	45.94	14.25	10.22	82.97

Panel B. Change in Subindices of TCGI *over 2006–2012*

Year	*Board Structure*	*Disclosure*	*Board Procedures*	*Shareholder Rights*	*Ownership Structure*
2006	42.57	23.34	49.77	31.21	43.47
2007	42.62	24.73	51.43	32.12	43.75
2008	43.54	25.61	52.84	32.81	43.95
2009	43.31	28.19	42.18	32.78	40.14
2010	44.58	29.35	43.24	35.32	40.20
2011	46.38	30.43	45.50	36.33	40.26
2012	81.07	41.91	71.54	38.74	43.01
2006–2012	49.15	29.08	50.93	34.19	42.11

Source: Ararat, Black and Yurtoğlu (2017)

Note: In Panel A, the table presents number of observations, sample mean, and other statistics for *TCGI* (0~100) by year. In Panel B, each subindex is expressed 0 ~ 100 one independent director; firm has more than one independent director; audit committee has an independent member and has a non-executive or independent chair) became mandatory in 2012, under new rules that required firms to have at least two independent directors, at least 1/3 independent directors, and a higher proportion in some cases. The table shows that the improvements in the Shareholder Rights have been limited to slight increases in 2011 and 2012 and that the Ownership Structure Subindex is fairly stable from 2006 to 2012.

7.3 The Effects of Corporate Governance Practices

One principal question addressed in the literature on corporate governance in emerging markets is whether better firm-level governance can reduce or offset the market value discount in firms domiciled in countries with weak legal protection for shareholders. Such a discount has been documented by empirical studies,[38] and is often attributed to the ability of dominant shareholders to expropriate the minority shareholders.

There is evidence that firm-level governance arrangements that go above the minimum required by law have a sizeable effect on firm behavior and firm value. For example, there is strong evidence that an overall corporate governance index is an important and likely causal factor in explaining the market value of Korean public companies.[39] A worst-to-best change in this index predicts a 0.47 increase in Tobin's q, which is the ratio of the market value of equity and book value of debt to the book value of total assets of the firm. The increase in Tobin's q translates into a 160% increase in share price. A similar analysis yields much stronger effects for Russian listed companies.[40] A cross-national comparison corroborates this finding in a panel data setting for four other emerging markets, albeit with lower effect sizes than in Russia.[41] Related research suggests that the positive relation between firm-level governance and valuation is systematic across a large set of countries and firms.[42] The following section provides a summary of the empirical evidence of the relationship between corporate governance characteristics and performance of Turkish firms. We start with empirical papers that predominantly focus on ownership structures. Then we turn to other aspects of governance.

Studies that analyze the impact of corporate governance practices of Turkish listed firms have uniformly documented higher firm value, higher profitability, and higher returns on invested capital for firms that exhibit corporate governance practices that facilitate better protections to outside shareholders. One study analyzes the effect of deviations from one share—one vote and the mechanisms that large shareholders use to maintain it.[43] These mechanisms include dual (or multiple) class shares, and corporate charters containing provisions that stipulate a disproportionate voting power in the nomination and election of the board of directors and audit committee members. Some studies also analyze preemptive rights, which serve as a remedial device through which existing shareholders can buy the shares of the company when new capital is raised at usually below market prices. These studies analyze the impact of these mechanisms on firm value and returns on invested capital using an empirical setting with panel data and controlling for various firm characteristics, including business group membership and report that, on average, firms with deviations from one-share-one-vote have lower returns on invested capital, whereas being part of a business group improves the investment performance by almost 16 %. More importantly, firms that have very large deviations from one-share-one-vote (those exceeding the 75th percentile of the sample distribution) have much worse investment performance than those with moderate levels.

Turning to individual mechanisms that are used to maintain the deviations from one-share-one-vote, they report that the use of dual or multiple classes of shares leads to an average return on investment that is 22% smaller than its the cost of capital. Similarly, companies that enhance their insiders' power in the election of the board of directors and companies with charter arrangements that stipulate special rights for the election of the members of the audit committee have substantially worse investment performance of the same order of magnitude. On the other hand, there is evidence that companies that give their minority shareholders the preemptive right to buy new issues of stock have substantially higher estimated returns on investment than their costs of capital. While there is a small number of companies with such arrangements (6% of 218 sample firms), they exhibit a return on invested capital that is 8% above their cost of capital. Qualitatively similar evidence is obtained in additional analyses that use Tobin's *q* as the dependent variable. Taken together these findings indicate that such ownership structures create substantial agency costs.

Direct (and not ultimate) ownership structures can affect returns and risk-taking behavior. Using data from 1992 to 1998, one study report that firms with concentrated ownership have higher P/E ratios and higher average returns.[44] Firms affiliated with holding companies and with the state have higher returns and higher earnings multiples. Family owned firms, on the other hand, experience lower returns with low P/E ratios. With respect to risk-taking behavior, this study reports that highly concentrated and less diffuse firms had higher risk, proxied by larger standard deviation of monthly stock returns. Government-owned firms and firms with foreign ownership displayed higher risk, although they were on average larger. Family owned firms, on the other hand, had lower risk. There is also a significantly positive association between institutional ownership and return on assets.[45] A related study reports insignificant differences between the performance of index constituents and other listed firms.[46]

There has been limited research on board independence in Turkey. An empirical study reports that between 2006 and 2008, a higher proportion of independent directors predicted lower Tobin's *q* and was unrelated to equity issuances.[47] Independent directors, when they are present, rarely own any shares in the company.[48] A study of the relationship between four board structure characteristics (independence, CEO duality, board size, and board tenure) and accounting performance for 27 Turkish banks from 2001 to 2004 reports that the presence of insiders has a positive impact on return on assets, while duality and board tenure correlate negatively with performance.[49] Related research examines the effects of CEO duality, board independence, board size, and foreign ownership on the extent to which firm-specific information is incorporated into share prices, as measured by stock price synchronicity. The sample consists of the constituents of the Borsa Istanbul 100 Index during the 2009–2014 period and find that firms with higher board independence and higher foreign ownership have more firm-specific information incorporated into stock prices and less stock price synchronicity. These findings suggest that foreign ownership and board independence improve the information environment of Turkish listed firms.[50]

A more recent study analyzes whether TCGI (as detailed in section 7.2) predicts firm value and profitability.[51] This paper uses panel data with firm fixed and random effects with extensive covariates to minimize the potentially confounding effect of unobservable factors. In the firm fixed effects specification, a one-standard deviation increase in TCGI predicts a 7.7% increase in Tobin's *q*. TCGI also predicts firm profitability, measured as current year EBIT over prior year assets. The firm fixed effects coefficient implies that a one-standard-deviation increase in TCGI predicts a 0.010 increase in EBIT/Assets, which is economically meaningful relative to mean EBIT/Assets of 0.046. When TCGI is replaced by its subindices, then the Disclosure Subindex stands out, which is significant across different specifications. In addition to the Disclosure Subindex, the Ownership Structure Subindex is marginally significant. Hence, this study concludes that Disclosure Subindex is the principal driver of the overall relationship between TCGI and firm value.

7.4 Corporate Social Responsibility

As discussed earlier in this chapter, CSR has become a strategic issue since the 2000s. A series of surveys document the increasing role of CSR in companies' market and non-market strategies. These surveys indicate both a public demand that companies should contribute to social goals beyond shareholder value,[52] and a willingness by corporations to satisfy societal needs and to protect the interests of future generations.[53] Perhaps more interestingly, the public view reflects a firm perception that business can pursue its self-interest while doing good work for society.[54]

Scholarly perceptions of CSR have evolved in line with these perceptions as well. While the early work emphasized the limitations of markets to ensure efficient pricing and provision of nonprivate goods and externalities, it also suggested that firms could not and should not be expected to voluntarily act in a socially or environmentally responsible manner, leading to the famous "classical dichotomy."[55] In this view, the only responsibility of firms is maximizing profits and governments, not managing externalities and serving the public good. Other scholars challenged this view and argued that firms should to consider the implications of their actions for all constituencies even if such considerations reduced shareholder wealth. These studies included the social issues in management perspective,[56] as well as the stakeholder theory perspective.[57] More recent research emphasizes that CSR can be compatible with profit maximization. While the practice of CSR activities to satisfy managerial preferences may be a manifestation of moral hazard problems, CSR activities to satisfy nonclassical preferences of various stakeholders such as investors, employees, and consumers do not.[58] Similarly, companies may be involved in CSR activities in order to influence outcomes driven by public and private politics in a way that is consistent with value maximization.

Given this background, this section provides an overview of the limited literature on corporate social responsibility practices in Turkey. Modern Turkey has a rich history of philanthropy rooted in the institution of "*waqf*," (a form of charity for the sake of Islamic goals) which played a central role as an instrument of public policy in the social and economic life of pre-modern Ottoman cities.[59] Given the absence of municipal authorities until the mid-19th century, the *waqf* proved the principal means by which Ottoman sultans and senior state officials could provide their citizens with the most basic public services. The activities of *waqf* spanned various spheres of life, ranging from the field of religion to education, from public health to public works. Starting with the modernization efforts of the Ottoman Empire in the mid-19th century, various activities originally organized by *waqf* have been transferred to the central government, an effort that became more intense under the new Turkish Republic founded in 1923. In 1937 a "Committee for the Abolishment of the Awqaf" was established within Central Waqf Administration, which led to a takeover of educational *waqf* activities by the Ministry of Education. In 1954 all (cash) *waqf* activities were abolished and their capital put in Bank of Awqaf. At that time, neither the Turkish Civil Code nor the Code of Commerce made use of the Turkish word for *waqf* (*vakıf*). Instead, they used the term *tesis*, which means establishment. This process continued until 1967 when a new legislation allowed establishment of secular *waqf* with Islamic principles. It amended the Turkish Civil Code to replace the word *tesis* with *vakıf* and authorized the Civil Tribunal to register a *vakıf* and give it a judicial personality.[60]

Following these changes in the legal framework, most of today's largest foundations were established, starting from the 1970s, by the families owning Turkey's largest diversified business groups, which are allowed to allocate a maximum of 5% of their profits to the foundation, for redistribution to social projects. The government may grant tax exemption for donations made to organizations certified as working towards the "public good," which extends to four areas: education, health, scientific research, and arts and culture. Only about 200 out of approximately 3,500 private foundations have been classified as serving "public good."[61]

There has been limited research on the nature, determinants, and effects of such corporate philanthropy.[62] The available body of evidence is largely based on large company or not-for-profit organization case studies, which present historical accounts.[63] The concept of philanthropy is often used interchangeably with CSR.[64]

One driver of corporate prosocial behavior seems to be the need of big business owners to achieve social legitimacy. An analysis of the historical development of the Turkish business class suggests that it emerged as the result of deliberate state policy.[65] Hence, the business community did not have strong roots in civil society and was always dependent on state policies for its legitimacy and well-being. The willingness to sacrifice money for a good cause can be seen as a rational response to the need to achieve and maintain social legitimacy, rather than as a strategic tool motivated by stakeholders' demands. Indeed, a study that investigates the CSR activities of Turkish companies argues that traditional practices have a strong influence on CSR reporting, whereas international influences are weaker and work mainly through market-driven norms rather than institutionally imposed mechanisms.[66] Another study of CSR initiatives of Turkey's 30 largest companies suggests that these activities are used to construct a moral identity.[67] This study also suggests that global CSR trends, rather than immediate local needs, influence the CSR agendas of these companies. The results of these two studies suggest varying degrees of international influence on different types of firms. Other scholars argue and predict that the drivers for CSR in Turkey will be exogenous and institutional rather than endogenous and cultural.[68]

Some other work documents industry-level differences across CSR engagements. For example, there is evidence that companies in the automotive and pharmaceutical industries engaged in "green" philanthropic activities more than textile corporations did.[69] More recent research on the philanthropic activities of Turkish banks offers insights on how Turkish banks allocate their philanthropic resources.[70] In this study bank profitability is positively associated with the diversity of philanthropic efforts, but at the same time, profitability has no significant effect on social performance. Older banks and banks that have higher media visibility have significantly better social performances. One important finding offered by this study is that business group affiliated banks are more likely to have superior social performances.

Distinct from corporate philanthropy, the introduction of Corporate Governance Guidelines in 2003 by the CMBT constitutes an important effort to promote CSR by recognizing various stakeholders, whose interests and rights had to be protected by corporate governance practices. The guidelines define a stakeholder as "any person, entity or party who has an interest in the operations of the company and achievement of its targets," and list employees, creditors, customers, suppliers, trade unions, various nongovernmental organizations and potential investors as examples. Furthermore, the guidelines recommended a code of ethics that stipulated that the operations of the company must be executed within the framework of ethical rules that had to be developed by the board of directors, announced and approved in the general shareholders meeting, and disclosed to the public. Practices regarding how these rules are implemented must also be publicly disclosed. Another recommendation was related to the social responsibility of the company towards the environment, consumer protection, and public health. While the guidelines did not mandate the companies to comply, and hence are unlikely to cause a measurable change in CSR activities, the inclusion of CSR related recommendations improved the transparency of listed firms' stance towards CSR.

A survey of the 30 largest listed companies in 2004[71] reports that 2/3 of the companies did not recognize any of the stakeholders explicitly mentioned by the CMB, while the remaining ones overwhelmingly mentioned employees as the most important stakeholder group.[72] Ethical Codes disclosed by the companies exhibited a high degree of similarity, most focusing on simple rules for employees. The codes did not reflect commitments to fair play, and they did not address boards or management. A later survey of the vast majority of listed firms between 2006 and 2012 reports that only 16% disclosed their code of ethics or code of conduct.[73] Similarly poor disclosure of CSR activities is observed in the banking sector, where environmental and social performance indicators are much less frequently disclosed than economic performance indicators.[74]

7.5 Discussion and Directions for Further Research

In closing, it is perhaps useful to put the current state of Turkish corporate governance in the broader context of Turkey's development trajectory from a rural and agricultural economy in the late 19th century to a mostly urban middle-income country at the start of the 21st century. While some observers see this change as an improvement, others consider it as a failure.[75]

The institutions and governance structures that accompanied Turkey's growth for over 100 years failed repeatedly over the last 40 years, ending up in a series of economic crises. They also do not yet allow and incentivize Turkish firms to become truly world-class players, able to achieve global scale either by expanding domestically or by partnering with foreign companies. Turkey's economic growth is erratic, showing how a system that works under one set of economic conditions fails miserably under another. Furthermore, there is still no consensus at the political level on the desirability of legal and institutional preconditions of a market-led economic system. Perhaps as a result of these inconsistencies, legal and regulatory changes in the area of governance have been unpredictable and produced a set of rules that lack a unified approach.

Given these fundamental weaknesses, investors have not surprisingly demonstrated limited trust in Turkey's controlling shareholders. One measure of this distrust is the premium that investors are willing to pay for better governed firms. One study estimates that, over the last decade, firms that offered one standard deviation more protections to outside shareholders were worth substantially more.[76] This high value attached to good governance suggests that investors discount Turkish listed companies as a reflection of embedded agency problems. While the evidence compiled in this paper documents some improvement in both country-level laws and regulations as well as firm-level practices over the last decade, much more needs to be established to create the preconditions of strong capital markets.

Strong corporate governance systems rely on a complex network of legal and market institutions that ensure that minority shareholders receive reliable information about the value of companies, and have confidence that insiders will not expropriate them. A country whose laws and related institutions fail on either count cannot develop a strong capital market, forcing firms to rely on internal financing or bank financing—both of which have important shortcomings.

While this chapter reviews the most salient characteristics of Turkish corporate governance and social responsibility, it does not cover a number of other important institutions. These include the roles played by the regulators, prosecutors, and courts in various aspects of corporate governance and their structural connection to political actors and institutions. Equally important is the function of reputational intermediaries, such as accounting firms, investment banks, law firms, and stock exchanges. Also omitted from this chapter is the broader role of culture and other informal institutions, such as an active and independent financial press and securities analysis profession that can uncover and publicize misleading disclosure and criticize company insiders and other agents. Somewhat paradoxically, research on the roles of such institutions is much less scarce. Examining how these institutions facilitate change or inertia for Turkish corporate governance and social responsibility provides an important research agenda.

Notes

1. See A. Shleifer and R. Vishny, "A Survey of Corporate Governance," *Journal of Finance*, v.52, 1997, pp. 737–783.
2. L. Zingales, "Corporate Governance," in *The New Palgrave Dictionary of Economics and Law*, London: MacMillan, 1998.

3. See S. Claessens and B. Yurtoğlu, "Corporate Governance in Emerging Markets: A Survey," *Emerging Markets Review*, v.15, 2013, pp. 1–33.
4. See A.M. Çolpan, "Business Groups in Turkey," in A.M. Çolpan, T. Hikino, and J.R. Lincoln (eds.) *The Oxford Handbook of Business Groups*, Oxford: Oxford University Press, 2010, pp. 487–523; A. Karaevli, "The Evolution of Diversification Strategies in Turkish Business Groups," *Journal of Management Research* (In Turkish), v.8, 2008, pp. 85–107.
5. B. Black, "The Legal and Institutional Preconditions for Strong Securities Markets," *UCLA Law Review*, 2001b, argues that another aspect of corporate governance is related to the question of how good a country's institutions are at ensuring that corporate insiders are competent to seek value maximization rather than other objectives. While governance debates in developed countries often revolve around this question, it is less important than the more basic disclosure and legal protection issues addressed in this section.
6. For surveys, see R. Levine, "Finance and Growth: Theory and Evidence," in P. Aghion and S. Durlauf (eds.) *Handbook of Economic Growth*, Amsterdam: Elsevier, 2005, pp. 865–934; J. Ang, "A Survey of Recent Developments in the Literature of Finance and Growth," *Journal of Economic Surveys*, v.22, 2008, pp. 536–576.
7. See World Bank, "Finance for All? Policies and Pitfalls in Expanding Access," Washington, DC: World Bank Policy Research Report, 2008; A. Demirgüc-Kunt and R. Levine, "Finance and Inequality: Theory and Evidence," *Annual Review of Financial Economics*, v.1, 2009.
8. This literature started with the seminal work of P. Gompers, J. Ishii, and A. Metrick, "Corporate Governance and Equity Prices," *Quarterly Journal of Economics*, v.118, 2003, pp. 107–158.
9. This view has been stressed by C. Doidge, A. Karolyi, and R. Stulz, "Why Do Countries Matter So Much for Corporate Governance?" *Journal of Financial Economics*, v.86, 2007, pp. 1–39.
10. See *Turkey Investment Climate Assessment: From Crisis to Private Sector Led Growth*, World Bank, 2010.
11. The statistics are from the 2016 Annual Report published by the Capital Markets Board of Turkey.
12. See "The Crisis in Turkey," *The Economist*, December 6, 2000; E. Alper and Z. Önis, "Soft Budget Constraints, Government Ownership of Banks and Regulatory Failure: The Political Economy of the Turkish Banking System in the Post-capital Account Liberalization Era," 2002, http://ssrn.com/abstract=303220
13. See M. Ugur and M. Ararat, "Does Macroeconomic Performance Affect Corporate Governance? Evidence from Turkey," *Corporate Governance: An International Review*, v.14, 2006, pp. 325–348.
14. See M. Ararat and H. Orbay, "Corporate Governance in Turkey; Implications for Investments and Growth," 2006, https://ssrn.com/abstract=2375767
15. See M. Ararat, "'Comply or Explain' Without Consequences: The Case of Turkey," in C.A. Mallin (ed.) *Handbook on International Corporate Governance*, Cheltenham, UK and Northampton, MA: Edward Elgar, 2011, pp. 355–370.
16. See M. Ararat, E. Suel, and B. Yurtoğlu, "Sustainable Investment in Turkey: The Case in Context—An Update," 2004, SSRN, https://ssrn.com/abstract=2447937
17. See Shleifer and Vishny, "A Survey of Corporate Governance".
18. See Y. Güney, A. Ozkan, and K. Yalciner, "Dynamic Capital Structure Decisions: Evidence from Firms in an Emerging Economy," in S. Altug and A.

Filiztekin (eds.) *The Turkish Economy: The Real Economy, Corporate Governance, and Reform and Stabilization Policy*, Routledge Curzon Studies on Middle Eastern Economics, 2006, pp. 149–171; B. Yurtoğlu, "Ownership, Control and Performance of Turkish Listed Firms," *Empirica*, v.27, 2000, pp. 193–222.

19. B. Yurtoğlu, "Ownership, Control and Performance of Turkish Listed Firms."
20. H. Orbay and B. Yurtoğlu, "The Impact of Corporate Governance Structures on the Corporate Investment Performance in Turkey," *Corporate Governance: An International Review*, v.14, 2006, pp. 349–363.
21. M. Ararat, B. Black, and B. Yurtoğlu, "The Effect of Corporate Governance on Firm Value and Profitability: Time-Series Evidence from Turkey," *Emerging Markets Review*, v.30, 2017, pp. 113–132.
22. A. Karaevli and B. Yurtoğlu, "Founding Family Effects on Business Group Growth: Longitudinal Evidence from Turkey (1925–2012)," *Long Range Planning*, v.51, 2018, pp. 831–864.
23. A. Goto, "Business Groups in a Market Economy," *European Economic Review*, v.19, 1982, pp. 53–70.
24. R. Morck and B. Yeung, "Agency Problems in Large Family Business Groups," *Entrepreneurship Theory and Practice*, v.27, 2003, pp. 367–382.
25. B. Üsdiken, this volume.
26. See N.S. Gökşen and B. Üsdiken, "Uniformity and Diversity in Turkish Business Groups: Effects of Scale and Time of Founding," *British Journal of Management*, v.12, 2001, pp. 325–340.
27. A. Karaevli and B. Yurtoğlu, "Founding Family Effects on Business Group Growth."
28. See M. Ararat and A. Balic, "Turkish Transparency and Disclosure Survey 2008: A Year of Little or No Progress," Standard & Poor's, 2008.
29. M. Aksu and A. Kösedag, "Transparency and Disclosure Scores and Their Determinants in the Istanbul Stock Exchange," *Corporate Governance: An International Review*, v.14, 2006, pp. 277–296.
30. M. Ararat, B. Black, and B. Yurtoğlu, "The Effect of Corporate Governance on Firm Value and Profitability."
31. See, J. Dahya, O. Dimitrov, and J.J. McConnell, "Dominant Shareholders, Corporate Boards, and Corporate Value: A Cross-Country Analysis," *Journal of Financial Economics*, v.87, 2008, pp. 73–100.
32. A. Klein, "Economic Determinants of Audit Committee Independence," *The Accounting Review*, v.77, 2002, pp. 435–452.
33. For a review, see E. Farvaque, C. Refait-Alexandre, and D. Saïdane, "Corporate Disclosure: A Review of Its (direct and indirect) Benefits and Costs," *International Economics*, v.128, 2011, pp. 5–31.
34. R. Lambert, C. Leuz, and R.E. Verrecchia, "Accounting Information, Disclosure, and the Cost of Capital," *Journal of Accounting Research*, v.45, 2007, pp. 385–420.
35. For a review, see S. Claessens and B. Yurtoğlu, "Corporate Governance in Emerging Markets."
36. B. Yurtoğlu, "Ownership, Control and Performance of Turkish Listed Firms."
37. See "Principles of Corporate Governance," Paris: OECD, 2004.
38. For a systematic overview of such results, see S. Claessens and B. Yurtoğlu, "Corporate Governance in Emerging Markets."
39. B.S. Black, H. Jang, and W.C. Kim, "Does Corporate Governance Predict Firms' Market Values? Evidence from the Korean Market," *Journal of Law, Economics and Organization*, v.22, 2006, pp. 366–413.

40. B.S. Black, "The Corporate Governance Behavior and Market Value of Russian Firms," *Emerging Markets Review*, v.2, 2001, pp. 89–108.
41. See B.S. Black, A.G. de Carvalho, V.S. Khanna, W.C. Kim, and B. Yurtoğlu, "Methods for Multicountry Studies of Corporate Governance (and Evidence from the BRIKT countries)," *Journal of Econometrics*, v.183, 2014, pp. 230–240.
42. A. Durnev and H. Kim, "To Steal or Not to Steal: Firm Attributes, Legal Environment, and Valuation," *Journal of Finance*, v.60, 2005, pp. 1461–1493; S. Claessens and B. Yurtoğlu, "Corporate Governance in Emerging Markets."
43. H. Orbay and B. Yurtoğlu, "The Impact of Corporate Governance Structures on the Corporate Investment Performance in Turkey," *Corporate Governance: An International Review*, v.14, 2006, pp. 349–363.
44. G. Gürsoy and K. Aydoğan, "Equity Ownership Structure, Risk Taking, and Performance: An Empirical Investigation in Turkish Listed Companies," *Emerging Markets Finance & Trade*, v.38, 2002, pp. 6–25.
45. See A.O. Gürbüz, A. Aybars, and Ö. Kutlu, "Corporate Governance and Financial Performance with a Perspective on Institutional Ownership: Empirical Evidence from Turkey," *Journal of Applied Management Accounting Research*, v.8, 2010, pp. 21–37. They report an association between (domestic and foreign) institutional ownership and financial performance of BIST CG constituents from 2005 to 2008.
46. See, E.D. Sengur, "Do Corporate Governance Index Companies Outperform Others? Evidence from Turkey," *International Journal of Business and Social Science*, v.2, 2011, pp. 254–260.
47. M. Ararat, H. Orbay, and B. Yurtoğlu, "The Effects of Board Independence in Controlled Firms: Evidence from Turkey," *SSRN*, 2010, https://ssrn.com/abstract=1663403
48. See E. Arioglu, "A Different Perspective on Ownership in Firms Quoted at Borsa Istanbul," *İktisat İşletme ve Finans*, v.30, 2015, pp. 65–80.
49. T. Kaymak and E. Bektas, "East Meets West? Board Characteristics in an Emerging Market: Evidence from Turkish Banks," *Corporate Governance: An International Review*, v.16, 2008, pp. 550–561.
50. O. Tas and S.D. Tan, "Corporate Governance, Foreign Ownership and Stock Price Synchronicity: Evidence from Borsa Istanbul," *Journal of Finance and Accounting*, v.3, 2016, pp. 156–165.
51. M. Ararat, B. Black, and B. Yurtoğlu, "The Effect of Corporate Governance on Firm Value and Profitability."
52. See Environics International Ltd, *The Millennium Poll on Corporate Social Responsibility: Global Public Opinion on the Changing Role of Companies*, 1999; Ipsos MORI, *Ethical Companies, MORI Corporate Social Responsibility Research* (Published: 21 November 2003).
53. PwC 17th Annual Global CEO Survey, 2014, www.pwc.com/gx/en/sustainability/ceo-views/assets/pwc-ceo-summary-sustainability.pdf
54. Edelman Trust Barometer, 2014, www.edelman.com/p/6-a-m/2014-edelman-trust-barometer/
55. M. Friedman, "The Social Responsibility of Business Is to Increase Its Profits," *The New York Times Magazine*, September 13, 1970.
56. See, S.L. Wartick and L.C. Philip, "The Evolution of the Corporate Social Performance Model," *The Academy of Management Review*, v.10, 1985, pp. 758–769; D.J. Wood, "Corporate Social Performance Revisited," *The Academy of Management Review*, v.16, 1991, pp. 691–718.
57. R.E. Freeman, *Strategic Management: A Stakeholder Approach*, Cambridge: Cambridge University Press, 1984.

58. M. Kitzmueller and J. Shimshack, "Economic Perspectives on Corporate Social Responsibility," *Journal of Economic Literature*, v.50, 2012, pp. 51–84.
59. See, Ağır, this volume; O. Peri, "Waqf and Ottoman Welfare Policy," *Journal of the Economic and Social History of the Orient*, v.35, 1992, pp. 167–186; T. Kuran, "The Provision of Public Goods Under Islamic Law: Origins, Impact and Limitations of the Waqf System," *Law & Society Review*, v.35, 2001, pp. 841–898; A. Singer, *Constructing Ottoman Beneficence: An Imperial Soup Kitchen in Jerusalem*, State University New York Press, 2002.
60. Survival & Restoration of Waqfs in Turkey, https://islamicmarkets.com/education/survival-restoration-of-waqfs-in-turkey, accessed March 30, 2019.
61. M. Ararat, "A Development Perspective for 'Corporate Social Responsibility': Case of Turkey," *Corporate Governance: The International Journal of Business in Society*, v.8, 2008, pp. 271–285.
62. F. Küskü and A. Zarkada-Fraser, "An Empirical Investigation of Corporate Citizenship in Australia and Turkey," *British Journal of Management*, v.15, 2004, pp. 57–72.
63. See, for example, D. Cetindamar, "Corporate Social Responsibility Practices and Environmentally Responsible Behavior: The Case of the United Nations Global Compact," *Journal of Business Ethics*, v.76, 2007, pp. 163–176.
64. F. Akyildiz, "Comparative Corporate Social Responsibility in the United Kingdom and Turkey," in G. Aras and D. Crowther (eds.) *Business Strategy and Sustainability (Developments in Corporate Governance and Responsibility*, Volume 3), Emerald Group Publishing Limited, 2012, pp. 115–153.
65. A. Buğra, *State and Business in Modern Turkey*. SUNY Series in the Social and Economic History of the Middle East, Albany: State University of New York Press, 2004.
66. B. Ertuna and A. Tukel, "Traditional Versus International Influences: CSR Disclosures in Turkey," *European Journal of International Management*, v.4, 2010, pp. 273–289.
67. E. Ozdora-Aksak and S. Atakan-Duman, "Gaining Legitimacy Through CSR: An Analysis of Turkey's 30 Largest Corporations," *Business Ethics: A European Review*, v.25, 2016, pp. 238–257.
68. M. Ararat Melsa, "Turkey: Social Responsibility in a State-Dependent Business System," in A. Habisch, M. Wegner, R. Schmidpeter, and J. Jonker (eds.) *Corporate Social Responsibility Across Europe*, Berlin and Heidelberg: Springer, 2005.
69. F. Küskü, "From Necessity to Responsibility: Evidence for Corporate Environmental Citizenship Activities from a Developing Country Perspective," *Corporate Social Responsibility and Environmental Management*, v.14, 2007, pp. 74–87.
70. F.N. Senol, *Relational Pluralism and Practice Variation*. PhD Thesis submitted to Sabancı University, Graduate School of Management, 2016.
71. M. Ararat and C. Göcenoğlu, *Drivers for Sustainable Corporate Responsibility, Case of Turkey*, Sabancı University, Corporate Governance Forum of Turkey, unpublished manuscript, 2005; M. Ararat, "A Development Perspective for 'Corporate Social Responsibility': Case of Turkey."
72. These results are consistent with Aşçıgil (2004), who reports that 75% of the managers give priority to economic motives when making decisions about CSR. Customers are considered to be the primary stakeholders by 75.8% of managers, employees being the second by 50.8% and society at large by 24.3%.
73. M. Ararat, B. Black, and B. Yurtoğlu, "The Effect of Corporate Governance on Firm Value and Profitability."

74. A. Akin and I. Yilmaz, "Drivers of Corporate Social Responsibility Disclosures: Evidence from Turkish Banking Sector," *Procedia Economics and Finance*, v.38, 2016, pp. 2–7.
75. See S. Pamuk, "Economic Change in Twentieth-Century Turkey: Is the Glass More Than Half Full?" in R. Kasaba (ed.) *Turkey in the Modern World*, Cambridge: Cambridge University Press, 2008.
76. M. Ararat, B. Black, and B. Yurtoğlu, "The Effect of Corporate Governance on Firm Value and Profitability."

8 Owners and Salaried Managers in Large Turkish Enterprises

Behlül Üsdiken

> Sakıp *bey* sometimes introduced me as the sixth brother. I have also seen myself as a member of the family. . . . Compared to other groups, I think I was the CEO with the greatest authority. Because of the trust in me, I could sign a 500 million US dollar contract on my own.[1]
>
> Sakıp *bey* wanted the cigarette factory dearly. . . . I was reluctant. . . . It did not seem ethical to me. He asked me to see him. He said, "You do not want this, but I want it." When he said something like this there was nothing you could say.[2]

When Hasan Güleşçi made these remarks, he was the highest ranking salaried manager in one of the largest business groups in the country. He had held this position for 15 years and had enjoyed a 40-year long tenure in the group. The post he occupied was labeled "General Coordinator" until a few months before he retired, in 2000, when it was changed to Chief Executive Officer (CEO), a title that the group has retained since.

My epigraph provides Güleşçi's interpretations of his relations with the second-generation leader of the family owning the business group in which he eventually worked as the top salaried manager. As such, it underscores the central issue that drives the present study. The question this chapter asks is "What is the nature of the relationship between owner families and high-level salaried managers in Turkish family business groups?" In more specific terms, the chapter examines the decision-making powers held by family members and salaried managers, the roles that each performs, and the influence strategies that they employ in their relationships. These issues are addressed with reference to family business groups, as they have come to constitute the largest private sector enterprises in Turkey since the 1950s.[3] Like their counterparts in various other societal settings, family business groups in Turkey have been characterized by extensive unrelated diversification, family ownership, and centralized control through a holding company located at the apex of the group.[4]

Although the focus is on Turkish family business groups, the present study is likely to be relevant for other contexts where similar types of organizations continue to be preponderant. An expanding literature has emerged over the last two decades or so on this form of big business organization and its varieties in different settings.[5] Despite this increasing interest, however, the question of "professionalization" in top management has remained rather tangential, leading to various calls for more research.[6] Moreover, much of this limited attention has been geared towards examining to what extent salaried managers have been able to attain directorship or top management positions. Although these studies have been informative in showing that there was notable, and possibly expanding, presence of salaried managers in higher echelons, they have had much less to say on what such involvement actually meant with respect to influence on the ways in which the family business groups were run. It is this gap in extant research that the present study addresses within the context of family business groups in Turkey.

The next section provides an overview of the international as well as the Turkish literature on salaried management in family business groups. The section that follows introduces the theoretical ideas that frame the study. The methodology is described next. This is followed by the presentation and discussion of the findings, and, in the final section, a conclusion.

8.1 Literature Background

8.1.1 Family Business Groups and Salaried Managers

In broad terms, extant international literature suggests that family business groups are in essence "family businesses." Yet, family business groups have also, albeit in varying degrees, accommodated hierarchies of salaried managers. In one of the early contributions, for example, Biggart surmised that the South Korean *chaebol* blended personal rule by a family leader with professionalized management.[7] Professionalization was deemed the incorporation of non-family managers in top leadership as well as the introduction of elaborate managerial systems and methods. Likewise, studies on various East and South-East Asian countries have shown that, even in early stages in the development of family business groups, higher ranks were not entirely closed to salaried managers.[8]

More recent research evidence from business groups in a broader range of countries indicates that the presence of salaried managers at top levels may have been expanding further.[9] Yet, these studies do not shed much light on the degree to which this numerical expansion has been accompanied by a retreat in family involvement in the management of business groups. As Hattori points out for the South Korean *chaebol*, it is difficult to know what the rise of salaried managers to top positions in affiliate enterprises actually implies regarding authority relationships with family members occupying higher ranks.[10] Likewise, in a recent study on Thai family business groups, for example, Wailerdsak Yabushita and Suehiro conclude that increasing employment of salaried managers in high-level positions does not necessarily imply a shift in the balance of power vis-à-vis the owner family.[11] Neither does it indicate a steady movement towards the so-called Chandlerian managerial enterprise, defined as "managed [and controlled] by a hierarchy of full-time salaried executives."[12] Wailerdsak Yabushita and Suehiro attribute the persistence of established power structures to the reluctance of owner families to forego control, a motive labeled in some of the family business literature as the preservation of "socioemotional wealth."[13]

A somewhat different picture emerges from historical studies on the Japanese *zaibatsu*, the forerunners of present-day family business groups elsewhere. Morikawa, for example, has claimed that after the turn of the 20th century, not only were salaried managers employed in larger numbers in the *zaibatsu* but had also begun to extend their influence.[14] The same was arguably the case in the so-called *gappon* enterprises, which had emerged during the Meiji period as the *zaibatsu's* alternative. *Gappon* enterprises were stand-alone joint-stock companies established by a number of large but non-controlling investors. The shares of these companies were also traded in the stock market.[15] Notably, though, Morikawa has argued that salaried managers had greater opportunities to rise to higher levels in the *zaibatsu* relative to *gappon* enterprises because of the struggles in the latter among large shareholders for top positions.[16] Still, according to Morikawa, by the 1930s salaried managers had gained marked ground in both the *zaibatsu* and the non-*zaibatsu* companies.[17]

Morikawa has tended to attribute the expansion of salaried management, more so in the larger and the older *zaibatsu*, mainly to the "forward-looking, progressive attitude" of the owner families, which, he argues, led them to "recognize the need for managerial talent."[18] This attitude, he claimed, became even more conspicuous after later generations took over.[19] Hattori, however, has argued that the somewhat greater inclination in Japan to share authority with salaried managers may have had to do with historical influences.[20] Specifically, he is referring to an institutionalized conception of the family that did not prioritize blood ties but rather its continuation. This established belief led to the *banto seido* (head clerk) tradition dating back to the pre-Meiji era, which involved choosing the most fitting person to carry out the family's business.

Morikawa does also recognize that the increase in the influence of salaried managers was not a process without tensions and resistance on the part of the owners.[21] Neither did control and monitoring by the founder or the owner families readily wane. The following statement by Yataro Iwasaki, the founder of the Mitsubishi group, appears to be indicative of the position taken by at least some of the owners of the *zaibatsu*:

> Our company should remain in reality as a family business, although it may have the title and formality of a corporation. All the businesses

related to the corporation should be consulted to the president who makes specific decisions [*sic*].[22]

Thus, Morikawa too regards the period until the mid-1930s as transitional, evolving towards the managerial enterprise, and uses the term "cooperative" to describe the relationships between families and salaried managers, particularly in the *zaibatsu* that he considers as more favorably disposed towards professionalization.[23] Economic recession and military pressures in the 1930s appear to have advantaged salaried managers not only due to the old *zaibatsu* families having to relinquish their shares and decentralize structurally, but also because of the emergence of the new *konzerns* in the form of joint-stock companies.[24] Still, the transition to the managerial enterprise could only be complete after the *zaibatsu* were dismantled after World War II by the occupation forces.[25]

8.1.2 Salaried Managers in Turkish Family Business Groups

Studies on Turkish family business groups have also shown that there was a notable presence of salaried managers in upper echelons. Focusing on proportions of family vs. non-family high-level managers and board members, Selekler-Gökşen and Üsdiken, for example, found that on average only about 10% of the managers in the holding companies at the apex of business groups were members of the owning family.[26] Family representation was higher at the board level. Still, family members constituted on average about 40% of the directors at the holding board and 20% in the boards of the affiliate firms.[27] In extending this line of research, Üsdiken and Yildirim-Öktem showed that some salaried managers were able to enter into the family leader's "inner circle."[28] These were managers who not only occupied high-level managerial posts in the group, but also had board memberships in an extensive number of affiliate firms. Colpan also suggested that there was an increasing presence of salaried managers in upper echelons of Turkish family business groups, indicated not least, she argued, by non-family managers assuming the so-called CEO positions.[29] She did note, however, that this pattern was more apparent in older business groups where later generations from the family were also involved. Likewise, Yildirim-Öktem and Üsdiken found that there was variation in the extent to which affiliate firm boards were "professionalized."[30] Their findings demonstrated that the ratio of salaried managers on boards was likely to be higher in affiliate firms operating in regulated industries (such as banking). There was, on the other hand, an inverse relationship between affiliate firm age, size and the presence of other large shareholders (as in joint ventures with foreign firms) and the proportion of salaried managers on the board.

Going beyond the question of the extent to which salaried managers occupied high-ranking positions, Selekler-Gökşen and Üsdiken have shown that operational decisions concerning affiliate firms were more likely to be decentralized in larger business groups. However, strategic decisions pertaining to affiliates were likely to be taken at the group level irrespective of size.[31] This finding confirmed an earlier observation by Buğra that owner-families were inclined to delegate to salaried managers only decisions of a non-strategic kind.[32] More specifically, Buğra argued, affiliate firm managers could neither make any investment decisions on their own nor deviate from financial and personnel policies devised at the holding company, which remained under the close control of the owner family. Furthermore, based on her interviews, Buğra suggested that salaried managers in Turkish family business groups were not really decision-makers but operated to a large degree as aides or advisors to the founder and/or later generation family members. In a similar manner, Colpan, reporting on her interviews, suggested that ostensible professionalization did not necessarily result in family directors refraining from involvement in the execution of strategies and policy. Indeed, it was not unlikely that the family member heading the business group as the chairperson of the holding board would be regarded in the group as the "invisible CEO."[33] Similarly, in a study on the founding and development of Turkey's largest family business group, Colpan and Jones observed that the founder "remained firmly in control as the unconditional authority for the whole group in the 1980s, with key strategy-formulation processes and decision-making mechanisms left in the hands of the family."[34] Within the context of Turkish family business groups, it is perhaps only a few seasoned salaried managers who enjoy some notable influence and decision making authority. And these would be the ones who have been able to gain the confidence of the owner family and come to be seen as close associates (akin to Üsdiken and Yildirim-Öktem's "inner circle") or even as quasi-family members.[35]

To conclude, the summary offered in the preceding paragraph seems to be all we know about what transpires in the highest echelons of Turkish family business groups. The indications are that the increase in the number of salaried managers at higher levels may not be adequately capturing what is actually taking place in relation to decision-making powers.

8.2 Theoretical Framing

In theoretical terms this study is framed by the institutional logics approach that has developed as an extension of institutionalist theorizing in organizational analysis. The notion of institutional logics was introduced by Friedland and Alford, who conceived of society as an "interinstitutional system" and institutions as "both supraorganizational patterns of activity through which humans conduct their material life in time and space, and symbolic systems through which they categorize that activity and infuse it with meaning."[36] Taking the "capitalist West" as their frame of reference, Friedland and Alford posited that its "central institutions" are the "capitalist market, bureaucratic state, democracy, nuclear family and the Christian religion."[37] Each of these institutions, according to Friedland and Alford, has a "central logic," defined as "a set of material practices and symbolic constructions, which constitutes its organizing principles and which is available to organizations and individuals to elaborate."[38] Also notable in Friedland and Alford's formulation is the idea that societal institutions are "potentially contradictory" and thus "make multiple logics available to individuals and organizations."[39] Likewise, again as Friedland and Alford have put it, "institutional logics are symbolically grounded, organizationally structured, politically defended, and technically and materially constrained, and hence have specific historical limits."[40]

The notion of institutional logics was soon appropriated by studies taking an institutional perspective in organizational analyses, employed particularly in examining inter-organizational field level phenomena and their interaction with organizations. Building on these studies, Thornton and her colleagues have proposed a reformulation of Friedland and Alford's initial conception by identifying central societal institutions as the family, community, religion, state, market, professions and corporations.[41]

Ideas pertaining to institutional logics have also been extended to studies of family business. Miller, Le Breton-Miller and Lester, for example, used the notions of "family" and "market" logics to differentiate between what they referred to as "family" and "lone founder" firms.[42] In doing so, they re-formulated the idea of the market logic as "entrepreneurial," which they claimed shaped and distinguished the two types of firms. Reay, Jaskiewicz and Hinings examined how the institutional plurality engendered by the co-existence of family, business, and community logics influenced the organizational arrangements and the behavior of wineries in Western Canada.[43] They were able to show that different types of firms (traditional family, lifestyle family and non-family) drew upon and combined these logics in varying degrees and ways.

The present study is also framed along these lines. To start with, the chapter argues that not only the structures and practices of family business groups but also the nature of the relationships between owner families and high ranking salaried managers will bear the effects of entrepreneurial, family, and corporate logics. What each of these logics entails is provided in ideal-typical terms in Table 8.1. The depictions in this table have parallels with some of the literature mentioned above and in the previous section of this chapter. It was Miller et al. who distinguished between entrepreneurial and family logics, associating the former with founders and suggesting that it had greater affinity to Friedland and Alford's logic of the capitalist market.[44] Gomez-Meija et al.'s notion of socioemotional wealth includes factors such as "emotional attachment, sibling involvement, sense of legacy, family control, and concern for reputation."[45] It is, thus, a manifestation of the family logic. Though not couched in those terms, the transition from founder to family enterprises has been one of the main issues addressed by Morikawa.[46] And the Chandlerian managerial enterprise has served as a representation of Thornton et al.'s logic of the corporation.[47]

Three main implications that can be derived from the institutional logics literature inform this study. First, as family business groups develop they may become infiltrated by more than one of the logics identified in Table 8.1. A plurality of logics implies multiple influences as well as the possibility of contradictions among them.[48] Second, it is likely that different sets of actors associated with business groups (founders, the owner family and non-family managers) are differently guided by these varying logics. Given their potentially contradictory character, the existence of multiple logics is likely to generate political struggles as different groups of actors defend and promote the logics that they are imbued with. Thirdly, the salience of these logics does not remain static.[49] Their relative significance may change in time, leading to alterations in the

Table 8.1 Institutional Logics Impinging Upon Family Business Groups

Categories	*Entrepreneurial logic*[a]	*Family logic*[b]	*Corporate logic*[b]
Root metaphor	Solo player	Family as firm	Hierarchy
Sources of legitimacy	Constituencies (e.g., the state, partners)	Unconditional loyalty	Market position of firm
Sources of authority	Founder	Patriarchal domination	Top management
Sources of identity	Business creator, deal maker	Family reputation	Bureaucratic roles
Basis of norms	Class of entrepreneurs	Household membership	Firm employment
Basis of attention	Status in business	Status in household	Status in hierarchy
Basis of strategy	Growth, wealth accumulation	Increase family honor	Increase size of firm
Informal control mechanisms	Social approval	Family politics	Organization culture
Economic system	Market capitalism	Family capitalism	Managerial capitalism

[a] Based on Miller et al., "Family and Lone Founder Ownership," p. 5
[b] Source: Thornton et al., *The Institutional Logics Perspective*, p. 56

power bases of the actors in their political struggles within family business groups.

8.3 Methodology

8.3.1 Source Material

The empirical material for this study comes from memoirs, biographies and life-story interviews of the founders and senior salaried managers in major family business groups in Turkey. After an extensive search in university libraries and internet bookstores, 44 such sources were identified, constituting in all likelihood an exhaustive list.[50] Thirty-three of these source materials are authored by or concern owner family members (more so the founders) and only 11 involve salaried managers. As the Appendix shows, dates of publication range between 1973 and 2016. Notably, though, most (exactly three-quarters) were published after the year 2000, thus providing "data" not only on the earlier days of respective business groups but also their more recent past.

Altogether, sources related to 19 family business groups. Of these, 14 are among the largest in Turkey, as identified by Colpan.[51] The founders of four had entered business during the interwar years. The origins of the remaining ten date back to the period of 1942 to 1957.[52] Of the five smaller groups four were close followers, emerging between 1955 and 1972. Only one was a latecomer, founded in 2003 when a branch of the owner-family broke away from one of the oldest and largest business groups.[53] Thus, in all, sources used in the study do provide a rich documentary base on the owners and senior managers of the older and larger family business groups, which constitute the prototypical instantiations of this organizational form in Turkey.

As research material, memoirs and biographies have both limitations and advantages. To start with, they are typically published for purposes other than those of the researcher.[54] They are also retrospective, as there is often a long time lapse between the events and the developments that are recounted and the time of writing. Accuracy may, therefore, be compromised due to lapses in memory and selectivity in recollection.[55] They may also be biased, as there may be inclinations towards self-justification and self-aggrandizement.[56] Self-censorship is not unlikely either, especially with regard to personal issues and family matters.

Despite these potential limitations, memoirs and biographies can be valuable sources for research. Most notably, they provide an insider's perspective of the phenomena that are being researched.[57] They offer direct access to the experiences, views, norms and concerns of actors, including those who may no longer be alive. As Tosh observes, they may be less solid as historical documents but "may be very revealing of mentality and values."[58] Likewise, they are not only about the individual author but, equally importantly, about his or her relationships with others.[59] Memoirs and biographies are, therefore, apposite for a study like the present one, where they are not treated as historical documents but rather as sources that can provide insights about the relationships between owners and salaried managers. Examining not only a single case but a number of such sources should also avoid some of the mentioned pitfalls and provide the opportunity to seek similarities in outlook, norms and values.[60] Moreover, the availability of source materials for both owners and salaried managers made it possible to take into account and compare both sets of actors' interpretations of their experiences and interactions.

8.3.2 Analysis

As sources were relatively few, all could be included in the analysis. In each of them, only parts that were most pertinent for the research question were examined—namely, those sections that related to the family members' and salaried managers' lives in the world of business.[61] These parts were closely read with a focus on instances where statements were made that pertained to the specific issues set out at the beginning of the chapter. These were occasions in which (a) some kind of a decision was made or referred to, (b) actors performed a particular role in the context of the position that they held, and (c) some type of an influence strategy was at play among actors.

Following Gioia, Corley and Hamilton, the analysis proceeded in three steps (see Figure 8.1).[62] In the first stage, portions of text that pertained to the three sets of instances mentioned earlier were recorded verbatim. The entire excerpt was then coded, which in some cases involved simultaneous coding, meaning that more than one code was assigned to the particular piece of text.[63] The coding scheme was developed inductively. Additional codes were included when suggested by new pertinent textual evidence. This first round of coding was provisional, sometimes involving longer phrases.[64] In each case, additional attributes were also coded by identifying who the "subject" was with respect to the position s/he occupied (founder, later generation family member, rank of the salaried manager) and who s/he was referring to, and, to the extent indications were available, when the particular incident took place. The coding scheme was then reviewed to ensure consistency in the phrases that were used. As this was done, the excerpts were also split so that a single code was assigned to each. In all, this first round generated a total of 119 codes. This was followed by interpreting the relationships between these codes, together with the associated textual evidence and the attributes that had been coded for each text excerpt.[65] Through this process, the first-order codes were reduced to 21 broader categories (first column, Figure 8.1).

In the second-order analysis, the focus was on the connections across the first-order codes. The aim in this interpretive attempt was

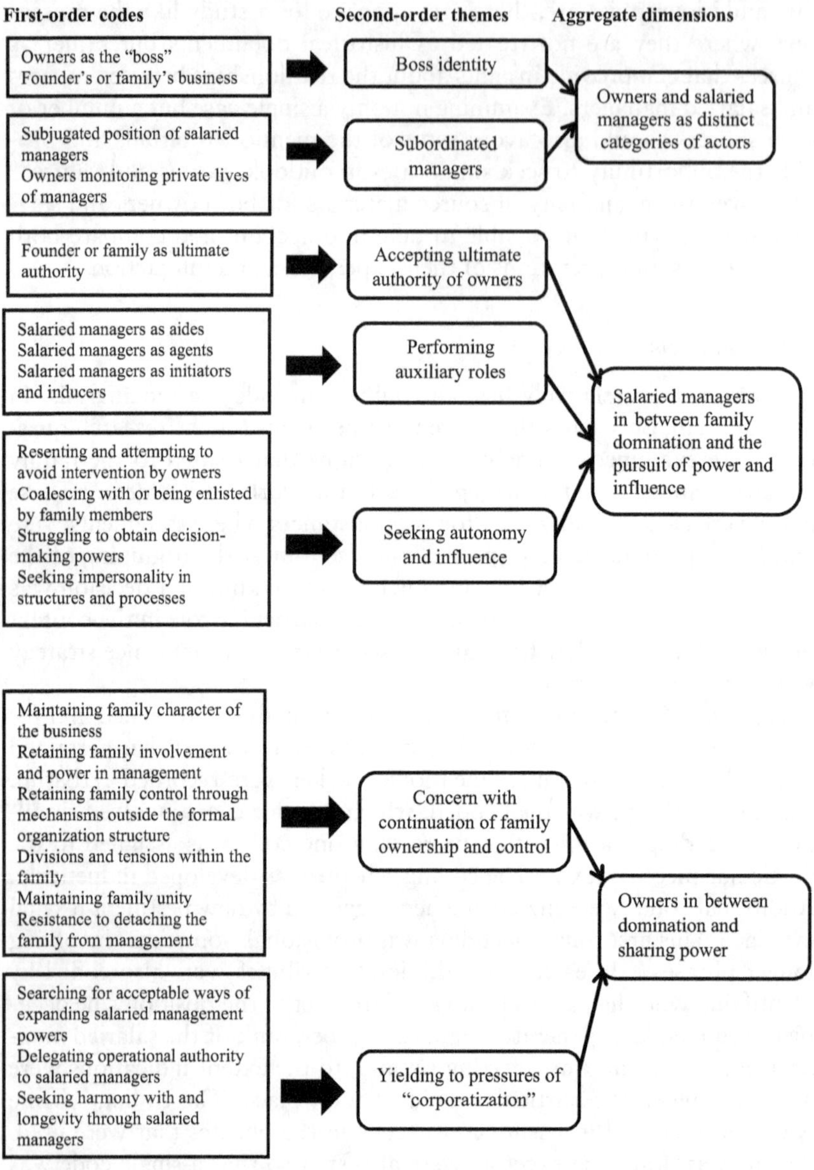

Figure 8.1 The Analysis Process: Development of Aggregate Dimensions

to synthesize these codes into substantive themes that captured the key aspects of the interrelationships between owners and salaried managers. A subset of the first-order codes suggested, for example, that a central concern for the owners was to maintain family control. Yet at the same time, there appeared to be tendencies on the part of the owners towards some degree of power sharing with the salaried managers (second column, Figure 8.1).

The third step in the analysis involved examining whether the second-order themes could be further assembled into a smaller number of theoretically significant overarching categories. The three aggregate dimensions that emerged capture, on the one hand, the way in which the relationship between owners and salaried managers has become established and, on the other hand, the tensions that were involved in this relationship. As shown in Figure 8.1 (third column), these dimensions were (a) owners and salaried managers as distinct categories of actors, (b) salaried managers in between family domination and pursuit of power and influence, and (c) owners in between domination and sharing power.

8.4 Findings and Discussion

The evidence in the memoirs, biographies and the life-story interviews shows that, without exception, the founders or family members have throughout been involved not only in the governance but also the management of the business groups in which they are the principal owners. The participation of the founder or the members of the family in management does appear to vary in extent and form. Yet, that they are involved in one way or another is independent of the particular ownership structure, the stage in the development of the group, or its scale.

Overall, the evidence also supports the argument that Turkish family business groups have been influenced concomitantly by more than one of the entrepreneurial, family, and corporate logics. There is also some indication that the impact of these logics has undergone some change together with the evolution of family business groups and the broader national and international environment in which they have come to operate. The transition from the lone founder to the involvement of the second generation, for example, implies a strengthening of the family logic vis-à-vis the entrepreneurial logic. Likewise, the national and, more notably perhaps, international currents calling for alterations in governance structures lead to a strengthening of the corporate logic in the institutional environment of family business groups.[66] The greater visibility that salaried managers began to gain in the Turkish media in the last decade or so, through the popularization of the term CEO (in its original version) for example, is one indication of the increase in the influence of the corporate logic within society at large.

As discussed in the section on the theoretical basis of the study, the existence of multiple logics implies that they may be generating potentially contradictory pressures on family business groups. The ramifications are twofold. First, actors within family business groups (founders, family members and salaried managers) may be imbued, albeit in different degrees, by more than one of these logics. This, in turn, can lead to contradictions in their decisions as well as their actions. Secondly, there may be differences among these groups of actors with respect to how strongly they subscribe to these conflicting logics. This could, then, serve as a source of political struggle among the carriers of these different logics.

With these broad observations in the background, findings are presented in the following section, based on the three aggregate dimensions that emerged from the analysis of the data derived from the source materials used in the study.

8.4.1 Owners and Salaried Managers as Distinct Categories of Actors

Within the organizational context where both the family and salaried managers partake in running the enterprise there is a distinct separation between these two groups of actors. And this division (a manifestation of family as well as entrepreneurial logics) is accepted, indeed, taken-for-granted by both the family and salaried managers. This clear-cut separation finds its expression in the way both sets of actors speak about themselves and the other group of actors. The owners readily and comfortably use the Turkish term *patron* (boss) borrowed from French. One of the founders of a group, for example, in a life-story interview in 2012, says the following in praising salaried managers who have apparently complained to him about some of his public appearances and the statements that he had made:

> *My professional manager* writes a letter to me and says "Why are you doing this? You are harming the company." I am the *patron* [boss] but my professional manager takes this stance. I say well done! He is doing his job and protecting the company.
>
> (Emphasis added)[67]

Neither do the salaried managers seem to have any problems with this, as a seasoned manager writing a biography after his retirement about the founder of the business group for which he worked for more than 40 years entitled the book *My Patron*. The salaried managers are typically referred to as the "professionals" or "professional cadres" (in the Turkified version of a term again borrowed from French). As the above quotation shows, they are the *patron's* managers. Writing in the mid-2000s, the general manager of a major firm affiliated with an old and large family business group voices his strong resentment of this distinction in the following way:

> One of the established viewpoints that I cannot accept is the *patrons'* approach to professional managers . . . as clerks and their view of this clerkship as serfdom, as it were.

For owners to view of their relationship with even the highest-ranking salaried managers in such terms put the latter in a subjugated position. A one-time "CEO" of one of the larger business groups remembers the following statement by the founder after a disagreement they had about whether they should enter a new line of business:

> This company is mine, I am the *patron* and you do what I tell you to do.

The domination of the founder or of the family stretched even to the private lives of high ranking salaried managers. The manager who wrote a biography about his business group's founder recounts his observations in the following way:

> The founder got worried when the earnings of someone working for him rose above his expectations and tried to figure out how things had gone wrong. . . . He believed that the owner had the right to closely monitor the private lives of high-level managers.

Possibly indicating owners' lack of trust in non-kin, salaried managers in return felt the obligation to account for what they did with the money that they earned. The same manager mentions that in the mid-1970s, after having worked in the group for more than 20 years, he "informed the owner family about his intention to buy a plot of land and obtained their approval," adding that he did this "because of his own rules." As if to attest that not much has changed over the years, a "CEO" of a major affiliate firm in another large group openly says, after about 25 years of employment there, that:

> Only the founder knew what I earned. . . . As a precaution, when I was to make any significant purchases in my private life, I first told him. . . . For example, when I decided to buy a Jaguar car I told this to him too.

The boss vs. employee distinction is not purely one of "hierarchy," as it would be understood under the corporate logic (see Table 8.1). It reflects the difference in the nature of the relationship with the enterprise. The *patron* is *the* owner. It is *his* (rarely her) business. It is *his* money. The "CEO" of an important affiliate firm, for example, remembered how in the late 1980s, while a group of high-ranking managers, including himself, were trying to persuade the founder to float some of the shares of the company, he made them think "that if the shares were to be sold he would feel as if he was sharing his firm with other people."

8.4.2 *Salaried Managers in Between Family Domination and the Pursuit of Power and Influence*

The data reveals that in various ways salaried managers found themselves in the midst of conflicting logics. On the one hand, salaried managers do appear to have been groomed by the entrepreneurial and the family logic in that they find it legitimate that the founder or the family leader has the ultimate authority in decision making. For example, as a highly prominent "CEO" of one of the largest affiliate firms of a business group throughout the 1990s put it:

> In the end, both in the group and in the affiliate firm the first and the last word was the founder's. . . . He knew very well that what came out of his mouth would be the final decision.

A seasoned manager in one of the largest groups, who had headed one of the most important affiliate firms and then rose to a high level position at the group, eventually ending up on the holding board, thought very much the same way when commenting in a life-story interview in 2015:

> If a family or any other group has 60–70% majority share in an organization in the end what they say prevails. . . . I have no problems with that. . . . That the majority shareholder has the final say is both *natural* and legal.
>
> (Emphasis added)

Opposing the founder or the family member in charge was also unthinkable. Again as the "CEO" quoted earlier conceded,

> There was no way you could suddenly say no to the founder; so before anything came to that stage. . . . I had to prevent him from taking a decision in the opposite direction.

Thus, within a context in which the founder or later generation family members had the ultimate authority, high-ranking salaried managers typically performed auxiliary roles. A prevalent one was what Buğra earlier referred to as the aide role.[68] It still constituted an important part of what the salaried managers did, especially during the rule of the founders. They conducted studies for family leaders and provided technical know-how and advice. The aide role also included carrying out administrative tasks mainly for the founder or the family leader, which even included serving as translators or taking care of the arrangements for their foreign travels. Not only was this the case in the founder-led formative stages in the development of business groups, but also when they had become sizeable. This is what a "CEO" of a large affiliate firm recollects from the meeting he had with the founder when the latter told him in the early 1990s that he had made up his mind about appointing him as general manager:

> Even if I decide to be a grocer and put on an apron, you will also wear an apron and we shall work together. Whatever business we do, I want to see you next to me as *my aide*.
>
> (Emphasis added)

Salaried managers could also be acting as the family's "agents," particularly in negotiating with third parties. This role enabled them to enjoy a considerable degree of authority, though always within the limits prescribed by the family members. As a "CEO" of a major affiliate firm proclaimed in relation to negotiations in 1996 for an important acquisition, "I had to be involved and take decisions within my authority. In issues that exceeded my authority I called the founder and obtained his approval." However, the agent role could also entail doing things that the owners did not want to do, as in the example given by the co-founder of one of the groups in a recent life-story interview:

> I never fired anybody. . . . There are always others who will perform this unpleasant role. . . . They did all this by letting me know and telling me their reasons.

High-level managers also performed what can be called an "inducer" role, through which they created opportunities for exercising influence on family-decision makers. This involved developing strategies and projects and attempting to convince members of the family to put them into action. At times, they were successful in doing so and did get the approval of the family. However, sometimes they could not have it their way or it took very long to have the founder or the family convinced. As a "CEO" of an affiliate firm commented on a proposal that he had made to the founder soon after he was appointed in the early 1990s,

> He initially listened to me and said nothing. I am sure that after our meeting he spoke to the managers of the other affiliate firm that was involved. My proposal was rejected. Yet, for about five or six months I kept on raising my proposal at every opportunity. This period gave him time to think. And, seeing that I was insistent and the premises of what I was proposing were correct, he eventually said "yes" to me.

So, salaried managers were in a precarious position. On the one hand, they were bred under the entrepreneurial and/or the family logic. On the other hand, they were influenced by the logic of the corporation. The latter was possibly due to the business education they may have had, the executive seminars they attended, and the business books and magazines they read. The managerially controlled foreign firms they interacted with are likely to have served as additional powerful yardsticks.

The in-between position in which salaried managers found themselves led to resentment, especially when the domination of the family members extended to decisions they considered minutiae. A "CEO" of one of the largest business groups in the early 2000s, for example, complained, possibly also aggrandizing his decision-making powers:

> We could decide on investments involving billions of liras, but in three issues the approval of the family leader was a must: . . . company cars, mobile phones and foreign travel (which had to be economy class).

Seeking the support of or siding with one or the other member or wing of the family became a way for salaried managers to influence owners' decisions. Examples abound. One manager, for instance, remembers an oil exploration project that a group of managers had developed in the early 1980s: "The founder was lukewarm. He thought that it was going to be an adventure. We managed to secure his son's support and the result was positive." Indeed, willing or not, managers were often enlisted by one of the owners against another, as the co-founder of a mid-sized group remarks about an incident that took place in the 1980s: "I could barely convince my partner. Thankfully, I had the support of our general coordinator."

Although an effective way for salaried managers to get the results that they wanted, these kinds of maneuvers led to political struggles and to winners and losers. A "CEO" of one of the large business groups in the early 2000s complained that during his time "some professionals in the holding were getting close to some family members and that this led to factions within the organization." A high-ranking manager from another large business group believed that because his views were often in line with those of one of the second generation family members, the elder brother who had become the chairman tended to see him as the "opposing team's man [*sic*]." Another manager from the same group remembers, apparently as a painful experience, an incident where he was firmly against an acquisition but his deputy, bypassing him, managed to convince the founder and her daughter to buy the firm in question.

The corporate logic also led salaried managers to seek greater autonomy. They wanted to have the authority to decide on their own. They expected to work in hierarchies and well-defined chains of command to which family members adhered too. They believed that impersonal rules should govern the functioning of the group and the affiliate firms. It was not that they did not realize the strength of the family logic on the part of the owners, but they seemed to be encouraged by the image of "modern management" that corporatization conveys, which they probably believed would help to convince the family to take steps in that direction. The managers' claim was always that what they were advocating was for the good of the enterprise. A "CEO" of one of the largest business groups in the early 2000s, in recounting his attempts to consolidate the CEO position, says:

> My aim as a professional manager was to establish within the group a *corporate* management style to ensure sustainable performance and at the same time to understand the dynamics and the sensitivities within the family well enough in order to create a balance. As you can imagine this was not that easy a task.
>
> (Emphasis added)

Indeed, it did not turn out to be. None of what was hoped for actually happened. Instead, the sector presidencies became occupied to a large degree by family members and their spouses. The "CEO" who had initiated the project left after only three years in office.

In any case, despite subscribing to the corporate logic, salaried managers' aspirations never seemed to entail hopes of a move towards the Chandlerian managerial enterprise. Realistically in a sense, the prospects that they could envisage and seemed to advocate were the detachment of family members from executive positions and from interference in implementation. With regard to the former, a highly senior salaried manager, for example, commented in 2015 that

> Family members should not have management positions. . . . Their place should be the board of directors, where they can represent the shares that they hold.

Even this was difficult to achieve, however, until perhaps recently and only in a small number of cases. The co-founder of a mid-sized business group, for example, who did seem to agree with this manager, had to concede in the early 2010s that "successors in the family tend to prefer being managers and to be in charge of execution rather than becoming *patrons*," which for him meant only sitting on boards.

8.4.3 Owners in Between Domination and Sharing Power

The owners of business groups were also influenced by entrepreneurial, family, and even corporate logics. It is probably the family logic that has been most influential, though there was in every case a period in which the business group was run by the lone founder or, in a few instances, by co-founders. That the family logic penetrated into all of these business groups is indicated by there being none within the "sample" of this study that had no later generation involvement. As mentioned earlier in the chapter, the influence of the corporate logic on founders and their families were rather late coming, possibly in the last couple of decades or so.

Formative periods of the business groups, old and new alike, were when the entrepreneurial logic triumphed. When founders spoke about the enterprise, major decisions, and business achievements at these early stages, they used, almost invariably, the first person singular. The founder of currently a mid-sized business group, for example, notes that "I sometimes shift to plural expressions, but unfortunately I was the only person contemplating and deciding on these matters." Not only were the founders the sole decision makers on any significant issue (such as entry into a new business), but they made almost all operational decisions on their own and attempted to monitor virtually all the activities. The same founder reminisces in a way that embodies the entrepreneurial logic:

> I had to look for new business areas and opportunities on my own. . . . I believed that I knew everything better or could do everything better. So I interfered a lot. I did everything on my own.

It was not that there were no other influential people around the founders at these early stages. There were; but they were more likely to be partners, friends, or advisers. There could also be some rudimentary family involvement by sons, siblings, and possibly spouses and other relatives. Yet none of these participants in the enterprise were in a position to challenge the founder.

Beginning during these formative stages and increasing after the involvement of the later generation, the strongest indicator of the dominance of the family logic is the invariable and almost obsessive emphasis on the continuation of the enterprise as the family's business as well as the companion hopes that it will remain in the hands of the future generations. The founder just quoted says the following in his "retirement" days:

> Currently, there are no outsiders in the management of our business group. After me, the management is now in the hands of one person—my son. . . . I am sure that, as he says, he will retire at the age 65. I hope that by that time the grandchildren will be ready to take over.

The wife of the founder of a larger business group expresses her very similar wishes:

> After us, our children will sustain and expand our business. I hope they will elevate their father's holding to a European scale, a world scale enterprise. There is no reason why it should not be so. Their father brought it from a small business to this level. They will make it even bigger.

Integration of the next generation into management was the way to ensure that family control and direction persisted. Sons and daughters, as the case might be, were placed not only on the board of the holding company at the apex of group, but also the boards of the affiliate firms. Founders' children were also entrusted with key management positions both at the holding and the affiliate firm levels. A salaried manager who had worked as a general manager of an affiliate firm in one of the largest groups and rose to high-level positions at the holding company, including its board, accounted for the unwillingness of owner families to relinquish control in the following way:

> One thing that pleases people most is probably *power*. To be able to say that "X is not good; s/he should go and Y should be appointed instead" is something people like.
>
> (Emphasis in the original)

When more seats and positions had to be allocated to non-family members with growth in the size of the group and the expansion of managerial hierarchies as well as the infiltration of the corporate logic, the tendency was to turn to "family committees," "family assemblies," or less formal gatherings of the family members. The accounts provided by top level salaried managers even in the largest groups clearly indicate that the locus of power within the group resided in these family-based arrangements. One of them described his experiences as a holding board member in the 2000s in the following manner:

> Decisions about most of the issues on the agenda would have been taken previously at the Family Assembly. Information was shared at the Board of Directors' meeting and the decisions were approved . . . The family would have already made the decision, having conferred with their advisers and people whose views they valued.

The same manager also added, as an example, that despite being a director at the holding board, he heard of a major acquisition by the group in 2005 only in the newspapers. What he further says about the nature of this acquisition provides a clear example of how the weakened entrepreneurial logic may be revived as the family too may respond to a sudden opportunity that promises growth and wealth accumulation (see Table 8.1). The soft critical position that the same manager takes towards this acquisition, claiming that it did not fit into the existing strategy of the group (which he interpreted as being close to the final consumer), serves additionally as an example of the tension between the entrepreneurial and the corporate logics.

The transition from the lone founder to the family, though not creating much of a challenge to the "patriarchal domination" of the founder (see Table 8.1), did seem to engender dual or perhaps even triple lines of authority within the business group. This happened as the second generation and then the third began to assume senior management or board positions. Such a state engendered at times inter- or intra-generational tensions. These possibly conflict-ridden situations and the political activity that they generated then tended to heighten another invariable and obsessive concern: the maintenance of family harmony and unity. The overwhelming and widespread belief was that if such harmony could not be preserved, the enterprise would not be able to survive. This is not to suggest that attempts to keep the peace were always successful and divisions within the family and ensuing departures could be avoided. Yet this emphasis on harmony and unity does indicate how the family logic overrides the corporate logic, especially among members of the family. One example is provided by one of the largest business groups as they embarked on a "corporatization" project in the 2000s. The "CEO" at the time recounts a meeting with the family leader, who is quoted as saying:

> What we are doing is right. Our objective was to set up a very solid structure for the group. And you put a lot of effort into this. However, let us for a while put this project in the icebox. Otherwise, I will not be able to restore the unity of the family.

The same family leader was also explicit in his views about the priority of the family vis-à-vis the corporate logic:

> The thing called "corporatization" does not mean that all the members of the family who have created, expanded, maintained and brought to the fore the business group will be purged, pushed aside and not allowed to enter the enterprise. This however neither means that all members of the family will necessarily be placed in high level management seats irrespective of their skills and education.

The last part of this statement can also be read as a concession to the corporate logic. While the family did not seem to be willing to forego control and management, they were also looking for ways to grant somewhat greater authority to salaried managers. Quite often family owners refer to how significant the salaried managers are, how important it is to find competent ones, and how the enterprise benefits from them. It appears that owners at least felt the need to express such views, possibly, both to elicit the commitment of salaried managers and to show that they had a "modern" approach to management. Looking back to the days when he established a holding company as the apex unit, the founder of a major business group proudly proclaims that this constituted the "first instance in the private sector of *handing over* management to professional management" [emphasis added]. When these words appeared in print (some twenty-five years or so after the founding of the holding company), the founder had only just stepped down as the chairman, handing over the position to his son. Moreover, for quite some time the son had been the president of what was at the time called the "executive committee," a role that would nowadays be referred to as the "CEO." So what this founder seemed to be referring to or seeking was "controlled professionalization," as one of his daughters put it succinctly (and critically) in the late 1980s, whereby "the weight of the family continued to be felt in top management." In an interview conducted some ten years later and after the founder had passed away, she said that they were still working towards "complete professionalization."

Nevertheless, although wholescale corporatization did not seem to be forthcoming, salaried managers were delegated some decision-making powers, more so possibly at the affiliate firm level, though at times at the group level too. The manager making the comment that he did not have any problems with the family exercising ultimate authority, talking about his own and his colleagues' experiences also says, for example:

> The business group I worked in gave us the opportunity to make decisions and to make mistakes. I found the opportunity to devise strategy. . . . Because we took the strategic decisions, working as a manager was very enjoyable in these firms.

Quite a few of the founders or later generation family leaders were also inclined to agree that salaried managers had a part to play in the continuation of their business, though, as always, not on their own but together with family members. The founder of one of the largest business groups, also quoted earlier, speaking after his official "retirement," remarked, again proudly it seems:

> I have entrusted the management of our group to my esteemed colleagues who have worked for many years and gained experience in our companies and *my children*.
>
> (Emphasis added)

Notable as it may seem that he refers to salaried managers first, not only did he hand over, as mentioned previously, the chairmanship of the holding board to his son but he himself remained highly involved with management until his death some ten years later. After another ten years or so, the founder's son did the same and his eldest son became the chairman.

8.5 Conclusion

The analysis presented in the preceding section shows that business groups in Turkey, large or small, long-standing or recently established, are still owned, controlled and managed by families. The Chandlerian managerial enterprise, in which salaried top management makes strategic and operational decisions, appears to be very far from view. Indeed, it seems so remote that it cannot even be imagined, either by the owner families or the high ranking salaried managers. The engagement of founder(s) in day-to-day activities in early stages and ensuing family involvement in management have led to the institutionalization of the "boss" identity both in the self-perception of the owners themselves and in the minds of those around them. This has been accompanied by the predominant view on the part of the founders or the owner families that the business group is *their* enterprise. The ultimate authority in running the business still resides, therefore, with the founder or the family, the salaried managers having made limited strides in acquiring authority and power. The latter are still viewed as the "hired hands," to use Khurana's expression.[69]

One way that this continuing state of affairs can be accounted for is by pointing to the persistent concentrated ownership of the families. The founder of one of the oldest groups was quoted by a salaried manager as having said some four decades or so ago that "in our [the Turkish] system, the majority ownership of families will continue for many years to come." His prophesizing appears to have come true. There has indeed not been much change in that respect until now. The result, as the various quotes in the previous section have shown, is that in this context of continuing concentrated ownership, the most that even salaried managers could envisage was the detachment of family members from executive positions and involvement in implementation.

The findings of this study suggest a different perspective: the family business group, including the persistence of concentrated ownership, has been and continues to be shaped by the interplay among the institutional logics of entrepreneurship, family, and corporation. Available textual evidence suggests that all the business groups included in this study have transited or are in the process of transition from a lone founder to a family firm. This implies a weakening of the entrepreneurial logic and the strengthening of the logic of the family. There is also evidence though, that the corporate logic has been making inroads, possibly increasingly so.

The existence of these multiple logics accounts for both the changes and the tensions described in the prior section. In most cases the family logic appears to have the upper hand. Nevertheless, although weakened, the entrepreneurial logic is still there, as exemplified in this chapter by the sudden and opportunity-driven major acquisition by one of the largest business groups. Likewise, the infiltration of the corporate logic, albeit in checkered ways, appears to have been a significant source of tension as it confronted established arrangements and practices resting on entrepreneurial and family logics.

These multiple logics also appear to have engendered dualities in the thinking, decisions and the actions on the part of both the owners and the high-ranking salaried managers. For the owners, there was the weight of the entrepreneurial or family logics. Yet, there was also the, possibly increasing, influence of the logic of the corporation. Arguably, this has had to do in part with the growing scale of their enterprises and an economic context that purportedly was becoming more competitive and internationalized. There were also normative pressures, however. One or one's enterprise had to be, or at least had to look, "modern" and "professionalized." That owners tended to readily endorse the term "CEO" roughly after year 2000 and allowed some more visibility to their high-ranking salaried managers, attests to the felt need for their enterprises to be, or rather perhaps look, corporatized. Yet the influence of the entrepreneurial and, possibly even more, the family logic has always been present. Owners seemed to be searching for a somewhat uneasy combination of retaining their ultimate authority and active involvement in management together with structures and practices shaped by the corporate logic. The latter appears to have been achieved, though possibly variably across the business groups, with respect to the use of formal management methods and techniques, particularly in lower, operational levels. Relinquishing power, however, still appears to remain difficult.

High-ranking salaried managers were not immune to dualities either, though in ways different from those of the owners. Often internally long-tenured, managers too were strongly imbued with entrepreneurial and family logics. They, therefore, typically took for granted the structures and practices shaped by these logics, some even seeing the founder as a "father" or an "elder brother." Yet they also had stronger affinities to the corporate logic, more strongly than the owners. This was accompanied by aspirations for greater autonomy and, more importantly perhaps, an enterprise that was run on the basis of formalized structures and procedures that were also adhered to by the owners. As has been shown, salaried managers' struggles towards these ends were typically justified with reference to economic and sustainability considerations. There was never even a hint that what they envisioned also meant that the balance of power would be tilting towards them. It is difficult to know whether this did not occur to them or whether this possibility could not be voiced even after one retired and no more had relationships with the group in which one had worked.

The brief review of the international literature on family business groups in this chapter suggests that what has been found in this study may not be unique to Turkey, though clearly more research along these lines is required on business groups elsewhere. It may well be that the history of the transformation of the Japanese *zaibatsu* towards the managerial enterprise still remains an exception. This is not only because of the intervention carried out by the occupation forces after World War II. Hattori, for example, argued that even if it were not for the purge by occupation forces, Japanese enterprises were set on a course of evolving towards the managerial enterprise.[70] Although this trajectory was arguably also facilitated by the politico-economic environment in Japan during the 1930s, Hattori has interestingly suggested that its roots may lie in the conception of the family in Japan and the associated traditions about running enterprises that date back to the pre-Meiji era. Most importantly perhaps, again as Hattori has argued, the pattern that Morikawa, for example, has identified for Japanese enterprises may be along Chandlerian lines, but the "mechanism" producing a similar outcome may have been different.[71]

These considerations raise questions about the "universality" and the "inevitability" of the evolution towards the managerial enterprise. The Turkish case confirms widespread evidence that, despite much rhetoric, family businesses even after a period of more than half a century are not on any kind of fast track to convert to managerial enterprises. The institutional logics view adopted in this chapter would imply that owner families are likely to resist moves in the direction of the managerial enterprise and will not readily relinquish the powers they have. Nevertheless, historical sensitivity requires the acknowledgement that in this case too, the study presented here pertains to a particular era. What the future may hold remains to be seen.

Notes

1. Hasan Güleşçi at the press conference announcing his retirement—reported in the daily *Hürriyet*, 14 July 2000.
2. Hasan Güleşçi, in an interview with his high school alumni magazine—*Buluşma*, n. 23, Winter 2015, p. 23.
3. See A. Buğra, *State and Business in Modern Turkey: A Comparative Study*, New York: State University of New York Press, 1994, p. 171; A.M. Colpan, "Business Groups in Turkey," in A.M. Colpan, T. Hikino, and J.R. Lincoln (eds.) *The Oxford Handbook of Business Groups*, Oxford: Oxford University Press, 2010, p. 487.
4. A.M. Colpan and T. Hikino, "Foundations of Business Groups: Towards an Integrated Framework," in Colpan, Hikino, and Lincoln (eds.) *Oxford Handbook*, pp. 17, 20.
5. See e.g., Colpan, Hikino, and Lincoln (eds.), *Oxford Handbook*; A.M. Colpan and T. Hikino, (eds.), *Business Groups in the West: Origins, Evolution and Resilience*, Oxford: Oxford University Press, 2018.
6. See e.g., A. Colli and A. Colpan, "Business Groups and Corporate Governance: Review, Synthesis, and Extension," *Corporate Governance: An International Review*, v.24, n. 3, 2016, p. 295; B. Üsdiken, "The Kin and the Professional: Top Leadership in Family Business Groups," in Colpan, Hikino, and Lincoln (eds.) *Oxford Handbook*, pp. 712–713.
7. N.W. Biggart, "Institutionalized Patrimonialism in Korean Business," in Craig Calhoun (ed.) *Comparative Social Research*, Greenwich, CT: JAI Press, v.12, 1990, p. 124.
8. See e.g., H. Morikawa, *A History of Top Management in Japan: Managerial Enterprises and Family Enterprises*, New York: Oxford University Press, 2001, pp. 43–46.

9. See Üsdiken, "The Kin and the Professional" for a review.
10. T. Hattori, "The Rise of Salaried Managers: Comparing Japan and South Korea," *Japanese Yearbook on Business History*, v.14, 1997, p. 24.
11. N. Wailerdsak Yabushita and A. Suehiro, "Family Business Groups in Thailand: Coping with Management Critical Points," *Asia Pacific Journal of Management*, v.31, n. 4, 2014, p. 1015.
12. A.D. Chandler, *Scale and Scope: The Dynamics of Industrial Capitalism*, Cambridge, MA: Harvard University Press, 1990, p. 14.
13. L.R. Gomez-Mejia, C. Cruz, P. Berrone, and J. De Castro, "The Bind That Ties: Socioemotional Wealth Preservation in Family Firms," *Academy of Management Annals*, v.5, n. 1, 2011, pp. 654–658.
14. H. Morikawa, *Zaibatsu: The Rise and Fall of Family Enterprise Groups in Japan*, University of Tokyo Press, 1992, p. 55.
15. See Chapter 1.
16. Morikawa, *Zaibatsu*, p. 245.
17. H. Morikawa, "The Increasing Power of Salaried Managers in Japan's Large Corporations," in Y. Cassis (ed.) *Business Elites*, Aldershot, UK: Edward Elgar, 1994, p. 479.
18. Morikawa, *Zaibatsu*, p. xxiv; Morikawa, "The Increasing Power," p. 462.
19. Morikawa, *Zaibatsu*, p. 246.
20. Hattori, "The Rise of Salaried Managers," p. 28.
21. Morikawa, "The Increasing Power," p. 480.
22. Quoted by T. Hikino, "The Development of Large Industrial Enterprises in International Perspectives," Working Paper, 2016, p. 4.
23. Morikawa, *Zaibatsu*, p. 216.
24. M. Shimotani, "The History and Structure of Business Groups in Japan," in T. Shiba and M. Shimotani (eds.) *Beyond the Firm: Business Groups in International and Historical Perspective*, New York: Oxford University Press, 1997, pp. 15–16.
25. Hattori, "The Rise of Salaried Managers," p. 8.
26. N. Selekler-Gökşen and B. Üsdiken, "Uniformity and Diversity in Turkish Business Groups: Effects of Scale and Time of Founding," *British Journal of Management*, v.12, n. 4, 2001, p. 338.
27. These figures pertain to the late 1990s. For similar findings on family member presence in affiliate firm boards in the first decade of the 2000s, see B. Üsdiken and Ö. Yildirim-Öktem, "Changes in the Institutional Environment and 'Non-Executive' and 'Independent' Members of the Boards of Directors of Firms Affiliated with Large Family Business Groups," *Amme İdaresi Dergisi*, v.41, n. 1, 2008, p. 62; N. Selekler-Goksen and Ö. Yildirim-Öktem, "Countervailing Institutional Forces: Corporate Governance in Turkish Family Business Groups," *Journal of Management and Governance*, v.13, n. 3, 2009, p. 207.
28. B. Üsdiken and Ö. Yildirim-Öktem, "Multiple Board Memberships and the Inner Circle in Family Business Groups," in J. Gabrielsson, W. Khlif, and S. Yamak (eds.) *Research Handbook on Boards of Directors*, Cheltenham, UK: Edward Elgar, 2019, pp. 266–267.
29. Colpan, "Business Groups in Turkey," p. 515.
30. Ö. Yildirim-Öktem and B. Üsdiken, "Contingencies Versus External Pressure: Professionalization in Boards of Firms Affiliated to Family Business Groups in Late-industrializing Countries," *British Journal of Management*, v.21, n. 1, 2010, p. 125.
31. Selekler-Gökşen and Üsdiken, "Uniformity and Diversity," p. 337.
32. Buğra, *State and Business*, p. 176.

33. Colpan, "Business Groups in Turkey," p. 520.
34. See Chapter 4.
35. Buğra, *State and Business*, p. 208; Üsdiken and Yildirim-Öktem, "Multiple Board Memberships," pp. 266–267. See also the epigraph.
36. R. Friedland and R.R. Alford, "Bringing Society Back in: Symbols, Practices and Institutional Contradictions," in W.W. Powell and P.J. DiMaggio (eds.) *The New Institutionalism in Organizational Analysis*, Chicago, IL: University of Chicago Press, 1991, p. 232.
37. Ibid., p. 232.
38. Ibid., p. 248.
39. Ibid., p. 232.
40. Ibid., pp. 248–249.
41. P. Thornton, W. Ocasio, and M. Lounsbury, *The Institutional Logics Perspective: A New Approach to Culture, Structure and Process*, Oxford: Oxford University Press, 2012, p. 56.
42. D. Miller, I. Le Breton-Miller, and R.H. Lester, "Family and Lone Founder Ownership and Strategic Behaviour: Social Context, Identity, and Institutional Logics," *Journal of Management Studies*, v.48, n. 1, 2011, pp. 1–2.
43. See T. Reay, P. Jaskiewicz, and C.R. Hinings, "How Family, Business, and Community Logics Shape Family Firm Behavior and 'Rules of the Game' in an Organizational Field," *Family Business Review*, v.28, n. 4, 2015, p. 299.
44. See Miller, Le Breton-Miller, and Lester, "Family and Lone Founder Ownership," pp. 2, 5.
45. Gomez-Meija, Cruz, Berrone, and De Castro, "The Bind that Ties," p. 692.
46. See Morikawa, *A History of Top Management in Japan*, pp. 18–22.
47. Thornton, Ocasio, and Lounsbury, *The Institutional Logics Perspective*, p. 67.
48. Friedland and Alford, "Bringing Society Back in," p. 232.
49. Thornton, Ocasio, and Lounsbury, *The Institutional Logics Perspective*, p. 103.
50. See the Appendix for the full list.
51. Colpan, "Business Groups in Turkey," pp. 491–494.
52. Ibid.
53. For three of these five business groups founding data comes from A. Karaevli and B. Yurtoğlu, "Founding Family Effects on Business Group Growth: Longitudinal Evidence from Turkey (1925–2012)," *Long Range Planning* v.51, n. 6, 2018, p. 838. In the case of two groups that were not in this list either, information on founding was obtained from web sites.
54. G. McCulloch, *Documentary Research in Education, History and the Social Sciences*, London: Routledge Falmer, 2004, p. 2.
55. Ibid., p. 27.
56. D. Bjorklund, *Interpreting the Self: Two Hundred years of American Autobiography*, Chicago, IL: The University of Chicago Press, 1998, pp. 20–21.
57. McCulloch, *Documentary Research*, p. 101.
58. J. Tosh, *The Pursuit of History: Aims, Methods and New Directions in the Study of Modern History*, 6th ed., London: Routledge, 2015, p. 77.
59. McCulloch, *Documentary Research*, p. 103.
60. Bjorklund, *Interpreting the Self*, p. 9.
61. See J. Saldaña, *The Coding Manual for Qualitative Researchers*, 2nd ed., London: Sage, 2013, p. 16.
62. D.A. Gioia, K.G. Corley, and A.L. Hamilton, "Seeking Qualitative Rigor in Inductive Research: Notes on the Gioia Methodology," *Organizational Research Methods*, v.16, n. 1, 2013, pp. 20–22.

63. Saldaña, *The Coding Manual*, p. 80.
64. Ibid., p. 101.
65. Gioia, Corley, and Hamilton, "Seeking Qualitative Rigor," p. 20; Saldaña, *The Coding Manual*, p. 194.
66. See e.g., Colpan, "Business Groups in Turkey," p. 516.
67. Translations from Turkish are by the author.
68. Buğra, *State and Business*, p. 213.
69. R. Khurana, *From Higher Aims to Hired Hands: The Social Transformation of American Business Schools and the Unfulfilled Promise of Management as a Profession*, Princeton: Princeton University Press, 2007.
70. Hattori, "The Rise of Salaried Managers," p. 27.
71. Ibid., pp. 27–28.

Appendix: Sources

Akkaya, Feyzi (1989). *Ömrümüzün Kilometre Taşları: STFA'nın Hikayesi*. İstanbul: Cep Kitapları.

Akman, Haşim (2012). *Saf ve Bakir Anadolu Çocuğu: "Güngör Uras Kitabı."* İstanbul: Türkiye İş Bankası Kültür Yayınları.

Bayraktar, Hüseyin (2004). *Şansı Arayacak Vaktim Olmadı: Öz Yaşam Öyküsü*. İstanbul: Bayraktar Kültür Yayınları.

Betil, İbrahim (2002). *Hafiften Bankacılık*. İstanbul: Ana Yayıncılık.

Candaner, Pembe (2015). *Türk Sanayiinde Bir Uzun Yol Kaptanı: "Hasan Subaşı Kitabı."* İstanbul: Türkiye İş Bankası Kültür yayınları.

Çarmıklı, Nurettin (2006). *Babama Söz Verdim: Hayatım, Anılarım*. Ankara: Arkadaş Yayınevi.

Çetiner, Yılmaz (1996). *Otomobilin Öyküsü: Otomotiv Sanayii Nasıl Kuruldu?* İstanbul: Milliyet Yayınları.

Darbaz, Tufan (2010). *CEO'luğa Uzanan Yol*. İstanbul: Sistem Yayıncılık.

Đikić, Ivica (2013). *Şarık Tara: A Life* (translated from Croatian by Michael Gable). Zagreb: Novi Libe.

Dündar, Can (2006). *Özel Arşivinden Belgeler ve Anılarıyla Vehbi Koç*. İstanbul: Doğan Kitapçılık.

Dündar, Can (2008). *Özel Arşivinden Belgeler ve Anılarıyla Vehbi Koç, 1961–1976 (2. Cilt)*. İstanbul: Yapı Kredi Yayınları.

Eczacıbaşı, Nejat (1982). *Kuşaktan Kuşağa*. İstanbul: Dr. Nejat Eczacıbaşı Vakfı.

Eczacıbaşı, Şakir (2010). *Çağrışımlar, Tanıklıklar, Dostluklar*. İstanbul: Remzi Kitabevi.

Ekşioğlu, Uğur (2015). *Kendi İşini Kendin Bul*. İstanbul: İnkilap Kitabevi.

Garih, Üzeyir (2001). *İş Hayatımdan Kesitler ve Gençlere Tavsiyeler*. İstanbul: Hayat Yayıncılık.

Gökyiğit, Ali Nihat (2016). *Doğa ve İnsan Sevdam*. İstanbul: ANG Vakfı Yayınları.

Gündem, Mehmet (2012a). *Lüzumlu Adam: İshak Alaton*. İstanbul: Alfa yayınları [also available in English: *An Essential Man: İshak Alaton*. İstanbul: Butik Yayınları, 2014].

Gündem, Mehmet (2012b). *Lüzumsuz Adam: İshak Alaton*. İstanbul: Alfa yayınları [also available in English: *A Redundant Man: İshak Alaton*. İstanbul: Butik Yayınları, 2015].

Gürbüz, Firuzan (2007). *Alnımın Teriyle—İbrahim Polat*. İstanbul: Doğan Kitap.

Kamhi, Jak (2013). *Gördüklerim Yaşadıklarım*. İstanbul: Remzi Kitabevi.

Kantarcı, Hazım (2014). *CEO Kantarcı* (genişletilmiş 4. Basım). İstanbul: Ofset Yapımevi Yayınları.

Karaca, Emin (2003). *Plazaların Efendisi Aydın Doğan: Bir Medya İmparatorunun Öyküsü*. İstanbul: Karakutu Yayınları.

Karaca, Emin (2015). *Ben de Kelkitliyim—Bir Medya Patronun Öyküsü: Aydın Doğan*. İstanbul: Asikitap.

Karaçam, Burhan (edited by Cem Akaş) (2006). *"Orası Yapı Kredi Fark Oradaydı", 1987–1999*. İstanbul: Yapı Kredi yayınları.

Kıraç, Can (1995). *Anılarımla Patronum Vehbi Koç*. İstanbul: Milliyet Yayınları.

Kıraç, Can (2004). *Anılar Olaylar*. İstanbul: Apa Yayıncılık.

Kıraç, Suna (edited by Rıdvan Akar) (2006). *Ömrümden Uzun İdeallerim Var!* İstanbul: Suna ve İnan Kıraç Vakfı.

Koç, Vehbi (1973). *Hayat Hikayem*. İstanbul: Apa Ofset Basımevi.

Koç, Vehbi (1987). *Hatıralarım, Görüşlerim, Öğütlerim (1973–1987)*. İstanbul: Vehbi Koç Vakfı.

Kocabıyık, Asım (2004). *Tazlar Köyünden Borusan'a*. İstanbul: Doğan Kitapçılık.

Nahum, Bernar (1988). *Koç'ta 44 Yılım: Bir Otomotiv Sanayii Kuruluyor*. İstanbul: Milliyet Yayınları.

Ofluoğlu, Filiz (2008). *İki Dünya*. İstanbul: Cumhuriyet Kitapları.

Okan, Bekir (2010). *Barak'tan Avrasya'ya: "Yaşadıklarım, Gördüklerim, Öğrendiklerim,"* İstanbul: Doğan Egmont Yayıncılık.

Öngör, Y. Akın (2010). *Benden Sonra Devam: Geleceğin Liderine Sürdürülebilir Başarı için İpuçları*. İstanbul: Alametifarika.

Sabancı, Sakıp (1985). *İşte Hayatım*. İstanbul [also available in English: *This is My Life*. Saffron Walden, UK: World of Information, 1988].

Sabancı, Sakıp (2004). *Bıraktığım Yerden Hayatım*. İstanbul: Doğan Kitap.

Selamoğlu, Esra Üstündağ (2011). *"90'a yaklaşırken" Asım Kocabıyık Kitabı*. İstanbul: Türkiye İş Bankası Kültür Yayınları.

Streather, Adrian (2011). *Mösyö Bernar Nahum: Türk Otomotiv Endüstrisinin Duayeni* (translated by Güniz Büyüktür). İstanbul: Çitlembik Yayınları [also available in English: *Monsieur Bernar Nahum: A Pioneer of Turkey's Automotive Industry*. İstanbul: Çitlembik Publications, 2011].

Tanju, Sadun (1983). *Hacı Ömer*. İstanbul: Apa Ofset [also available in English: *The Life of Hacı Ömer Sabancı*. Saffron Walden, UK: World of Information, 1988].

Tüzün, Çiğdem (2015). *Şarık Tara Anlatıyor*. İstanbul: Doğan Kitap.

Tüzün, Çiğdem ve Sühan Muratlı (2013). *Şarık Tara Sınırların Ötesinde: İş Yaşamı ve Uluslararası İlişkiler*. İstanbul: Doğan Kitap [also available in English: *Şarık Tara Beyond Borders: Career and International Relations*. İstanbul, 2014].

Yaşar, Selçuk (1996a). *Hayatım*. İzmir: Tükelmat [also available in English: *My Life*, İzmir: Tükelmat].

Yaşar, Selçuk (1996b). *Hayat Okul Gibidir*. İzmir: Tükelmat.

Yazıcı, Kâmil (2007). *Ortak Akıl: Tahtakale'deki bir Hırdavatçı Dükkânından Anadolu Holding'e Uzanan Azmin Öyküsü*. İstanbul: Anadolu Grubu.

9 Ethics and Corruption

Contrasting Perspectives of the General Public and Business Community in Turkey

Ali Çarkoğlu

Schumpeter's perspective on economic development is largely recognized for its acknowledgment of the entrepreneurial spirit that creates technological advances.[1] In creative destruction, the innovations of entrepreneurs push existing firms into competition with newly introduced inventions that render current technologies and products obsolete. The literature on economic development not only recognizes the contributions of private business towards building a competitive economy, technological advances, and job creation, but also recognizes the challenges businesses typically impose upon provision of public goods as well as building and developing public welfare. A peculiar set of ethical problems arise when private, and public sector players interact.

Discussion of the role of the business sector and entrepreneurs in capitalist development in responding to ethical problems arising from intense interaction between businesses and public administrators has attracted special attention.[2] The case of Turkey is a particularly intriguing experience among the developing economies. In the founding years of the country, the Republican elite chose to remain an integral part of the capitalist world economy by agreeing to pay back the debts of the precursor Ottoman Empire.[3] The Republic not only tried to stimulate the economy through public investments, but also aimed at building a new economic system based on private ownership, and abolished direct taxes on the rural sector. The economy reverted to more controlled economic governance during the Great Depression and World War II. Soon after the War, the Turkish economy was reoriented towards a market system. However, only with the measures introduced on January 24, 1980, did the Turkish economy fully commit itself to the market system. Nevertheless, the Turkish business community had its roots in the pre-market system with respect to development strategy, and most of the large Turkish business groups organized around family holding companies were founded before this policy shift. As such, the incentive structures in place during the state-led and -planned economic development along with the traditional principles of import substitution policy molded the character of Turkish business.

Although the large corporate players were well-established prior to the introduction of the reform package, a public debate concerning the substantial role of the business community in the development of the Turkish economy was at best superficial. The potential of private corporate initiative for developmental ideas beyond profit-making came to be realized by the Republican elites only relatively recently. The objective in this chapter is primarily to trace public opinion concerning the bold economic policy alternatives of market-led development versus to state initiatives designed to spur growth. First, a summary of public attitudes towards private initiative in economic policy will be assessed with the available *World Values Survey* data collected since 1990. Next, a descriptive account of public perceptions concerning corporate social responsibility will be given, again by using data only available from 2011 to 2015. Lastly, the public's lack of confidence in private initiative will be linked to their perceived prevalence of corruption in the country among both the public as a whole as well as private sector players.

9.1 Attitudes Concerning the Economy

World Values Surveys (WVS) provide extensive data on the Turkish public's attitudes and preferences concerning economic issues.[4] Turkey has been a partner in WVS since the second wave of data collection in 1990; the Turkish data has been available to researchers for a total of five cross-sectional data collections representative of the voting age population in the country. In WVS waves two through four (that is in 1990, 1996 and 2001 in Turkey) a question was asked about how business and industry should be managed.[5] The first pattern that arises from this particular framing of the question is that there is little support for state ownership of business and industry (14.4% in 1990 and 12.1% in 2001), and there is a declining trend in this preference for the first decade of data collection.[6] The overwhelming majority appear to take private ownership of businesses as granted. There are differences in the way respondents say the management of these enterprises should be handled. A dominant group seems to emphasize a partnership between the owners and employees in the selection of managers for the businesses. Rather than owner-run enterprises (which is preferred by only 26 to 32%), a larger group of about 38 to 41% prefer that owners and employees should select professional managers. A group significantly larger than those who support the state owning business and industry prefer that employees should own the businesses and elect managers. Hence, there appears to be a higher level of support among the voting age population for a version of workers' enterprises. Between 1990 and 2001, we also observe that while owners' and employees' participation in the selection of managers remains stable, at around 38 to 41%, those who assert that owners should run their business grow from about 27% to 32%.

When the question-wording shifts to preferences concerning changes in the status quo of the economy, we diagnose various other trends in public preferences. Should private or government ownership of businesses, for example, be increased? We see from Table 9.1 that in 2011 42% of people prefer that government ownership increase, whereas only 33% prefer increasing private ownership. In the same vein, as of 2011, more than twice as large a group of people (56%) prefer that the "state should take more responsibility to ensure that everyone is provided for," compared to those who assert that individuals should take "more responsibility for providing for themselves" (22%). Nevertheless, we also observe that there is no contradictory view of competition as harmful. In the first observation, from 1990, 60% of the respondents preferred the option that "competition is good," while only 23% found competition harmful. By 2011, those considering competition good fell slightly, to 55%, while those holding the view that competition is harmful remained stable at 22%. We also observe that nearly twice as large a group, 53 to 59%, prefers the view that "in the long run, hard work usually brings a better life" over the view that "hard work doesn´t generally bring success—it´s more a matter of luck and connections" (24 to 29%). As such, one could claim that inherent in these findings is an underlying belief in competition and meritocracy—a quasi-Protestant ethic in economic aspects of Turkish society.

However, we also see that while early observations from the 1990s show a more naïve belief in the possibility of win-win growth in the economy being possible, the 2000s reveal a disillusionment and rising support for the view that "people can only accumulate wealth at the expense of others." We also observe an interventionist approach when it comes to providing for greater parity in income distribution. A comfortably larger proportion of respondents prefers that "incomes should be made more equal" over the need for a "larger income differences as incentives."

When we look into several questions concerning material well-being, the importance of money, family, and new technologies, as well as respect for authority, we again observe some intriguing patterns. For instance, we see that less emphasis on money and material possessions appears increasingly more as a good thing. 70% in 2001 compared to only 56% in 1990 finding this as a good thing. Although this question was discontinued in Turkey after 2001, in this tendency we get the first glimpse of a post-materialist value emphasis. Instead of valuing money and all the effort that goes into bringing more money to one's life, people seem to place more value on less material alternatives. However, we see a complementary tendency in evaluations of "decrease in the importance of work in our lives" as a good thing rising from 16% in 1990 to 27% in 2011, while those who consider this statement as a bad thing fell from 74% in 1990 down to 45% in 2011. We also see that the predominance of the family continues with almost no change throughout the two decades

Table 9.1 Public View on Corporate Ownership and Wealth Accumulation

	1990	*1996*	*2001*	*2007*	*2011*
Incomes should be made more equal	53%	46%	56%	49%	55%
Middle	16%	13%	16%	16%	19%
We need larger income differences as incentives	31%	40%	28%	35%	26%
	100%	100%	100%	100%	100%
	1990	*1996*	*2001*	*2007*	*2011*
Private ownership of business should be increased	35%	50%	46%	30%	33%
Middle	23%	17%	22%	30%	25%
Government ownership of business should be increased	42%	34%	32%	41%	42%
	100%	100%	100%	100%	100%
	1990	*1996*	*2001*	*2007*	*2011*
Individuals should take more responsibility for providing for themselves	29%	40%	26%	29%	22%
Middle	21%	14%	18%	23%	22%
The state should take more responsibility to ensure that everyone is provided for	50%	46%	55%	48%	56%
	100%	100%	100%	100%	100%
	1990	*1996*	*2001*	*2007*	*2011*
Competition is good	60%	70%		55%	55%
Middle	17%	12%		26%	23%
Competition is harmful	23%	18%		18%	22%
	100%	100%		100%	100%
	1990	*1996*	*2001*	*2007*	*2011*
In the long run, hard work usually brings a better life	55%	59%		53%	55%
Middle	17%	11%		21%	21%
Hard work does not bring success—it is more a matter of luck and connections	28%	29%		26%	24%
	100%	100%		100%	100%
	1990	*1996*	*2001*	*2007*	*2011*
People can only accumulate wealth at the expense of others	30%	24%		38%	38%
Middle	24%	21%		27%	26%
Wealth can grow so there´s enough for everyone	46%	55%		35%	37%
	100%	100%		100%	100%

Source: Compiled by author based on World Values Survey

under consideration. Respect for authority at large appears in decline. A similar development is observed with respect to the development of technology. More and more people seem to move from seeing developing technology as a beneficial innovation to a suspicious phenomenon. However, as of 2011, the number of those who see developing technology as negative remains less than 10%.

Table 9.2 provides a guideline for macro policy objectives according to popular preferences. Maintenance of a high level of economic growth remains a predominant preference among the voting age population for the whole period under consideration. When those surveyed are asked in a different way, we still observe that "stable economy" is preferred over both progress towards "a less impersonal and more humane society" and "a society in which ideas count more than money." Options emphasizing participation in politics and freedom of speech appear less salient for people when compared with maintaining order and fighting against rising prices. In other words, given the economic fluctuations and uncertainties of the period under consideration, public preferences remain focused on stability and the maintenance of order with a high level of growth. As such, Turkey remains firmly on the materialist side of the debate rather than on the post-materialist side.

9.2. Looking at the Business Community: Evaluations of Corporate Social Responsibility

We see from the ensuing analyses that the overall attitude of the Turkish public towards economic issues and the market system is mixed with a strong belief in competition, but also a growing desire for an interventionist economic policy to bring about results that are more egalitarian. From the perspective of the management modalities, state ownership is not preferred over private enterprise, but participatory mechanisms bringing business owners and employees together appears to be evaluated more favorably. Hence, a business community with a more responsible approach towards management of enterprises might be assessed more favorably. In this section, we use a unique dataset collected with the initiative of the *Capital* magazine since 2011. The following section presents the analyses of the findings of this data collected by GfK (www.gfk.com/tr/) with a sample of about 1200 to 1500 respondents over the age of 15 across geographic regions of Turkey between 2011and 2015.[7]

The first open-ended questions asked in these surveys concern respondents' understanding of corporate social responsibility (CSR): "What is corporate social responsibility for you? How would you define corporate social responsibility?" Those who could not give an answer to this question in 2011 represent 52% (Table 9.3). In 2015, this group declined to about 27%. Hence, the dissemination of information and resulting self-confidence in the conceptualization of the concept of CSR have increased

Table 9.2 Public View on Macro Developmental Objectives

	1990	*1996*	*2001*	*2007*	*2011*
Maintaining a high level of economic growth	42%	42%	43%	41%	43%
Making sure this country has strong defense forces	15%	23%	22%	24%	26%
Seeing that people have more to say about how things are done at their jobs and in their communities	18%	16%	20%	19%	20%
Trying to make our cities and countryside more beautiful	25%	18%	15%	16%	10%
	100%	100%	100%	100%	100%
	1990	*1996*	*2001*	*2007*	*2011*
Maintaining order in the nation	22%	31%	25%	36%	35%
Give people more say	25%	24%	25%	21%	23%
Fighting rising prices	31%	22%	27%	24%	26%
Protecting freedom of speech	22%	24%	22%	20%	15%
	100%	100%	100%	100%	100%
	1990	*1996*	*2001*	*2007*	*2011*
A stable economy	29%	34%	31%	36%	40%
Progress towards a less impersonal and more humane society	30%	26%	28%	22%	27%
Progress towards a society in which ideas count more than money	23%	22%	22%	18%	18%
The fight against crime	17%	19%	18%	24%	16%
	100%	100%	100%	100%	100%

Percentages and totals are based on responses.

Note: The actual questions in the questionnaire from top to bottom are as follows: "There is a lot of talk these days about what the aims of this country should be for the next ten years. On this card are listed some of the goals which different people would give top priority. Would you please say which one of these you, yourself, consider the most important?" "If you had to choose, which one of the things on this card would you say is most important? And which would be the next most important?" "Here is another list. In your opinion, which one of these is most important? And what would be the next most important?

Since figures are rounded, they may not exactly equal to 100%"

Source: Compiled based on the World Values Survey

considerably in the short period. We see that CSR is primarily regarded as aid provided by corporations to those who are in need. In a sense, these answers leave the impression that CSR is perceived by ordinary Turkish citizens of voting age primarily as charity rather than anything else. Corporate activities that address social, cultural, or educational needs and problems are also represented in these answers. This group remains between 15 to 24% of the voting age population and hence, compared to the respondents who do not have a response, they remain a smaller group but obviously larger than those underlining charity as the definition of CSR.

The open-ended nature of this question renders the grouping of the answers into categories a tough task. Especially, considering the incoherent and sometimes incomprehensible answers noted from a reply in the field are not easily categorized in the analysis. Rising self-confidence among the respondents is perhaps reflective of the fact that the public increasingly recognizes the term CSR, but the precise meaning of the term remains largely unclear.

The capital-GfK survey also specifically asks "whether or not the respondent thinks that private sector companies bear responsibility concerning social problems." In 2011, the number of those who responded that private sector enterprises bear responsibility was 66%. In 2015, this group rose to about 73%, with non-respondents declining. Only about 10% assert that industry bears no responsibility concerning social issues. At the same time, the group of respondents indicating that they had no information about CSR activities of private sector companies declined from 42% in 2011 to about 35% in 2015. During the same period, those who considered the CSR activities in the private sector as inadequate declined from about 24% to about 11%. In other words, the public appears to have become not only better informed, but while attributing more responsibility to the private sector concerning social issues the country faced, also in general considered the activities of the private sector as increasingly adequate.

What then are the priority activity areas in the eyes of the Turkish public as a whole for private sector CSR activities? One clear pattern that emerges from the answers to this question in Table 9.4 over the 2011–2015 period is that the priority emphasis on charity work (comprising 16% of the answers in 2011) slowly turns in favor of activities that aim to prevent violence within the family or against women (comprising 20% of the answers in 2015). Emphasis on environmental protection together with charity work declines significantly. While activities that support education remain around 12 to 15%, we see a significant rise for activities that support arts and culture.

In short, we observe that CSR activities are slowly becoming better known and understood as reflected in declining non-response rates for the question concerning the meaning of the term. At the same time, we

Table 9.3 The Meaning of "Corporate Social Responsibility" for the Layman in Turkey

	2011	*2012*	*2013*	*2014*	*2015*
Don't know/cannot answer	52.4%	47.8%	41.3%	33.3%	26.9%
Aid provided by corporations	10.6%	25.6%	33.6%	23.3%	20.4%
Responsibilities of corporations towards the needs and problems of their society	8.1%	3.2%	8.4%	5.8%	3.6%
Activities of corporations concerning social problems	6.1%	9.0%	1.9%	7.4%	8.7%
Activities of corporations concerning social and cultural issues	4.2%	4.4%	1.9%	3.6%	5.3%
Proper delivery of the duties of corporations as an institution	3.5%	0.1%	0.2%	1.7%	2.3%
Activities of corporations concerning educational problems	2.1%	1.8%	3.2%	1.4%	2.4%
Other	13%	8%	10%	23%	30%

Note: The actual questions in the questionnaire are: "What is corporate social responsibility for you? How would you define corporate social responsibility?"

Source: Compiled based on Capital-GfK Survey

also observe that expectations concerning the CSR activities are also changing over time from basic charity activities to more activity areas such as prevention of violence against women, arts and culture.

As underlined in the previous paragraphs, with emphasis on the ethically responsible business community and belief in state intervention for better income distribution and open competitive business sector, the third main question shaping the views of the public towards the corporate sector in Turkey concerns the capacity of the public and private sectors to meet these expectations. Widespread corruption is one factor that limits the ability of both the public and the private sector to meet expectations concerning competitive and redistributive engagement in the economy.

Table 9.4 Priority CSR Activities for Private Sector Firms

	2011	*2012*	*2013*	*2014*	*2015*
Charity/voluntary work	16%	9%	9%	11%	10%
Contributions to the health sector	12%	11%	11%	15%	12%
Activities to prevent violence in the family or against women	12%	15%	15%	14%	20%
Activities to contribute to education	12%	10%	12%	15%	15%
Activities to contribute to the protection of the environment	12%	8%	9%	8%	8%
Activities to contribute to the protection of human rights	8%	10%	9%	4%	6%
Activities to contribute to the development of sports	6%	6%	3%	8%	4%
Activities to ameliorate work condition and security of their employees	5%	6%	6%	0%	0%
Support for the civil society	5%	6%	5%	7%	6%
Support for arts and culture	4%	5%	5%	10%	9%
Other	7%	13%	14%	9%	10%

Source: Compiled based on Capital-GfK Survey

9.3 Corruption and Business Community

"The use of power by political authorities and/or public servants outside their duties, in order to serve personal interests or the interests of those who, they feel, belong to the same group as themselves"[8] can be used as the simplest definition of political and administrative corruption. As such, corruption covers a huge space in public and private sector interaction and directly influences the behavior of the business community.

Although bribery and favoritism are the widest forms of corruption, politicians and civil servants abuse their authority in a variety of other ways.[9] Politicians might use their position to perform transactions they should not perform, accelerate some transactions at the expense of others, or make decisions regarding quality and quantity of work that serve their own or their party's interests. A special kind of corruption benefits not only individual politicians involved in activities such as accepting bribes, nepotism, cronyism, and rent-seeking, but also other constituencies with political motives—under the protection of politicians, voters or potential voters or "clients" constantly trade benefits with their "patrons" or politicians. Typically, business opportunities are provided in return for loyalty to a party rather than because they are in the public interest. Favoritism expands possibilities in the distribution of services in exchange for political support.[10] Besides "political corruption" that builds patronage relations between politicians and different constituencies, "administrative corruption" occurs when individual civil servants violate the principles of public impartiality, justice, and equality which makes it relatively easier to observe the illegality of these transactions.[11] The narrower definition of corruption, where engagement in bribery is illegal, will be followed here in the ensuing discussions.

It is important to note, however, that all the types of corruption underlined here lead to enormous damage to a country's social, economic, and political life. From a purely economic perspective, at least four major costs can be identified. First and foremost is the neglect of public benefit in the allocation of resources favoring purely private gain. Secondly, corruption lowers productivity by emphasizing unproductive activities like lobbying for favoritism. By also lowering transparency and information concerning public spending, corruption also raises uncertainty in economic life. Thirdly, corruption biases the distribution of income towards relatively wealthier groups. Fourthly, corruption typically leads to a hostile investment environment for foreign capital sources and hence reduces international investment that could help promote development efforts.

From a political perspective, the costs of corruption are also tremendous. Perhaps most significantly, corruption violates equality and undermines the most basic principle of democratic rule by destroying transparency and thus rendering citizens' opportunity to monitor the actions of the public administration tough if not impossible. As a consequence, corruption diminishes public accountability, which in turn tends to lower the quality of government performance. Corruption feeds populist policies and prevents more responsible policy making. By creating clientelistic dynamics, corruption destroys intra-party competition to bring responsible and accountable politicians to power and hence degrades the functioning of democracy.

Given the enormous costs corruption imposes upon a country's social, economic, and political life, the question about the extent to which patronage and corrupt relationships play a role in business community's relations with the public sector becomes critical.[12] The following section will first focus on public attention upon corruption in Turkey in order to underline its fluctuating influence on setting the political as well as business agenda. Then, using a survey with the Turkish business community from the early 2000s, we will examine the corporate sector's perception and experience of corruption.

9.4 Public Attention on Corruption

In Turkey, public attention to corruption changes drastically over time. Sometimes petty corruption in the form of bribes offered by regular citizens' engages the public's attention. At other times higher level grand corruption, such as "siphoning of banks," "rent-seeking," and "patronage networks," occupies the center of focus. Figure 9.1 shows the fluctuations of the Turkish public's attention to bribery and corruption among the top two most important problems the country has faced at different points between 2000 and 2016.

As early as 2000, corruption and bribery were in the minds of the voting age population as the third most significant problem Turkey faced

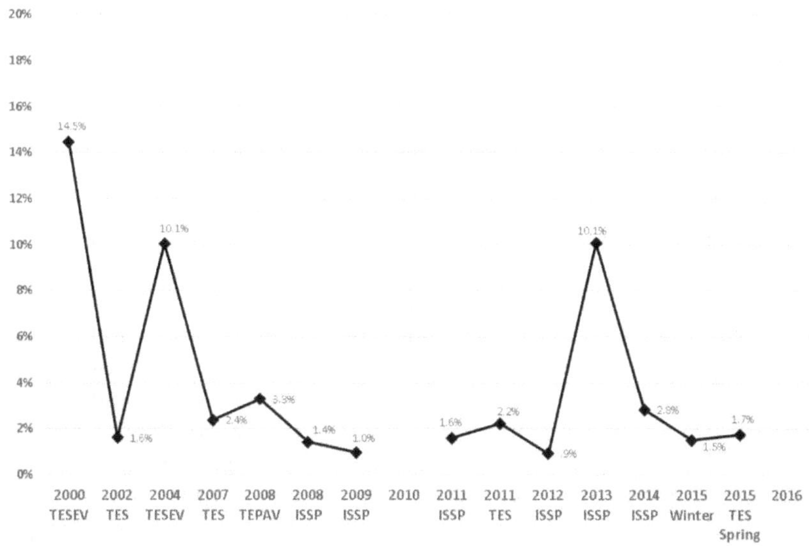

Figure 9.1 Bribery and Corruption as the Most Important Problem of Turkey, 2000–2016

Source: Compiled and drawn based on the following sources:

2000 TESEV from Adaman, F., Çarkoğlu, A. and Şenatalar, B. *Hanehalkı Gözünden Türkiye'de Yolsuzluğun Nedenleri ve Önlenmesine İlişkin Öneriler* (Causes and Policies against Corruption in Turkey from the Perspective of Households) in Turkish, Turkish Economic and Social Studies Foundation (TESEV) publications, 2001; 2002 TES from Turkish Election Study-2002; 2004 TESEV from Adaman, F., Çarkoğlu, A. and Şenatalar, B. *Toplumun Kamu Yönetimine, Kamu Hizmetlerine ve Reforma Bakışı* (Turkish Society's Evaluation of Public Administration, Public Services and Reform), Türkiye Ekonomik ve Sosyal Etüdler Vakfı (TESEV) publications, 2005. Available at http://tesev.org.tr/wp-content/uploads/2015/11/Toplumun_Kamu_Yonetimine_Kamu_Hizmetlerine_Ve_Reforma_Bakisi.pdf; 2007 TES from Turkish Election Study-2007; 2008 ISSP Religion III survey; 2008 TEPAV from Adaman, F., Çarkoğlu, A. and Şenatalar, B. *Hanehalkı Gözünden Kamu Hizmetleri ve Yolsuzluk* (Household View on Public Services and Corruption) in Turkish, TEPAV (Economic Policy Research Foundation of Turkey) Publications, 2009. Available at www.tepav.org.tr/upload/files/1295967822-8.Hanehalki_Gozunden_Kamu_Hizmetleri_ve_Yolsuzluk.pdf; 2009 ISSP Social Inequality IV survey; 2011 TES from Turkish Election Study-2011;

2011 ISSP Health and Healthcare survey; 2012 ISSP Family and changing gender roles IV survey; 2013 ISSP National Identity III survey; 2014 ISSP Citizenship II survey; 2015 TES Spring from Turkish Election Study 2015 Spring;

2016 from Populism in Turkey Survey.

after inflation (34%) and unemployment (26%). As such, it attracted more attention than deficiencies in the education system (8%) or terror and the (Kurdish) southeastern problem (6%). This first observation came about a year and a half before the Justice and Development (*Adalet ve Kalkınma Partisi*-AKP) came to power in November 2002. The pre-election data in Figure 9.1 from 2002 show that the relative importance of corruption and bribery had significantly shrunken in response to the rising salience of economic issues in the aftermath of the financial crisis of 2001. Attention in the months before the general election of 2002 was focused on the economy and almost nothing else. However, about two years after the 2002 election, as the country was approaching the local elections of 2004, the dominating influence of inflation and unemployment had declined, effectively pushing bribery and corruption up. Nevertheless, the group who placed bribery and corruption among the top two most important issues Turkey faced at the time was about four percentage points lower than in the observation for 2000.

From that point on, we observe that corruption and bribery lost its importance in the public mind. The TEPAV study in 2008 prior to local elections of March 2009 shows that only about 3% place bribery and corruption among the top two most important issues Turkey faced at the time. This issue remains of importance for only about 2% of the voting age population until the aftermath of the December 2013 allegations of graft concerning prominent AKP cabinet members. The scandal necessitated a late December cabinet reshuffle, effectively ousting the ministers accused of corruption. By the end of January 2014, eight AKP parliament members had left the party over the row. Istanbul deputy Muhammed Çetin summed up the developments by saying that, "with these corruption scandals the AK Party has turned black,"[13] warning of unrest within the party ranks, which at the time was expected to lead to further resignations. However, these expectations were not realized, and slowly the issue has dropped out of public attention. As the country moved into the presidential election in August 2014 and then to the chaotic 2015 double elections in June and November, the problem of corruption and bribery simply did not attract any significant public attention. As of 2016, for the very first time since 2000, the issue of corruption and bribery did not appear as an answer to the same question concerning the most important problem facing the country. In other words, this issue seems to have vanished from public interest.

One important point to keep in mind concerns the measurement of public attention or importance given to different issues. The measurement strategy of TESEV (Türkiye Ekonomik ve Sosyal Etüdler Vakfı) and TEPAV (Türkiye Ekonomi Araştırmaları Vakfı) studies in the early 2000s entailed a closed-ended format where respondents were read some issues pre-determined by the researchers to obtain the top-two most pressing problems. Starting with the TES (Turkish Election Studies) 2002 and in all the remaining ISSP surveys this question was asked in an open-ended format where respondents could articulate the problems Turkey was facing at the time in whatever way they liked, and the researchers later re-coded these responses into different categories. With an open-ended format, without reminders concerning the researchers' agenda, the respondents tend to focus on the most salient issues, and bribery and corruption may be just dropping from the list more easily. However, the overall trend in these results clearly shows that corruption and bribery drop out of the public agenda over the past fifteen years. The notable exception is when the graft allegations concerning cabinet ministers surfaced in December 2013, but these quickly disappeared primarily in response to shifting attention to economic and security issues from 2014 to 2016.

Another major issue to keep in mind concerns the short-lived focus of public attention on different issues. Unless supported by the sustained attention of the media, even as comprehensive an issue such as bribery and corruption could disappear from the public agenda. As the media attention shifted its focus away from corruption towards primarily economic and security issues surrounding the Syrian crisis and the Kurdish opening in 2014 to 2016, corruption and bribery simply disappeared from the most important problem list.

Figure 9.2 shows that the pattern observed in public perception of the most significant problems facing Turkey between 2000 and 2015 is reflected in the experiences of the same respondents concerning unruly payments (that is payments they would legally not have to make under normal circumstances) they report to have made to public officials. While in the year 2000 about 18% report they made an unruly payment to a public official to obtain certain benefits over the previous year, this figure continuously shrank over the next 15 years. So much so, that just prior to the June 2015 and November 15 general elections, only about one to two percent reported such unruly payments. Since this figure is within the survey's margin of error, it corresponds to almost no significant group in the country. In other words, unruly payments or bribery also appear to have disappeared from the personal experience of the average citizen. Whatever level of corruption there exists in the elite circles of the business community and politicians is perceived as a problem only when these come to be reported and discussed in the media. As media coverage of these issues also disappeared, general public attention to the issue of bribery and corruption also dropped from discussions in the public agenda.

9.5 The Survey

The ensuing analyses use data collected using a questionnaire designed to disentangle the business-state relationship in general and corrupt linkages therein.[14] The fieldwork was carried out in September-October 2001.

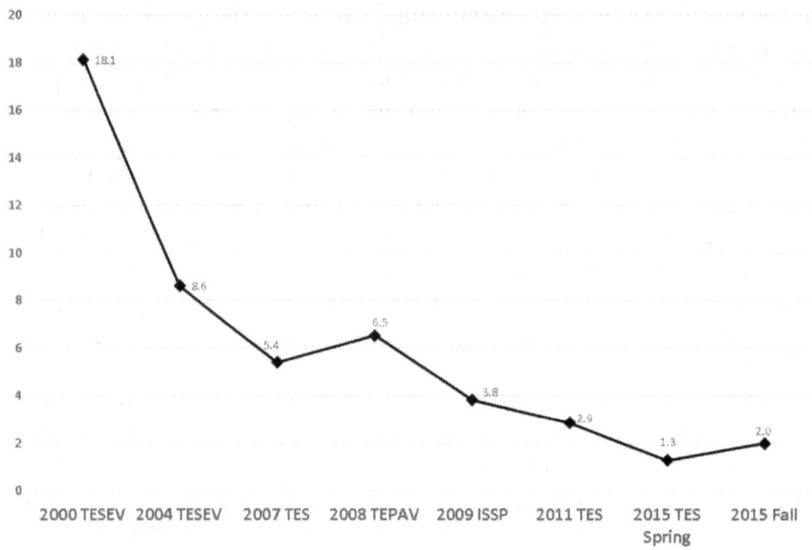

Figure 9.2 Unruly Payments or Bribery Experience, 2000–2015

Source: Compiled and drawn based on the following sources:

2000 TESEV from Adaman, F., Çarkoğlu, A. and Şenatalar, B. *Hanehalkı Gözünden Türkiye'de Yolsuzluğun Nedenleri ve Önlenmesine İlişkin Öneriler* (Causes and Policies against Corruption in Turkey from the Perspective of Households) in Turkish, Turkish Economic and Social Studies Foundation (TESEV) publications, 2001;

2004 TESEV from Adaman, F., Çarkoğlu, A. and Şenatalar, B. *Toplumun Kamu Yönetimine, Kamu Hizmetlerine ve Reforma Bakışı* (Turkish Society's Evaluation of Public Administration, Public Services and Reform), Türkiye Ekonomik ve Sosyal Etüdler Vakfı (TESEV) publications, 2005. Available at http://tesev.org.tr/wp-content/uploads/2015/11/Toplumun_Kamu_Yonetimine_Kamu_Hizmetlerine_Ve_Reforma_Bakisi.pdf;

2007 TES from Turkish Election Study-2007;

2008 TEPAV from Adaman, F., Çarkoğlu, A. and Şenatalar, B. *Hanehalkı Gözünden Kamu Hizmetleri ve Yolsuzluk* (Household View on Public Services and Corruption) in Turkish, TEPAV (Economic Policy Research Foundation of Turkey) Publications, 2009. Available at www.tepav.org.tr/upload/files/1295967822-8.Hanehalki_Gozunden_Kamu_Hizmetleri_ve_Yolsuzluk.pdf; 2009 ISSP Social Inequality IV survey; 2011 TES from Turkish Election Study-2011;

2015 TES Spring from Turkish Election Study 2015 Spring; 2015 Fall from TES post-election survey.

Although this is a relatively old survey, there is no more up-to-date follow-up survey conducted with the members of the business community on this topic, and the results obtained herein remain relevant and interesting for the understanding of business world and corruption in Turkey. A total of 1,219 businesspeople, representing six sectors—industry, construction, trade, transportation and communication, financial institutions, and trade and personal services—were interviewed face to face.

The survey was conducted in 12 cities categorized as Large Western, Small Western, Large Eastern, and Small Eastern. The firms from each city were chosen through a random sampling procedure, and each firm in a sector of a town had the same probability of being chosen. As a result, mainly small- and medium-sized enterprises were selected in our sample. There is no firm from the top 500 largest companies in the country represented in our sample. As such, our sample only considers the business environment that lies below Turkey's very top-level firms. Dynamics of interactions at the very highest tier might be parallel in certain regards to those this section will be describing and analyzing. However, in other respects, an entirely different state of affairs might obtain. Similarly, the survey looks at the state of affairs at the end of 2001 and hence reflects the pre-AKP period. To what extent these dynamics remain the same today or have changed is hard to judge.[15] What we can safely conclude from the data is that the importance attached to corruption by the public as a whole has considerably declined over the years. Despite the recent rise in how seriously the public views corruption due to graft allegations in December 2013, electoral dynamics, as of the end of 2016, appear to have pushed the issue once again away from the public attention.

As Figure 9.3 shows, the business community back in 2001 was far more concerned about bribery and corruption as a problem that the country had to deal with than was the public at large. Bribery and corruption were seen by about 22% of the respondents as the second most significant problem Turkey was facing. Because the survey was conducted during a period of economic turmoil, it is unsurprising that some 45% of respondents considered inflation and unemployment among the top three problems. However, deficiencies in the education system and moral degeneration, the latter of which is directly linked to corruption and bribery, are also seen as amongst the top two most significant problems. When corruption and moral degeneration are considered together, they almost tie the largest category of challenges for the business community—that is inflation. In other words, from the perspective of the business community, the issue of corruption and moral degeneration together with inflation appears to be amongst the most significant issues Turkey faced back in 2001.

In order to gauge attitudes about bribery and unruly payments, as part of our survey we created two hypothetical scenarios and asked respondents how they would react to them. An assessment was obtained of a hypothetical situation that involves a decision on the part of our respondent that may involve making an unruly payment or make a bribe offer to a public officer or a policeman. Our two scenarios run as follows:

Police scenario: Assume that you are caught by the police traveling on the highway above the speed limit. Police tell you that you have to pay a ticket fine of about $25 (40 million TL at the time). Would

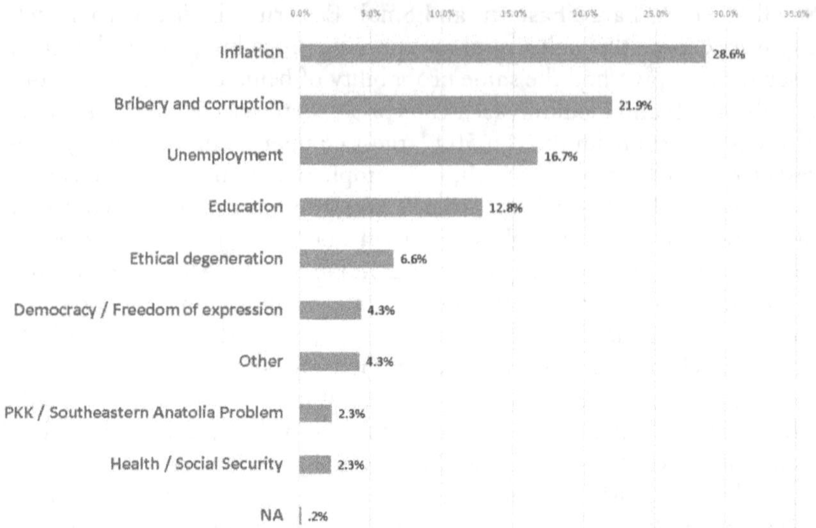

Figure 9.3 Top Two Most Important Problems Turkey's Business Community Faced, 2001

Source: Compiled and drawn based on Adaman, F., Çarkoğlu, A. and Şenatalar, B. *İş Dünyası Gözünden Türkiye'de Yolsuzluğun Nedenleri ve Önlenmesine İlişkin Öneriler* (Causes and Policies against Corruption in Turkey from the Perspective of Business Community) in Turkish, Turkish Economic and Social Studies Foundation (TESEV) publications, 2003. Available at http://tesev.org.tr/wp-content/uploads/2015/11/Is_Dunyasi_Gozunden_Turkiyede_Yolsuzlugun_Nedenleri_Ve_Onlenmesine_Iliskin_Oneriler.pdf

you offer the police about $7 (10 million TL at the time) or would you rather pay the full ticket without making such an offer?[16]

Public Bidding Scenario: Assume that your firm is participating in a public bid. You see that unless you make an unruly payment, your success is very unlikely. Under these conditions would you approach the public administrators with an unruly payment or benefit offer in order to win the bid?

Respondents were given four options. They could choose either to provide a bribe or make the unruly payment, they could wait for a move of an intermediary (a trusted third party) or a signal from the public official requesting an unruly payment, or they could choose to shun any unruly behavior and live with the consequences of their decision. The fourth option was to remain undecided as to how to behave. Those who unilaterally chose to make an illegal payment offer formed a group of 29% in the police scenario and 19% in the public bidding scenario. We observed that 18% in the police scenario and 10% in the public bidding scenario reported that they would wait for a signal from the public official to offer an unruly payment. As such, we see that 47% (police) to 29% (public bidding) appear to be open to offering an unruly payment in the two scenarios they were presented with. Nearly one in three respondents from the business sector was also ready to make a potentially grand corruption payment in a public bidding scenario is significant. In a similar vein, the fact that nearly one in two respondents from the business sector were ready to make an unruly payment offer for what could be considered a petty corruption case is also quite significant.

Using a multinomial logistic regression model, this study analyzes the determinants of choices between these options given in the question posed in each scenario. Younger respondents appear to have a significantly higher likelihood of choosing the unruly behavior as opposed to the reference category of avoiding such choices and living with the potentially adverse consequences of either paying a ticket or not winning the public bid. Gender appears to be significant for the scenario involving a speeding ticket. Men are more likely to adopt unruly behavior and offer a bribe to avoid paying the full ticket. However, when it comes to the scenario involving public bidding, differences between men and women disappear. Hence, men appear to be more likely than women to engage in small-scale corruption, whereas gender differentials vanish when it comes to large-scale corruption.

Respondents' level of education is in general insignificant with respect to their likelihood of engaging in unruly behavior. The only exception is for larger scale corruption, where university graduates are more apt to seek intermediation for getting involved in unruly behavior in securing a win in open bidding. A more persistent negative influence appears to exist between trust in the business community to keep their promises and the likelihood of engaging in unruly behavior in both scenarios. Lastly, in the scenario concerning making small bribery payments to police, as the retrospective economic evaluations of the respondents get better, the likelihood of choosing to offer a small bribe gets lower. However, economic condition evaluations of the respondents do not appear to make a difference in larger scale corruption choices.

The nature of a firm's business affected how its employees reacted to the scenarios. Respondents engaged in foreign trade (import or export) were more likely to offer bribes. Similarly, if the respondent worked in the communication or transport sector, then again the likelihood of bribe offering was significantly higher. The fact that respondents from different sectors were not found to be more prone to making unruly payments, unlike their counterparts involved in the foreign trade and transport and communication sectors, suggests that in these areas contextual or sectoral issues rendered bribing more likely. However, economic evaluations of the respondents appear insignificant in the actual reported bribing activity. Although in hypothetical scenarios there seems to be a linkage between small bribing inclinations and economic evaluations of the respondents, in actual practice, there appears to be no correlation.

When a similar analysis is conducted to see who actually appeared to be more likely to offer a bribe to any institution, a similar set of results are obtained. Older people were less liable to offer bribes. However, those who are at the highest level of education or university graduates appear to be more likely to offer them. Older respondents may simply be under more conformist pressure to give a proper answer that conceals bribing activity. University graduates comprise about 38% of the sample of respondents, and they appear to be more likely than primary or junior high school graduates to offer bribes. This might simply be due to the former being placed in more bribe-prone activities compared to less well-educated business community members.

9.6 Conclusion

The preferences of the Turkish public over the two decades between 1990 and 2011 places Turkey firmly on the materialist rather than the post-materialist side of the debate. During this period the public placed less value on political participation and freedom of speech than on the maintenance of order and control of inflation. They favored a more collaborative arrangement between business owners and employees as well as a greater role for government in the functioning of the economy rather than reliance on private initiative alone. More interesting is the stable, favorable view of competition and a belief that instead of luck and connections, hard work tends to be rewarded. As Turkey developed, with rising per capita income since the 1990s, a greater emphasis on equality of income as well as rising appreciation for the non-material aspects of life may be observed. In other words, despite reflections of solid materialist rather than post-materialist preferences, sound support for an active and interventionist public sector in the economy is seen.

Given this cultural predisposition, over the past few years the public has learned more about CSR and ceded more responsibility to the private sector for the handling of Turkey's social problems. The Turkish public increasingly sees CSR as a fundamental responsibility of the private sector towards Turkish society as a whole and are increasingly aware of these CSR activities. Most importantly, the problems of violence in the family and violence against women have emerged as an area in which the public feels the private sector can play a key role.

One important factor that limits the ability of both the public as well as the private sector to meet the expectations from the business community concerns corruption. The analyses in this chapter reveal first the public's fluctuating attention to Turkey's bribery and corruption problem. Despite the fact that the incidence of reported bribing experience of the average citizens continuously has declined from the 2000s, the importance attached to corruption as a problem on the country's public agenda fluctuates as a result of elite conflicts that raise or lower its prominence in public debates. Unless sustained media coverage is focused on this issue, corruption does not seem to remain salient in the public mind. One study's coding of the newspaper content for about two months prior to the June 2015 general election yielded about 20,000 news stories.[17] On average, in only about 4% of these was there any mention of the corruption allegations of December 2013. There is also much partisan coverage in these news items. For instance, in opposition newspapers such as *Zaman* and *Sözcü*, the share of stories concerning corruption rises to about 8% and 5% respectively. In the mainstream *Hürriyet* and *HaberTürk*, this proportion is close to the grand average of 4%. Clearly, corruption was not a salient issue for the June and November 2015 general elections and as such, tiny focus on this issue found among the average citizen in the country is not surprising.

From our hypothetical scenarios exploring whether or not respondents would prefer to make an unruly payment in order to avoid being punished or obtain a benefit and win a public bid by paying bribes very few distinct patterns emerge. Older people appear to be less inclined to make unruly payments, but men are more likely than women to do so. Trust in the business community dissuades respondents from unruly payments. Although non-persistent across our two hypothetical scenarios, deteriorating retrospective economic evaluations of respondents renders the inclination to make smaller unruly payments stronger. Similar observations are obtained for the influence of age upon bribe-offering behavior. However, most interesting is the observation that although hypothetical inclinations do not reflect much of persistent personal characteristics or firm level variables of influence, companies' characteristics such as foreign trade involvement, communication, and transportation sector activities appear significant in shaping likelihood to bribe. As such, firm-level characteristics, rather than individual-level features, reflect sector-specific structural features that shape the bribe-offering behavior.

The prevalence of corruption in the eyes of the public is, of course, especially important in shaping political reactions to the problem of bribery in Turkey. However, perhaps to a significant degree independent of the actual experience of the business community with widespread corruption in their dealings with the public sector, the public sector's focus is shaped primarily by the media. As the previously mentioned pre-election newspaper content data illustrates, if the media does not see the corruption as a public issue, corruption and bribery drop out of public attention. This, however, may not mean that the business sector is unaffected by corruption and its behavioral constraints.

The limited evidence this chapter offers from the early 2000s suggests that even when the level of public concern about corruption was at a much higher level than in more recent years, the business sector administrators' emphasis on and experience of corruption was even greater than the general public's. In other words, when one does not observe much emphasis on corruption among the public as a whole, the business community's perception and experience is likely to be different and more likely to be reflective of a critical perspective and more intense experiences with corrupt activities. Yet more data on this, especially in recent AKP years, is necessary to reach a more conclusive result.

Notes

1. J.A. Schumpeter, *The Theory of Economic Development*, Cambridge, MA: Harvard University Press, 1934. For an evaluation of Schumpeter's conception of entrepreneurs, see I.M. Kirzner, "Creativity and/or Alertness: A Reconsideration of the Schumpeterian Entrepreneur," *The Review of Austrian Economics*, v.11, n. 1–2, 1999, pp. 5–17.
2. Shibusawa Eiichi's perception of the idealized state of modern capitalism seeks a sense of harmony between morality and economy wherein no inherent contradiction exists between moral values and profit-seeking behavior by entrepreneurs. As such, Shibusawa's vision offers an alternative perspective on capitalist development for developing economies. See E. Shibusawa, *Rongo to Soroban* (The Analects and the Abacus), Tokyo: Kokusho Kanko Kai 1916, 1985, p. 12. For a discussion on Shibusawa's Gappon capitalism, see also Colpan and Jones, this volume.
3. On the economic history of modern Turkey, see S. Altug, A. Filiztekin, and Ş. Pamuk, "Sources of Long-Term Economic Growth for Turkey, 1880–2005," *European Review of Economic History*, v.12, n. 3, 2008, pp. 393–430; V. Balasubramanyam and S. Togan, (eds.), *The Economy of Turkey Since Liberalization*, Springer, 2016; B. Hansen, *The Political Economy of Poverty, Equity, and Growth: Egypt and Turkey*, Oxford: Oxford University Press, 1991; Ç. Keyder, *State and Class in Turkey: A Study in Capitalist Development*, London: Verso, 1987.
4. See www.worldvaluessurvey.org/wvs.jsp
5. WVS wording of this question is as follows: "There is much discussion about how business and industry should be managed. Which of these four statements comes closest to your opinion?" The four answer options given are as follows: i-) Owners should run their business, ii-) Owners/Employees participate in selection of managers, iii-) The State should be the owner, iv-) Employees should own the business and elect managers.
6. This question was not used in WVS for Turkey in the last two waves of data collection.
7. The author is thankful to the administrators of Capital and GfK who made the data available for these analyses. The sample of the questionnaire is balanced between male and female respondents. The youngest age groups, below the age of 25, consist of approximately 30% of the sample, while respondents above 45 represent about 25%. Socio-economic status (SES) also reflects a balanced grouping of about 70% in the middle SES category, with higher and lower SES groups having 10 to 15% shares in the sample. The largest metropolitan provinces of Istanbul, Ankara, and İzmir comprise about 38% while the East and Southeastern Anatolia regions comprise about 20%.
8. This chapter follows prior treatment in F. Adaman and A. Çarkoğlu, "Social Capital and Corruption During Times of Crisis: A Look at Turkish Firms

During the Economic Crisis of 2001," *Turkish Studies*, v.4, n. 2, 2003, pp. 120–145 in differentiating between two types of corruption behavior and relationship.

9. For a detailed exposition, see: S. Rose-Ackerman and B.J. Palifka, *Corruption and Government: Causes, Consequences, and Reform*, Cambridge: Cambridge University Press, 2016. For a review of the literature, see also: A.J. Heidenheimer, J. Michale, and V.T. LeVine, *Political Corruption: A Handbook*, 3rd ed., New Brunswick, NJ: Transaction Publishers, 2001. On the case of Turkey see: F. Adaman and A. Çarkoğlu, *Türkiye'de Yerel ve Merkezi Yönetimlerde Hizmetlerden Tatmin, Patronaj İlişkileri ve Reform* [Satisfaction with Services, Patronage Relations and Reform in Local and Central Governments in Turkey], Istanbul: TESEV Publications, 2000; F. Adaman, A. Çarkoğlu, and B. Şenatalar, *Hanehalkı Gözünden Türkiye'de Yolsuzluğun Nedenleri ve Önlenmesine İlişkin Öneriler* [Household View on the Causes of Corruption in Turkey and Suggested Preventive Measures], Istanbul: TESEV Publications, 2001; F. Adaman, A. Çarkoğlu, and B. Şenatalar. *Hanehalkı Gözünden Kamu Hizmetleri ve Yolsuzluk* [Household View on Public Services and Corruption] (in Turkish), TEPAV (Economic Policy Research Foundation of Turkey) Publications, 2009, www.tepav.org.tr/upload/files/1295967822-8.Hanehalki_Gozunden_Kamu_Hizmetleri_ve_Yolsuzluk.pdf
10. On vote buying experience in Turkey, see A. Çarkoğlu and S.E. Aytaç. "Who Gets Targeted for Vote-Buying? Evidence from an Augmented List Experiment in Turkey," *European Political Science Review*, v.7, n. 4, 2015, pp. 547–566.
11. See S. Rose-Ackerman, "Bribery," in *The New Palgrave: A Dictionary of Economics*, London: Macmillan, 1987, pp. 277–279.
12. See, for a detailed review, A. Dreher and T. Herzfeld, "The Economic Costs of Corruption: A Survey and New Evidence," 2005; P. Bardhan, "Corruption and Development," *Journal of Economic Literature*, v.35, n. 3, 1997, pp. 1320–1346; Welsch, H. "The Welfare Costs of Corruption," *Applied Economics*, v.40, n. 14, 2008, pp. 1839–1849.
13. The official acronym of the party adopted by the party establishment is AK, or unblemished pure white, party. See "AK Partili Muhammed Çetin Partisinden İstifa Etti (Muhammed Çetin from AKP Resigned from his party)," *Hürriyet*, January 31, 2014, www.hurriyet.com.tr/ gundem/25707298.asp, accessed February 26, 2014.
14. In addition to the present author, Professors Fikret Adaman (Boğaziçi University) and Burhan Şenatalar (İstanbul Bilgi University) were the other members of the team that conducted the survey on "Corruption: From the Business Perspective." More details on the results can be obtained from TESEV's web site, www.tesev.org.tr
15. On the precise new shape of business politics linkage during the AKP era see, A. Buğra and O. Savaşkan's, *New Capitalism in Turkey: The Relatiopnship Between Politics, Religion and Business*, Cheltenham: Edward Elgar Publishing, 2014.
16. These apparently odd amounts are just the corresponding US dollar equivalents of the Turkish Lira amounts that were more sensible.
17. See for details of this study: A. Çarkoğlu, L. Baruh, and K. Yıldırım, "Press-Party Parallelism and Polarization of News Media during an Election Campaign: The Case of the 2011 Turkish Elections," *International Journal of Press/Politics*, v.19, 2014, pp. 295–317.

10 Ethical Business, Corruption and Economic Development in Comparative Perspective

Janet Hunter and Geoffrey Jones

Turkey has historically been associated with the issue of corruption, even though as Chapter 9 showed, perceptions within the country of the importance of the problem have fluctuated greatly over time. "The existence of corruption in the Turkish political-bureaucratic system as a pervasive, entrenched, and enduring problem," one study written in 2009 noted, "has long been an "open secret" for anybody involved even scantly in the public affairs of the country."[1]

There appears plentiful quantitative evidence documenting the extent of corruption in Turkey, certainly for the recent past. Turkey has never fared well in the widely cited Corruption Perceptions Index published by Transparency International over the last two decades. In 2000, Turkey was ranked 50th out of the ninety countries surveyed. Finland, Denmark and New Zealand were at the top of the ranking for least corrupt, while Nigeria was ranked in last position as the most corrupt. In the 2018 rankings, Turkey was ranked 78 out of 180. The same three countries remained the least corrupt as in 2000, while Somalia held bottom position. Turkey was ranked as more corrupt than China and South Africa, equally corrupt as India, and better than Brazil and Russia. There were few developing countries amongst the top 30 least corrupt, but they included Singapore (3), Hong Kong (14) and Chile (27). Japan was ranked high, at 18.[2]

The nature of corruption in Turkey is also well-documented. Although Turkey has developed extensive anti-corruption laws, they have remained poorly and arbitrarily enforced. There is extensive evidence that Turkey's judiciary has been and remains highly corrupt, and has little independence from the government. A recent survey indicated that half of all Turks believed most or all police officers were corrupt.[3] Corruption, bribery and political interference became pervasive in the award of public contracts. During the years when public procurement was regulated under the State Procurement Law, between 1983 and 2003, the whole process was politicized and operated with no transparent framework, which resulted in continuous corruption scandals. A new Public Procurement Law, formulated as a strategy to harmonize Turkish law with the European Union, was enacted in 2003. However the new law coincided with the advent of the AKP government, which introduced multiple exemptions from open auctions and other transparent measures in support of Anatolian business interests.[4] Land, tax and customs administration also suffer from widespread corruption.[5]

This chapter places the experience of Turkey in a comparative and historical perspective. It begins with definitions. The following section explores why corruption, at least more recently, seems particularly associated with developing countries. The chapter then turns to the cases of Japan in the early stages of modernization, and India, which act as instructive comparators. Both, like Turkey, have had for at least part of the period since the mid-19th-century national governments committed to developmental strategies, strategies that have in turn been conducive to particular forms of interaction between the state and the private sector, and between business and non-state actors. They have been exposed to the same pressures exerted by developing economy status, and the shaping of institutions and organizations within the constraints of the interaction between indigenous cultural practices and external (mostly Western) influences and technologies. While what is construed as "corruption" may take different forms across these three economies, the comparison offers insights regarding the basic factors that may help to encourage or deter it, as well as the economic impact that it may have.

10.1 Defining Corruption

As Chapter 8 discussed, there are multiple definitions of corruption, but all of them raise conceptual issues. Perhaps the very first definition of corruption was offered by ancient Greek philosophers such as Aristotle and Plato, as Velasquez has noted, and it was focused on the corruption of political institutions, defined as failing to meet the idealized state of that institution. In contrast, today corruption is most frequently used in relation to individuals. These individuals, of course, function as parts of institutions, whether governmental or business, and the definition is still based on deviation from the ideal norm.[6] The problem for those pursuing a historical and comparative perspective is that ideal norms have varied over time and have tended to vary between societies. Morality is socially and culturally contingent, and this affects many things, such as price setting.[7]

A number of other definitions of corruption have been proposed, partly in response to such complexities, although each has its problems. Nye defined corruption as the violation of formal duties in pursuit of personal gain.[8] These formal duties might be specified in contracts or reflect public norms, although this does not really address the issue that such norms might not be agreed upon even within one society.[9] Friedrich defined "corruption" as inflicting damage on the "group or organization to which the functionary belongs."[10] However, the concept of damage is also open-ended.[11]

In much recent literature Rose-Ackerman's definition of corruption as "the misuse of public power for private gain" has been widely cited.[12] However, this definition, which assumes a distinction between the public and the private, raises particular issues when it is applied historically, and to certain non-Western economies today.[13] It reflects a distinction that only strongly emerged in the West in the nineteenth century with the rise of governmental bureaucracies. Prior to that, government offices were not considered public, but private. It has been argued that such "patrimonial" states continue in many parts of the developing world. Zolberg identifies regions and countries as diverse as sub-Saharan Africa, the Gulf and Thailand as falling into such a definition.[14] When the boundaries between the public and the private are blurred, definitions such as that of Rose-Ackerman are problematic.[15]

A final set of challenges is related to the nature of corruption itself, which is far from homogeneous. Corruption takes many forms: bribery, embezzlement, nepotism, and others. Many believe it is important to distinguish between "grand" corruption—occurring at the highest levels of power—and "petty" corruption—which involves lower level functionaries, and is typically associated with facilitating interactions with government bureaucracy.[16] Velasquez considers such facilitating payments as "morally permissible" under certain circumstances.[17]

10.2 Are Developing Countries Especially Corrupt?

Corruption, then, is an ambiguous concept that makes generalizations about its prevalence over time and between countries hazardous. With this major caveat in place, it needs to be emphasized that although developing countries as a group populate all the lower ranks of the recent Transparency International indexes, there has been plenty of corruption and ethical failure in Western business over the last two centuries.

Balleinsen has documented the rich history of fraud in the United States from the nineteenth century until the present day, much of which involved corruption of numerous kinds.[18] The twentieth century's greatest financial swindler was Ivar Kreuger, the Swedish "match king." Kreuger built a global match business, and from the mid-1920s engaged in sovereign lending to heavily indebted European and other governments in return for match monopolies, raising capital on the basis of fraudulent accounts. The scale of Kreuger's fraudulent practices was sufficient for the United States to pass the Securities Act which established the Security Exchange Commission in 1933.[19]

Western business and other interests have a particularly tarnished historical record of corruption, bribery and lawlessness throughout Africa, Asia and Latin America. Spectacular examples included the role of

British merchant houses such as Jardine Matheson in opium trading in China in the first half of the nineteenth century, and the brutal looting of the Congo under the King of Belgium, Leopold II, during the second half of that century. Western multinationals have been massive perpetuators of corruption and bribery when they operated in fragile developing economies. It was the behavior of the United Fruit Company, the largest banana producing and marketing company in Central America and one with a spectacular record over decades of dismal ethical behavior, which led to the United States passing the Foreign Corrupt Practices Act in 1976, designed to regulate such behavior.[20]

There is no suggestion, then, that business systems in developed countries do not have a sordid history of corruption. The case can be made that current corruption indexes, like the Transparency International data, exaggerate their current cleanness compared to developing countries. The United States, for example, has steadily fallen in rankings over the last decade, but it was still ranked at 22 in 2018. This almost certainly relies too much on evidence at the federal level, and fails to take into account huge levels of corruption in state and municipal governments across the country.[21]

If we set such concerns aside, and make the heroic assumption that over recent decades at least corruption has probably been more pervasive in developing economies, it is worth exploring why this should be so. The contemporary literature on business ethics sometimes suggests that the stage of economic development of a country should be taken into account in considering issues of business ethics and corporate social responsibility. A 2008 CSR baseline report on Turkey, for example, noted that the country was "in a different developmental stage and it has special economic and cultural characteristics when compared to other candidate countries seeking to join the European Union."[22] Ethical value systems may vary between countries too. Some empirical studies have suggested that contemporary Turkish business people may be less concerned with ethics than some of their counterparts in other countries.[23] Chapter 8, however, reports considerable concern about corruption among Turkish business leaders.

A number of studies have suggested that instability and economic hardship can lead to a sacrifice of ethicality.[24] Some authors on countries such as China have stressed that developing economies cannot be expected to move to any internationally determined criteria for ethical business within any short space of time. The concept of

> bread first and morals later has even been accepted by some moral philosophers, and the pressure for survival in the early stages of development can mean that moral considerations are often overridden by the prospect of material gain. Over time these imperatives decline, and it becomes more realistic for business to take moral

> considerations into account, but it remains difficult for many business people to shrug off this "survival mentality.[25]

If we move beyond the simplistic idea that high ethical standards are something of a luxury that only the rich can afford, however, it is apparent that there may be a number of features of developing economies that influence the ways in which economic actors approach the undertaking of transactions and any application of behavioral standards to them. Developing economies often suffer from shortages of resources. Consumer goods may well be in scarce supply, meaning that competition for them can be intense.[26] Low income economies are faced with a shortage of capital and formal capital-pooling institutions—hence, for example, the frequent reliance on family or other personal or informal networks. It may be that an entrepreneur or would-be entrepreneur has to bypass the formal framework to secure the capital that is required, but that bypassing may, in the longer run, lead to economic success. Finding a way of pooling scarce resources of expertise and capital can be critical to the development of a modern sector.

In the early stages of development the modern sector remains a small part of total economic activity. The growth of large enterprises and firms in the modern business sector in developing economies takes place in the context of a large number of traditional producers and sellers who may have very different values and criteria for survival. The widespread proliferation in contemporary developing economies of small-scale individual entrepreneurs has been identified as making the spread of high standards of business ethics particularly difficult. Such individual entrepreneurs may not only be ignorant of the benefits of developing social capital, but are lacking in education and have a low public status. The slim margins of their businesses allow no scope for philanthropy.[27] Reports have highlighted the difference between modern businesses adopting global best practices and small scale traditional businesses. "Faced with competition, traditional businesses circumvent tax or labor laws to save money."[28]

An absence of social knowledge and social capital has also been identified as another factor in developing economies that can cause problems in terms of ethical business behavior.[29] The trust that is fundamental to the smooth operation of market transactions is particularly likely to be in short supply.[30] At the heart of this lies the issue of institutions. Developing economies are often said to suffer from institutional voids, or at least fragility.[31] An economy needs a whole set of institutions if the operation of business is to be facilitated, and defining and building those institutions takes time, knowhow and money.

An absence of trust may be particularly associated with a weakness in legal institutions. Deficiencies in legal institutions have been identified as a major factor in failures to enforce business rights and address inappropriate transactional behavior in the Middle East and North Africa region.[32]

This forms an important component of what Acemoglu and Robinson define as extractive rather than inclusive economic and political institutions. The former, they assert, do not rule out economic growth, but nor do they provide the incentives to invest in new technologies and skills conducive to driving sustained modern economic growth.[33] Even where an economy has developed a functioning legal system, however, trust in that legal system may remain low due to a number of factors, including lack of familiarity with the new frameworks, a preference for informal rather than formal institutions, or a lack of trust in the impartiality of those who operate the rules. The role of the state is likely to be crucial in this process of institution-building, but the existence of a strong state that seeks to compensate for institutional weakness may generate its own problems in terms of the ability to wield patronage and distort issues of distribution and the public good.

Institutional problems in a developing economy are likely to be magnified in the context of rapid change. Faced by the challenges of transition to a new order, many economic actors encounter additional uncertainty. The borderline between what is illegal and what is immoral, a borderline that is at the best of times lacking in clarity, becomes even more blurred. An environment of major change breeds uncertainty about the actual rules of the game, and is conducive to the existence of many one-off, rather than repeated, transactions.[34] Studies of more recent economies transitioning from Communist to free market regimes present a particularly stark example of what such change can mean for social capital and market institutions, with the move to the market economy appearing to generate major ethical issues in post-transition Eastern European economies and China since the 1980s.[35]

Post-transition economies are an extreme example of rapid imposed change, but development itself is invariably associated with abrupt alterations in formal and informal institutions, organizations and patterns of belief and behavior. Increased international interactions are likely to enhance these difficulties. The greater geographic mobility and, in some cases, immigration, that accompanies growing global market integration also has the capacity to undermine transactions based on ethnicity, reputation and direct experience.[36] The net result is that within both national and global economies there is much complexity in determining what unethical actions in business are. That difficulty is further compounded in many developing and transition economies, particularly when those economies may be seeking to introduce from elsewhere elements of legal systems or other institutions that may be more or less suited to existing local systems.[37]

A final observation is that corruption, and the broader issue of extractive institutions, is not an inevitable fate for developing economies such as Turkey. Path dependency is powerful, but things change. Quah has explored why, atypically in Asia, Singapore and Hong Kong have become far less corrupt. He identifies the importance of institutions designed and supported to oppose corruption in politics and business. In particular, he stresses the importance of the British colonial government's decision in Singapore in 1952 to take anti-corruption policing away from the police and assign it to a separate agency. This agency received enhanced powers from the independent Singaporean government in 1960. In 1974 the British colonial government in Hong Kong took the same step after a major corruption scandal in the police. In both cases the agencies were given great autonomy, and fully supported by legal systems committed to punishing corrupt behavior regardless of position, status, and political affiliation.[38]

10.3 Corruption and Development: The Historical Case of Japan

Contemporary Japan appears well in the Transparency International rankings, but the country was not always lauded for high business ethics. Indeed, Japanese business was widely considered as highly corrupt in its international dealings during the era of modernization after the Meiji Restoration in 1868.[39] Japanese businesspersons, it was said, were lacking in ethics and honor. The challenge of how business could be moved from the dishonorable to the honorable was at the heart of the career of Shibusawa Eiichi, discussed in the Introduction to this volume.

Japan has a long history of ambiguity about corruption. During the Edo period, between the seventeenth and middle of the nineteenth centuries, the Tokugawa government considered bribery as illegal and it was condemned as immoral by the regime's dominant Confucian philosophy. Yet so-called "gift-giving" was widespread.[40] After the Meiji Restoration Japan was faced with the need to adjust to a new type of economy, both nationally and internationally. Those embarking on new ventures or becoming involved in international trade in the early Meiji period were just as unsure of the rules of the game as economic actors in post-socialist economies. Many commentators in the late nineteenth and early twentieth centuries lamented the lack of trust in business partners that contributed significantly to the poor reputation of Japanese traders. This was far removed from the alleged high trust levels observed in contemporary Japanese business.[41]

A simple explanation for this shift might be that Japan became more affluent. It also seems likely, however, that Japan relatively early on managed to tap existing sources of social capital and to find alternative ways of building relationships of trust, at least in relation to many domestic economic transactions. Early on this was often achieved through personal and family networks, as in many other industrializing economies; cheating one's friends and family was, in most cases, less likely and more difficult than cheating those whom one did not know. But for a developing

Japan, friends and family were able to offer far more than just more trustworthy business partners. Notwithstanding the appearance in the Meiji period of the joint stock company, personal networks remained a crucial source of capital for investment in a capital-scarce economy.[42]

However, the key development was probably Japan's success in institution building. By the early twentieth century, Japan had established institutions and forms of organization that shaped expectations and penalized those deemed to breach the established norms of honest dealing.[43] In the words of Acemoglu and Robinson, the country had embarked on building inclusive institutions. By 1900 the country had a fully functioning legal system that could provide redress for economic actors who felt that they had been wronged and penalize wrongdoers. This legal system was not necessarily trusted by non-Japanese, but by the early twentieth century, it was apparent even to such outsiders that Japan was moving towards having a respected set of legal institutions.[44] The legal institutions formed part of an eco-system of institutions and organizations that laid the basis for a market economy to function. Higher education institutions in Japan from the 1890s onwards sought to include training in business ethics in courses on commerce and business activity. Clear regulations framed the operation of joint stock companies and banks, and provided for the right of redress when those regulations were breached.[45]

Nevertheless, corruption did not go away, but rather evolved alongside Japan's developmental state. Much has been written about state intervention in developing economies in the pursuit of development, but it is less discussed how such intervention promoted rent seeking. Government policies often served to limit improvements in trust and ethical business behavior, and sometimes worked to encourage corruption and other breaches of accepted standards.

In fact, as a number of writers, including Rose-Ackerman have pointed out, corruption in the sense of misuse of public office for private gain has not only been relatively widespread in modern Japan, but could even be considered as structurally entrenched within Japan's economy.[46] Mitchell has traced this tradition back to the pre-modern period, concluding that "despite anti-bribery laws, moral restraints, and harsh punishments . . . bribery appears to have been ubiquitous. Two details in particular contributed to this situation: low salaries for officials and the long-standing custom of giving gifts."[47]

Attitudes towards the state, and the policies undertaken by the state in the industrializing period, provide essential context for any consideration of the causes and implications of corruption in Japan. Given the long tradition of government intervention in economic affairs, few objected to the principle that the state had a role to play in leading the industrialization process after the Meiji Restoration. The Meiji government took to this role with enthusiasm and commitment, portraying the Emperor as the father of the people and the state itself as a paternal ruler that knew what was best for the people. Constrained by the obstacles imposed by late development—inappropriate institutions, absence of knowhow, resources and human capital—the strategy of the Meiji state was to undertake initiatives that only the state could undertake, including institutional and organizational reform and the promotion of a national infrastructure. After the early Meiji years, most of manufacturing development and the service sector was entrusted to private enterprise. Almost the only exception to this was military-related industry and a few production areas of strategic importance.[48]

While the state remained a crucial actor, for modern business it was, therefore, above all, a facilitator. Even as a facilitator, however, the state was in a powerful position to use its interests to promote particular actors in the private sector, while those actors in their turn were able to identify the actual or potential benefits that could be derived from close relationships with officials and politicians, and the provision of inducements aimed at persuading those in decision-making positions to opt for a particular strategy or policy. The existence of the so-called "political merchants" (*seishō*) in the Meiji period is testimony to the extent to which political decision-making, industrialization strategy and the interests of individual businesses and entrepreneurs were closely entwined. Bureaucrats and politicians often moved into business, while business leaders in their turn might wield direct influence through institutions such as the Upper House of the Diet. There was plenty of what would now be called corruption.

Many of the corruption scandals that occurred during Japan's early period of modern industrialization, particularly during the interwar years, were closely associated with government development policies, which served as both cause of, and opportunity for, significant personal enrichment. The growth of urbanization and the associated development of local infrastructure proved fertile ground for potentially profitable deals between officials and businesspersons. As early as the turn of the century, the *Mainichi*, one of Japan's leading daily newspapers, was reporting that a company engaged in the manufacture of lead piping had offered bribes totaling ¥3,000 to Tokyo city officials.[49]

It was the national level scandals, however, that really grabbed both national and international attention. As with the case of urban infrastructure, these scandals were not only the result of individual greed and the desire for business profits, but were also associated with the developmental strategies of governments. The scandal involving the Greater Japan Sugar Refining Company that emerged from 1907—one of a number that occurred around this time, but which received limited exposure—was associated with the payment of bribes in an attempt first to influence national legislation and subsequently to get the state to nationalize what was effectively an unprofitable private company. No fewer than seven company officials and sixteen politicians were deemed to have committed punishable offences, including members of the Lower House of the Diet.[50]

It was the Siemens scandal of 1914–1915, however, that really exposed the extent to which it was possible for national policies to be exploited by both sides in the pursuit of personal gain. Early in 1914 Karl Richter, who had been employed at the Tokyo office of Siemens-Schuckert, was found guilty by a German court of having stolen company documents and attempted blackmail. Information released during the course of the trial suggested that not just Siemens, but also the British company Vickers, had "friends in the Ministry of Marine" and had paid bribes to high ranking Japanese naval officers in an attempt to secure valuable orders.[51]

This scandal offers two insights in particular. Firstly, the Navy Ministry was one of the government's big spending departments, and even a small "take" of the huge cost of purchasing a battleship, for example, could be a significant amount of money. One report at the time suggested that the fact that bribery permeated the great spending departments had long been known, but that it had been difficult to find supporting evidence, particularly evidence that could be taken to court.[52] In the case of large programs or items of expenditure, the returns to obtaining an order were disproportionately great, and the value of the order potentially made it easier to absorb any additional cost in a discreet way.

Secondly, the scandal suggests the degree of ambiguity with which illegal actions of this kind were often perceived, and the difficulty of pinning down any assignment of guilt. Although a number of employees of Mitsui Bussan had confessed to handling the illicit payments, one senior Mitsui director still asserted that since the purpose of the company was to make money, he saw nothing wrong in taking a "commission."[53] He was among a number of those involved who argued that what had happened was justified on the grounds that any monies that had changed hands had not been for individual enrichment, but rather for a higher collective purpose, whether the company or the country. On the government side, the acceptance of "commissions" by naval officers was said to date back to the Sino-Japanese War in the 1890s, and these were now regarded as legitimate payments, through which many naval officers had secured considerable fortunes. This ambiguity regarding what was, or was not, unacceptable behavior appears to have been shared by the legal system. Heavy sentences passed on the Mitsui employees involved in handling the illicit payments were subsequently overturned by the appeal court.[54]

Corruption scandals continued to occur through the 1920s and 1930s, involving senior government officials, and the situation was exacerbated as individual political parties fought for political advantage.[55] The developmental policies of the high growth period after 1950 were just as vulnerable to abuse and exploitation. The late 1940s and early 1950s saw reports of a succession of bribery attempts by Japanese business interests in relation to the awarding of government contracts, the introduction of new regulations and access to government loan schemes. According to one British journalist familiar with Japan, the country was "long inured to questionable relations between 'big business' and politicians."[56]

The substantial costs of corruption are laid out in Chapter 8, yet the scholarly literature remains deeply divided on the overall impact of corruption on economic development. A number of scholars have considered bribery and corruption to bring positive benefits, especially through enhancing efficiencies in complex bureaucratic situations, and enhancing knowledge spill-overs.[57] Others have stressed the downsides for economic growth. Banerjee, for example, points to the arbitrariness of corrupt politicians and bureaucrats.[58] Empirical attempts to measure the cost of corruption suggest that it reduces rather than enhances investment levels.[59]

There are measurement and definition problems in assessing the cost of corruption, but the case of Japan certainly raises questions concerning how serious corruption was as an impediment to growth. Despite the entrenchment of corruption in the Japanese economic system by the 1930s, Japan was Asia's leading industrial economy. Japan flourished even more during the high growth decades of the 1950s and 1960s, despite plentiful corruption scandals. Pascha has observed that there is insufficient evidence to prove that corruption was actually bad for the Japanese economy.[60] The same can be said about corruption in the West. As Bardhan has noted, the "gilded age" in the United States during the 1860s and 1870s saw massive corruption at state and city level, which did not prevent the rapid growth of the American economy.[61]

The existence of corruption is not an automatic brake on overall economic development. However, it would seem that the more extractive the overall institutional context, the more is the damage to development by corruption. The pervasiveness of corruption also matters a great deal. Meiji Japan had plenty of corruption, but it also had a significant number of business leaders such as Shibusawa Eiichi, and his contemporaries such as Sakichi Toyoda, the creator of the cotton spinning machinery business Toyoda, and Arinobu Fukuhara, the creator of the beauty company Shiseido. These figures were noted for high ethical standards, and they built modern firms, brands and technologies which drove Japanese growth.

This chapter now turns to the case of India, and makes a comparison with Turkey.

10.4 Corruption and Development: India and Turkey

The potential of development strategies to drive corruption comes out particularly well in the case of India. In 2018 India was ranked as equal to Turkey by Transparency International, although in the previous two decades Turkey usually was ranked slightly higher. There is plenty of supporting evidence of the prevalence of corruption in India. "Nobody really knows the exact extent of corruption in India," Arun Agrawal observed in a leading Indian political science journal in 2007. "However, everybody is aware that it is all pervasive and that it is eating inexorably in to the vitals of the nation."[62]

Like Japan, there is a long history of what would now be considered corruption in South Asia, although once the distinction between the public and the private spheres is relaxed, it is not clear what this really means.[63] The arrival of the British, in the initial form of the East India Company, exposed the region to rule by rapacious merchants with no interest in the country beyond making fortunes. However, after the establishment of direct rule by the British Crown in 1858, the senior levels of the government, at least, had strict rules against bribery and corruption. The colonial government was laissez-faire, and was involved in few parts of Indian life beyond the maintenance of law and order, revenue collection and infrastructure such as railroads.[64]

The problem of corruption intensified after Independence in 1947. There is a general acceptance that this was the unintended consequence of the era now known as the License Raj. This involved increasing centralized control over the economy with five-year plans, exchange controls, price controls, licensing and high levels of protectionism. There was a huge extension of the role of government in the economy compared to the colonial period.[65] Execution was also flawed, resulting in shortages and bottlenecks throughout the system. The need to secure licenses and to access scare resources drove many businesses into unethical practices. "Perhaps the most pernicious, though unintended, by-product of the system of control," a recent business history survey by Tripathi and Jumani concluded, "was widespread corruption in the bureaucracy."[66]

The problems of the License Raj peaked during the 1970s, as inflation and shortages intensified. The government of Prime Minister Indira Gandhi, facing growing political challenges, suspended Indian democracy during the so-called Emergency (1975–1977). "Inefficiency, mis-governance, sycophancy and corruption," Tripathi and Jumani noted, "were the inevitable consequences of such an environment."[67]

Gandhi's Congress Party was by then consumed by "galloping corruption."[68] By the 1970s Congress politicians were asking for commissions on arms deals with foreign suppliers. At the state level, there was widespread corruption with government ministers regularly bribed over securing licenses, real estate deals, and much else. Around 70–90 percent of funds allocated to rural development were siphoned into corruption.[69]

As in Japan, development policies delivered economic gains. There was much discussion of India's slow GDP growth, which was around 3.5 percent during the 1950s and 1960s and much lower in per capita terms, yet much was also achieved. As Roy has recently noted, "some of India's best-known consumer brands to emerge since the 1950s, from the Ambassador car to the Godrej typewriter, to the Bajaj Scooter or the Usha sewing machine, might not have survived at all but for the unbounded generosity of the state, which did everything in its powers to drive out foreign competition."[70]

However, the extensive government intervention also stimulated corruption. Jones and Comunale show, using an oral history database consisting of business leaders in emerging markets since the 1960s, that Indian business leaders ranked corruption as a bigger political risk than did leaders in eight other South Asian and Latin American countries.[71] There are plentiful testimonies to the spread of corruption in that database. Rahul Bajaj, then chief executive of the Bajaj Group who produced the Bajaj scooter, recalled one episode when he was pressured by a government minister:

> There was this Telecom Minister from Himachal Pradesh—I got a call from him one day. Mandi is one of the cities in Himachal. "Rahul Saab, we want a dealership in Mandi." I said, "Yes we can make a dealer, I think that is a hilly country, not a scooter country, but we will see. Let the person apply, give your reference." He said, "Sure, I will send him, but make him a dealer." I didn't know what he meant, so I said, "At Bajaj Auto, we deal on merit. I will give it to my marketing chief and tell him that other things being equal, Mr. So-and-So has recommended this case so we should give him preference, but if somebody else is better, then, you know . . ." He said, "Mr. Bajaj, do you know whom you are talking to, I am Minister of Telecommunications." I said, "Mr. So-and-So, you can go to hell" and I put the phone down.[72]

The Bajaj scooter was incredibly popular in India, but with waiting lists as long as a decade. The cost of corruption was clearer than in Japan. Bajaj went on in his interview to explain how difficult it was to access resources to expand his business during the License Raj. "You could expand," he explained, "but a lot of things were required—bribes—and we would never give a bribe, so our growth was slow."[73]

Petty corruption became the norm, rather than the exception, during the License Raj. Prithvi Raj Singh Oberoi, chairman of Oberoi Hotels and Resorts, a prominent luxury hospitality and tourism group in India, noted, "certain things could not be done unless you [engaged in] some sort of corruption. It was not always money—favors."[74]

The liberalization of policy after 1991 did nothing to stem the problem of corruption. "Corruption has now been institutionalized," Agarwal noted in 2007, "and has become a commonly accepted way of life."[75] This was because bureaucratic involvement in Indian life did not cease, even if five year plans did, reflecting the nature of law and institutions in India. The serial entrepreneur Jerry Rao, also interviewed in the CEM project, observed that the root cause of corruption in the real estate sector was the huge number of laws that were never taken off the statute book, all of which required approval for builders. Now, when you require approval," he noted, "particularly from a low-level or medium-level government functionary—trust me, there is going to be corruption."[76] While his own low cost housing company did not want to engage in corrupt practices, he went on to describe how the corruption eco-system works. Government officials "hit on our lawyers or architects—who are doing multiple projects and who probably need to keep (those officials) on their side."[77]

When laws against corruption and other matters were put on the statute book in India, they were seldom enforced. As Zia Mody, founder and senior partner at the leading law firm AZB & Partners, explained, often times, "The law is clear but the implementation has yet to happen."[78] Ratan Tata, who led the Tata group, India's largest business group, during the 1990s and 2000s, added:

> The greatest weakness of India is poor enforcement. . . . Why is the air being polluted? Because people are taking shortcuts on antipollution equipment or scrubbers at power plants and fertilizer plants, etc. . . . While everybody could determine what the cause is, the cause is skirted around. . . . We need to enforce the law where it's necessary, and we should do it irrespective of who is involved.[79]

Not surprisingly, Quah contrasted the independent anti-corruption agencies in Hong Kong and Singapore with law enforcement in India. India's Central Bureau of Investigation, the main body charged with fighting corruption, is a branch of the police. As a result, Quah observes, India relies on a "police agency to fight corruption in the midst of widespread police corruption." It is poorly funded, under-staffed, and widely believed to be in the service of whatever political party holds power.[80] In terms of the macro-economy, however, policy liberalization was followed by far higher annual GDP growth, often well in excess of 5.5 percent.

The impact of corruption on the development of India as a whole was distinctly nuanced. The country had partially fragile legal and other institutions, yet Independent India was also a flourishing democracy that met Acemoglu and Robinson's definition of possessing inclusive political institutions. It has had businesses that manifested a wide spectrum of ethical behavior. Among the largest family-owned business groups, some such as the Tata, Godrej and Bajaj were standout examples of high ethical standards and the avoidance of corruption. Certain religious values and devotion to Gandhian ethics were among the influences on these firms.[81] The ethical behavior of these business groups enhanced their reputations within the Indian business system, becoming one of their competitive advantages. There were other large groups at the opposite end of the ethical spectrum. The Ambani family, which built the Reliance group from the post-war decades into one of India's largest and most profitable business groups, was notorious for high level corruption. Dhirubhai Ambani's ability to grow his business fast during the License Raj, Tripathi notes in his classic business history of India, "was to a large extent due to Dhirubhai's ability to manipulate using fair and foul means alike, the government machinery to his advantage."[82] High levels of corruption did not automatically result in entirely corrupted business systems: it might even stimulate highly ethical responses. India, like Meiji Japan, had plentiful corruption. However, it also had business groups such as the Tata and the Bajaj that created highly successful businesses and much-admired brands.

Parallels between Turkey and India should now be evident. The Ottoman Empire was a patrimonial state in which the Sultan controlled national assets and wealth could only be generated in service to him. It had textbook extractive institutions. After the establishment of the Republic in 1923, the State pursued economic growth and again rewarded loyalty. Ethnic minorities lost their assets and foreigners were largely excluded. Supporters of the ruling Republican People's Party were rewarded, and opponents penalized. When the Democrat Party came to power in 1950, the system continued, with that party's supporters now rewarded. After 1960 multiple military coups further eroded the political and economic institutions framework of the country.

As noted in other chapters, from the 1950s, governments pursued Indian-style planning with exchange controls, price controls, high tariffs and discouragement of foreign ownership of assets. By the 1970s, this strategy had resulted, as in India, in high levels of inflation, shortages and political instability, and mounting corruption. Nor did the problem go away with subsequent liberalization. "It was arguably during the 1990s, Turkey's infamous 'lost decade,' that the issue of corruption loomed largest in the country's politics," one US study observed. "The tenure of Tansu Çiller remains synonymous with the financial and political impropriety generally associated with this era."[83] Subsequently the politicization and corruption of public procurement intensified.[84]

This turbulence had its consequence on ethical behavior. It is well-established that even the pioneer entrepreneur Vehbi Koç, the founder of what became Turkey's largest business group which has come to be known for its philanthropy and CSR efforts in the country, made considerable profits in grey markets during World War II, proving a major source of funds for the subsequent growth of the group.[85] Even Unilever, the Anglo-Dutch consumer products multinational that had very strong corporate policies against corruption, discovered in the late 1970s that its affiliate in Turkey had engaged in irregular payments.[86] The development state, which rewarded supporters and penalized opponents, worked to strongly re-inforce the long Turkish tradition that the state was the epicenter of rent seeking and rent providing.[87] By 2003, bribery was said to add something like 15% to contract prices in Turkey.[88]

Business leaders described the same sort of phenomena as in India, and experienced even greater difficulties in addressing them. The testimony of Cem Boyner, a prominent textile industrialist and chief executive of the large Boyner retailing group, is indicative. Boyner headed the Turkish Industrialists' and Businessmen's Association in the late 1980s, but his efforts to complain against corruption only resulted in his being taken to court:

> This being fed from the government's hand was such a dominant psychology that the Turkish bourgeoisie, unlike the European bourgeoisie, never developed. . . . I was chairman of the Turkish Industry and Business Association. I was asked to go to court several times because of criticizing the government. I then called the government a kleptocracy because they were stealing so much—there was so much corruption. I went to court. Then I came back and two months later, I said something else. As the top representative of Turkish business, I was again brought to the court.[89]

As in the case of India, the level of corruption did not deter well-respected business groups from emerging and growing. However, political contacts were essential for any business regarding government contracts. During the 1930s, Vehbi Koç had to work with a politically connected contractor while creating business in construction.[90] As noted at the beginning of this chapter, public contracts have continued to be dependent on contacts and corruption, and it is hard to imagine this as anything but distorting and hampering trust throughout society. The prevalence of corruption, alongside laws and complex regulations, might have been one factor that contributed to the low level of foreign direct investment in Turkey, although some statistical work on the recent past suggests its negative impact was concentrated in some sectors, like financial services and real estate.[91]

Evidently corruption did not prevent the overall economic development of modern Turkey. As in Meiji Japan and India, there were impressive business enterprises, such as the Koç Group, which developed modern business enterprises, created brands and developed technologies. However in the case of Turkey the political and economic institutions were particularly extractive, and productive counter-forces to corruption were weaker than in India. Pervasive corruption was a barrier to innovation and enterprise. For example, organic farmers avoided certifying their products as the certification process was seen as corrupt and debased.[92]

The overall trend was towards more corruption. In the case of public procurement, Gürakar shows that while during the 1980s and 1990s there was large-scale corruption, it took place at an individual level through the abuse of loopholes, whilst after 2003 corruption became "centralized" as the government employed it as a deliberate strategy to favor its business supporters.[93] The upshot, that author argues, was that "corruption is perceived as more normal and acceptable in Turkey." There were very real consequences in the shape of poor-quality construction and growing numbers of work-related accidents.[94] The extent of corruption is also likely to have been one influence behind the remarkably low level of interpersonal trust seen in Turkey. An OECD report in 2016 noted that the share of people reporting high trust in others was 12 percent, which was a third of the average level across the OECD.[95]

10.5 Conclusion

This chapter has sought to contextualize the issue of corruption in Turkey, particularly with comparisons to Meiji-era Japan and India. The conclusion is in one sense comforting, as there are many similarities. Turkey's experience was more the norm than the exception.

It has been suggested that despite all the differences between the three countries, there was a common driver of corruption—the developmental state. Catching-up by using extensive state intervention had the major downside that it served to facilitate corruption. The operation of the developmental state may have been constrained by factors beyond the control of the state, such as shortage of funds or external pressures. Yet it is apparent that the individual measures that made up the overall strategy of the developmental state are not only vulnerable to exploitation by those who are involved in their implementation, but can positively encourage such manipulation. The Japanese example suggests the building of inclusive political and economic institutions, and consequent trust levels, can help address the problem, but it also suggests that old habits die hard, and that respect for the state and its institutions is something that cannot be taken for granted. The fact that some places, such as Singapore and Hong Kong, were able to roll back corrupt practices is less comforting for Turkey. For one reason or another, Turkey, like India, has not yet taken the necessary steps needed to disrupt corrupt practices.

There remain, though, considerable uncertainties in this subject. As this chapter has emphasized, the very term corruption is ambiguous, because there are many grey areas that result from variations in cultural norms. The existence of corruption does not stop development. It did not stop Japan's economic growth over the long-term. It has not stopped India's rapid growth in recent decades, which appears, if anything, as correlated with growing corruption rates since the 1970s. Indeed, if the prevalence of corruption were always associated with a lack of development and growth, the incentives to solve the problem would be far clearer. It would appear, though, that the more extractive the institutions of a society, and the fewer the countervailing forces of productive business enterprise, the more potential there is for negative outcomes. In the case of twentieth century Turkey, corruption has not prevented significant economic growth, but it has had negative consequences, such as poor quality building construction, and distortions, such as helping one sector of the business community grow at the expense of others. However its prevalence may be part of the explanation why Turkey has struggled to build innovative businesses able to drive forward the development of the country and break out of the middle-income trap.

Notes

1. M. Acar and U. Emek, "Preventing Corruption in Turkey: Issues, Instruments and Institutions," in T. Gong and S.K. Ma (eds.) *Preventing Corruption in Asia. Institutional Design and Policy Capacity*, New York: Routledge, 2009, pp. 164–188.
2. www.transparency.org/research/cpi/cpi_2000/0; www.transparency.org/cpi 2018
3. http://seldi.net/fileadmin/public/PDF/Publications/CAR_Turkey/CAR_Turkey_2016/CAR_Turkey_1_Corruption_Perception_English.pdf, accessed February 3, 2019.
4. E.C. Gürakar, *Politics of Favoritism in Public Procurement in Turkey: Reconfigurations of Dependency Networks in the AKP Era*, New York: Springer, 2016, especially chapter 3.
5. GAN Business Anti-Corruption Portal, June 2018, www.business-anti-corruption.com/country-profiles/turkey, accessed February 1, 2019.
6. M. Velasquez, "Corruption and Bribery," in G.G. Brenkert and T.L. Beauchamp (eds.) *The Oxford Handbook of Business Ethics*, Oxford: Oxford University Press, 2012, pp. 473–474.
7. D.L. Szanton, "Contingent Moralities: Social and Economic Investment in a Philippine Fishing Town," in R.W. Hefner (ed.) *Market Cultures: Society and Morality in the New Asian Capitalisms*, Boulder: Westview Press, 1998, pp. 251–267; R. Mandel and C. Humphrey, *Markets and Moralities*, London: Bloomsbury, 2002, Introduction; P. Bardhan, "Corruption and Development: A Review of Issues," *Journal of Economic Literature*, v.35, n. 3, Sept. 1997, pp. 1320–1346, p. 1330; T. Donalson, "Values in Tension: Ethics Away From Home," *Harvard Business Review*, Sept.–Oct.1996, pp. 52–58.
8. J.S. Nye, "Corruption and Political Development: A Cost Benefit Analysis," *American Political Science Review*, v.61, 1967, pp. 417–427.
9. Velasquez, "Corruption," p. 476.
10. C.J. Friedrich, "Corruption Concepts in Historical Perspective," in A.J. Heidenheimer, M. Johnstone, and V.T. LeVine (eds.) *Political Corruption: A Handbook*, New Brunswick, NJ: Transaction, 2007.
11. Velasquez, "Corruption," p. 477.
12. S. Rose-Ackerman, *Corruption and Government: Causes, Consequences, and Reform*, New York: Cambridge University Press, 1999, p. 91.
13. Velasquez, "Corruption," pp. 476, 482–484.
14. A.R. Zolburg, *Creating Political Order: The Party States of West Africa*, Chicago: University of Chicago Press, 1966; G. Roth, "Personal Rulership, Patrimonialism, and Empire—Building in the New States," *World Politics*, v.20, 1968, pp. 194–206.
15. Valesquez, "Corruption," p. 490.
16. D. Hardoon and F. Heinrich, *Bribe Payers Index*, Berlin: Transparency International, 2011; Rose-Ackerman, S. "'Grand' Corruption and the

Ethics of Global Business," *Journal of Banking and Finance*, v.26, n. 9, 2002, pp. 1889–1918; A. Argandoña, "Corruption and Companies: The Use of Facilitating Payments," *Journal of Business Ethics*, v.60, n. 3, 2005, pp. 251–264.

17. Valesquez, "Corruption," p. 490.
18. E.J. Balleinsen, *Fraud: An American History from Barnum to Madoff*, Princeton: Princeton University Press, 2017.
19. F. Partnoy, *The Match King: Ivar Kreuger and the Financial Scandal of the Century*, London: Profile Books, 2010.
20. G. Jones, *Multinationals and Global Capitalism*, Oxford: Oxford University Press, 2005, pp. 220, 263.
21. Jonathan Chait, "Why the Worst Governments in America Are Local Governments," *New York Magazine*, September 8, 2014, accessed January 27, 2019; Ray Woodcock, "State and Local Government Corruption in the U.S.," February 15, 2016, https://thefailedsystem.wordpress.com/2016/02/15/corrupt-states, accessed February 2, 2019.
22. *Turkey Corporate CSR Baseline Report*, 2008, p. 61, http://kssd.org/site/dl/uploads/CSR_Report_en.pdf, accessed February 2, 2019.
23. S. Burnaz et al., "An Exploratory Cross-Cultural Analysis of Marketing Ethics: The Case of Turkish, Thai and American Businesspeople," *Journal of Business Ethics*, v.90, suppl. 3, Dec. 2009, pp. 371–382; R. Sims and A.E. Gegez, "Attitudes Towards Business Ethics: A Five Nation Comparative Study," *Journal of Business Ethics*, v.50, n. 3, 2004, pp. 253–265.
24. G. Rice, "Islamist Ethics and the Implications for Business," *Journal of Business Ethics*, v.18, n. 4, February 1999, p. 353.
25. G.J. Rossouw, "Business Ethics in Developing Countries," *Business Ethics Quarterly*, v.4, n. 1, 1994, pp. 43–51.
26. Rossouw, "Business Ethics," p. 46.
27. F. Azmat and R. Samaratunge, "Responsible Entrepreneurship in Developing Countries: Understanding the Realities and Complexities," *Journal of Business Ethics*, v.90, n. 3, 2009, pp. 437–452.
28. Cited in M. Ararat, "A Development Perspective for Corporate Social Responsibility: The Case of Turkey," *Corporate Governance*, v.8, n. 3, 2008, pp. 271–285.
29. Rossouw, "Business Ethics," p. 49.
30. M. Casson, *Entrepreneurship and Business Culture. Studies in the Economics of Trust*, volume 1, Brookfield, VT: Edward Elgar Publishing, 1994, Chapter 4; T. Khanna, *Trust. Creating the Foundation for Entrepreneurs in Developing Countries*, Oakland: Berrerr-Koehler, 2018.
31. C. Gao, T. Zuzul, G. Jones, and T. Khanna, "Overcoming Institutional Voids: A Reputation-Based View of Long Run Survival," *Strategic Management Journal*, v.38, n. 11, 2017, pp. 2147–2167; G. Austin, C. Davila, and G. Jones, "The Alternative Business History: Business in Emerging Markets," *Business History Review*, v.91, n. 3, 2017, pp. 537–569.
32. J.B. Nugent and C. Glezakos, "Why Does It Take So Long to Collect on a Bad Check Through the Courts? A Case of Institutional Path Dependence with Special Reference to the MENA Region," in S. Sayan (ed.) *Economic Performance in the Middle East and North Africa: Institutions, Corruption and Reform*, London and New York: Routledge, 2009, pp. 67–93.
33. D. Acemoglu and J.A. Robinson, *Why Nations Fail. The Origins of Power, Prosperity, and Poverty*, New York: Currency, 2012.
34. J. Humphrey and H. Schmitz, "Trust and Inter-Firm Relationships in Developing and Transition Economies," *Journal of Development Studies*, v.34, n. 4, April 1987, pp. 32–61.

35. J.L. Hanafin, "Morality and the Market in China: Some Contemporary Views," *Business Ethics Quarterly*, v.12, n. 1, January 2002, pp. 1–18; Mandel and Humphrey (eds.), *Markets and Moralities.*
36. Humphrey and Schmitz, "Trust," p. 38.
37. Nugent and Glezakos, "Why," p. 72; Humphrey and Schmitz, "Trust," p. 45.
38. J.S.T. Quah, "Combating Corruption in Asian Countries: Learning from Success & Failure," *Daedalus*, v.147, n. 3, 2018, pp. 202–215.
39. J. Hunter, "'Doing Business by Fair Means': Putting Shibusawa Eiichi's Views on Business Ethics in Context," in P. Fridenson and T. Kikkawa (eds.), *Ethical Capitalism*, Toronto: University of Toronto Press, 2017, pp. 93–120; J. Hunter, *"Deficient in Commercial Morality"? Japan in Global Debates on Business Ethics in the Late Nineteenth-Early Twentieth Centuries*, Basingstoke: Palgrave, 2016.
40. R.H. Mitchell, *Political Bribery in Japan*, Honolulu, HI: University of Hawai'i Press, 1996, p. 9.
41. M. Sako and S. Helper, "Determinants of Trust in Supplier Relations: Evidence from the Automotive Industry in Japan and the United States," *Journal of Economic Behavior and Organization*, v.34, n. 3, March 1998, pp. 387–417.
42. See J. Hunter, "Reviving the Kansai Cotton Industry: Engineering Expertise and Knowledge Sharing in the Early Meiji Period," *Japan Forum*, v.26, n. 1, March 2014, pp. 65–88; M. Sawai and M. Tanimoto, *Nihon Keizai Shi*, Tokyo: Yūhikaku, 2016, pp. 168–178.
43. See J. Hunter, "Institutional Change in Meiji Japan: Image and Reality," in M. Blomstrom and S. La Croix (eds.) *Institutional Change in Japan*, London and New York: Routledge, 2006, pp. 45–70; T. Okazaki (ed.), *Torihiki Seido no Keizai Shi*, Tokyo: Tokyo University Press, 2001.
44. See W. Röhl (ed.), *History of Law in Japan since 1868*, Leiden: Brill, 2004.
45. Ibid.; M. Ikema et al. (eds.), *Hitotsubashi University, 1875–2000: A Hundred and Twenty-Five Years of Higher Education in Japan*, Basingstoke: Macmillan, 2000.
46. W. Pascha, "Corruption in Japan: An Economist's Perspective," Duisberger Arbeitspapiere Ostasienwissenschaften Issue 23, Institut für Ostasienwissenschaft, 1999, p. 10.
47. Mitchell, *Political*, p. 8. See chapter 1 for the pre-modern period. Mitchell's book is the most comprehensive work in English on the major corruption scandals of Japan from the Meiji period through to the end of the 20th century. See also M. Carlson and S. Reed, *Political Corruption and Scandals in Japan*, Ithaca, NY: Cornell University Press, 2018. For the latter 20th century see B. Woodall, *Japan Under Construction: Corruption, Politics, and Public Works*, Berkeley, CA: University of California Press, 1996; W.K. Black, "The *Dango* Tango: Why Corruption Blocks Real Reform in Japan," *Business Ethics Quarterly*, v.14, n. 4, 2004, pp. 603–623.
48. P.G. Francks, *Japanese Economic Development: Theory and Practice*, 3rd ed., Abingdon: Routledge, 2015, chs.4–5.
49. Mitchell, *Political*, p. 19.
50. Ibid., pp. 22–23; *Manchester Guardian*, January 10, 1910.
51. Mitchell, *Political*, p. 28; *Manchester Guardian,* January 22, 2014.
52. *Manchester Guardian*, February 21, 1914.
53. Mitchell, *Political*, p. 29.
54. Ibid.
55. Ibid., pp. 42–77; *Manchester Guardian*, November 2, 1929. R.H. Mitchell, *Justice in Japan: The Notorious Teijin Scandal*, Honolulu, HI: University of Hawai'i Press, 2002.

56. H. Tiltman, "Japanese Political Storm over Corruption Scandals," *Manchester Guardian*, February 27, 1954.
57. F. Lui, "An Equilibrium Queuing Model of Bribery," *Journal of Political Economy*, v.93, n. 4, 1985, pp. 760–781; S. Braguinsky, "Corruption and Schumpeterian Growth in Different Economic Environments," *Contemporary Economic Policy*, v.14, n. 3, 1996, pp. 14–25.
58. A.V. Banerjee, "A Theory of Misgovernance," *The Quarterly Journal of Economics*, v.112, n. 4, 1997, pp. 1289–1332.
59. P. Mauro, "Corruption and Growth," *The Quarterly Journal of Economics*, v.110, n. 3, 1995 pp. 682–712.
60. Pascha, "Corruption in Japan."
61. Bardhan, "Corruption," p. 1328.
62. A. Kr. Agrawal, "Corruption in Historical Perspective: A Case of India," *The Indian Journal of Political Science*, v.LXV111, n. 2, 2007, p. 325.
63. Ibid., pp. 329–332.
64. Ibid., pp. 331–332.
65. T. Roy, *A Business History of India. Enterprise and the Emergence of Capitalism from 1700*, Cambridge: Cambridge University Press, 2018, Chapter 7.
66. D. Tripathi and J. Jumani, *The Oxford History of Contemporary Indian Business*, New Delhi: Oxford University Press, 2013, p. 28.
67. Ibid., p. 94.
68. R. Guha, *India after Gandhi*, London: Picador, 2008, p. 470.
69. Ibid., pp. 682–683.
70. Roy, *Business History*, p. 156.
71. G. Jones and R. Comunale, "Business, Governments and Political Risk in South Asia and Latin America since 1970," *Australian Economic History Review*, v.58, n. 3, 2018, p. 242.
72. Interview with Rahul Bajaj, interviewed by Srikant M. Datar, July 8, 2014, Creating Emerging Markets Project, Baker Library Historical Collections, *Harvard Business School*, www.hbs.edu/creating-emerging-markets (hereafter CEM); Jones and Comunale, "Business," p. 249.
73. Interview with Rahul Bajaj, CEM.
74. Interview with P.R.S. Oberoi, interviewed by Ryan Buell and Ananth Raman, August 25, 2015, CEM; Jones and Comunale, "Business," p. 248.
75. Agarwal, "Corruption," p. 333.
76. Interview with Jaithirth (Jerry) Rao interviewed by Geoffrey Jones, June 1, 2016, CEM; G. Jones and R. Comunale, "Oral History and the Business History of Emerging Markets," *Enterprise & Society*, v.20, n. 1, 2019, p. 29.
77. Interview with Jaithirth (Jerry) Rao, CEM.
78. Interview with Zia Mody, interviewed by Tarun Khanna, February 14, 2017, CEM.
79. Interview with Ratan Naval Tata, interviewed by Tarun Khanna, April 27, 2015, CEM.
80. Quah, "Combating Corruption," pp. 208–210.
81. Austin, Davila, and Jones, "Alternative," pp. 27–28.
82. D. Tripathi, *The Oxford History of Indian Business*, New Delhi: Oxford University Press, 2004, p. 302.
83. B. Misztal, N. Danforth, J. Michek, and R. Gingeras, "Power and Corruption in Erdoğan's Turkey: Context and Consequences," November 2017, https://bipartisanpolicy.org/wp-content/uploads/2017/11/BPC-National-Security-Power-and-Corruption-in-Erodgans-Turkey.pdf, accessed February 3, 2019.

84. E.Ç. Gürakar and T.B. Ildiri, 2016. "Political Connections and Public Procurement in Turkey: Evidence from Construction Work Contracts," Working Papers 1053, Economic Research Forum, 2016; E.Ç. Gürakar and E. Meyersson, "State Discretion, Political Connections and Public Procurement: Evidence from Turkey," *Working Paper*, March 31, 2016, https://drive.google.com/file/d/0BxGIkxI0T-q7SzRLSDNaVjZhYk0/view, accessed February 4, 2019.
85. See Chapter 4.
86. G. Jones, *Entrepreneurship and Multinationals. Global Business and the Making of the Modern World*, Northampton, MA: Edward Elgar Publishing, 2013, p. 169.
87. Z. Baran, "Corruption: The Turkish Challenge," *Journal of International Affairs*, v.54, n. 1, Fall 2000, p. 130ff.
88. M. Ararat and C. Göcenoğlu, "Drivers for Sustainable Corporate Responsibility: The Case of Turkey," Report for MDF 5, www.gocenoglu.net/CSR-TurkeyMDF5.pdf, accessed February 3, 2019.
89. Interview with Cem Boyner, interviewed by Felix Oberholzer-Gee, September 16, 2014, Creating Emerging Markets Project, Baker Library Historical Collections, *Harvard Business School*, www.hbs.edu/creating-emerging-markets/
90. See Chapter 4.
91. E. Öğrül and M. Eryiğit, "The Factors That Affect on Foreign Direct Investments in Turkey (Sectoral Comparisons)," *Theoretical and Applied Economics*, v.22, n. 3, 2015, pp. 251–272.
92. G. Jones, *Profits and Sustainability. A History of Green Entrepreneurship*, Oxford: Oxford University Press, 2017, pp. 244–245.
93. Gürakar, *Politics*, p. 109.
94. Ibid., p. 110.
95. OECD, "Society at a Glance 2016. A Spotlight on Youth. How Does Turkey Compare?" October 2016, www.oecd.org/turkey/sag2016-turkey.pdf, accessed February 26, 2019.

Contributor Biographies

Seven Ağır is an Assistant Professor in the Department of Economics, Middle East Technical University, Ankara, Turkey. Her research interests include economic history, business history and economic thought in the Middle East, with special focus on the late Ottoman Empire and early Turkish Republic. She has published in journals including *Journal of Interdisciplinary History*, *Economic History Review*, and *Journal of Economic History*.

Efe Murat Balıkçıoğlu is a Lecturer in Islamic History in the Department of Religion, Wellesley College, Wellesley, United States. He holds a PhD in History and Middle Eastern Studies from Harvard University and his research focuses on early modern philosophy in the Ottoman Empire and the rise of political Islam in modern Turkey.

Ayşe Buğra is Emeritus Professor of Political Economy at Boğaziçi University, Istanbul, Turkey, and an affiliate of the Boğaziçi University research center Social Policy Forum, which she co-founded in 2004. She has taught and published in the areas of economic methodology and socio-economic history, state-business relations, and social policy. Her books in English include *New Capitalism in Turkey: The Relationship between Politics, Religion and Business*, Edward Elgar Publishing, 2014, (co-authored with O. Savaşkan), *State and Business in Modern Turkey: A Comparative Study*, State University of New York Press, 1994, and *Reading Karl Polanyi for the 21st Century: Market Economy as a Political Project*, Palgrave Macmillan, 2007 (co-edited with K. Ağartan). She is a member of the Science Academy Society of Turkey.

Ali Çarkoğlu is a Professor of Political Science at Koç University, Istanbul, Turkey. He previously taught at Boğaziçi and Sabancı universities in Istanbul. His areas of research include voting behavior, elections, public opinion and party politics in Turkey. He is the founding director of the Center for Survey Research at Koç University and is on the editorial board of Turkish Studies, South European Society and

Politics and Insight Turkey. His publications have appeared in journals including *International Journal of Communication*, *European Political Science Review*, *Democratization*, *European Journal of Political Research*, *Turkish Studies*, and *Middle Eastern Studies*.

Asli M. Colpan is a Professor of Corporate Strategy at the Graduate School of Management and Graduate School of Economics, Kyoto University, Kyoto, Japan, and Visiting Professor at Koç University, Istanbul, Turkey. Previously she was the Alfred Chandler Visiting Scholar at Harvard Business School, Boston, and Visiting Scholar at the Department of Political Science and Sloan School of Management at MIT, Cambridge, United States. Her research interests include corporate strategy, corporate governance, and especially the evolution of large enterprises in developed and emerging economies. Her work has been published in journals including *Industrial and Corporate Change*, *Journal of Management Studies*, *Business History*, *Strategic Management Journal*, and *Journal of Business Ethics*. She co-edited (with T. Hikino and J. R. Lincoln), *The Oxford Handbook of Business Groups* (Oxford University Press, 2010) and (with T. Hikino), *Business Groups in the West: Origins, Evolution and Resilience* (Oxford University Press, 2018).

Kristin Fabbe is an Assistant Professor in Business Administration at the Harvard Boston School, Boston, United States. She researches comparative politics, with a regional focus on the Middle East and southeastern Europe, particularly Turkey. Her book *Disciples of the State: Religion and State-Building in the Former Ottoman World* (Cambridge University Press, 2019), examines the role of religious elites, institutions, and attachments in modernization initiatives in Greece, Turkey, and Egypt. In her other research, she examines legacies of violence, post-conflict reconciliation, refugees and forced-migration, and state-business relations.

Patrick Fridenson is Professor Emeritus of International Business History, École des Hautes Études en Sciences Sociales, Paris, France. His recent publications in English include (with P. Scranton) *Reimagining Business History* (Johns Hopkins University Press, 2013) and (edited with T. Kikkawa), *Ethical Capitalism: Shibusawa Eiichi and Business Leadership in Global Perspective* (University of Toronto Press, 2017). He is editorial adviser of the journal *Entreprises et Histoire*. In 2018 he was awarded the title of honorary foreign member of the American Historical Association.

Janet Hunter is Saji Emeritus Professor of Economic History at the London School of Economics and Political Science, London, United Kingdom. She has published widely on the economic and business history of modern Japan, focusing in particular on the female labor market during industrialization, Anglo-Japanese economic relations, technology transfer and business ethics. She is the co-editor (with P. Francks) of *The Historical Consumer: Consumption and Everyday Life in Japan, 1850–2000* (Palgrave Macmillan, 2012), and author of *"Deficient in Commercial Morality"? Japan in Global Debates on Business Ethics in the Late Nineteenth and Early Twentieth Centuries* (Palgrave Macmillan, 2016), and "Obtaining Wealth Through Fair Means": Putting Shibusawa Eiichi's Views on Business Morality in Context', in P. Fridenson and T. Kikkawa (eds.), *Ethical Capitalism: Shibusawa Eiichi and Business Leadership in Global Perspective* (University of Toronto Press, 2017).

Geoffrey Jones is Isidor Straus Professor of Business History at the Harvard Business School, Boston, United States. His research interests include the history of global capitalism, the environmental and social responsibility of business, and the business history of emerging markets. His more recent books include *Multinationals and Global Capitalism: From the Nineteenth to the Twenty-First Century* (Oxford University Press, 2005), *Beauty Imagined: A History of the Global Beauty Industry* (Oxford University Press, 2010), (edited with Andrea Lluch), *The Impact of Globalization on Argentina and Chile: Business Enterprises and Entrepreneurship* (Edward Elgar, 2015), *Profits and Sustainability: A History of Green Entrepreneurship* (Oxford University Press, 2017), and *Varieties of Green Business: Industries, Nations and Time* (Edward Elgar, 2018).

Ümit Özlale is a Professor of Economics at Özyeğin University, Istanbul, Turkey. His research focuses mainly on macroeconomic policy in developing economies with a focus on the Turkish economy. In the past, he served as an executive board member of European Association of Development Research Institutes (EADI). He is also the recipient of "The Young Investigator Award" by The Scientific and Technological Research Council of Turkey, which has been awarded to outstanding academicians under 40 years old. He has published widely in journals including the *Journal of International Money and Finance*, the *Journal of Economic Dynamics* and *Control and Energy Policy*.

Behlül Üsdiken is a Professor of Management and Organization at Sabancı University, Istanbul, Turkey. His work has appeared in journals including *Academy of Management Annals*, *Business History*, *Journal of Management Studies*, *Organization Studies* and *Strategic Management Journal*. He has recently co-authored (with L. Engwall and M. Kipping), *Defining Management: Business Schools, Consultants, Media* (Routledge, 2016).

B. Burçin Yurtoğlu is a Professor of Finance at WHU—Otto Beisheim School of Management, Vallendar, Germany. He has conducted research and consulting projects with major companies, regulatory agencies and research centers in Austria, Turkey and at the IFC at the World Bank. His research interests include corporate governance, corporate finance and competition policy with a focus on emerging markets. He has published in journals including the *Economic Journal*, *European Economic Review*, *Journal of Econometrics*, *Journal of Accounting and Economics*, *Journal of Corporate Finance*, and *Journal of Law and Economics*.

Index

Page numbers in *italics* indicate figures; page numbers in **bold** indicate tables.

For Product Safety Concerns and Information please contact our EU
representative GPSR@taylorandfrancis.com
Taylor & Francis Verlag GmbH, Kaufingerstraße 24, 80331 München, Germany

www.ingramcontent.com/pod-product-compliance
Lightning Source LLC
LaVergne TN
LVHW011122300926
849160LV00008B/472

* 9 7 8 0 3 6 7 7 7 7 0 8 1 *